FASCISM IN EUROPE AND BEYOND

FASCISM IN EUROPE AND BEYOND

A HISTORY OF THE FIRST HUNDRED YEARS

Paul Baxa

BLOOMSBURY ACADEMIC
LONDON • NEW YORK • OXFORD • NEW DELHI • SYDNEY

BLOOMSBURY ACADEMIC

Bloomsbury Publishing Plc, 50 Bedford Square, London, WC1B 3DP, UK
Bloomsbury Publishing Inc, 1359 Broadway, New York, NY 10018, USA
Bloomsbury Publishing Ireland, 29 Earlsfort Terrace, Dublin 2, D02 AY28, Ireland

BLOOMSBURY, BLOOMSBURY ACADEMIC and the Diana logo are trademarks of
Bloomsbury Publishing Plc

First published in Great Britain 2025

Copyright © Paul Baxa, 2025

Paul Baxa has asserted his right under the Copyright, Designs and Patents Act, 1988, to be
identified as Author of this work.

For legal purposes the Acknowledgments on p. x constitute an extension
of this copyright page.

Cover image: Fascist rally at Mussolini's Tomb a century after the March on Rome
© Photo by Andrea Savorani / Getty Images

All rights reserved. No part of this publication may be: i) reproduced or transmitted in any form, electronic or mechanical, including photocopying, recording or by means of any information storage or retrieval system without prior permission in writing from the publishers; or ii) used or reproduced in any way for the training, development or operation of artificial intelligence (AI) technologies, including generative AI technologies. The rights holders expressly reserve this publication from the text and data mining exception as per Article 4(3) of the
Digital Single Market Directive (EU) 2019/790.

Bloomsbury Publishing Plc does not have any control over, or responsibility for, any third-party websites referred to or in this book. All internet addresses given in this book were correct at the time of going to press. The author and publisher regret any inconvenience caused if addresses have changed or sites have ceased to exist, but can accept no responsibility for any such changes.

A catalogue record for this book is available from the British Library.

A catalog record for this book is available from the Library of Congress.

ISBN: HB: 978-1-3502-4224-1
PB: 978-1-3502-4223-4
ePDF: 978-1-3502-4225-8
eBook: 978-1-3502-4226-5

Typeset by Newgen KnowledgeWorks Pvt. Ltd., Chennai, India
Printed and bound in Great Britain

For product safety related questions contact productsafety@bloomsbury.com.

To find out more about our authors and books visit www.bloomsbury.com
and sign up for our newsletters.

To the memory of my mother, Anna Saccucci Baxa (1928–2013)

CONTENTS

List of Illustrations — viii
Acknowledgments — x

Introduction — 1

  1 The Culture Wars of the *Fin-de-Siècle* — 15

  2 Trenchocracy — 31

  3 Red Years, White Terrors — 47

  4 The Fascist Seizure of Power — 67

  5 Weimar and the Rise of the Nazi Party — 81

  6 Fascism and the State — 101

  7 Fascism and Society — 119

  8 Fascism and Culture — 141

  9 Fascism and Its Imitators — 157

  10 The Second World War: Fascism's Playground — 181

  11 Cold War Fascism — 207

  12 Hobbits, Skinheads, and Gurus: Neofascism after 1968 — 225

  13 Fascism in the New Millennium — 249

Conclusion: One Hundred Years On — 275

Works Cited — 285
Index — 301

ILLUSTRATIONS

I.1	Giorgia Meloni waves to her supporters at a Brothers of Italy rally during the 2022 election campaign	2
I.2	Fascist sympathizers display a banner commemorating the 100th anniversary of the March on Rome in Predappio, Italy	3
1.1	Georges Boulanger: The strongman on his horse *c.* 1880	17
2.1	The First Duce: Gabriele D'Annunzio addresses his admirers in Fiume	34
3.1	Adolf Hitler and other Nazi leaders lead a procession commemorating the anniversary of 1923 Beer Hall Putsch	48
3.2	Flame thrower squad of *Freikorps* in action during the Spartacist Uprising, 1919	52
4.1	Blackshirts enter the Eternal City through the Porta del Popolo during the March on Rome, 1922	68
4.2	The body of Giacomo Matteotti is removed from the shallow grave he was buried in by his fascist assassins north of Rome. August 1924	74
4.3	The Cult of the Duce goes to the beach. Anzio, July 1929	79
5.1	The first Nuremberg Party Rally, 1927	82
5.2	Adolf Hitler addresses members of the Reichstag at the Garrison Church during Potsdam Day, 1933. Opposite him sits Reich President Paul von Hindenburg	94
6.1	Mussolini addresses the "oceanic crowd" of supporters from the balcony of Rome's Palazzo Venezia during the year of the Decennale, 1932	102
6.2	The "Long Hall" of Hitler's Reich Chancellery Building. Part of the long trek visitors had to make before reaching Hitler's office	116
7.1	Opening of the Summer Olympics in Berlin, 1936	120
7.2	Mussolini rides a Fiat tractor at the foundation of Aprilia, one of the new towns on the Agro Pontino, 1936	126
7.3	Hitler examines a Mercedes-Benz Grand Prix car. This was one of the "Silver Arrows" cars that dominated Grand Prix racing under the Nazi banner in the 1930s	132
8.1	Hitler and Goebbels visit the Degenerate Art Exhibition in Munich, 1937	145

8.2	The Palazzo della Civiltà Italiana in Rome as it looks today in Rome's EUR Quarter. The building is an example of the *Stile Littorio*, a monumental mix of classicism and modernism that characterized Italian Fascist architecture	154
9.1	Masked members of the Cagoule celebrating, 1937	167
9.2	Plaque commemorating the Battle of Cable Street in London's East End	169
9.3	Corneliu Codreanu gives the fascist salute in peasant costume	173
10.1	Hitler's Berghof with the massive picture window in full display	183
10.2	*Waffen-SS* recruitment poster for the Charlemagne Division in France	196
11.1	Francisco Franco's tomb under the altar in the monastery of the Valley of the Fallen. Franco's body was exhumed in 2019 and moved to a family plot in Madrid	208
11.2	A massive crowd greets President Juan Perón in Buenos Aires in 1948	214
11.3	The aftermath of a terror bombing perpetrated by neofascists in Brescia in 1974	221
12.1	Nazi salutes for Ian Stuart and his band Skrewdriver in Stockholm, 1986	228
13.1	George Lincoln Rockwell makes a speech at an American Nazi Party rally in Chicago, August 21, 1966	255
C.1	The opening of the Tolkien exhibition sponsored by Giorgia Meloni's government. Rome, November 2023	276

ACKNOWLEDGMENTS

This book would not have been possible without the help and support of many people. I am indebted to my colleagues at Ave Maria University (AMU), especially Roger Nutt, Dan Davy, Mary Blanchard, Michael Breidenbach, Thomas Maurer, Alex Crawford, Michael Dauphinais, and Gabriel Martinez and to the late and lamented Michael Sugrue. I am especially grateful to James Patterson and Joseph Pearce for their many insights into this subject matter. Many thanks as well to the administrators and library staff at AMU, especially Megan Hare and Judyta Mielnicka. I am grateful for the hard work and dedication of Aaron Weisel, whose keen editorial eye proved invaluable. To the editorial staff of Bloomsbury and to the anonymous reviewers I owe a special thanks, especially to Gabriella Cox and Rhodri Mogford for their patience and assistance. Finally, I am eternally grateful to my wife Patrizia for her love and support.

INTRODUCTION

The Return of the Flame

On October 22, 2022, during a somber ceremony in Italy's presidential palace, the country's first female prime minister, Giorgia Meloni, was sworn into office. Immediately following the ceremony, Meloni got into an Alfa Romeo sedan and was taken to the prime minister's palace, the Palazzo Chigi, for the official handover ceremony. This involved the outgoing prime minister, Mario Draghi, handing over a little bell to Meloni, who rang it for the assembled photographers. With that simple ceremony completed, Meloni took her place in the prime minister's office while Draghi was escorted out of the building. Apart from Meloni being a woman, there was nothing new in this ritual. Indeed, for the sixty-eighth time in seventy-six years, Italians were treated to a display of the peaceful transition of power in a democracy.

Three days later, on October 25, Meloni gave her inaugural address to the Italian parliament. In this speech, Meloni focused on pressing matters, such as the financial and economic fallout of the Covid-19 pandemic and the persistent refugee crisis. She also addressed Italy's fascist past, declaring that she had no sympathy for antidemocratic regimes and that Italy's lowest point was the antisemitic racial laws of 1938, issued by Mussolini's fascist regime. These points were meant to assuage any fears that Meloni aimed to resurrect Italy's fascist past, fears linked to her party, the Brothers of Italy (FdI), which traced its genealogy back to the neofascist Italian Social Movement (MSI). This was a party founded by ex-fascists in the wake of Italy's loss in the Second World War. Throughout the election campaign and in her political autobiography, *I Sono Giorgia* (I Am Giorgia), Meloni reassured Italians that fascism was consigned to the past and that her party was democratic. There were no ambitions to bring Italy back to fascism. Her critics were not so sure. After all, her party's emblem bore the same flame of the MSI (Figure I.1). Meloni's FdI also included members of the old party, many of whom had expressed admiration for Italy's fascist past; Meloni, too, had expressed a similar admiration during an interview she had given to French television in her youth.

Notably, toward the end of her speech to the Assembly, Meloni claimed that she was an outsider, someone who had "come from a cultural area that has often been confined to the margins of the Italian Republic ... an underdog not helped by family background or political friendships" (Reuters 2022). It made sense for Meloni to present herself and her party as outsiders. First, she was a woman, in a country with a powerful masculinist political and social culture. Second, she was born and raised in a working-class part of Rome by a single mother. Third, her party was barely a decade old and had received only negligible support in general elections until breaking out with a quarter of the national vote in 2022. Finally, the term "cultural area" was a reference to the perceived marginalization of conservative culture in Italy where the left was considered to have cultural hegemony

Figure I.1 Giorgia Meloni waves to her supporters at a Brothers of Italy rally during the 2022 election campaign. The flame logo of her party can be seen behind her.
Source: Getty Images.

in the media and in education. Critics noted that this promotion of outsider status, while technically correct on some levels, was also a dog whistle to those old neofascists that the time had come for historical wrongs to be corrected. Since the 1990s, a process of historical revisionism had been underway in Italy led by academics, popular historians, writers, and politicians to relativize Italy's past by suggesting that all Italians had been victims in the Second World War, including fascists who had fought against communist partisans in Italy's northeastern borderlands (Broder 2023). Fascists and neofascists were not only outsiders who were kept out of Italy's political establishment for decades but also victims of history. In consigning fascism to the past, Meloni was denying that anti-fascism had played a fundamental role in the establishment of Italian democracy.

The problem was that the past was still very present. Three days after making this speech to parliament came the centennial of the March on Rome, which had brought another self-described outsider—Benito Mussolini—to power in 1922, thus launching Italy's fascist era. He too was seen as an underdog and outcast by the political establishment. While Meloni's government ignored the anniversary, neofascists and neo-Nazis in Italy did not, and many of them made their annual pilgrimage to a small hillside village near the Adriatic coast to mark the occasion (Figure I.2).

Pilgrimage

Every year, on the anniversary of the March on Rome, neofascists and curiosity seekers come to the sleepy village of Predappio of two thousand people to visit the tomb of

Figure I.2 Fascist sympathizers display a banner commemorating the 100th anniversary of the March on Rome in Predappio, Italy.
Source: Getty Images.

Benito Mussolini, the founder of fascism. Predappio has become a site of pilgrimage for those who still believe in fascism and revere Mussolini as a man of vision. The irony is that Predappio and the Romagna region have been left-wing bastions since the end of the Second World War.[1] Mussolini himself began his career as a socialist. Yet, in this "red region" of Italy, a small enclave has become a sacred site of the far right.

If one wants to know how the fascist flame has been kept alive in Italy, a visit to Predappio is a must. Here, the cult of the Duce is alive and well. Souvenir shops on the town's main road sell all manner of items celebrating Mussolini and even Hitler. An effort was made in 2009 to close these shops, but the effort proved futile, and the shops continue to do a brisk trade. On the anniversaries of Mussolini's coming to power, his death, and his birthday, Pullmans arrive with pilgrims and tourists. To be sure, these have not gone uncontested and have often led to violence (Storchi 2019). There are counterdemonstrations from left-wing groups and the pilgrims who want to recall the Italian Resistance of the 1940s. As fate would have it, counterdemonstrations of the March on Rome also fall on the same date of Predappio's liberation by the Allies in 1944. The marches and demonstrations are lively affairs. In recent years, they have mostly been peaceful with men and women, young and old, gathering at the Mussolini family crypt

---

[1] Predappio elected its first right-wing mayor in 2019.

in the San Cassiano cemetery, listening to speeches and giving the occasional fascist salute, *Presente!*, a gesture that remains illegal under the Scelba Law of 1952 and that made the "apologia" of fascism a crime.

The "pilgrims" carry banners with fascist era slogans, and many of the pilgrims are dressed in period costume with blackshirts and fezes. There is a festive atmosphere, and to the uninitiated, this looks completely harmless and even ridiculous. One could even find it amusing if it were not for the fact that these people were admiring a movement that brought ruin to Italy and to Europe. Some argue that the regime did positive things, while others recognize it as a thing of the past that must not be repeated, with a tinge of regret. However, a closer look at the pilgrims reveals some disturbing signs. Interviews conducted by Italy's media outlets demonstrate that this is more than an exercise in misplaced nostalgia. In fact, many of these people look forward to the return of fascism in some guise or other. The language the pilgrims use mimics that of the 1920s. They talk of the need to "purge" Italy of its enemies. They hope for another strongman like Mussolini to restore order and a sense of patriotism. In the twenty-first century, this means ridding Italy of immigrants. It also means settling scores with the Left, whom they accuse of pushing false narratives of Italian history. In Predappio, these ideas can be flaunted in the open without any concern of being arrested.

Historical circumstances allow for the undertone of menace beneath the nostalgia and kitsch to come out into the open. In 2018, shock waves were sent across Italy when the news showed a woman wearing a T-shirt that read "Auschwitzland" with Disney-style lettering. She was taking part in the anniversary of the March on Rome in Predappio. When asked about the T-shirt, the woman called it "black humor." Her name is Selene Ticchi, a well-known activist of the far-right *Forza Nuova* movement. In 2019, she ran for mayor in the town of Budrio, not far from Predappio. After questions were raised in parliament following an international outcry, Ticchi was arrested and put on trial for wearing the shirt. Given a suspended sentence of four months, the conviction was later commuted to a fine of €9,000.[2] The sentence was handed down on October 28, 2019. Ticchi's T-shirt represented a new sense of confidence among supporters of the extreme right. In March 2018, the far-right *Lega* Party won a substantial number of seats in Italy's general election and became a part of Italy's government. *Lega*'s leader, Matteo Salvini, an outspoken critic of Italy's immigration policies, became minister of the Interior. Neofascists interviewed at the Predappio march expressed sympathy for Salvini.

The grotesqueness of equating Auschwitz with Disneyland seems fitting in Predappio, which has become a kind of theme park of Italian fascism. It is not much different than Stone Mountain in the United States, a literal theme park that celebrates the racist heritage of the Confederacy. Modern Predappio was built by Mussolini's fascist regime. Mussolini was born in a stone house on the main road to Forlì in a hamlet called Dovia, just below the village of old Predappio. In 1924, two years after Mussolini's

---

[2] "FN woman tried for 'Auschwitzland' T," *Ansa.it*, October 28, 2019, ansa.it/english/news/general_news/2019/10/28/fn-woman-tried-for-auschwitzland-t_6d97b065-4f3b-4db6-a72b-d136c7c931c0.html.

coming to power, the town was hit by a mudslide, giving the regime the opportunity to rebuild it. Rather than reconstructing the old town, the regime decided to build the "New Predappio" on the main road, around the Mussolini homestead. The result was a microcosm of fascist architecture and urban planning, seen on a larger scale in most of Italy's major cities.

Well into the 1930s, Predappio Nuovo (now simply known as Predappio; the older town is now referred to as Predappio Alta) became the focus of new construction in the fascist *Stile Littorio*, a style that mixed classical motifs with modern lines, all on a monumental scale. Built on the axis of straight road, the town's focal point is a piazza dominated by the Casa del Fascio (Fascist Party headquarters, a landmark of virtually every town in Italy) and a neo-Baroque church across from it. Overlooking the vast square is the town hall, a repurposed building once the home of a school where Mussolini's mother, Rosa, was a teacher. Along the main road are large residential buildings, schools, and the home of the fascist youth organizations, laid out on a rational grid. The layout of the new town is in stark contrast to its older namesake, made up of a collection of old houses on a winding mountainous road.

Predappio is a place of fantasy. Here, one can pretend to be in an ideal fascist city even though they are really in a village. The square and the buildings, especially the Casa del Fascio, are disproportionate to the location. They are too large for what remains of a small agricultural community. To feed the illusion, the regime built the Caproni aircraft factory in the town. Today, both the factory and the Casa del Fascio are abandoned. In the case of the Caproni factory, the abandoned structure still bears the marks of its wartime damage. Everything is oversized. The small house where Mussolini was born still stands. To give it some sense of grandeur, an exedra was built in front of it on the main road. Today, the house is a museum not without controversy. In 2013, a proposal was made by the left-wing city council to turn the unused Casa del Fascio into a museum and document center on fascism. Stiff resistance met this proposal by those worried that Predappio would become a literal fascist theme park. In 2020, the project was put on hold due to the Covid-19 pandemic. Its future remains unclear.

With or without the museum, the town of Predappio is a gateway into understanding the complicated legacy of fascism in Italy. Despite Italy's laws against fascist apologia, Predappio is a place where fascism and its founder are celebrated. In contrast, it is impossible to find an equivalent for Hitler and the Nazis in Germany and Austria. A memorial stone taken from the Mauthausen concentration camp sits in front of Hitler's birthplace in Braunau, Austria. It reads, "For Peace, Freedom and Democracy/Never Again Fascism/Millions of Dead Warn Us."[3] No such warning appears in Predappio. The Mussolini family crypt in the museum does not help. Sculptures and photos that echo

---

[3] The fate of the house remains uncertain after the Austrian Ministry of the Interior announced its demolition in 2016. As of this writing, the house remains standing and there is some controversy over its fate. In 2020, it was announced that the house would be converted into a police station; this proposal did not go over very well with the locals. Emily Schultheis, "This Old House: Austria torn over what to do with Hitler's birthplace," *Politico.eu*, September 21, 2020, politico.eu/article/this-old-house-austria-torn-over-what-to-do-with-hitlers-birthplace/.

the propaganda of the fascist regime surround the tombs of the Mussolini family. Indeed, Predappio became a fascist pilgrimage site only after Mussolini's body was returned to the town in 1957 in a ceremony attended by Mussolini's widow and many of his former disciples (Luzzatto 2005).

Material traces of fascism, Nazism, and the various other extreme right-wing movements of the twentieth century remain standing in Europe. While fascism was defeated in 1945, it continues to haunt the twenty-first century. The concentration camps remain standing as mute witnesses to the atrocities committed in its name. Meanwhile, a fascination for all things fascist and Nazi persists not just in the souvenir shops of Predappio but also in films, documentaries, websites, video games, and books. In other words, fascism is not dead even after the downfall of the Hitler and Mussolini regimes in 1945. While the world entered the binary conflict between communism and democracy during the Cold War, the memory of fascism remained, as did true believers who kept the fascist flame burning. With the end of the Cold War in the early 1990s, space was opened for fascism to reemerge in new and different ways. In 1994, the old neofascist party, the MSI, came into power as part of a coalition led by the Italian media mogul Silvio Berlusconi. Fascism, it seemed, was back.

A New History of Fascism

In fact, fascism never went away. One hundred years after Mussolini's rise to power, fascist-type movements proliferate in many parts of the world. What explains this continued fascination for a movement that was roundly discredited? Scholars continue to produce articles and monographs in great quantities trying to get at the surprisingly elusive meaning of fascism. This book is another contribution to that scholarly output. Rather than coming up with a new definition of fascism, this book will provide a narrative history of fascism, from its origins in the late nineteenth century to the present. It will tell the story of a movement born in the immediate aftermath of the First World War and its powerful influence on the interwar period, its ruinous climax in the Second World War, and its persistence as an idea to the present day.

Why a narrative history? In myriad scholarly literature produced on the subject, few have approached it from this perspective, preferring a topical or thematic approach. Existing narrative histories are also dated or not comprehensive (Eatwell 1995; Laqueur 1996). So caught up are scholars in the so-called "definitional wars" that simply telling the story of the galaxy of ideas, people, and places that make up the extreme right has been pushed to the background.

A narrative approach provides some important benefits to understanding fascism. The centenary of Mussolini's rise to power in Italy calls for a study of how and why such a movement came to be and why it continues to inspire fear despite its relatively small numbers in the present. In his famous definition of fascism from 1932, Mussolini (via the idealist philosopher Giovanni Gentile) declared that the twentieth century would be "Fascism's Century." What about the twenty-first century? A narrative of fascism must consider its trajectory into the present. A narrative history is also the best way to understand fascism in the different contexts in which it is embedded. David Roberts has recently called for historians to consider the "epochal nature" of fascism while at the same time attempting to give the movement some sense of shape and meaning (D. Roberts 2016).

Several historians and theorists have placed fascism in its political and social context, but few have examined the cultural context of fascism (R. Paxton 2004). A narrative history of fascism places it within the so-called "spirit of the times" without historicizing it. This book contends that fascism is one manifestation of modernity, and it seeks to demonstrate that the challenges of fascism persist through modernity to the present day (Jarausch 2015). Finally, a narrative history is best able to demonstrate the varieties of fascism and, in the words of Roberts, their interactions, not just among themselves but also with other conservative and right-wing movements.

What Is Fascism?

Briefly, this book approaches fascism as the product of a political culture that began taking shape in the late nineteenth century in Europe. It was the product of a series of "cultural wars" that consumed Europeans over a variety of issues, including the changes wrought by modernization and industrialization, the perceived decline of traditional values in the face of modernity, and the rise of Social Darwinism with its so-called "scientific racism." What became fascism was a cocktail of ideas, resentments, feelings, and fantasies that arose out of the experience of the First World War. The challenge it posed to the established political order made it, in the words of one influential historian, "neither right nor left" (Sternhell 1994). Taking its cue from the war experience, fascism brought together men and women from various places on the political spectrum into a new, elemental, self-styled movement that viewed itself as existing outside the traditional parameters of politics. From there, figures like Mussolini and Hitler, among others, formed new movements aimed at challenging the postwar political settlement by using violent tactics made acceptable by the prolonged violence of the First World War. Fascism became an increasingly attractive movement for those concerned with the weakness of liberal democracies in the face of the communist threat. It also provided an "alternative modernity" that manifested itself in different ways, depending on the country (Ben-Ghiat 2001; Griffin 2007). This situation called for a national renewal based on traditional values allied with modernization. In other words, it sought to create a new, stronger cultural identity, something the liberal interwar order had failed to inspire.

Despite this narrative, fascism has proved notoriously difficult to define. One historian has argued that fascism is akin to pornography: one knows it by sight, but it is difficult to put into words (Laqueur 1996). What has befuddled scholars are the contradictions found in fascism. It did not have an intellectual ancestor as communism had in Karl Marx. Mussolini waited ten years while in power before he laid down the official definition of fascism in the *Treccani Encyclopedia*, ghostwritten by Giovanni

Gentile. Meanwhile, National Socialism had Hitler's rambling *Mein Kampf* as a guide. The incoherence in fascist ideology has led scholars to a variety of conclusions and generated a myriad of approaches over the decades, which will be discussed below. Additionally, many commentators from various disciplines have felt compelled to spell out what they believe fascism is and means. These commentators have included political theorists, philosophers, journalists, and ideologues of varying stripes. Indeed, the first group to attempt to decipher fascism was Marxists, who viewed fascism as nothing more than a rearguard action by capitalism to stave off the inevitable communist revolution. Finally, there is the sheer number of variations that have existed between the different fascist movements and the inability to distinguish between, on the one hand, fascist and conservative and, on the other, fascist and socialist.

The thinking on fascism has become more nuanced and advanced over the years, but a clear definition still seems elusive. For the purposes of this book, a summary of the various "schools" of thought will be presented here before it provides a working definition of the movement. Although the study of fascism has produced a vast literature, it is possible to identify seven approaches that have retained an important explanatory value and thus continue to shape our understanding of the movement. The first approach ignores fascist ideology altogether or tries not to make any sense of it. The second views fascism as a sui generis phenomenon that does not fit into any accepted political convention. The third searches for a "fascist minimum" that overlooks national idiosyncrasies and contradictions. The fourth views it as a form of totalitarianism, which renders any distinctions between it and communism irrelevant. The fifth sees fascism as a "political religion," and the sixth sees it as a revolutionary and modernizing force. Finally, there is the notion of a "generic fascism" that can be found in any society at any time.

As to the first approach: if fascism is riddled with contradictions and does not appear to have a coherent set of ideological principles, should it be taken seriously on that level? According to some scholars, the answer is no. This approach denies that fascism contributed anything positive to politics and culture. The Italian philosopher Norberto Bobbio once famously remarked that fascism had no culture. Historians like Richard Bosworth warn scholars not to take what fascists said at face value (Bosworth 1998). The important thing is to look at what fascists did as opposed to what they said (R. Paxton 2004). This notable gap between fascist ideals and practices suggests that whatever fascism said about itself is irrelevant in the face of its actions, which amounted to nothing more than an authoritarian dictatorship just as corrupt as the liberal regimes it claimed to have destroyed. There is a certain degree of continuity between fascism and the political order that preceded it. The style was different, but the substance largely remained. This argument that fascist ideology mattered less than what they did has also been made by cultural historians like Jeffrey Schnapp, who claims that the "overproduction of aesthetics" conceals the "unstable core" at the heart of fascist ideology (J. Schnapp 1996).

The second approach calls for fascist ideology to be studied on its own terms. It was, in the words of Zeev Sternhell, "neither right nor left" (Sternhell 1994). This is the fascism as a sui generis ideology. It borrowed from other ideologies and ideas and put them together in novel and experimental ways (D. Roberts 2016). For this reason, a name like National Socialism makes sense. It also explains why fascist movements cannot be placed in the same category as more traditional conservative movements or socialist ideas. While fascist ideas resembled those of other ideologies, fascism itself does not belong to any of them. While such an approach emphasizes the uniqueness of fascism, it also removes it from its historical context. It also fails to explain neither the convergences between fascism and other conservative movements, nor the at times stark differences between the different fascist movements in different countries.

An understanding of these differences leads us to the third approach, that of searching for a so-called "fascist minimum" that recognizes fascism as a coherent set of principles underneath the differences. This has led to the famous typology or "elements of a retrodictive theory" of fascism proposed by Stanley Payne (Payne 1995). Payne divides this typology into five factors; all five had to be present in each historical circumstance for fascism to emerge. For Payne, only five countries—Italy, Germany, Austria, Hungary, and Romania—presented these conditions in the twentieth century (Payne 1995, 488). Payne's important work set the tone for the "definitional wars" in fascist studies. Almost all historians of fascism have contributed to this search for a "fascist minimum" to some degree (Passmore 2014). Put simply, this approach aims at minimizing contradictions in search of essential ideas that make spotting fascism easier. While the "fascist minimum" school has contributed enormously to our understanding of fascism, its taxonomic thrust has led to a downplaying of the variety of fascisms that exist outside the central core of fascist movements, nor does it account for the dynamic nature of fascism. It also does not explain the persistence of neofascism since the Second World War.

Another way of explaining (away) the contradictions within fascism is found in the fourth approach, which classifies it as part of a larger process. One may, for instance, view fascism as part of the modernization process found in countries that fell behind more advanced nations. Thus, fascism is a kind of "developmental dictatorship" that makes economic and industrial development paramount (Gregor 1979). A political equivalent is the totalitarian thesis. This thesis argues that fascism is an ideology that seeks to create a state outside of which nothing exists (Arendt 1968). In both cases, the details of fascism and the variations between the movements matter less than the grand process they serve. This approach also lumps fascism in with other movements, especially on the left. In this reading, fascism and communism are very much alike in their approach to state building and governance. Their respective tactics and repressive policies, too, are similar, aiming for the same regimented society, empty of free individuals (Arendt 1968). Some critics object to these metanarrative approaches to fascism as products of a Cold War approach.

The fifth approach attempts to understand fascism as a "political religion." Emilio Gentile's book on the "sacralization of politics" has had an enormous influence on fascist studies in this way (Gentile 1996; Burleigh 2007). This view holds that fascism was a secular form of millenarianism that drew upon religious traditions. In the case of fascist Italy, the Catholic Church served as a model for Mussolini. Fascism became a "liturgy" and dead fascists became "martyrs." This sacralization argument suggests that fascism was not a modernist or modernizing force.

An opposing view sees fascism as revolutionary school. The leading scholar in this camp has been Roger Griffin, who has argued that, while fascism drew upon religious themes like "rebirth," it was presented as a modernist and modernizing force (Griffin 1991). Griffin's "palingenetic thesis" has since enormously contributed to the study of fascism, spawning numerous books and even a specialized journal published by Brill.[4] Griffin has also claimed that this view of fascism has caused a "new consensus" to emerge in fascist studies (a claim that has been challenged) (Griffin 2002; Roberts et al. 2002). This view rightly recognizes the radical nature of fascism. It also insists that fascism be taken at its word. Even though fascists did not always accomplish their goals, they were still deadly serious about transforming society and creating the so-called "New Man." Griffin's view, like that of Gentile, also contends that fascism had a coherent ideology. These claims have generated significant pushback from historians like Richard Bosworth, who have criticized Griffin and Gentile and their search for a "final pure load that will identify fascism in a few words or paragraphs" (Bosworth 2009, 5).

Finally, there is the "Ur-Fascism" approach. This term is taken from a famous essay by the Italian semiotician Umberto Eco, who argued that the fascism temptation is something ever present in culture and can be manifested in fourteen different ways, ranging from the "cult of tradition" to "obsessions with plots" (Eco 2001). Eco's essay, originally published in the *New York Review* in 1995, has been rediscovered with the rise of right-wing extremism since the 2010s. The revival of Eco's work is part of a trend to view fascism as a cultural tendency that exists in most Western cultures, always ready to rise up when circumstances permit. Recent trends have led to similar works by philosophers and politicians (Albright 2018; Stanley 2018;). Fascism is viewed as something universal, and these works have served less as histories than as warnings of fascism's return, albeit in a different guise.

The above summary of approaches is not exhaustive, but these approaches do constitute the main views that affect current scholarly and non-scholarly discussions of fascism today. It should be noted that the approaches often overlap, and scholars can be found straddling two or more of these camps. It is best not to be too schematic here and recognize the remarkably diverse approaches. All these views have some merit, and this book will not privilege one over the others. Additionally, this book is not intended to provide a novel thesis on the subject. It is informed, however, by some recent publications that have tried to reconcile these diverse approaches in some way. António Costa Pinto and Aristotle Kallis have called for a more "transnational" view of fascism that both recognizes the unique and experimental nature of fascist ideology and considers how that ideology crossed over into the more mainstream and traditional right. Rather than viewing fascism as either revolutionary or conservative, they argue that a "cross fertilization" of ideas occurred (Costa Pinto and Kallis 2014). One of the contributors to Costa Pinto and Kallis's volume, David D. Roberts, published his own book, in which he proposes a new approach that takes into account fascism's interaction

---

[4] *Fascism: Journal of Comparative Fascist Studies.*

with other right-wing movements. His method is one that attempts to harmonize the theoretical with the empirical by recognizing the "fluidity" of fascist ideology while avoiding the fixed and rigid classifications provided by other scholars (D. Roberts 2016). In both cases, the studies end with the defeat of fascism in 1945, but they can be applied to the entire history of fascism right to the present.

The Fascist "Cocktail"

As mentioned above, the scope of this book does not allow for the proposal of a new theory of fascism. It will approach fascism as a primarily cultural phenomenon, as a cocktail of assumptions and attitudes that had developed in the late nineteenth century and that coalesced into a political program after the First World War. In the spirit of the approaches outlined above, this book proposes the following set of characteristics that constitute fascism in the past, present, and future. Fascism emerged in the nexus between culture and politics born in the late nineteenth and early twentieth centuries and was shaped by the tension between tradition and modernity. This gave rise to a unique movement that appealed to many in the aftermath of the Great War. Getting at the root of this appeal is the main challenge of understanding fascism. This book's narrative on fascism presupposes several key characteristics taken from the main schools of thought discussed earlier.

First, fascism must be understood as a political cult whose appeal is primarily emotional and atavistic, an appeal linked to what Robert Paxton has called a "set of mobilizing passions" (R. Paxton 2004). It appeals to fantasies, dreams, and myths. It also taps into resentments and fears. One can argue that trauma caused by the shock of modernity is at the root of fascist phenomena. As with all cults, fascism involves a kind of retreat from ordinary society and "flight" into a fantasy world made up of rituals and symbols that only the initiated can truly understand. This is symbolized by the desire to stand apart from society. All fascist movements require distinctive clothing or markers, such as colored shirts, songs, and gestures that identify them as different. These involve distinctive gatherings, such as rallies and political meetings that have unique choreography. At the center of these rallies is a charismatic speaker who can tap into the emotions of the crowd. He or she is a kind of political shaman who is there to give the faithful a glimpse of the glorious future awaiting them.

Out of this cult comes Gentile's "sacralization of politics" mentioned earlier. Like communism, fascists tend to prefer the millenarian approach to politics, hoping that the "decadence" of the present will give way to a utopian future in which the nation will be reborn and society and culture purified of its "degenerate" elements. To be reborn society requires "purging" of some kind. Thus, violence is a positive and necessary tactic. Whereas Marxists believed that history would lead to a future of communism, fascists called for immediate action, lest the nation be taken over by its enemies. Once victory was secured, then the "anthropological revolution" would take place. A fascist New Man would be forged from the purest and noblest elements of society and become a new aristocracy. Friedrich Nietzsche, a major influence on many fascist leaders such as Benito Mussolini, argued that the root of all cultural achievement was a "creative destruction" carried out by an "overman" (Sznajder 2002).

The influence of Nietzsche points to another key characteristic of fascism. While fascism can claim no single founding father, numerous thinkers can be seen as godfathers of fascism, such as Nietzsche, Jean-Jacques Rousseau, Georges Sorel, Gustave Le Bon, and many others. The point is that fascism cannot be seen as a coherent ideology but rather as a movement that reflects its time; it is a movement rather than a fixed set of principles. Mussolini defined his creation precisely as a movement in 1919 and, although he transformed the *Fasci di Combattimento* into the more organized *Partito Nazionale Fascista* (PNF) in 1921, "movement" remains the best way to describe fascism, capturing its heterogeneous nature. The multiple influences—or what Stanley Payne calls "strands"—that have gone into the fascist cocktail accounts as well for the contradictions found in fascism. It also accounts for its transnational nature and the different forms it took in different national contexts. Rather than finding some reductive generic fascism or attempting to find some coherence in the contradictions, this book will examine the variety of fascisms as they developed in time. It will also look at how the various fascist movements interacted with conservative and far-right movements as well as between each other.

Conclusion

The book opens with a study of fascism's pre-origins in Europe's *fin-de-siècle*. This chapter focuses on the Boulanger and Dreyfus Affairs in France and the rise of far-right populism in Austria-Hungary. The various assumptions, attitudes, and ideas that informed this era and made their way into fascism—antisemitism, Social Darwinism, hyper-nationalism, and militarism—are examined as well. At the root of these movements lay the tension between modernity and tradition, a tension that was a product of the rapid acceleration of social, political, and economic change that took place in the nineteenth century. Out of this era came new ideas on how to mobilize the masses, the obsession with decadence and degeneration, and restlessness. Violent reactions against progressive movements like socialism and women's suffrage reflected deep anxieties about modernity, while the expansion of colonialism heightened racist sentiments. In short, the turbulent "cultural wars" that marked this era became the fertile ground out of which fascism grew.

The crucial step that made fascism possible was the First World War and the immediate postwar period. The years 1914–22 created the conditions for political experiments like fascism. The rise of Bolshevism and the success of the Russian Revolution added an extra layer of urgency and fear in Europe. The weakening liberal contingent in Germany did nothing to put minds at ease, especially after the world economy collapsed after 1929. The seeming success of fascist Italy and Nazi Germany in the 1930s appeared to give credence to a Third Way between capitalism and communism. From this apparent economic success, along with the dynamic nature of the fascist regimes, came a prestige that many sought to imitate in Europe and elsewhere.

The second part of the book examines the culmination of fascism's historic period: the Second World War. This section examines the Axis powers' dream of a New World Order in action and the impact of the fascist worldview on Europeans and beyond. The racial policies and genocide they produced were an integral part of the fascist vision, even if not all fascist movements made racism a central pillar of their movements. Only after the war began and the fascist vision seemed to come to fruition did the annihilation of the Jews and other enemies come to be accepted by all fascist collaborators.

The final section of the book examines the fate of fascism since 1945. Although the movement was largely discredited by the events of the war, true believers have remained in Italy, Germany, and elsewhere, not to mention that prewar fascist states in Spain and Portugal outlasted the war, as did fascist movements in South America. Fascism persisted through the Cold War, and it continues to attract interest to this day. This section studies the neo-Nazi and neofascist groups that have sprouted in various countries since the war. The book also places these groups in the context of extreme right-wing populist movements that have emerged since the end of the Cold War. The point is that, even one hundred years since the rise of Mussolini's fascists in Italy, fascism continues to exist. This book considers fascism's future possibilities.

As the book proceeds with the narrative, great attention is paid to the people, events, and places that have marked fascism's history. Each chapter begins with a snapshot that introduces that chapter's material. Separate boxes are set aside for biographies and primary documents, not to mention maps and photographs. An effort is made to explore the ideas and artifacts of fascism, from the political philosophies to the esoteric symbols. The contradictions of fascism are explored, and no attempt is made to reconcile them. Fascism was both modern and traditional; it was anticlerical and pro-religion, pagan and Christian, reactive and proactive at the same time. It celebrated violence in the framework of a conservative ethos. It resembled the dynamism of the city and machine while idealizing agrarianism.

Finally, it was both elitist and populist at the same time. Ernst Nolte famously wrote of fascism's "three faces"—but fascism had many faces (Nolte 1966). There were the notorious Hitlers, Mussolinis, and Francos, but a large cast of characters both famous and not so famous supported them. One of the recent trends in fascist studies examines the lesser-known voices that have contributed to the rise of fascism rather than its prominent leaders (Duggan 2013). This book argues that fascism can only be understood as a movement made up of many people, places, and ideas that have coalesced into one of the most powerful and disastrous political ideologies ever conceived—and it is not dead yet.

CHAPTER 1
THE CULTURE WARS OF THE *FIN-DE-SIÈCLE*

The Man on the Black Horse

At noon, on September 30, 1891, Georges Boulanger visited the grave of his late mistress in a cemetery in Brussels, Belgium. Alone, Boulanger pulled out a gun and put a bullet in his head. Thus, ended what one historian has called the "semi-comic opera" of the Boulanger Affair (Wright 1987). In truth, the affair had ended two years previously, but the man after whom it was named remained a famous figure and his death was reported internationally. "By nature, a *poseur*," claimed the obituary in *The Illustrated American*, Boulanger "died by his own hand in a thoroughly melodramatic manner at the grave of the woman who had sacrificed her name and fortune for his sake."[1] While Georges Boulanger's fame outlived the movement named after him (Boulangism), the effects of that movement lingered long after Boulanger himself was forgotten. In fact, Boulangism, which gripped France for three years in the late 1880s, may have been the West's first glimpse of what later became known as fascism.

Georges Boulanger hardly fits the image of the Fascist New Man. He was a man of his time, and his "operatic" end fits the Romantic era in which he grew up. He was handsome, a ladies' man, aristocratic in manner if not in pedigree, and a career soldier. Although Boulangism became a political movement, Boulanger was not the political type. Indeed, his fame began as a warrior. Leading a group of colonial soldiers from Tunisia, Boulanger was wounded in the Italian Wars of Independence in 1859. He later took part in wars against China, Prussia, and finally Parisians, as part of the force that ended the Paris Commune in 1871. Boulanger also learned how to win over public opinion. At every opportunity, he let it be known that he was a French nationalist and a guardian of the Jacobin tradition of Republicanism. In 1885, one of the leading Radical Republican leaders, Georges Clemenceau, convinced the French government to appoint Boulanger as War Minister.

In the sixteen months Boulanger served as War Minister, he established himself as a reformer. Like a good heir of the Jacobins, he made conditions better for enlisted men and penalized aristocrats. He also pressured his government to adopt a more aggressive attitude towards Germany. Boulanger's *révanchism* (revengism) gained a certain degree of popularity within a government that was made up of Opportunists or moderate Republicans anxious not to get involved in external wars with an increasingly powerful Germany. Things get strange here. In the spring of 1888, Boulanger's name was written into ballots for a series of by-elections. He won them all. Technically, Boulanger was

---

[1] "Boulanger's Dramatic End," *The Illustrated American*, October 17, 1891, p. 395.

not allowed to run as a politician while being a member of the military. His surprising successes in what were Bonapartist areas led to his dismissal from the military. Emboldened rather than weakened by this, a movement began to coalesce around the general, known for his frequent public appearances on a black horse (Figure 1.1). Opponents claimed he stood for nothing specifically. Thus, in 1888, a political program was published, listing the principles of Boulangism.

This *Programme du Général Boulanger* added little detail to what Boulanger would do if he ever became France's leader. What it offered instead was a series of slogans followed by exclamation points. A series of six slogans answered the question: "What is Boulanger?" A litany of six answers followed: "Boulanger is Work! Boulanger is Liberty! Boulanger is Honesty! Boulanger is Rights! Boulanger is the People! Boulanger is Peace!"[2] The rest of the program repeated these slogans without much in the way of substance. What it did was remind "honest, working Frenchmen" that internal and external enemies surrounded them. Externally, the Germans were always a threat because of their friends inside France. Internal enemies kept French workers in bondage, and they were found in the world of finance and politics. If the French were not free, it was because the political class was afraid of them and the consequences that awaited them if the French were given their rights. What these rights were remained unclear.

The vagueness of the program seemed to reinforce the Jacobin tradition at the heart of Boulangism. So why was Boulangism succeeding in traditionally conservative districts? If Boulanger was a radical republican, why were Bonapartists voting for him? Furthermore, why were Royalists funding the movement? The odd feature of Boulangism is that it came to represent the interests of conservatives who rejected the very existence of the republic. This scenario led to Boulanger's ousting from the Radical Republicans— or so they thought. In January 1889, to the astonishment of Republicans, Boulanger won the by-election in Paris, a city dominated by radicals. Not only did he win the election, but he won it comfortably against a well-credentialed Radical Republican. So strong was Boulanger's position after this that many of his supporters—especially those in the *Ligue des Patriotes*—called on Boulanger to lead a coup d'état. Fortunately, for the Third Republic, Boulanger rejected these calls and hoped instead to win the general election slated for later in the year. In the meantime, rumors circulated that Boulanger was going to be arrested for treason. Convinced that this was true, Boulanger fled to Belgium with his mistress. He never returned to France, and the Boulangist movement fizzled.

The demise of Boulangism demonstrated that the movement was nothing without the man it was named for. Meanwhile, the whole affair became a fascinating if troubling episode in the history of the Third Republic. What did it all mean? Historians have argued that Boulangism was ultimately a movement of the left, the last gasp of the Jacobin tradition that went back to the French Revolution. Republicanism was now established, and its leaders, like the Opportunists, had become conservative. The older conservatives, the monarchists and Bonapartists, faded into history. Boulangism, therefore, seemed the

---

[2] "Programme du Général Boulanger," *Gallica*, gallica.bnf.fr/ark:/12148/bpt6k1128115/f1.item.r=georges%20boulanger.zoom.

Figure 1.1 Georges Boulanger: The strongman on his horse *c.* 1880. Credit: Getty Images.

end of something. However, the events of the twentieth century—specifically, the rise of fascism—have led to a reevaluation of the Boulanger Affair, seeing in it the beginning of something new. Zeev Sternhell has argued that the Affair spawned the origins of fascism, specifically the fusion of the left and the right (Sternhell 1994). Others, like William Irvine, have argued that the Boulanger Affair saw the birth of the new, radical right. It was the moment when conservatives embraced mass politics (Irvine, The Boulanger Affair Reconsidered: Royalism, Boulangism, and the Origins of the Radical Right in France 1989).

Either way, it is possible to see the Boulanger Affair as a protofascist episode. Like fascism in the twentieth century, it was able to amass an eclectic base made up of left- and right-wing elements. Its main constituents were those who rejected the Third Republic. Created after the French fell to the Prussians, the Third Republic was little loved even by its supporters, the Republicans. Radical Republicans viewed it as a sellout to conservative elements, especially the so-called Notables in the provinces. Socialists, meanwhile, had little hope that the Third Republic would take the interests of industrial workers seriously. On the right, the Republic was rejected in principle. Legitimists (supporters of the Bourbon Restoration), Orléanists, and Bonapartists wanted their pretenders back on the throne of France. Boulangism aimed at overthrowing the state.

Immediate circumstances, such as an economic crisis and a farming crisis, explains to some extent how these strange bedfellows came together in 1888–9. More significant was a broader cultural crisis that was looming in France. What today is called a "culture war" was making itself felt in the 1880s. Those on the right were furious with the Ferry Laws, which established free, mandatory, and secular education run by the state. Named after the moderate Republican Jules Ferry, these laws had been passed in 1882. The opposition to the Ferry Laws mostly came from the Catholic Church, allied with the Monarchists, who saw this as an attempt to destroy Catholicism in France since the church had been mostly responsible for education. Added to this was the rivalry with Germany, a rivalry not only political and diplomatic, but also cultural. Boulanger worked to ban German music in France, coloring German *kultur* as a destructive force. Boulanger appealed to those Frenchmen who believed their own culture was being threatened and, in so doing, set the stage for radically xenophobic campaigns in the future.

Boulangism was an example of populism that was not in itself fascist; still, it was a populism that depended on the charisma of a leader who was a political outsider. In 1889, the famous Pellerin studio of engravers produced a biography of Boulanger in the Épinal style. The *images d'Épinal* were vivid cartoons of popular subjects. They were invariably sentimental and traditional, often exalting religious and military themes. The Boulanger "biography" illustrated the general's career in sixteen vignettes. The scenes focus exclusively on Boulanger's military career, including his actions in battle. He is shown leading colonial troops, getting shot, and being given a medal for heroism in battle. We also see him on his horses, visiting the United States on the centennial of the Battle of Yorktown, and addressing the Chamber of Deputies in military dress. One scene shows Boulanger being celebrated by the inhabitants of Clermont-Ferrand as he rides on his horse. His actions as War Minister are also celebrated. Notably, nothing is said about Boulanger's political ambitions, nor about Boulangism. It is as if this dimension of Boulanger did not exist.

The Épinal illustration contributed to the cult of personality that emerged around Boulanger. It was important to show Boulanger not as a politician but as a military man. In every scene he is in uniform, and the number of medals increases as the story goes on. He is presented as a man of destiny whose military credentials are enough to convince the French that he would save the country. The complete absence of political scenes—apart from the one in which he addresses the Chamber of Deputies—are an indication that parliamentarism was not important. The depictions on horseback indicate a new Renaissance *condottiero* or a new Bonaparte. The Boulanger Program is not explicitly mentioned but it is implied in the actions of the general. The last scene shows the effects of Boulanger the reformer. He is shown surrounded by soldiers of different ranks while the caption below mentions his "amelioration of the lives of non-commissioned officers and the mess halls for the troops."[3]

Notably, Boulanger's inability to live up to the cult around him spelled the end of Boulangism. This indicated that the leader of a movement—and his persona—was essential to the movement's success. While it can be argued that France had seen something like this already with Bonapartism, the new context of mass politics in the Third Republic made this something new. Boulanger's vague program did not make the specific references to social and economic conditions that had helped Louis Napoleon Bonaparte come to power (Wright 1987). The Épinal illustrations laid the groundwork for the motifs that would shape fascist cults of personality. The idea of a "man of destiny riding in on a horse" became a familiar image of Mussolini. Boulanger's military background and disdain for politics as usual combined with his zeal for the nation, feeding into the fascist image of the leader. That he could bring together opposing political groups helped reinforce his image as a *taumaturgo* (miracle worker) sent by Providence to heal a nation reeling from a traumatic war defeat (Fogu 1997). Boulanger held secret dealings with Royalists and received money from foreign sources; such practices came to prefigure the fascism of the twentieth century. In short, Boulanger created a movement that depended on mass appeal, sui generis politics, antiestablishment sentiment, and elite financial support. This mixture of ingredients, unprecedented before the 1880s, became the recipe for fascism.

France: Birthplace of Fascism

The Boulanger Affair suggests that France was the birthplace of fascist ideology. The deep cultural contrasts and rise of a new dynamic on the right was first seen in France. It is telling that the climax of the Boulangist crisis came in 1889—the year France was celebrating the centennial of the French Revolution. For some, notably Radical

---

[3] "Une biographie," *Gallica.fr*, gallica.bnf.fr/ark:/12148/btv1b6938670w/f1.item.r=boulanger%20epinal.zoom#.

Republicans, the France of the Third Republic seemed to pale in comparison with the glorious events of the revolution. Few of them believed that this new republic could claim the heritage of that event. For conservatives, the French Revolution had destroyed an even more glorious past of Throne and Altar. These two competing visions of the past had in common a rejection of the present. As the Eiffel Tower went up on the banks of the Seine River in anticipation of the World's Fair of 1889, a fair that exalted innovations and technologies, France was divided between two competing visions of the past.

Thus, Boulangism was a harbinger of things to come. At the heart of this cultural crisis was a fear that France was losing its way and that modernity was uprooting French culture. Modernity, for all its accomplishments, was a source of anxiety. The Boulangist opposition to the Third Republic and the parliamentary system at its center reflected this fear. In a speech to the French Assembly, a Boulanger supporter had noted that while Great Britain had taken centuries to get used to parliamentary politics, France did not have such long time to wait (Peukert 1987). The sense of urgency, the feeling that events were racing towards some apocalyptic end where the very existence of the nation was at stake, gripped some parts of French society at the end of the century. A pervasive sense of national decline fed into the next dramatic crisis, the Dreyfus Affair. Many of the elements that fed into Boulangism were stoked again by this new crisis, which emerged over the supposed discovery of an espionage network within the French army.

In 1894, a captain in the French Army, Alfred Dreyfus, was convicted of spying for the Germans and sent to Devil's Island to serve his sentence. Dreyfus was Jewish and hailed from the province of Alsace, lost to the Germans after the Franco-Prussian War. Four years after his conviction, while he languished in solitary confinement, a campaign was started in France to exonerate Dreyfus. Led by the writer Emile Zola, who accused the French government of a cover-up in the case, the Dreyfusard campaign eventually led to a full exoneration by France's High Court in 1906. In the meantime, France had been divided, and old wounds reopened. The Dreyfus Affair, as it was called, plunged France into another culture war that had far-reaching consequences. The Dreyfus Case continues to fascinate, producing films and books, including a recent film by Roman Polanski, *J'accuse*. Several scholarly and popular history works have been published on the case and the affair. What interests us here is the role the Dreyfus Case played in the rise of fascism.

On the surface, there appears to be little connection between the Dreyfus Affair and fascism. Moreover, unlike the Boulanger Affair, the Republic was in no immediate danger. However, that shift in the right catalyzed by Boulanger came into prominence during the Dreyfus Affair. The Anti-Dreyfusard movement—a Boulangist mix of royalists, revanchists, and Catholics—saw the attempt to exonerate Dreyfus as a plot to destroy France. Against Dreyfus and Zola—both Jews—these groups were brought together by their antisemitism. The Anti-Dreyfusards saw in this fight a chance to roll back history. It was also an opportunity to attack France's Jewish minority. The Dreyfus Affair, then, played a significant role in the rise of fascism because it fanned the flame of the antisemitic activism of the new, radical right. This was demonstrated in the work of two men: Édouard Drumont and Charles Maurras.

Drumont's credentials as an antisemite were established with the publication of his book, *La France Juive*, in 1886. Three years later during the centennial of the French Revolution and at the height of the Boulanger Affair, Drumont founded the Anti-Semitic League of France based on the arguments he made in his book. Running over one thousand pages in two volumes, Drumont's book drew upon the traditional anti-Judaism found in Catholicism. Jews as "Christ killers" was a familiar refrain going back deep into the Middle Ages. However, Drumont added to this a more distinctly modern form of antisemitism. Drawing upon the work of Arthur de Gobineau, Drumont claimed the Jews formed a distinct race that opposed the "Aryan" race. Drumont held the Jews responsible for the enslavement of workers via "finance capitalism. These three poles of antisemitism, with an emphasis on the latter two, would feed into fascism. Drumont's book had great appeal because it used traditional antisemitism and updated it to explain modern problems (Ravitch 1990, 101). Drumont's updating of an ancient prejudice stood as a condemnation of the modern world. He associated the Jews not only with finance capitalism, but also with liberal values. In short, the Jew now equaled modernity, and modernity was the equivalent of French national decline.

The Dreyfus Affair gave Drumont the opportunity to become a national figure and the leading voice of the anti-Dreyfusards. In 1892, Drumont launched a newspaper called *La Libre Parole*. The journal was pointedly antisemitic allowing it to capture the attention of the anti-Dreyfusards. Drumont's anti-capitalism made it attractive to some socialists as well as ultraconservatives and Catholics. At the height of the Affair, both Drumont's journal and book sold in enormous quantities. The success of the *La Libre Parole* can be attributed not just to the content of the articles, but also to its distinctive cover pages. These invariably showed caricatures of Jews as money-hungry, rapacious, and evil. The exaggerated features that became a staple of Nazi propaganda in later years were ubiquitous here. The Jew is shown as hook-nosed and grotesque. By contrast, the French are shown as simple and wholesome, in the tradition of the naïve images of the Épinal illustrations discussed earlier. The Jews represented the immorality and greed of the city, while the noble Frenchman was one who was rooted in the soil. The image of the Jew as *déraciné*, or "uprooted," represented an implicit threat to France and its national identity. The Jew, if left unopposed, would eventually enslave all of France, as shown in one of the journal's most notorious covers.

Drumont's notoriety encouraged him to enter politics. In 1898, helped by the endorsement of antisemitic activists, Drumont was elected to the Chamber of Deputies as one of the representatives of French Algeria. His margin of victory resembled the kind of landslides enjoyed by Boulanger, proving antisemitism's political power. As a deputy, Drumont made antisemitism the guiding theme of his political career. This got him into trouble with French law during the Panama Canal Scandal, but it demonstrated how antisemitism could be used to advance anti-parliamentary and anti-Republican feeling.

Drumont died in obscurity in 1917, but he started a movement that influenced other antisemites, like the Franco-Spanish aristocrat Antoine de Morès. After numerous failed business ventures in America, De Morès returned to France in 1889, where he came across Drumont's *La France Juive*. Inspired by Drumont's antisemitism and seeming to find in it the root of his own problems, De Morès became one of Drumont's main financial backers. De Morès's activities were wide-ranging. He founded societies that united antisemitism with Catholic socialism. Like Boulangism, De Morès's and Drumont's ideas appealed to an eclectic audience bringing together aristocrats, lower-middle-class merchants, and workers—in other words, a coalition of people who felt disenfranchised by the Third Republic. Influenced by his time living in the Badlands of the Dakotas, De Morès had his supporters wear purple cowboy shirts and sombreros. Significantly, De Morès called his ideology the *doctrine du faisceau*. De Morès's life as an adventurer foreshadowed, in some ways, the Fascist New Man embodied by such figures as Gabriele D'Annunzio. An attempt at politics failed, and De Morès ended up dying while trying to cross the Sahara Desert. If nothing else, the Marquis de Morès can be seen as an early progenitor of the fascist style.

A substantive influence on the future fascist movement was Charles Maurras. The way Drumont harnessed antisemitism for political gain became a key feature of the life and work of Charles Maurras. Raised in a lower-middle-class family in Provence, Maurras aspired to a literary career. As a young man, he moved to Paris, living on the Left Bank and writing literary criticism. Maurras was critical of Romanticism and hoped for a return to a classical form of literature. After reading Drumont, Maurras too became a convert to the antisemitic cause. The Dreyfus Affair further radicalized Maurras, who became a fanatical anti-Dreyfusard. In 1899, he cofounded the *Action Française* (AF), an association or league aimed at educating the French masses on the virtues of classical culture, royalism, and Catholicism. In 1908, the AF produced a journal in which Maurras contributed numerous articles calling for a renewal of France and a repudiation of the French Revolutionary heritage. Although he had been a Boulangist, Maurras was not a Republican, calling instead for the restoration of the monarchy.

Although royalism was a political project, Maurras was more interested in broader cultural values, and it was here that he had his greatest influence. Looking for the cause of France's cultural malaise, Maurras blamed Jews, foreigners, Freemasons, and Protestants. These four "powers," according to Maurras, had undermined the traditionalism France needed to remain true to itself and its heritage. This undermining was done mostly through culture, specifically urban culture, which had split France in two. Influenced by what he saw during the Dreyfus Affair, Maurras claimed that there were two Frances, the *pays réel* (the true France), and the *pays legal* (the artificial or legalist France). The True France was Catholic, rural, and royalist. Artificial France was parliamentary, republican, and urban. A nation, then, was divided into true, authentic citizens on the one hand and imposters, on the other. This dialectic between true citizen and imposter developed into a key theme in later fascist discourse. The imposters were subverters of culture, taking France away from its roots in the soil.

Maurras's integral nationalism would also be instructive for future proponents of the radical right. A believer in tradition and the importance of the Catholic Church (despite his own agnosticism), Maurras was influenced by the idea of a medieval, hierarchical society where the masses were kept in check by an elite. Maurras's ideal society was one based on order and hierarchy. Significantly, the more modern ideas associated with the

French positivist Auguste Comte also influenced Maurras's ideas. The order that Maurras called for was not simply a nostalgic one of a medieval past, but one based on objective, concrete, and scientific facts associated with Naturalism. Instead of a wholesale rejection of modernity, Maurras advocated for the eradication only of modernity's destructive elements. For Maurras, individualism was a corrosive and anarchic factor that needed to be subsumed to the higher good of the community. Maurras's AF was also successful in creating a fusion between nationalism and the Marxist revisionism of Georges Sorel (Sternhell 1994).

Maurras's debt to Sorel also accounted for his positive view of violence. In several of his writings, Maurras called for violent actions against Jews and politicians, incitements which landed him in jail. In his book, *Reflections on Violence*, Sorel advocated for the "myth of violence" as something anarchist unions could use to start a General Strike. Maurras came to support the idea of the General Strike. Although he did not enter politics, preferring a position of alterity, Maurras's support of violent action had some direct influence. In 1908, a group of young supporters of the AF created the *Camelots du Roi*. This group was made up of young activists who took their messages to the streets where they often engaged in violent confrontations with their opponents. These included shouting down professors at the Sorbonne, whom they accused of giving antipatriotic lectures (Nolte 1966, 101). As we shall see later in the book, this group had a role to play in the attempted fascist coup of February 1934.

The *Camelots du Roi* bears some resemblance to the Blackshirts of Italian Fascism and the Brownshirts of Nazism. Organized gangs of men specifically to bully, threaten, and beat up opponents is one of the hallmarks of the extreme right. To be sure, violence as a positive tool in political disputes was not a monopoly of the right. Suffragists in the United Kingdom demanding the vote also resorted to violence, as did anarchists. For Maurras and the AF, however, violence was not merely anarchic; rather, for them, violence contributed to social order. Maurras was able to bring together conservative calls to order with revolutionary tactics. The AF was also not an exercise in nostalgia but aimed at creating a new order that would appeal to conservatives and radicals at the same time.

Historians debate as to whether Maurras and his AF were fascist or not. To be sure, there are several dissimilarities between Maurras's movement and later fascist movements. For one thing, the AF never became a mass party. In fact, it never became a party at all. It remained a mostly literary and intellectual movement. Its attachment to traditionalist elements like Royalism and Catholicism made it seem reactionary. Moreover, Maurras lacked the charisma to develop the Cult of Personality so essential to fascism. However, a closer look shows that a few essential attributes of fascism were central in AF. Maurras's royalism, like that of Boulanger, was not identical to that of most French Royalists. This was not simply Restorationism. Maurras's interest in positivism suggested his ideas were more modern than those of the average reactionary. His Catholicism was also very different in some ways. He himself had fallen away from the Church and often proposed pagan ideas. Rather than simply delivering power to the Church, Maurras saw it as a bulwark of order, thus *de facto* putting the interests of the state first. This got the AF condemned by the Vatican in 1926. Like Italian Fascism later, Maurras's AF found in the Church an ally against the enemies of order but disagreed on other issues.

Maurras's flirtation with modern ideas—such as his support for workers' right to strike and his sympathy for the anarcho-syndicalism of Georges Sorel—also made him more than just a reactionary. AF was a movement of contradictions and was not a systematic ideology. It only made sense in the moment because of the context in which it was forged—namely, the Dreyfus Affair. Maurras was not the kind of charismatic leader requisite in any successful fascist movement, yet the AF persisted into the 1940s and was involved in the attempted coup of 1934 in Paris. In short, the AF mixed modern and traditionalist ideas and looked not to return to some idealized past but to forge a new society and culture. Like the Boulangist movement, the AF was part of the so-called New Right that emerged from the cultural clashes of the *fin-de-siècle*. It lacked a populist dimension, though, which prevented it from ever getting close to power. That dimension was found in the Lueger movement in Vienna.

A Political Experiment in Vienna

The *Ringstrasse* in Vienna is a ring road circling the old city. Built in the 1860s, the road represented the triumph of liberal modernity for the city's bourgeoisie. Just before the *Ringstrasse* meets the banks of the Donau Canal, near the *Stadtpark*, there is a square with an imposing monument dedicated to Karl Lueger, mayor of Vienna from 1897 to his death in 1910. One of the city's longest serving mayors, Lueger's memory is still alive in the modern city that he helped build. For the uninitiated, the monument seems a remembrance of a key figure in the city's history. A plaque at the foot of the statue, however, reveals that the mayor was a "controversial figure." Placed there in 2012, the modern plaque is a work of contextualization. Lueger's achievements as mayor are listed. They include the "expansion of municipal infrastructure," the modernization of the city's administration, and the "municipalisation (sic) of public transport." He protected the meadows and woods around the city and established a system of pensions for widows and orphans. He was, therefore, a modern politician who helped improve the city at a time when "waves of migrants from across the Habsburg Empire" began flooding into the city.

After this long list of accomplishments, however, the plaque concludes that Lueger "reinforced the antisemitic and nationalist trends of his time." Many tourists would probably not reach this final section after the exhausting celebratory remarks. It comes across as an afterthought. Surrounded by the splendor of the *Ringstrasse* monuments and palaces, one could be forgiven for not noticing that postscript, instead celebrating a man who contributed to a capital city that continues to inspire sentimental nostalgia for the lost Habsburg Empire. Lueger's modernization of Vienna included a bold new experiment in populist politics. While this is often overlooked, his mixture of populism, civic activism, and antisemitism represented the first successful implementation of protofascism. So successful was it that it did not escape the notice of a young man from

The Culture Wars of the *Fin-de-Siècle*

Linz, Adolf Hitler, who had migrated to the city, like millions of others, looking for an identity. The plaque only obliquely recognizes that this is a statue to a man whose legacy greatly influenced what later was called National Socialism.

Vienna was, in the late nineteenth century, a teeming city. The center of a sprawling, multiethnic empire, the city became a polyglot metropolis, taking in numerous immigrants from the provinces. The city embraced both modernity and tradition. *Fin-de-siècle* Vienna was, then, one of the most exciting cities in Europe, housing new artistic styles, sciences, and political experiments (Schorske 1981). Inevitably, Vienna became a flashpoint for the culture wars. The Viennese establishment panicked when, in May 1890, a group of socialists went on procession on the Prater. Although peaceful, the march struck fear in the Viennese bourgeoisie who feared that a Paris Commune was in the making (Kuna 1991). In the final years of Lueger's mayoralty, the modernist architect Adolf Loos began construction on a bank opposite the Habsburg Palace; the bank building sparked controversy with its modernist lines. The influx of Jewish immigrants, meanwhile, instigated an antisemitic backlash that would influence the young Hitler, who was lapping up the numerous racist pamphlets circulating the city.

The clash between the new and the old opened the door for KL and his CSP, politically and culturally. Late-nineteenth-century Vienna became a laboratory for the new shifts in politics—and Lueger took full advantage of these shifts. He came from a humble background but managed to obtain a law degree from the University of Vienna. He then went into politics as a liberal, but after meeting the Pan-German politician Georg von Schönerer, he began to shift toward the left, embracing social democracy. A supporter of the extended voting franchise in 1884, Lueger won a seat in the national parliament in 1885. There, he embraced the interests of the so-called "little man" who made up the petit bourgeoisie of the city. Lueger became one of the first politicians to realize the importance of the city's lower middle classes, made up of shopkeepers, artisans, lower officials, and municipal employees. This group of people proved essential for the rise of fascism in the twentieth century. Vulnerable to economic shifts without enjoying the privilege and protections of the upper classes, this group fell prey to fear and resentment, often expressed against immigrants and Jews. Slowly, Lueger, an eminently pragmatic politician, adopted antisemitism as a main platform in his campaigns for mayor.

In the late 1880s, Lueger created the Christian Social Party. While he was influenced by the style and politics of Schönerer, Lueger did not share his Pan-Germanism. In shaping his anti-liberal ideology, he instead looked to the monarchy and to the Catholic Church. Lueger brought Drumont's antisemitism to bear upon an Austrian Catholicism looking to orient itself in the increasingly liberal Austria-Hungary. Lueger's party brought Catholic aristocrats and lower-middle-class democrats together. According to Carl Schorske, Lueger was the "political chemist who fused the elements of Catholic social disaffection into an organization of the first magnitude" (Schorske 1981, 143). Like Boulanger, Lueger took traditional and conservative elements and refashioned them into something new and radical. Unlike Boulanger, Lueger was not hesitant to take charge of this new political formulation and put it into action. In 1897, he was elected mayor of Vienna despite serious misgivings from the monarchy and other conservatives who attempted to block his election;[4] he was still much too left wing for their comfort.

Lueger's time as mayor represented a political experiment. Mass politics had wrought new political tensions; Lueger's election—and the resistance offered by the Liberal establishment—made these tensions manifest. As would happen in Germany and Italy after the First World War, the liberals, who normally supported parliamentary government and liberal ideas, relied on authoritarian tendencies to block the will of the democratic electorate. This was especially true when that electorate was willing to vote in a radical and new movement, such as the Christian Socialists. Although Lueger was loyal to conservative forces—the monarchy and the church—some remained suspicious of his mass appeal. However, unlike Schönerer, Lueger was able to use a more calculating approach, creating a consensus even among some liberals who appreciated his attacks on the wastefulness of his predecessors. Since he was not known as a devout Catholic himself (like Maurras), he was able to win the support of those suspicious of clericalism. Lueger's shrewdness, in other words, allowed him to create an effective political organization that went beyond the more truculent Schönerer, who never came close to achieving power with his Pan-German movement.

What made Lueger's movement protofascist? In *Mein Kampf*, Adolf Hitler recognized Lueger as a major influence, along with Schönerer. Lueger's ability to mobilize the lower middle classes and create an effective political organization impressed Hitler, as did the mayor's ability to win traditional institutions over to his side. Hitler also noted Lueger's charisma and ability to gain unswerving loyalty from his base. He was critical, however, of Lueger's expedient approach to antisemitism, noting Lueger's famous quote: "I decide who is Jewish." Hitler's qualified praise has influenced historians' ambivalence regarding Lueger's protofascist credentials. Like Maurras, Lueger is often depicted as a pragmatic politician who used antisemitism without being a convinced antisemite. Moreover, Lueger's movement became increasingly conservative once its appeal spread to the countryside, leaving behind some of the more radical democratic elements of the early movement.

Yet there is much to recommend Lueger as a protofascist. To be sure, his party did not engage in the dynamic and violent actions of the later fascists. Nor did they promote anything approaching revolution, given Lueger's attachment to throne and altar. However, Lueger's mobilization of resentment and prejudice in the service of a positive, forward-looking program of reform hinted at the future. The plaque on his statue points at the public works projects his government accomplished. Like Maurras, Lueger did not want to turn back the clock to a feudal Austria run by the aristocracy. Rather, he aimed at creating a modern movement that appealed to the masses, albeit through attacks on the Jewish and Magyar elements in the empire. Refusing the aristocratic alterity practiced by Maurras, Lueger worked hard to express the frustrations and dreams of the lower middle classes. His skill at oratory allowed him to become the muse of the lower classes

---

[4] Lueger had been elected in 1895 but the emperor, Franz Josef, refused to ratify his electoral victory until 1897. The Liberal establishment backed the Emperor's resistance to Lueger's victory.

who felt alienated from the world of big business and finance, a frustration expressed via antisemitic tropes.

Lueger, therefore, was profoundly modern but also archaic. He appealed not only to the masses but also to the traditional elements in the aristocracy and Church who realized that the way forward involved some alliance with the masses and not a retreat into a sentimental view of the lost past. Lueger's promotion of public transportation and preservation of forests outside of Vienna helped him put his stamp on both the past and the present. His policies harmonized technology and nature in a way that would characterize Nazism in later years. All of this was carried out by vilifying both the Jews (associated with modernity) and the non-Germans in the empire. Lueger, in effect, discovered the "suburbs," a feature that would dominate twentieth-century politics. The suburb formed a space between the urban and the countryside. It became a liminal space where identities overlapped and where its inhabitants lived undefined lives.

While Lueger's movement did not have the trappings of fascism, the substance of the movement was clearly present. He appealed to those who felt culturally threatened, yet he also wanted to continue the path of progress. He also personified what one historian has called Vienna's "reactionary progressivism." This was a city that welcomed the modern, but always checked by tradition, a fact that frustrated many of the city's most illustrious artists, such as Gustav Mahler (Kuna 1991). In short, Vienna was a front in the European culture wars, and Lueger's skill was to be modern while at the same time expressing some of the cultural resentments against modernity.

Conclusion

The movements described in this chapter can best be classified as protofascist. They were novel experiments that hinted at things to come even if they cannot be formally described as fascist proper. The elements that made up the fascist cocktail were present in these movements; these elements were the cult of personality (Boulanger and Lueger), xenophobia, antisemitism, populism, and an elusive political classification. They mixed left-wing and right-wing ideas, an appeal to the workers with support from the aristocracy and middle classes. They claimed allegiance to traditional institutions such as the monarchy and the church without promising any real restoration of these institutions. They appealed to nostalgia but did not advocate a return to the past, instead exalting modern and even, at times, progressive ideas. Finally, these movements were fueled by the culture wars produced by mass society.

The early years of the twentieth century produced the conditions that made these novel movements possible. In France, struggles over national identity and the heritage of the French Revolution provided the backdrop to events such as the Boulanger and Dreyfus Affairs. The French population was not growing fast enough to keep pace with the Germans and Russians, instigating French fears of national decline. France feared not only external invasion but also internal subversion from foreigners and Jews. In

Germany, meanwhile, dreams of imperial conquest shared by the Kaiser and middle classes after 1890 fueled tensions with France and Great Britain.

The development of the *Kaiserreich* after German Unification in 1871 created the conditions that made fascism possible. Bismarck's identification of "enemies"—beginning with Catholics in the 1870s and then shifting to socialists in the 1880s—was a cynical tactic that fostered national unity. Despite the cynicism, this tactic succeeded, as it played into the fears and anxieties produced by a rapidly changing society. Germany's industrialization and the growth of a dynamic middle and working class challenged the older Prussian aristocracy. Mass society in Germany, as elsewhere, produced tensions. However, as a new nation, Germany had an additional level of anxiety, an anxiety expressed, by the rising middle classes, in calls for imperial conquests. This anxiety fueled the formation of various leagues (such as the Navy League with its millions of members).

The rapidly changing nature of German society made many fear that something essential was being lost. While Germany was advancing industrially and technologically, intellectuals were expressing a growing sense of unease. The so-called classical school of German sociology, produced by the German universities, began to examine the stresses and strains of their culture. Max Weber raised concerns about the "iron cage of rationality" that characterized modern society, while Georg Simmel pondered the impact of the modern city. Ferdinand Tönnies, meanwhile, published an influential tract in 1887 entitled *Gemeinschaft und Gesellschaft*, in which he argued that society can be divided into two groupings called "community" and "society." The former corresponds to a traditional society whereby the individual's will is in unison with the will of her neighbors; the latter is a modern phenomenon made up of isolated individuals chasing their own self-interests. Community unifies; society disintegrates. Relationships in society are based on money, while those in communities are grounded in mutual togetherness.

While the reading public for such works never went beyond those of specialists, their ideas circulated and were adapted to many of the prejudices of the time. Modernity was castigated as impersonal and harmful to traditional roots, thus threatening national identity. These critiques struck a chord with those obsessed with the ideas of decadence and degeneration, a uniquely "European disorder," according to Daniel Pick, that afflicted not just Germany but most Western countries in the years leading up to the First World War (Pick 1993). Informed by psycho-medical ideas as well as Social Darwinism, notions of decline and degeneration began to permeate all levels of public opinion. Fears of the crowd, or "mobs," driven by sexual deviancy, found their way into fiction and art. In France, the work of sociologists like Émile Durkheim began to probe into pathologies like suicide. In Italy, Cesare Lombroso, inspired by the banditry found in the south, gave rise to criminal anthropology. Crime and deviance became the subject of modern social science and the nightmare of bourgeois society. As Pick suggests, the politics of these works are "complex and plural" (Pick 1993), but they reflected a general anxiety among the middle and ruling classes around degeneracy. These were often linked to new political movements on the extreme left, such as socialism, Marxism, and anarcho-syndicalism.

France, Spain, and Italy, all faced the similar challenges of mass society; the syndicalist movements produced a wave of labor strikes in the first decade of the new century. In every case, they were met with stiff resistance from the state. The Italian army in Milan killed striking workers in 1898, while similar events occurred in France and Spain. Anarcho-syndicalist ideology, inspired by the writings of Georges Sorel, called for the violent General Strike as a positive tactic and even a "myth" to be exploited to forge a new society based on self-governing workers' communes. The General Strike was the basis for creating a new culture. Individual anarchists, meanwhile, embarked on a campaign to assassinate political leaders of and heads of state. In a wave of violence that would today be termed terrorism, anarchists assassinated the King of Italy, the President of the United States, and the heads of state of Spain, France, and Russia. Known as "propaganda of the deed" by its adherents, these events were inspired by the Paris Commune of 1871, when anarchists murdered the Archbishop of Paris along with other prominent citizens.

The anarchist wave of violence, which stretched from the late nineteenth century well after the First World War, played a dual role in the rise of fascism. The campaign, which included bombings, instilled fear especially among the ruling classes of the West. The specter of violence increasingly made state repression of anarchism attractive. For example, the assassination of Czar Alexander II of Russia in 1881 ended an era of reform and ushered in a period of harsh rule by his successor. They also stoked new rounds of xenophobia. In some cases, these acts were carried out by members of an ethnic minority, such as the assassination of US President William McKinley in 1901. In the United States, anarcho-syndicalism was increasingly associated with foreigners who became the targets of violence and xenophobia. The revival of the Ku Klux Klan at Stone Mountain, Georgia, in 1915 was aimed at targeting foreigners and Jews just as much as blacks.

However, the influence of these violent events on the rise of fascism was more ambiguous. While fear of the left fed into the later rise of fascism, many anarcho-syndicalists later became fascists, as Zeev Sternhell has pointed out. While middle-class society and the ruling establishment feared the disorder and crime instigated by left-wing movements, the violent tactics also proved attractive for preserving that sense of order. Anarchism's "myth" of violence—aimed as it was at producing a new and regenerative culture—proved appealing to a world beset by the unprecedented nature of the First World War, a war precipitated by the assassination of the Archduke Franz Ferdinand. This assassination, carried out by an anarchist group, was motivated not by left-wing ideals but by nationalism. By 1914, nationalism had become the preserve of the xenophobic right in places. The shift in nationalism from a republican left to a radical right has already been noted in France in the Boulanger Affair. While the Bosnian Black Hand group was motivated more by a romantic nationalism found in the mid-nineteenth century, their anarchist approach suggested a political shift to a new, radical right. This shift was made more evident with the First World War.

CHAPTER 2
TRENCHOCRACY

A Funeral in Fiume: "City of the Holocaust"

In October 1919, the entire city of Fiume, the former Austro-Hungarian port on the Adriatic, seemed to take part in a solemn funeral rite for two fallen aviators, Aldo Bini and Giovanni Zeppegno. The pair died on a reconnaissance flight when their plane crashed over Fiume. Thousands, including distinguished visitors from Italy, attended the funeral. Two platoons of *bersaglieri* (a unit of the Italian infantry) led the cortège through the streets, followed by bands and high military officials. These, in turn, were followed by long rows of citizens and trucks filled with flowers and wreaths. The two caskets were draped with flags. "The procession seemed endless," reported the Official Bulletin of the High Command. "It's a true plebiscite of love and pity."[1] The funeral was an impressive public spectacle not only for the number of participants but also its martial spirit: Bini and Zeppegno were First World War heroes, and the funeral procession was led by military figures. Moreover, rather than being a somber affair, the funeral was of almost festival-like quality. According to Michael Ledeen, "the funeral procession was a blaze of colors, composed of flowers, flags, and uniforms" (Ledeen 2002).

Overseeing this funeral spectacle was Gabriele D'Annunzio, poet, aviator, war hero, and adventurer, D'Annunzio was the "commander" of Fiume, which became an open city after the First World War. Leading a group of Italian war veterans, D'Annunzio "took" control of the city in September 1919. Despite some half-hearted resistance by the Italian army, D'Annunzio was allowed to lead a growing number of followers in the city and establish what he called the Regency of Carnaro. From September 1919 to December 1920, D'Annunzio and his band of Italian war veterans, mostly from the assault squads known as the *Arditi* ("Ardent Ones"), ran the city of Fiume while the Allies tried to come up with a proper solution for the city's future. D'Annunzio had no doubts about the city—it was Italian and should belong to Italy as one of the so-called "irredentist" (un-redeemed) territories that Italian soldiers had fought and died for between 1915 and 1918. At a speech given at the funeral, D'Annunzio declared Fiume to be a "holocaust city"—a martyred city—offered up as a sacrifice to the ambitions of the Allied powers with the complicity of the Italian government.

The funeral of the aviators was the first of what was to be a steady stream of festivals and commemorations that marked D'Annunzio's Regency. The poet became the choreographer-in-chief, keeping the citizens of the city engaged in a constant

---

[1] "Le solenni onoranze di Fiume ai suoi primi morti gloriosi," *Comando di Fiume d'Italia*, Series 1, no. 8 (Ottobre 11, 1919).

mobilization of passions and political spectacles. Speeches, processions, and spectacles abounded, and D'Annunzio was always at the center of things. A cult of personality emerged around the poet—known as the *vate* (bard) by his disciples—which became quasi-religious. D'Annunzio stoked this enthusiasm through his constant use of religious imagery. In his eulogy for the aviators, D'Annunzio told his audience that these "young Italians had fallen over the heart of the city, had died over the heart of the city, had been consummated over the heart of the city. Their faith has been converted into an eternal flame."[2] Anyone familiar with D'Annunzio's poetry and novels would have recognized these as typically D'Annunzian high diction rhetoric; it seemed to work in convincing his followers that something transcendent was happening in Fiume.

The experiment that was D'Annunzio's Fiume attracted observers from all over Europe and beyond. It became a magnet for those who were looking for something new in the wake of the most destructive war the West had seen. Adventurers, artists, diplomats, and ideologues descended on Fiume to have a look at the strange spectacle that surrounded D'Annunzio. War veterans fed up with the "old order" came to see what Fiume was all about. Men like Guido Keller, an aviator from the Great War, soon surrounded D'Annunzio. Known for his eccentric habits, such as walking on the beach naked, Keller established a "Ministry of the Coup" with which he planned military actions and plotted the overthrow of the Italian government. The leader of the Futurists, F. T. Marinetti, whose 1909 manifesto called for the destruction of museums and art galleries and praised war as the "great hygiene," called on D'Annunzio. Meanwhile, D'Annunzio lived out his reputation as a "decadent," as stories of orgies and drug use emanated from the governing palace. This hedonistic atmosphere attracted many of the visitors, while others simply wanted to bask in the aura of D'Annunzio, who had become an Italian national hero and an international celebrity. Still others, like Benito Mussolini, came to observe the political experiment that was Fiume.

Ostensibly, Mussolini had come to D'Annunzio to get the poet's blessing for his fascist movement, founded the previous March in Milan. He had also come to see what D'Annunzio had to offer and why his Regency seemed so successful. At first glance, D'Annunzio did not offer much in the way of substance. The poet, born in 1863 in Pescara, Abruzzo, a region in southern Italy, was known mostly for his decadent lifestyle and for his florid prose and poetry. He wrote erotic stories that scandalized respectable opinion, until the first decade of the century when he became an avowed Italian nationalist. In 1907, he published a play called *La Nave*, set during the mythical origins of the Venetian Republic. In 1915, D'Annunzio returned to Italy from exile in France to become one of the leading representatives for the interventionist cause, calling on the Italian government to enter the First World War.

D'Annunzio did not seem naturally skilled at politics. Before Fiume, D'Annunzio had tried his hand at conventional politics. In 1897, he was elected to the Italian Chamber of Deputies on a conservative platform, despite his anti-parliamentary views. Not an

---

[2]Ibid.

active participant in the daily workings of the chamber, D'Annunzio instead used his time in politics to make dramatic gestures. For example, in 1899 he crossed the floor to join the socialists in protest against the government's heavy-handed repression of a labor strike in Milan. He did not bother with reelection when his term was up. This brief foray into politics demonstrated D'Annunzio's lack of interest and even contempt for parliamentary politics and suggested that his notion of politics was a mostly aesthetic concern. Ideological consistency mattered less than the grand gesture. The way D'Annunzio shifted from right to left marked the futility of practical politics.

D'Annunzio's time in Fiume was more political theater than anything else. For D'Annunzio, the First World War was an opportunity to carry out bold actions, regardless of their practical military results. He became known for dropping leaflets over Vienna in October 1918 and his involvement in a raid on the Austrian fleet at Buccari the previous February. In both cases, D'Annunzio understood the psychological impact that these ventures had on morale, even if they accomplished little materially.

D'Annunzio brought this attitude to politics as well. Fiume became an experiment in the psychological appeal to the masses. Through the ceremonies and rituals, he devised, appealing to the war experience, D'Annunzio was able to construct a new kind of politics far removed from the staid world of parliamentary liberalism. This is what caught Mussolini's attention and influenced his development of fascism.

Historians have argued that, while D'Annunzio was never a fascist, his Regency of Carnaro represented a prototype of the fascist state. D'Annunzio's Fiume experiment included at least five characteristics that were later appropriated by fascist movements. These were the cult of personality, politics as religion, the development of a new language, a distaste for liberal, parliamentary politics, and a belief in the corporate state. Just like his military exploits, D'Annunzio's Regency amounted to little, but it left an influential legacy, rallying around a charismatic leader. While Fiume attracted an eclectic and eccentric cast of characters, D'Annunzio was always the central figure. Everything revolved around him. The cult of personality that D'Annunzio built up in Fiume was a product of his literary and military fame. The deliberate way he made public appearances and spoke to the crowds contributed to this cult as well. Appearing on the balcony of Fiume's municipal palace, D'Annunzio developed a style that was more than just words, employing a theatrical and rhetorical style (Figure 2.1). He tended to dialogue with the crowds. He would ask them questions and wait for their response. He would then respond to them with ad-libs, often breaking from his prepared remarks. In short, his speeches demanded from his audience not only passive reception, but also active participation.

Audience participation was also common in the rituals and celebrations mentioned earlier. These rituals became in the hands of D'Annunzio a kind of liturgy, shaping what was a distinctly religious approach to politics. Although he was an agnostic, D'Annunzio was obsessed with religion. A room in his home on the Lake Garda, the Vittoriale, is dedicated to religious objects he acquired during his lifetime. D'Annunzio's use of religious imagery predated his time at Fiume. In 1915, during the interventionist campaign, when he advocated for Italy's entry into the First World War, D'Annunzio gave a famous speech

Figure 2.1 The First Duce: Gabriele D'Annunzio addresses his admirers in Fiume. Credit: Getty Images.

in which he used the form of the Beatitudes. The funeral for Bini and Zeppegno clearly showed D'Annunzio's religious approach to ceremonies of state. Politics as liturgy was not new, born as it was during the French Revolution. D'Annunzio's contribution to this modern tradition was significant, though, because it not only applied to the ceremonials but also to the rhetoric he used in his speeches, along with the religious imagery which defined the very meaning of the Fiume expedition. Fiume was about "redemption," not only of the territory to Italy, but also of the incompleteness of the Risorgimento (the national movement to unify Italy in the nineteenth century). This idea of "redemption," a Judeo-Christian concept, forged an important link between D'Annunzio's Fiume and the rise of Italian Fascism (Gumbrecht 1996).

A key element in the D'Annunzian experiment was the deliberate use of language. In D'Annunzio's case, this was an eclectic mix of the religious and the modernist. D'Annunzio borrowed heavily from the Catholic lexicon familiar to most Italians. He used words like "sacrifice," "passion," "redemption," and "eternal flame" in abundance. He came across as a Christ figure ready to die for the redemption of Fiume. His favorite Catholic martyr was Saint Sebastien, a figure that he often referred to in his speeches. Mixed in with Catholicism were the many festivals which drew upon pagan Greek and Roman rituals, such as the Bacchanalia. Here, D'Annunzio was influenced by Friedrich Nietzsche and the philosopher's evocation of the Dionysian sources of culture. D'Annunzio's use of language also appealed to modernists—such as the Futurist and Dadaist supporters— who came to the city and surrounded figures like Guido Keller. Inspired by the modernist critique of bourgeois language, D'Annunzio invented nonsensical words like "*Eia, Eia, Alalà!*" as the battle cry of the Legionnaires. This phrase, like the dismissive phrase "*me ne frego…*" (I don't care) were later appropriated by Mussolini.

Drawing on his literary background, D'Annunzio used language to bring down the old world and build a new one in its place. His language directed at the Italian Liberal government and establishment was violent. He characterized Rome as a cesspool afflicted with pestilence. He baptized the Italian Prime Minister Francesco Nitti with the nickname *cagoia* (shit) contrasting him with the *teste di ferro* (Iron Heads) who made up his followers in Fiume. This duality, the division of the world into pure and impure, virtuous and corrupt, characterized most of D'Annunzio's speeches. The Legionnaires were the "chosen ones" who understood D'Annunzio's messianic appeal. Everyone was an enemy to be disparaged with violent and scatological language. D'Annunzio, in effect, founded what George Mosse called the "brutalization of politics," which, as a direct consequence of the First World War, eventually came to profoundly shape fascism (Mosse 1990).

This language served to denigrate not only the political establishment of Italy, but also the parliamentary system. However, the constitution devised by the anarcho-syndicalist, Alceste de Ambris, included a bicameral legislature. Its powers were limited, and the system was designed as a collective structure. Each citizen of the Regency had to belong to one of the nine corporations based on sectors of the economy. A tenth corporation, added by D'Annunzio, was reserved for the so-called "supermen" based on the philosophy of Nietzsche. The system reflected De Ambris's left-wing ideology, which included remarkably progressive notions, like women's rights. De Ambris's constitution, therefore, seemed to belie the brutality of D'Annunzio's rhetoric and represented a positive—and progressive—contrast to the Fiume experiment.

D'Annunzio's apologists—those who wish to minimize his influence on Italian fascism—often point out this leftist tilt. They remind us that he was never a fascist and notably refused to become the leader of Italian fascism when approached by some of Mussolini's opponents. D'Annunzio was also repulsed by the violent tactics of the fascist *squadristi*—or Blackshirts—and had a difficult relationship with Mussolini, whom he often disparaged. Some historians have pointed out the similarities between D'Annunzio's and fascism's respective styles, noting how Mussolini opportunistically appropriated the poet's style as a means of building up his own movement. D'Annunzio's support for representative government and women's rights—not to mention the generally hedonistic atmosphere at Fiume—also helped distinguish D'Annunzio's Regency of Carnaro from the regime Mussolini was later to build. Public memory of D'Annunzio maintains this separation between the poet and fascism. Today, the Vittoriale on Lake Garda is a state-run museum. When the author visited the museum in 2019, the tour guides did not mention fascism—except to note how D'Annunzio would keep Mussolini waiting when the Italian dictator made one of his frequent visits. The current director of the museum, the historian Giordano Bruno Guerri, goes out of his way to point out that the link between Mussolini and Fiume was very tenuous.

So why is D'Annunzio's Fiume experiment important for understanding fascism? As we shall see, fascism had a peculiarly defining style. Far from being a superficial aspect of the movement, its style was central to understanding how the movement itself worked. The gestures, rituals, and language pioneered by D'Annunzio at Fiume profoundly shaped fascism, especially in the absence of any definable and coherent ideology. Aesthetics also played an important role. D'Annunzio was an artist who, inspired by Nietzsche, made politics into an art. Walter Benjamin famously defined fascism as politics made into art; this can be traced back to D'Annunzio (Benjamin 1968). Jeffrey Schnapp, meanwhile, has argued that fascism's "aesthetic overproduction" served to mask its unstable ideological core (J. Schnapp 1996). The fact that D'Annunzio surrounded himself with an eclectic group of artists that included Futurists and even some Dadaists resembled Italian fascism's openness to different styles (although this was certainly not true of German Nazism and other fascist movements).

While it is true that fascism did not adopt the more progressive elements of the Regency constitution, it did—as we shall see—adopt the corporatist model, defining it as a middle way between communism and capitalism. The violent anti-parliamentary speeches by D'Annunzio and the general disparagement of the political establishment in Italy became a common trope for Mussolini's movement, and indeed for all fascist movements. D'Annunzio's populist appeal and his insistence on mobilizing the masses would feature prominently in fascism. Although D'Annunzio did not appear to aspire to the totalitarianism of fascism, his desire to fashion a new order centered on a Nietzschean superman became the prototype of the Fascist New Man. For all of his disavowal of violence, D'Annunzio did not object to groups of young men prowling the city to ensure that all citizens remained enthusiastic about the experiment. (This was under the direction of Guido Keller.)

It is possible to argue that Mussolini merely copied all of this to bolster his own movement. In other words, fascism rode on the coattails of D'Annunzio, who became a reluctant "John the Baptist" of the fascist regime. However, there remained a crucial organic link between Fiume and fascism: the war experience. Both D'Annunzio's and Mussolini's movements drew upon war veterans as their core support. For both, peacetime was a continuation of the First World War. Both referred to it constantly, using it to inspire the attitude and language of their respective movements. The so-called "mutilated peace"—a phrase coined by D'Annunzio to describe Italy's inability to claim all the "unredeemed territories"—was the prime factor that led to his seizure of Fiume. In fascists' eyes, the Italian government's weakness at the Paris Peace Conference was of a piece with the bitter perception that many Italians had profited from the war without donning the uniform; this fueled the formation of the *Fasci Italiani di Combattimento* in March 1919.

A military aesthetic pervaded these movements. Mussolini organized his supporters—all veterans—into squads wearing black shirts, carrying clubs and rifles. The tactics of the assault troops of the First World War, the *Arditi*, informed both D'Annunzio's Legionnaires and Mussolini's Blackshirts. The violent words used by D'Annunzio at Fiume against the Italian establishment became violent actions in the hands of Mussolini's squads.

This is intriguing because Mussolini's fascist movement predated D'Annunzio's taking of Fiume. In fact, the idea that the war—and specifically the war veteran—would form the basis of a new political experiment dates from December 1917, when Mussolini published an editorial in his newspaper, *Il Popolo d'Italia*, titled, "The Aristocracy of the Trenches."[3] Published two months after the Italian defeat at Caporetto—at which an Austro-German army broke through the Italian front and nearly reached Venice—Mussolini, who was serving in the trenches with the Bersaglieri regiment, argued that the trench experience was producing a "new aristocracy of the future." Parodying the medieval nobility, this aristocracy's coat of arms would be made up of a Friesian horse, a trench, and a hand grenade. Mussolini adopted the rhetorical style of the Futurists, praising the beauty of the hand grenade and the thrill of tossing them at the enemy. From there, Mussolini pointed out the polarization that was becoming evident in Italy. The country was splitting into two camps, argued Mussolini: those who fought and those who did not fight. This division would be sharpened once the war was over.

Although the creation of the fascist movement was still many months in the future, one can see the idea of such a movement taking shape in Mussolini's mind. He noted the groups of war veterans, most of them wounded, emerging in the cities such as Milan, Turin, and Bologna to protect their interests and defend themselves from those who might want to take advantage of their experiences to advance a pacifist agenda. Mussolini predicted that once the war was over, the old parties would disappear to be replaced

---

[3] Benito Mussolini, "Trincerocrazia," *Il Popolo d'Italia*, dicembre 15, 1917, p. 1.

by new formations that would renounce the terms "liberalism," "republicanism," and "socialism" (and the like). In its place, an anti-Marxist socialism would arise that would discover the virtues of nationalism. The workers returning from the trenches, predicted Mussolini, will realize that the supposed antitheses of class and nation would produce a new synthesis; this, in turn, would shape the politics of the future. Mussolini used musical metaphors to describe the kind of politics this would produce. It would be "*fortissimo*" in a key with "many sharps."

Although D'Annunzio's Fiume experiment differed in many ways from fascism, his choice to draw upon the war experience was already predicted in Mussolini's "trenchocracy." Here was the celebration of war, the belief that it created a higher form of humanity, which came from the trenches of the First World War. Here, too, the anger at contemporary politics and culture was expressed. In his editorial, Mussolini expressed the hope that a school for hand grenade throwing would result from the war to replace the useless education that most were receiving. In this essay, Mussolini exalts technological progress and hopes for a cultural rebirth, long before D'Annunzio used the same themes at Fiume. The notion of a new style of politics based on art also predated Fiume. To be sure, Mussolini's writing is derived from the Futurists and their love of war and cultural upheaval, but crucially, it predates D'Annunzio's Fiume, and it suggests that both men found inspiration in the same fundamental experience—the war.

1914

Images of cheering crowds have become famous. It is difficult for us today to imagine people celebrating in the streets after a declaration of war; it is just as difficult to imagine thousands of men rushing to the colors so that they can experience the fighting before Christmas. To be sure, many of the images of 1914 have become clichéd, and many historians have argued that the enthusiasm for war has been exaggerated. In fact, most people in Europe did not cheer for war. It was a vocal minority, mostly, and not entirely representative of popular feeling (Winter 1996). Everything about 1914 has become mythological, from the enthusiastic crowds to the supposedly beautiful weather of that final summer before the cataclysm that ensued. 1914 has been held up as a mass delusion believed by a young and naïve generation who saw in war the release needed from the boring and stultifying world of bourgeois Europe. The reality was much more complex, as Robert Wohl demonstrated in his classic study of the so-called "Generation of 1914" (Wohl 1979).

Whatever the reality of 1914, its importance in informing the future rise of fascism cannot be overlooked. Peter Fritzsche has demonstrated that the "myth" of 1914 was one of the key moments that shaped Germany's postwar future, regardless of what happened in the intervening years (Fritzsche 1999). The so-called "August Days" of 1914 lingered in the memory of Germans as a moment of national unity and common purpose. The compliance of the German Social Democrats, the largest party in the German Reichstag and staunch opponents of "imperialist wars," evidence how this unprecedented moment brought Germans of all political stripes together.

A similar myth spread in Italy but in a different way. Whereas Germans seemed spontaneously united in 1914, Italy was a divided country, and its government declared itself neutral when war broke out, even though it formally belonged to the Triple Alliance with Germany and Austria-Hungary. The country did not officially enter the war until the spring of 1915 on the side of the Triple Entente. This came only after secret negotiations with the Allies who promised to recognize some of Italy's territorial claims against Austria-Hungary.

The myth of 1914 in Italy was that popular pressure on the liberal government led to Italy's intervention. D'Annunzio, Mussolini, and the Futurist F. T. Marinetti were all public figures in what was called "Radiant May." D'Annunzio's famous speech at Quarto in the spring of 1915 came during the unveiling of a monument to Giuseppe Garibaldi's Expedition of the Thousand in 1860, seen as a key moment in Italian unification. D'Annunzio's speech connected the Wars of Unification with the need to intervene in the First World War. Only Italy's participation in this war, claimed D'Annunzio, could complete Italian unification, as the "unredeemed territories" would be added. The interventionist campaign created a "myth" that men like D'Annunzio formed an avant-garde minority that managed to, in the words of Robert Wohl, impose a revolutionary war "on a reluctant and hopelessly bourgeois nation" (Wohl 1979).

D'Annunzio's Quarto Speech was infused with Christian imagery, but his participation in the interventionist campaign—joined by other prominent figures—was also informed by modernist themes coming from the Italian avant-garde movement. These included Marinetti's Futurism and a group of nationalist, futurist, and idealist writers based in Florence. Born in Alexandria, Egypt, to Italian parents, Marinetti was influenced by the French Symbolists during his time as a student in Paris. In 1909, he published the "Futurist Manifesto" in a French newspaper where he called for the destruction of museums and libraries and their replacement with industries. Marinetti praised modern technology like the racing car (more beautiful than the Victory at Samothrace) and expressed a love for war (the world's only hygiene). He inveighed against the *passeism* (past-ism) that obsessed the Italian bourgeoisie. Although the manifesto was a political statement, Marinetti called for a cultural revolution, in which professors would be replaced by technicians, and politicians replaced by warriors. Like D'Annunzio, Marinetti liked to use religious analogies to make his arguments. In another manifesto, he called for a new religion-morality of speed. Violence permeated Marinetti's writings, from the car crash in the Futurist Manifesto, to the desire to "murder the moonshine" and wipe away the vestiges of Romanticism. When Italy entered the war, Marinetti and his followers joined up. Some of them, like architect Antonio Sant'Elia, were killed. Marinetti survived and wrote a memoir celebrating his time in the trenches. In 1919, he became one of the first to join Mussolini's *Fasci Italiani di Combattimento*.

One of Marinetti's influences found its way to Florence, where groups of young intellectuals were exploring avant-garde ideas in opposition to the bourgeois liberalism of the city's establishment. There, Futurist ideas mixed in with the Idealism of Benedetto Croce and Giovanni Gentile, as well as the nationalism of Enrico Corradoni. These young idealists/activists congregated around journals such as *Leonardo*, *Lacerba*, and

La Voce, where new ideas were explored and affirmed. Writers like Giovanni Papini, Giuseppe Prezzolini, and Ardengo Soffici, to name a few, used the new ideas to call for a renewal of Italian culture and an affirmation of Italian identity in the world. Taking as inspiration Corradoni's idea that Italy was the proletarian among nations, the *Vociani* condemned the current Italian establishment as weak and corrupt. Prezzolini took aim at Giovanni Giolitti, Italian Prime Minister, as the "Minister of the Malavita," accusing him of corrupt bargains with local elites in the south to maintain power. Not surprisingly, the Florentine intellectuals advocated Italy's entry into the war in 1914. In a way that prefigured Mussolini's trenchocracy article in 1917, the *Vociani* and *Lacerbiani* distinguished between two "Italies": the so-called "real Italy" and the "official Italy." The former consisted of avant-garde nationalists and revolutionaries, mostly young, while the latter was bourgeois, old, and liberal.

As with D'Annunzio, the Futurists and Florentines have their apologists. Although many of the individuals became lifelong supporters of fascism, not all of them did. Figures like Croce and Prezzolini became noted anti-fascists, as did Curzio Malaparte. Some of them, like Giovanni Papini, became fellow travelers. Papini supported Mussolini's regime but intellectually he was a defender of traditional Catholicism after his disenchantment with Futurism. To be sure, these movements had varied and widespread influences. Elements of Futurism, for example, made their way to the Soviet Union in the 1920s under the name of Constructivism. However, the intellectual pedigree of these movements found their way into fascism. As Walter Adamson has shown, several figures from this group went on to fight in the war and came back to Florence, where they founded groups like the *Fascio Politico Futurista* (Adamson 1993). Florentine modernism also contributed enormously to the vocabulary of fascism. Activists like Mario Carli, who served in the assault squads of the Italian army, became the founders of Roman Futurism after the war, where they, too, became fascist supporters.

The mixture of conservative and modern ideas needed an event like the First World War to synthesize them into a new movement like fascism. In Germany, a somewhat different process occurred, but it too required the forge of war to become Nazism.

The Rise of *Völkisch* Culture

In Germany, the expansion of so-called folkish thought made its way into areas of bourgeois life. Influenced by the Romantics, composers (such as Richard Wagner), and a host of lesser literary figures, German youth were exposed to a folk culture that put itself in opposition to modern, urban, and industrial life. The work of George Mosse has demonstrated how prevalent this attitude was in the years leading up to the war and how many of the young men who volunteered in 1914 were, to some extent, influenced by this idea (Mosse, *The Crisis of German Ideology: Intellectual Origins of the Third Reich* 1999). Folkish ideology resembled to some degree the ideas of Maurras and Drumont: they were both critical of modern culture, but it was pagan rather than Christian, and it focused on youth. It celebrated the forests of Germany and living "close to nature," especially with the Wandering Youth movement (*Wandervogel*). Writers like Walter Flex came out of this movement. He wrote a famous memoir called *Wanderer between Two Worlds*, describing his experiences in the war. He was later killed in action, but his book played an important role in linking folkish ideas with the war experience, describing it in idealistic terms. Based on the life of Flex's wartime friend, Ernst Wurche, the novel exalts a soldier who was a graduate of the *Wandervogel* and who fought with the works of Nietzsche and Goethe in his backpack.

Flex's hope that the war would usher in a new world and a new man was shared by Ernst Jünger, who ran away from home to join the French Foreign Legion when he was young, after having taken part in the *Wandervogel*. Like many war veterans who moved toward fascism after the war, Jünger found meaning and self-realization in the war. Wounded several times, and the winner of some of the most important military decorations handed out by the *Kaiserreich*, Jünger served in the assault squads known as the Stormtroopers. This experience was the basis for his war memoir, the *Storm of Steel*, which presented the war experience as something glorious and transcendent. Unlike many war memoirs that came out in the 1920s and 1930s, Jünger's account celebrated the war without sentimentalizing it. It was also clear that he saw in the war something new and constructive, an opportunity to forge a new man who would oppose the bourgeois world whence he had come. The Nazis found inspiration in his work. Like Gabriele D'Annunzio, who never joined the Italian Fascist Party, Jünger also refused to participate in any Nazi organizations, despite the opportunity to do so, something that allowed him to carve out a distinguished literary career after the Second World War.

Jünger's account of the war exalts such technology as the submachine gun, bombs, artillery, and airplanes. His mixture of modern technology with the sensibility of the folkish thinker formed a key element in Nazism as well as in fascism. Like D'Annunzio, a fascination with death accompanied the cult of technology. Flamethrowers, tanks, and guns dominate Jünger's imagination. War is presented as a fortifying trial where the superior man emerges from the trenches. Regardless of what Jünger's views on Nazism were in the 1930s, his book exemplified Nazi values. Jünger's mixture of Romanticism and Modernism in celebrating the war experience amounted to what Jeffrey Herf has called a belief that the Front Experience's (*Fronterlebnis*) pervasive death was necessary to bring forth a new man (Herf 1986, 15).

Writers like Jünger, D'Annunzio, Marinetti, and others reveled in the cult of the war experience. For them, the war was a life-giving moment, a moment which made the supposed betrayals of their governments more stinging. Whether it was Germany's Treaty of Versailles or Italy's Mutilated Peace, the outcome of the war did not correspond to the exaltation they experienced while in the trenches. Fascists generally viewed the war experience as affirming and the subsequent peace as insulting. The home front, especially the politicians, profiteers, and workers who preferred to go on strike rather than serve in the military, were viewed as traitors or *imboscati* (shirkers). To be sure, the anger against profiteers and shirkers was universal. Some of the poetry of Siegfried Sassoon, for example, expressed hatred against civilians. Sassoon, contrary to some of the writers mentioned above, did not exalt the war experience, although he preferred to return to the front rather than stay home in England. The British war poets, and even anti-war writers like Erich Maria Remarque in Germany, could not resist reliving the war in a way that was exciting—a strong contrast to the misery of the home front.

The First World War provided a powerful aesthetic, both for those who reveled in it and reviled it. This fascination for the aesthetic experience made its way into extreme politics after the war. As mentioned above, Walter Benjamin has noted the prevalence of the aesthetic in fascism. The British Futurist Wyndham Lewis depicted the First World War as a mechanized utopia, where even the soldiers become mechanical. Lewis demonstrated a fondness for the artillery, and it is no accident that he named his Vorticist journal *Blast*. In the 1930s, Lewis demonstrated an enthusiasm for Nazism and for Hitler. Lewis, like the writers mentioned above, was a modernist who searched for a new, modernist aesthetic to express the inexpressible—this led him to Nazism. The Front Experience proved crucial to the synthesis of the technological and reactionary that fascists came to embody. The horror of war even found validation in the fascist imagination as a means of warning Germans of the "monsters" that existed outside of Aryan society (Poole 2018). The war's horror and waste made the desire for order sharper. In his classic study of Expressionist films after the First World War, Siegfried Kracauer argued that such films—like *The Cabinet of Dr. Caligari*—paved the way for Nazism by instilling in German audiences the fear of disorder and death coming from without, and as such, these films appealed to autocratic tendencies (Kracauer 2004). The war also fed the technocratic imagination and sowed the seeds for what Omer Bartov has called the "industrial killing," characteristic of the Final Solution in the Second World War (Bartov 1996).

This fascination for technology and its ability to kill in mass numbers manifested itself in the modern, centralized state. The impact of the war on the fascist imagination went beyond the personal experience of the trenches. Important too were the lessons taught about mass regimentation and the channeling of a society's resources to the cause of war, or Total war. It was practiced, to varying degrees, by the major combatants in the war. It was not necessarily new. Glimpses of Total war could be seen in the American Civil War and in the French Revolutionary Wars. The scope of Total war in 1914–18 was, however, unprecedented. As the war progressed, millions of men were put into uniform and millions of women were employed in factories.

The application of Total War varied in each country, but each instance involved some degree of synergy between the state, private business, and the military. The volunteerism that had marked the first months of the war eventually gave way to conscription. Again, each country's experience was unique on this front, but most combatants at some point had to use coercive measures to get men into uniform. These coercive powers of the state increased as a result; conscientious objectors like Bertrand Russell in the UK, for example, were thrown into prison. Civil liberties were severely curtailed in all countries where emergency powers were invoked. The Italian military treated desertion severely under the leadership of Luigi Cadorna. In Germany, the elected government of Bethmann Hollweg was largely swept aside by a military dictatorship in league with big business. The state's ability to direct the economy without nationalizing industry would be instructive for future fascist regimes. Private business and enterprise mostly remained intact during the war, but businesses could be directed through the supply of government contracts. The war effort brought private enterprise and the state together in a manner that had enormous consequences for the future. It simply demonstrated that war could be good for business. The "military-industrial complex" about which future American president Eisenhower warned found its origins here.

The First World War did not only reveal the coercive potential of the state, but it also greatly shaped and informed the modern definition of propaganda. Total war required both coercion and persuasion to sustain the massive and sustained effort. The enthusiasm of 1914 eventually disappeared and was replaced by grim determination on the part of governments to keep the war effort going. Many of the combatants relied upon the citizen-soldier model that had developed since the eighteenth century (Mosse 1991). Other liberal state traditions also proved useful. Creating an Other—an enemy which a nation could identify and stand against—proved crucial for governments justifying the ongoing war effort to its citizens. This required dipping into the Culture Wars that had marked the *fin-de-siècle* and had already created the conditions for protofascist movements discussed earlier.

In the early months of the war, campaigns in Great Britain warned against the dangers of German *kultur*. Germany was painted as an aggressive, militarist nation that was setting out to brutalize the Anglo-Saxon West. Anti-German sentiment proliferated in the United States as well when the country entered the war in 1917. Propaganda posters depicted the Germans as "brutes" carrying off American women. This thinly disguised racist appeal was the same kind used against African Americans during the Reconstruction period. That the German is represented as an ape left little to the imagination. Though depicting the enemy as an animal dead set on the destruction of Western Civilization found great appeal in the fascist imagination after the war, it was already widely shared in the West. The events of the Dreyfus Affair in France, the pogroms in Russia against Jews, and the Nativist and racist campaigns in the United States demonstrated that modernity had created opportunities for mass campaigns of hate. These forces were now mobilized by the modern state in the First World War.

Total war also implied war by any means. Atrocities and war crimes have always occurred; however, the West went into the First World War with a set of rules, understanding that there were limits. The rise of industrial warfare made these ethical concerns even more urgent. The Geneva Conventions, detailing the treatment of war prisoners, dated back to the mid-nineteenth century and reflected the "benevolent empire" beliefs of bourgeois, liberal culture. Meanwhile, the Hague Conventions against the use of poison gas were signed in the decades leading up to the First World War. Once Total war became the norm, however, all sides flouted these conventions. Alongside the breaking of conventions came atrocities. The Germans committed several in Belgium in the early weeks of the war. The British government exploited these acts for propaganda purposes, suggesting to some historians that they may have been exaggerated. Examining the diaries of German soldiers, Alan Kramer has convincingly argued that the German Army did in fact commit atrocities, as did Germany's ally Austria-Hungary (Kramer, 2007). They were not alone.

War crimes trials did not, as sometimes thought, originate after the Second World War. The Allies held war crimes trials after the First World War as well (Kramer 2006). One of these trials was held in Istanbul, former capital of the Ottoman Empire. It dealt with the genocide of the Armenians committed by Turkish troops in 1915–17. Attacks on the Armenian minorities in Istanbul predated the war and were partially a consequence of a renewed Turkish nationalism after the Young Turk Revolution of 1907. In 1914, the Ottoman Empire's ally, Germany, helped broker a treaty that ended the ethnic violence, but the outbreak of the First World War prevented this deal from being implemented. Instead, the Ottomans used the war as a justification for genocide. The genocide itself forced Armenians through marches into the Syrian Desert. Those who survived the marches were placed in concentration camps. According to Stefan Ihrig, the Germans knew about these killings but did not protest, in the interests of keeping the alliance strong (Ihrig 2016). The Nazis, too, would later use war as a cover for genocide. Originating in a revolutionary nationalism desirous of ethnic purity, the Armenian genocide inspired the Nazis profoundly. (Not for nothing, either, did the Nazis note the lack of international protest due to preoccupation with the war effort.)

Conclusion

The D'Annunzio episode in Fiume demonstrated that the First World War thus served as a laboratory out of which the experimental politics of fascism emerged. While none of the above-mentioned factors were in and of themselves fully fascist, all of them were united in fascism after the war. The experience of trench warfare—coupled with the dramatic changes ushered in by the war—ignited the fascist imagination. This is perhaps best captured in a war painting. In 1918, the British war artist John Nash painted an image of no-man's-land. Slightly abstract, the painting depicted the lunar landscape created by the war, illuminated by the rising sun just beyond the hills. It is an image at once desolate and hopeful. Nash titled it *We Are Making a New World*. Although Nash never became a fascist, his painting encapsulates the two images that would dominate the fascist mind. On the one hand, a world was ending and left in ruins—out of these ruins, however, came the chance to build a new order of things. The war, far from being a waste of human life and material, was a forge out which a new humanity was born. Nash's compatriot and fellow war painter, Wyndham Lewis, who did develop fascist sympathies, saw this new humanity as made of steel, machine like, engaged in the industrial slaughter that was the First World War. While both artists painted what Samuel Hynes has called "anti-monuments" to the war, these artists saw in the war the birth of a new world (Hynes 1990). The cultural turmoil caused by the war provided the opportunity for future fascists to contemplate both the destruction of the old world and the birth pangs of the new. The Nietzschean vision of "creative destruction" that already informed many of the generation of 1914 seemed borne out by the events of the war.

The end of the war offered a spectacle that seemed to confirm this dyad of apocalypse and rebirth. With the wholesale destruction and massive loss of life (more than nine million dead), the war brought down centuries-old institutions. The Habsburg, Hohenzollern, and Romanov dynasties had all collapsed under the weight of Total war. In Russia, the world's first communist regime rose to power, a fact that would have an enormous influence on the rise of fascism. The familiar order of empires and dynasties was replaced by new states in central and Eastern Europe, theoretically expressing the nationalist aspirations of different ethnic groups. Dissatisfaction and anger with the peace settlements—especially in Germany and Italy—gave the new order of things a provisional character that allowed adventurers like Gabriele D'Annunzio to make their own, temporary order.

The political collapse of the European state system provided one of the "shocks" caused by the war and set up what Alan Kramer has called the "nexus between sacrifice, utopian expectations, and the outcome of the war" (Kramer 2009, 45). Kramer warns against making a too easy connection between the First World War and fascism, noting that the trauma of war provoked several different responses. This is correct, but the war was the necessary event that made fascism (and Bolshevism) possible. As we shall see in the upcoming chapters, the radical politics and extremism that spawned fascism was largely due to the experience of war and its political and cultural legacy. Fascist movements drew mostly upon war veterans (as did left-wing movements), and they incorporated a positive and energized view of the war experience. The anger and resentment caused by the outcome of the war was directed at civilians and politicians who were seen as having benefited from the war and betrayed those who fought it. The First World War sparked the fascist imagination, providing the element missing from the protofascist movements discussed in Chapter 1. When the Italian Prime Minister Giovanni Giolitti sent a gunship to Fiume in December 1920 to smoke out D'Annunzio and his followers, it simply confirmed the world that the Fiuman Legionnaires understood—that of the war. In an example of that sacralization of politics that made D'Annunzio such an influence on fascism, the poet declared this to be Fiume's "Bloody Christmas." The Fiume experiment could not have ended any other way, and in ending that way, it birthed a new movement that would bring about an even greater Holocaust.

CHAPTER 3
RED YEARS, WHITE TERRORS

Munich: From Beer Halls to Greek Temples

Munich, city of art and culture. City of Nazism. On November 9, 1935, the Nazi Party staged a solemn procession through the streets of the Bavarian capital, commemorating the twelfth anniversary of the failed Beer Hall Putsch, Hitler's first attempt to seize power in Germany. It was an impressive spectacle from a movement now firmly in power since Adolf Hitler was appointed Chancellor in January 1933. The putsch had been commemorated every year since then—but this one was different. On this occasion, the Nazis were laying to rest the sixteen putschists who had been killed in 1923. One of them had been marching right next to Hitler. The ceremonies began the night before, during a solemn evening procession when the sarcophagi were brought to the Feldherrnhalle on the Odeonsplatz. This memorial to Bavarian soldiers was now the initiation site of Heinrich Himmler's *Schutzstaffel* (SS). The sixteen caskets lay in state.

The next day, accompanied by some sixty thousand Nazi Stormtroopers, the caskets were carried to the newly built Temples of Honor at the Königsplatz. Designed by one of Hitler's favorite architects, Paul Ludwig Troost, these two structures resembled Greek temples. Next to them were the Nazi Party Headquarters, or Brown House, and two other prominent neoclassical structures designed to accommodate Nazi ceremonies. The Greek style reflected the Nazi obsession with the neoclassical, and it fit the Greek theme of the square. Built by the Bavarian King Ludwig I in the early nineteenth century, the square was a testament to an earlier era's love of ancient Greece. At the opposite end of the Troost temples, was a Greek-style gate called the Propylaea, built to commemorate the Bavarians who lost their lives in the service of the Greek War of Independence. Two large Greek-styled buildings flanked this gate, both housing art collections, a testimony to King Ludwig's desire to make Munich into an art capital.

The procession that led to this square began at the Bürgerbräukeller, a beer hall on the other side of the Isar river, near the train station. This was how the Beer Hall Putsch was reenacted each year by Hitler and the old guard Nazis. Nazism began in the beer halls of Munich, far away from the neoclassical pomposity of Ludwig's Munich. Nevertheless, the two worlds were intimately connected in the imagination of Hitler and thus for his movement. In his autobiography, *Mein Kampf,* Hitler celebrated Munich as the capital of German art, a truly German city in contrast to the larger and more cosmopolitan Vienna, where he had lived before moving to Munich in 1913. In Hitler's mind, Munich was a city that best embodied the Germanic spirit. "Most of all," wrote Hitler, "I was attracted by this wonderful marriage of primordial power and fine artistic mood … this single line from the Höfbrauhaus to the Odeon, from the October Festival to the Pinakothek"

Figure 3.1 Adolf Hitler and other Nazi leaders lead a procession commemorating the anniversary of 1923 Beer Hall Putsch. Credit: Getty Images.

(Hitler and Manheim 1971). From the beer halls to its Greek temples, Munich came to reflect the contrast between beer drinking and veneration of the classical past, from the tastes of an elite to that of the masses. For Hitler, there was no contradiction between these two worlds (Figure 3.1).

In May 1938, Hitler designated Munich as the Capital of the Movement and the Capital of German Art. A place for the muses and the masses, the spirit of the Bavarian capital was firmly imprinted on Nazism. However, Munich's influence was not just that of a place, but of a time. The famous beer halls of Munich, most of them built in the late nineteenth century—when the city was booming into a metropolis after being incorporated into Imperial Germany—became the site of the various right-wing *völkisch* groups that descended on Munich after the downfall of the Bavarian Soviet Republic in 1919. Coming from Berlin and Vienna, paramilitary groups made up of battle-hardened ex-servicemen found refuge in the large beer halls where they drank, sang, and conspired to eliminate their enemies on the left. In these cavernous halls, like the Höfbrauhaus, the members of the *Freikorps*, who had come from Berlin after liquidating the Spartacist Uprising in January, reveled in the violence that had brought down the Bavarian Soviets. In the smaller rooms of the beer halls, groups of political activists met, plotting to establish a *völkisch* future for Germany. Not content to simply prevent Bolshevism from taking root, these groups aspired for a Germany that would revive the Germanic spirit, a pure community freed from Jews, Freemasons, and cosmopolitanism.

The atavistic atmosphere of the beer halls was the miasma that made Nazism possible. The architecture of the beer halls became metaphors for a movement that tried to create that "straight line" Hitler fantasized about. They were large buildings with spacious central halls, designed to hold thousands of beer drinkers spread out on long tables. The halls were decorous, often built with classical archways and Bavarian decorations. The Höfbrauhaus's walls were covered in illustrations of historical and hunting scenes. The buildings were either neoclassical, Renaissance, or Gothic in style, reflecting the historicism of the nineteenth century, when bourgeois architects borrowed from past styles. These were not seedy taverns, hidden away in the dark corners of Munich; rather, they were large, imposing buildings that celebrated Bavarian sociability in the veneer of high culture. They dominated the street corners of Munich and became landmarks. It was in one of these, the Bürgerbräukeller, that Hitler had hoped to launch his national revolution in 1923, because it was here that three high officials of the Bavarian government were meeting to plot their resistance to directives coming from the Social Democratic federal government in Berlin.

A decade later, the Nazi national revolution eventually came—but it was in the drawing rooms and streets of Berlin, not in the beer halls of Munich. Yet, that failed putsch remained deeply embedded in the Nazi psyche. The March to Berlin, hoped for in 1923, really did begin here in Munich. This was the significance of that solemn celebration in 1935. Frederic Spotts said the ceremony "turned a burlesque into a sacred celebration of heroism and rebirth"; it became a "melodramatic sacrament" (Spotts 2003). Munich was the site where Nazism showcased fascism's many sides. A hybrid of the elite and the masses, a tale of rebirth and vindication, and politics turned into a religious spectacle. Why Munich? "How was it," writes David Clay Large, "that this genial place, this center of beery good cheer and magnet of muses, came to play the crucial role it did in the development of National Socialism? How was it that the land of *Dichter und Denker* (poets and thinkers) became the country of *Mörder und Henker* (murderers and hangmen)?" (Large 1997, xvii) Furthermore, how could the failure of 1923 be transmuted into a triumph?

These questions are central to understanding the emergence of fascism, a new political and cultural phenomenon that gripped central and southern Europe after the First World War. As we saw in the previous chapter, the war experience is crucial in understanding this new movement. However, the war experience in and of itself did not cause fascism. The world of "murderers and hangmen" needed a context in which some individuals took their experience of the trenches and transformed them into something unprecedented. This chapter will examine how the experience of three countries—Italy, Germany, and Hungary—provided the space for fascism to rise. Although these countries presented their own unique situations, they also gave birth to a movement that became transnational due to similar experiences. In each case, the war was interpreted as a defeat. Even though Italy was on the winning side of the war, D'Annunzio's idea of a Mutilated Victory suggested that it may as well have been a loss.

Fascism in Europe and Beyond

The Allies treated Hungary as a war aggressor. Meanwhile, Germany was blamed for the war and handed a humiliating peace treaty. In all three countries, the postwar turmoil gave rise to the specter of Bolshevism, a movement that terrified the establishment and the middle classes. This, in turn, caused a counterrevolutionary backlash known as the White Terror. In Italy, Germany, and Hungary, the circumstances gave rise to the radical right. As one historian has noted—commenting on the transnational character of the White Terror—militant right-wing activists "were shaped by the common experiences of war, military defeat, unfulfilled imperialist ambitions, revolution, territorial amputation and irredentism" (Gerwarth 2008, 182). Not everyone who joined these counterrevolutionary movements became fascists, though, nor did they share a common political ideology apart from an opposition to Bolshevism. Yet, out of this fertile ground, fascism sprouted.

The Red Years

Munich was one of the first cities to fall to Bolshevism in Central Europe. On November 7, 1918, two days before the German Kaiser Wilhelm II abdicated his throne, the Wittelsbach dynasty in Bavaria was toppled. The Wittelsbach family had ruled Bavaria for eight hundred years. A democratic republic called the People's State of Bavaria replaced them. Its leader was the Independent Socialist, Kurt Eisner, who had only months before been arrested for spreading anti-war messages and encouraging war workers to put down their tools. Although Eisner proved himself a moderate, open to working with the Social Democrats, he was seen as a radical and Bolshevik by his enemies. To make matters worse, he was Jewish. In February 1919, Eisner was on his way to the Bavarian parliament to announce his resignation after a poor showing for his coalition in state elections. Before he got there, a right-wing radical nationalist shot him in the back. Eisner's assassination opened the floodgates to a period of violent unrest in Munich, which led to a more radical Bolshevik regime and an extremely violent right-wing backlash that ended in May.

The events in Bavaria struck fear into the hearts of German middle classes and convinced many of them that Bolshevism was on the rise. In January 1919, the Spartacist Uprising in Berlin seemed to confirm their fears. Since the armistice in 1918, waves of soldiers and workers councils, modeled on the events in Russia, had spread throughout Germany. In Berlin, a republic was declared on November 9, led by the Social Democrats, who immediately collaborated with the German Army to suppress the Spartacist uprising. With restrictions pending on the military, the government turned a blind eye while the militia units set up by returning soldiers, mostly middle-ranking officers, violently suppressed the uprising. Armed by the military, these units, known as the *Freikorps*, roamed throughout Germany in their uniforms with machine guns and armored vehicles, looking for Bolsheviks. After dispensing with the Spartacists and murdering their leaders, Rosa Luxemburg and Karl Liebknecht, the militia units turned to the south and stormed into Munich.

In Budapest, capital of the newly independent Hungary, a republic was proclaimed on November 16, 1918. Led by the aristocrat Count Mihály Károlyi, the new government was essentially a moderate democratic state, hampered by having to deal with the victorious Allies and their demands. Known as the "Red Count" by his enemies on the right, Károlyi resigned in March 1919 after the Allies made exorbitant demands on the Hungarians. A Soviet Republic proclaimed on March 21 by the journalist and Bolshevik Béla Kun replaced him. Kun was a revolutionary who had taken part in the Russian Revolution. A confidant of Lenin, Kun aimed to establish a system that mirrored Lenin's policies in Russia. The so-called Republic of Councils lasted a mere one hundred and thirty-three days before it was toppled by a combination of foreign invasion and right-wing insurgents.

In Italy, the so-called "Two Red Years" of 1919–20 were opened by the Occupation of the Factories in September 1920. After the war, socialist labor unions saw enormous increases in membership. Stoked by the success of the Russian Revolution and bitter about the profits made by industrialists off the back of the soldiers who fought the war, socialism spread rapidly among the industrial workers in the cities and the agrarian unions in the Po Valley. The leadership of the Italian Socialist Party (PSI), meanwhile, had officially opposed the war, a fact that gave them great prestige after the war ended. They also used violent and extremist language that often belied their more pragmatic practices. Nonetheless, the language of the PSI helped further radicalize the unions. Started by the metallurgical unions in the northern industrial cities, the occupation of the factories demonstrated the potential power of the labor unions but ultimately failed mainly due to a lack of support from the PSI. Despite this, socialist victories in local elections in November 1920 continued to haunt conservatives. The defeat of a nationalist coalition in Bologna was especially alarming, leading landowners to rely on fascist militias to defend against attacks from the socialists.

In each nation—in Germany, Hungary, and Italy—the leftist challenge ultimately failed. What they left behind, though, was a fear of revolution among the middle classes and a distrust of liberal democracy from conservatives, landowners, and industrialists. Nationalists came to believe that socialists were anti-national, working on the orders of the Soviet Union. Most alarming was the violence, either actual or potential, the left was willing to use, from the armed occupation of factories in Italy to the forced requisitions and seizure of land and industry that took place in Bavaria and Hungary in the brief period of Bolshevik rule. The tendency of the Bavarian Councils to use hostages, and the Hungarian Soviet's use of "Lenin's Boy" to attack opponents, raised fears of the kind of violence seen in Russia. These fears, both real and perceived, led to the counterrevolution known as the White Terror.

The White Terror

The pushback against Bolshevism in central and southern Europe after the war has become known as the White Terror because of the extreme violence often used by right-wing militia groups in Germany, Hungary, and Italy, not to mention Austria. The word "white" reflects the kinship these groups felt with the White Army that opposed the Red Army in the Russian Civil War (1918–21). The ferocity of that conflict came to characterize the White vs. Red struggles in central Europe. On April 29, 1919, as *Freikorps* units marched toward Munich, committing a series of atrocities along the way—such as the murder of twenty medical orderlies and the execution of several unarmed red soldiers—the Soviet regime in Bavaria ordered the execution of eight hostages held at the Luitpold gymnasium. This event sent shockwaves through Munich, especially among the middle classes who already viewed the Soviet Republic with horror. Known as the *Gieselmord* (hostage murder), this event touched off the civil war that would rage throughout May. Stories of atrocities circulated throughout Munich, justifying the rampages of the *Freikorps*, who entered the city on May 1 (Figure 3.2).

Many Bavarians welcomed the *Freikorps* as liberators. Crucially, as Joachim Fest has pointed out, they "appealed to the imagination of the public" (Fest 1974, 113). This was especially true of the Ehrhardt Brigade, a well-known *Freikorps* unit that had achieved fame suppressing the Spartacists. Their symbol was a swastika, an ancient runic sign that they carried with them as they marched on the Maximilianstrasse, one of Munich's main boulevards. The unit was named after its leader, Hermann Ehrhardt, a decorated war hero, who established the brigade's fame as the best of the Freikorps units. The Bavarian *Freikorps*, led by Franz Ritter von Epp—another war hero who was still on active duty with the German Army while he led his unit against the Bavarian Soviet

Figure 3.2 Flame thrower squad of *Freikorps* in action during the Spartacist Uprising, 1919. Credit: Alamy.

Republic—joined them. Out of this unit came the likes of Ernst Röhm, a captain in the German Army who had won the Iron Cross First Class at the Battle of Verdun in 1916, one of the First World War's worst battles. These units, along with several others, were decisive in overthrowing the Soviet Republic on May 3. They were also known for their brutality. When it was all over, the *Freikorps* may have been responsible for the deaths of some six hundred people, half of which were civilians (Kershaw 1998). This included reprisals against Russian POWs who were still being held in Munich. The murders were followed up by mass incarcerations of political opponents. Significantly, the *Freikorps* did not leave the city once the Soviet Republic was overthrown. They stayed and formed the nucleus around which a radical right-wing culture developed, especially in the Beer Halls.

The influence of the *Freikorps* on the fascist imagination was enormous. Not all *Freikorps* members became fascists; in fact, some of them became opponents of Hitler and the Nazis in the future. However, their style and their actions would leave their mark. Each of these units was identified with its commander, fostering a cult of personality. Individuals like Ehrhardt, von Epp, Röhm, and Wolfgang Kapp all harbored political ambitions. In March 1920, Kapp would lead his *Freikorps* unit to overthrow the German government in the failed Kapp Putsch. Since these militia groups were not officially part of the German Army, they would adopt their own symbols, like the swastika. Thus, each unit developed their own mystique, which only increased with their brutal actions. They promised to reestablish order and a sense of German nationalism. Their mimicking of the German Army—with their steel helmets, uniforms, and heavy military hardware—sowed terror in their opponents and admiration among their supporters. As Ian Kershaw has pointed out, the *Freikorps* units effectively simulated the First World War in Munich with such actions (which even involved aircraft) (Kershaw 1998).

In the months following the overthrow of the Soviet Republic, the *Freikorps* made Munich their home. Civil authorities allowed them to flaunt themselves in public and commit atrocities unhindered. Munich was the base of operations for a series of assassinations carried out by members of the Ehrhardt Brigade that targeted prominent Social Democrats blamed for the Treaty of Versailles. The *Freikorps* units were largely made up of ex-officers from the war trenches, most of whom hailed from the middle classes. They were also joined by younger men who had missed out on the war and wanted to share in the warring mystique. One such notable figure was Ernst von Salomon, who was completing his training in a military academy when the war ended. Von Salomon served in the Ehrhardt Brigade while in Munich and would later participate in the Kapp Putsch. He would serve time in prison for his part in the assassination of the Social Democrat Walther Rathenau. A German nationalist steeped in *völkisch* culture, no one did more to romanticize the *Freikorps* than von Salomon. He would write a series of books and screenplays in the 1930s extolling the actions of the Freikorps. He continued doing so even after the Second World War.

In his writings, the *Freikorps* were glamorized as "outsiders" who saved Germany from Bolshevism. After the units were dissolved following the suppression of the Bavarian Soviet, many of the men who made up the corps remained in Munich, becoming a part of diverse groups, leagues, and secret societies. Around these nuclei emerged *völkisch* and political groups. After ending Bolshevism, these groups fantasized about creating a new Germany based on extreme right-wing ideologies. Klaus Theweleit's classic psychological study of the ex-*Freikorps* relates how these male associations pursued masculinist ideas, ideas which often led to hatred of women (Theweleit 1987). Congregating mostly in the beer halls, these groups dreamed of a Germany purified of foreign and hostile elements, especially the Jews. When the fighting against Bolsheviks ended, Theweleit shows how the groups turned on each other, murdering their own comrades who were suspected of betrayal. Some of the associations valorized a vision of ruralism and a "return to the land," while others idealized labor. Racial and Darwinist views were common among the ex-*Kämpfer*. In short, these groups indulged in political and social fantasies that emanated from the cultural morass of *völkisch* thought. Culture, in the case of the ex-*Freikorps*, preceded politics.

To keep themselves afloat, these groups cultivated new members, committed crimes, and canvassed wealthier elites for donations. Cultivating the conservative establishment was a crucial element in the survival and influence of these groups. In one of the trends that marked fascism, elements of the revolutionary right cultivated establishment figures as a bulwark against the left. This was the case with the *völkisch* groups in Munich in 1919–23. One prominent example of a group that combined *völkisch* thought with esotericism and far-right politics was the Thule Society. Formed in 1918 by Count Sebottendorf, an adventurer who inherited his title by marriage, the society met in the swanky surroundings of one of Munich's most exclusive hotels. The group appealed to high society figures, such as aristocrats and wealthy industrialists, as well as lawyers, university professors, judges, and scientists. This well-heeled group met to discuss political and racial issues. They immersed themselves in pagan and Germanic mythology and believed in the pure Aryan ideal.

Aside from its ideas, the Thule Society was also well organized and connected with the counterrevolution in Bavaria. The group was involved in the White Terror via its support of the *Bund Oberland*, a *Freikorps* unit that fought in the Baltics against Polish communists. In May 1919, the *Bund Oberland* came to Bavaria to help overthrow the Soviet Republic. Several of its members belonged to Thule and the society helped finance and arm them. The Thule Society also developed a sophisticated propaganda apparatus to defend against the actions of the White Terror. Central to this was the creation of a newspaper called the *Beobachter*, the forerunner of the future Nazi newspaper, the *Völkischer Beobachter*. Ultimately, according to Nicholas Goodrick-Clarke, the occult Thule Society played a crucial role in the success of the Bavarian counterrevolution, helping to create a "raw and rancorous atmosphere" in which the counterrevolution thrived (Goodrick-Clarke and D'Olier Butler 1992, 149). Their most significant achievement, however, was laying the groundwork for the emergence of the Nazi Party.

To reach out to the workers and lower middle classes in the beer halls, the Thule Society sponsored the creation of the German Workers' Party (DAP) in 1918. Two of the society's members, Anton Drexler and Gottfried Feder, led this group, which styled itself as a discussion circle. Drexler was a machine fitter who had once been a member of the Social Democrats. Critical of Marxism and capitalism at the same time, Drexler aimed to create an anti-communist workers' movement. Feder, on the other hand, was the son of a civil servant and trained as a civil engineer. Like Drexler, Feder aimed for a socialism divorced from Marxism and married to German nationalism. Feder's political views were primarily anti-capitalist with a focus on finance capitalism. Like Drexler, Feder argued that German society was made up of producers and exploiters, with Jews belonging to the latter group. Antisemitism is the unifying theme of this group, which met in the Leiber Room of the Steinecker Beer Hall.

The DAP was one of several of these small groups meeting in the beer halls of Munich. Designed as a means of instructing workers in the finer points of *völkisch* thought and drawing them away from socialism, the DAP struggled to get any traction. This changed, however, when Adolf Hitler attended one of their meetings in September 1919. Serving army intelligence, Hitler was ordered by his superiors to spy on groups like the DAP. In *Mein Kampf*, Hitler recounts that he was unimpressed by what he witnessed and, at one point, even got involved in a heated discussion with one speaker who advocated Bavarian separatism. It was here that he discovered his "vocation" for politics, although he was already gaining a reputation among his fellow soldiers and superiors for his talents as a firebrand. Although unimpressed with the little party, he agreed to join it once he left the military after receiving an invitation from Drexler. As it turned out, Hitler was ideally suited to the party's ambitions of bringing political enlightenment to the artisans and workers who made up the bulk of the DAP's small membership.

Over time, the DAP would also begin attracting ex-members of the *Freikorps*, such as Ernst Röhm, who served with von Epp's unit as well as the Bund Oberland. Dietrich Eckart, a failed writer and journalist who had participated in the Kapp Putsch, also joined. A virulent antisemite, Eckart blamed both communism and capitalism on the "Jewish spirit." He would eventually become the chief editor of the Nazi newspaper, the *Völkischer Beobachter*, and one of the early propagandists for the Nazi movement. Members of the Thule Society such as Alfred Rosenberg and Rudolf Hess also joined the DAP in those earlier years. In March 1920, with the budding leadership of Hitler, the party changed its name to National Socialist German Workers' Party (NSDAP).

Hungary

The growth of violent paramilitary groups and their connections to political and cultural circles on the far right was also seen in the Hungarian cities of Szeged and Arad (now in Romania). These movements had in common with their German and Austrian brethren the sense of defeat in the First World War and a desire to extinguish Bolshevism. The Hungarian case, too, saw a mixture of culture and politics that made extremism inevitable. Here too was the exaltation of violence and a desire to return to some pure idea of being Hungarian that rejected many aspects of the modern world. As in Bavaria, the growth of paramilitarism in Hungary was the result of the toppling of the Soviet regime under Béla Kun. Exacerbating this situation was the significant loss of territory at the hands of Hungary's neighbors, namely Yugoslavia, Poland, and Romania, countries that formed a hostile ring around the country. Long before the Treaty of Trianon recognized Hungary's truncation, these countries had already seized the territory because of "claim jumping," or not waiting for the diplomats in Paris to sign treaties before claiming land. With the rise of the Soviet regime, there was little sympathy from the Allies, especially the French, who occupied the southern cities of Hungary like Szeged.

The immediate trigger of the Soviet collapse in Hungary was the occupation of Budapest by the Romanian army in August 1919. The occupation lasted until November with French support. When they left, Hungarian paramilitary units led by the so-called National Army occupied the city. Commanded by a former Austro-Hungarian admiral, Miklós Horthy, the militias went on a rampage. Horthy's gang, along with other units that joined him, went after Bolshevik leaders and sympathizers with violent zeal. However, the attacks were wide-ranging as Jews and Freemasons came under attack, reflecting the deeper cultural roots of the Hungarian White Terror. The attack on Hungarian Jews reflected the wave of antisemitism that swept through Hungary in 1919 and 1920. This was a surprise, as assimilated Jews had enjoyed a degree of liberty in prewar Hungary.

All of this arose out of a seething cultural discontent and economic crisis that was especially felt in the capital. Budapest, like Munich, had become a receptacle of the resentments and fears of the postwar period, a fact exacerbated by the Romanian occupation. The city saw an influx of some forty thousand deserters and 1.2 million demobilized soldiers looking for housing and employment (Kitchen 2006, 190). From this transient and potentially violent population arose the political clashes that led first to the Soviet Republic and then the White Terror. The violence unleashed by the militias set the stage for elections to a constituent assembly in January 1920, which saw a victory for a coalition of right-wing parties. Although the elections were held using a secret ballot, the "continued white terror made a mockery of the whole enterprise," according to one historian (Kitchen 2006, 193).

Although this new state in Hungary was not fascist, it reflected the kinds of contradictions that would show up in fascist movements. In the summer of 1921, the new government signed the humiliating Trianon Treaty, whereby nearly two thirds of Hungary's territory and three fifths of its population was lost, creating a situation where more Hungarians lived outside of Hungary than within it. The creation of the Little Entente alliance between the successor states against Hungary resulted in a siege mentality that fueled the rise of radically right politics. Opposition to Trianon came to dominate domestic politics, with the cry of "*Nem, nem, soha!*" (No, no, never!) appearing at far-right rallies. In 1921, Habsburg pretenders used this atmosphere to attempt a restoration of the monarchy; this failed, however, due to Allied opposition. Although Hungary was technically a monarchy, a fact that pleased the more traditional elites of the country, there was little interest from the radical right to bring back a monarch. Instead, the radical right, supported by Admiral Horthy, was able to push the politics of the country in the direction of a revisionist foreign policy—and an increasing antisemitism.

The attacks on Hungarian Jews arose from traditional antisemitism but were also driven by economic competition. The Hungarian middle classes, like the Viennese merchants at the turn of the century, viewed the Jews as a threat to their economic well-being, a fact exacerbated by the postwar economic crisis. As one historian has noted, it was mainly the professionally educated middle classes who fueled the antisemitism that gripped Hungary in the 1920s (Walters 1988). Such an economic crisis, coupled with a rise in antisemitic sentiment, brought fascism to power in 1932, when Horthy appointed Gyula Gömbös as prime minister. A former captain of the Austro-Hungarian General Staff, Gömbös was one of the so-called "Twelve Captains" in Szeged after the war. He founded the Hungarian National Defense militia corps in November 1918 and became one of Horthy's key supporters, defending the Regency against the Habsburg pretenders. He remained in power for four years until his death in 1936. During his time as prime minister, Gömbös did not pursue radical legislation against the Jews (at Horthy's request), but he did entangle Hungary in alliances with Nazi Germany and Fascist Italy. Such antisemitic legislation would be introduced by Gömbös's successors, who, on paper, were more moderate, aristocratic leaders. With Horthy as Regent and Gömbös as prime minister, the influence of Hungary's White Terror continued well into the 1930s and made Hungary a key member of the Axis.

The Rise of Italian Fascism

The emerging radical right in Germany and Hungary found inspiration in the 1922 appointment of Benito Mussolini as Prime Minister of Italy, who thus became Europe's first fascist leader. There was nothing inevitable about Mussolini's rise to power, but the forces of postwar Italy, like those in Germany and Hungary, created the conditions on which Mussolini's party fed. Although Italy was on the winning side of the war, figures like Gabriele D'Annunzio declared the peace a "mutilated victory" since Italy did not receive the irredentist territory it claimed. Furthermore, divisions on the home front left a legacy of bitterness and hostility. As we have seen with Mussolini's idea of "trenchocracy," some veterans saw Italy as a country filled with traitors, or *imboscati*. These ranged from the trade unions who called a general strike late in the war, to the "profiteers"—industrialists—who used the war to accumulate wealth while avoiding the trenches. Added to this was the general indifference and even opposition to the war found among the mass of Italians. Most of the troops were made up of Italian peasants from the south who showed little interest in the war effort. When the Austrians broke through at Caporetto in October 1917, they were helped by the mass desertions in the Italian Second Army. Against this background of defeatism and indifference came Italian fascism.

The *Fasci Italiani di Combattimento* was officially formed in Milan on March 23, 1919. The war veteran, journalist, and former revolutionary syndicalist Benito Mussolini gathered a group of around a hundred people in the Palazzo Castani in Milan's Piazza San Sepolcro to announce his new political association. It was an inauspicious beginning, as the meeting did not produce any definite statement of principles. As Adrian Lyttelton has noted, the name of the new association was vague since it did not clearly indicate a political position (Lyttelton 2004). It used the ancient Roman symbol of the fasces, a bundle of rods tied around an ax. Various groups in different countries had used the symbol previously. For example, fasces could be seen in various landmarks in the United States, such as the Lincoln Memorial (built between 1914–22). In the 1890s, a group of left-wing Sicilian peasants used it in their revolt against landlords. Most recently, it was the symbol of the *Fasci di Azione Rivoluzionaria*, a group of interventionist associations in 1914–15. It was from this group that Mussolini took inspiration when he adopted the fasces for his fledgling movement.

The individuals that met that day in March came from various backgrounds and professions, with the majority hailing from the left, specifically the revolutionary syndicalist movement. Like Mussolini, they had broken with their comrades in support of the war effort, the vast majority having fought in the trenches. In addition, they wished for a reformed socialism that harmonized with nationalism. Beyond that, there were precious few specifics given in the speeches of that day. One of the speeches came from the father of Futurism, Filippo Tommaso Marinetti, who hoped that this new movement would contribute to a Futurist vision. The new movement—not a party, as Mussolini emphasized—was an aspirational association that hoped to forge a new Italy out of the war experience. It would be made up of men who fought the war for those who "produced," in opposition to the "parasites" who profiteered from the war while not risking their own lives. When a manifesto was finally produced in June 1919, it reflected these progressive views, calling for an 85 percent tax on war profits, a progressive tax on capital, and the seizure of land from the Church and its subsequent redistribution to war veterans. Virtually all these demands would disappear as the fascist movement gradually moved toward the right in the next few years.

Whatever fascism was at the beginning, its defining characteristic came to be the paramilitary units known as the Blackshirts. Made up at first of ex-servicemen from the assault units known as the *Arditi*, these groups of armed men developed into *squadrismo*, since they organized themselves into squads. These units of 200–250 men made it their mission to attack socialists during the Two Red Years. Their first "action" came in April 1921, when they ransacked and burned the headquarters of the Socialist newspaper, *Avanti!* in Milan. The men of this assault belonged to the Arditi Association run by Ferruccio Vecchi, an early supporter of fascism who provided Mussolini's personal bodyguard. The attack by the *Arditi* proved popular with the new movement, and Mussolini gradually organized the first units in the summer of 1919. Over time, these squads of Blackshirts came to dominate the movement, and they became a major headache for Mussolini as they proved difficult to control.

The explosion of *squadrismo* in Italy, however, came in 1920–21, on the heels of the socialist occupation of the factories and their victories in local elections. The Occupation of the Factories in September 1920 by the metallurgical unions proved crucial. Industrialists, humiliated by the event, came to believe that the liberal state could no longer be trusted to defend their interests, and many of them turned to the Blackshirts, providing them with funds, weapons, and means of transportation. The growth of *squadrismo* in the major industrial cities like Milan and Genoa was accompanied by the even greater rise of the movement in the provincial centers of the north. Cities like Bologna, Cremona, and

Ferrara would all see *squadrist* activity in response to the perceived threat of the peasant leagues. The landowners of the Po Valley subsidized the Blackshirts to go out and attack these organized groups of farm laborers and sharecroppers in violent actions that often led to deaths.

By 1921, the Fascist movement had grown to over two hundred thousand members grouped in eight hundred local associations known as *fasci*. While the fascist movement failed to gain traction in elections, failing miserably in the November 1919 legislative elections, it was growing exponentially in the provinces via *squadrismo*. As in Germany and Hungary, the violence of the squads constituted the movement's appeal. Attacks on socialists and so-called "subversives" were met with the approval of the local elites and were even abetted by local police. They also appealed to young men from the lower middle classes, many of whom had missed out on the war and wanted to fight a war, wherever it might be. The squads developed a certain elan in their so-called "punitive expeditions." They adopted the D'Annunzio war cry and many of the squads borrowed his slogans such as "*Me ne frego*" (I don't care). Depending on the size of their coffers, some created standards with symbols, such as skulls or other insignia, much like the *Freikorps* in Germany. Their symbols of punishment were the *manganello* (club) and the *olio di ricino* (castor oil), a laxative that they forced their opponents to drink. Many of their actions also were in the nature of the *beffa*, an audacious act in the form of a prank or a joke.

These activities became part of the *squadrista* legend in later years. The romanticization of the Blackshirts in later years allowed apologists to suggest they were harmless compared to the brutality of the Nazi Brownshirts. Films like Federico Fellini's *Amarcord* (1974) contributed to this trivialization in later years. The reality of Blackshirt violence was quite different, of course. The clubs and the castor oil could inflict severe injury and even death. Moreover, the Blackshirts were equipped with surplus military hardware, often with the connivance of active service members. They traveled on Fiat 18BL trucks to make lightning ambushes on the headquarters of socialist organizations. Many of the squads had machine guns, rifles, revolvers, and bombs, which were used to simulate the war experience. The damage they caused was significant, and it resulted in the deaths and mutilations of their opponents. Armed socialists often fired back; Blackshirts who died this way became martyrs to fascism.

The "punitive expeditions" were later celebrated in fascist lore as "battles," such as the so-called "Battle of Parma" in August 1922 or the assault on the Balkan Hotel in Trieste in July 1920, when the fascists torched a building that housed the offices of Slavic associations. Both assaults caused numerous deaths. Those who supported such violence pointed to the imminent threat of a Bolshevik revolution. While the reality of such a revolution was minimal—proven by the failed occupation of the factories—the fascists played on the fears of industrialists, landowners, and middle classes of a coming "civil war." *Squadrismo* painted the Italian liberal establishment as a weak bunch unable to stop Bolshevism and labeled these liberals as shirkers. While the squads terrorized the countryside, they also participated in patriotic events and downplayed any kind of ideological discourse, in contrast to the anarcho-syndicalist fascists who still made up the movement in the big cities.

The success of *squadrismo* in drumming up support for fascism, especially in the provinces, caused some severe tensions within the movement. In his classic work on the rise of Italian fascism, Adrian Lyttelton has demonstrated how the early fascist movement was riddled with factions and tendencies, due largely to its lack of ideological focus. *Squadrismo* seemed to fill this ideological hole by its emphasis on action, confirming the *fascio*'s identification as a movement. In the meantime, the revolutionary syndicalists, many of whom belonged to the "Fascists of the First Hour," increasingly clashed with rural fascists, who were less interested in theory and more focused on protecting the property rights of the landowners. This fault line overlapped with those who wanted to keep the movement small and elite as opposed to those, mostly agrarians, who aimed for a mass party. Finally, contrasts developed between those who aimed for a revolutionary takeover of the state and those who, like Mussolini, hoped for a normalization of the movement as a parliamentary force working strategically with other parties. In 1920, several of the early fascists left the movement when Mussolini failed to support D'Annunzio's cause in Fiume. The movement's progressive shift to the right, culminating in the declaration of the PNF in November 1921, further alienated the republicans and anticlericals in the movement who were angered by the party's official support of the Church and monarchy.

Mussolini's transformation of the movement into a party in 1921 was his attempt to wrest control of the movement from the local fascist leaders. Much of the momentum enjoyed by fascism in 1920–21 was due to the rise of local leaders who organized their own *fasci*, often without direct support from Milan. These leaders developed their own cults of personality akin to that surrounding Mussolini. They were the ones who brokered the alliances between the Blackshirts and local elites, and they were the ones who dominated the provincial towns as fascism grew stronger. In cities like Trieste, where a "frontier fascism" was developing, leaders like Francesco Giunta became extremely powerful and *de facto* city leaders. Giunta divided the city into quarters and had squads patrol each quarter, ready to assault socialists and Slavs. Other local squad leaders, like Italo Balbo in Ferrara, Leandro Arpinati in Bologna, and Roberto Farinacci in Cremona, followed Giunta's example. These men attained a great degree of prestige through their ability to lead and commit ferocious acts of violence. Balbo achieved a reputation for assault-style tactics, learned from his time in the *Arditi*. His "Ring of Fire" exploit, where he and his group raced around the countryside setting fire to as many local socialist cells as possible, became part of his legend. Farinacci, meanwhile, was known for his brutality and ambition. He would become one of Mussolini's greatest rivals within the PNF in later years. Arpinati exemplified the kinds of compromises fascists were willing to make in the service of the cause. Although he came from a revolutionary syndicalist background, he was willing to hold his nose and make alliances with landowners whom he otherwise despised (Lyttelton 2004). The tactic worked, as the Bolognese *fascio* soon became the largest in the country.

Called *ras* (after Ethiopian chieftains), the local fascist leaders became the most dynamic and volatile element in fascism by 1922, so much so that they represented a threat to Mussolini's leadership of the movement. Their violent and insurrectionary methods increasingly clashed with Mussolini's pragmatism. Although he railed against democracy and parliamentary regimes, Mussolini aimed to use parliament as a launching pad toward national power. This proved increasingly difficult due to the provincial *ras*. In 1921, the crisis over the Pact of Pacification revealed the potentially explosive divide within fascism. This "pact" was a truce between the socialists and fascists brokered by the fascists who sat in parliament. It was mostly aimed at neutralizing the increasingly violent *squadrismo*, especially in Bologna. The Pact made the above-mentioned rifts clearer, as the old socialist and urban fascists largely supported it, while the agrarian reactionaries opposed it. Mussolini eventually dropped the pact when he realized the extent of provincial opposition to it at a conference of local fascists in Bologna in mid-August. Although he failed, Mussolini realized that now was the time to transform fascism into a party with a structured, hierarchical leadership. The movement had to be nationalized and the local influence of the *ras* neutralized through this process.

The paramilitary arm of fascism was thus both a cause of fascism's success and its potential disintegration. For Mussolini, any hope of "normalizing" fascism required it to make an alliance with more established parties on the right through parliament. He had to do this while maintaining fascism's potential for violence, for it was through violence that fascism grew, especially in the provinces. The paradox that Mussolini faced, as did Hitler in Germany, was to make fascism both revolutionary and reactionary. Rather than search for some doctrinal consistency or orthodoxy, Mussolini accepted that fascist doctrine had to be flexible and had to appeal to groups in Italian society that would see in fascism a salvation. It meant constructing a movement that found broad support from different social strata. It also required focusing on the class that came to dominate fascism: the lower middle classes, or petty bourgeoisie. This included shopkeepers, artisans, clerks, and middle-ranking officials in the military who felt that no one represented them. While the working class relied on socialist organizations and industrialists and landowners had their own associations, the lower middle class had no one to speak for them. Their condition was exacerbated by the persistent economic crisis of the postwar period. This was the group attracted to Karl Lueger in Vienna and to the *völkisch* groups in Bavaria. These groups had no political doctrine spelling out their interests; rather, they turned to fascism, which represented their fears and mobilized them against their enemies, real and perceived.

The Beer Hall Putsch

The rise of Hitler's NSDAP mirrored that of Mussolini's fascists. Beginning as a small group in beer halls, the Nazis eventually developed a paramilitary arm in Ernst Röhm's *Sturmabteilung* (Stormtroopers, or SA). While the Blackshirts started their campaign of terror by assaulting socialist newspapers and headquarters, the Nazis brawled with their socialist opponents. The first came on November 4, 1921, at the Hofbräuhaus, when an outnumbered group of Nazis took on a group of social democrats who had filled the hall to contest one of Hitler's speeches. The Nazis later celebrated this event as the "Battle of Hofbräuhaus" and the birth of the Brownshirts.[1] The militarization of the movement paralleled that of the Italian fascists, causing similar tensions. Some of the original members, like Drexler, eventually drifted away from the party, disagreeing as they did with this development.

Hitler's growing leadership became another source of tension within the NSDAP. At one point, when encountered with resistance, Hitler threatened to leave the party—but his skills as a propagandist and orator convinced the membership to keep him. As with Mussolini's movement, the more democratic origins of the movement clashed with the militarized hierarchy to which Hitler aspired. Furthermore, Hitler aimed for a mass movement and not the small, elitist, conspiratorial group Drexler and company had created in 1919. For Hitler, the NSDAP was primed to take over Bavaria and Germany; first, though, its numbers had to increase. The persistent economic crisis and the political instability of the Weimar Republic helped in the growth of the movement. Hitler's speeches in the beer halls attracted larger crowds of both supporters and of opponents, necessitating a move to the larger venues like the Hofbräuhaus.

Although the leaders of the Weimar Republic had worked with subversive elements on the far right to stop a Bolshevik revolution, there was no love for the republic on the radical right. Former *Freikorps* attempted to assassinate politicians who had signed the Treaty of Versailles—men they had dubbed as the "November Criminals." In August 1921, Matthias Erzberger, one of Germany's authorized representatives to sign the armistice, was murdered. The following year, former members of the Ehrhardt Brigade assassinated Walther Rathenau, who had signed the Treaty of Rapallo, renouncing Germany's territorial claims from the First World War. In all these cases, the perpetrators were brought to trial but invariably received light sentences if found guilty. As with the ex-*Freikorps* activities in Munich, in Germany criminal acts were either condoned, abetted, or dismissed by members of the judiciary and police. A growing sense of impunity among the far right resulted from the establishment's tacit approval of their actions.

Such impunity—and the continuing difficulties faced by the Weimar Republic—provided fertile ground for extremist movements like the NSDAP. In 1923, things came to a head when the German government defaulted on its reparations to the Allies and the French Army moved in to occupy the Ruhr. In the short term, the French occupation seemed to benefit Weimar, as it had the effect of uniting German public opinion against the French, and thus the republic. However, this was undermined by the ruinous inflation caused by the printing of *Reichsmarks* needed to pay off reparations. The spectacular inflation suffered by Weimar in these years effectively wiped out life savings. The middle classes felt the brunt of this inflation. The French occupation, meanwhile, was a national humiliation that aggravated the one felt under Versailles. The French proceeded to take its reparations in kind from the industrial output of the Ruhr factories, which further deepened the country's economic crisis.

---

[1] The Austrian painter Felix Albrecht immortalized this event in a work called "The Brawl" (1930).

The Crisis of 1923 provided Hitler's NSDAP with the opportunity it needed for a putsch. The fact that Hitler saw this as a chance is testament to his overarching self-confidence, a leadership trait that helped him win control of the movement. At the same time, Hitler also demonstrated an element of pragmatism. The NSDAP was still a relatively small and local organization and was in no way in a position to topple the Weimar Republic in Berlin. What matters here is context. The Weimar Republic was perceived as weak, easily humiliated. Its judiciary seemed to favor the far right against its own government. Meanwhile, in Bavaria, a conservative establishment was in a political struggle with the federal state in Berlin. Gustav Ritter von Kahr, a typical establishment figure who had been friendly to the paramilitary groups in Munich, headed the Bavarian government. He, along with the army commander in Bavaria, Otto Hermann von Lossow, and the chief of police, Hans Ritter von Seisser, seemed amenable to working with the Nazis when contacted by Ernst Röhm and Hermann Göring.

On the night of November 8, 1923, these three men were holding a meeting in the Bürgerbräukeller when Hitler and his Brownshirts crashed the meeting. Firing a shot into the ceiling, Hitler ordered the crowd to keep in place while he ushered the three government officials into a backroom. There, he demanded that the three men join him in leading a March to Berlin to depose the government, or he would shoot them and himself. Röhm had already, in the meantime, managed to secure the main army barracks in the city. The men agreed—but Hitler then left them with General Erich von Ludendorff, a commander of the German Army in the war who had become a far-right hero. While Hitler was gone, Ludendorff allowed the men to leave the beer hall, thus ending any chance they would help the cause.

The putsch should have ended then and there, but Hitler, after a night of indecision, finally decided to carry out the putsch on his own. The next morning, he and his fellow Nazis marched to the Felderrnhalle, the monument built to honor dead Bavarian soldiers. Before they reached the square, the Bavarian police confronted the Nazis and a brief gunfight ensued—when the smoke cleared, fourteen Nazis and four police officers were dead. The men standing on either side of Hitler were shot, but he was not. He was able to escape the police and went into hiding for the next little while.

The Nazi Beer Hall Putsch had, then, failed miserably. In its wake, the very existence of the NSDAP was uncertain. Hitler and several of his comrades were arrested. It was clear that Hitler's movement simply was not large enough to carry out a revolution. Hitler had been inspired by Mussolini's March on Rome in October 1922 (discussed in the following chapter) and believed that a similar coup could happen in Germany. He was badly mistaken. Even the conservative government officials of Bavaria were not willing to march with the Nazis despite their seemingly favorable disposition toward Hitler and the far right in Munich. Only the presence of Ludendorff, who had marched with Hitler during the putsch, gave the event some degree of prestige in conservative circles. In the end, not even Ludendorff was able to prevent the shooting. For those on the extreme right, the failure of Hitler's putsch, combined with that of Kapp three years previously, suggested that the moment for a *völkisch* coup had passed.

Despite the failure, the Beer Hall Putsch served some important lessons for Hitler and his party. Hitler's instincts, in contrast to those of some other members of the NSDAP, was to harness the support of the conservative establishment. Although this had failed during the putsch, Hitler remained committed to this strategy in the long term, and it would eventually bear fruit in 1933. The failure of the putsch also gave rise to an important element of fascist thinking—specifically, harnessing the rage of failure and humiliation to mobilize support. Hitler could, in the future, point to the putsch as a reminder of a corrupt and diseased society that had failed to appreciate what the Nazis had to offer. It was an occasion to demonstrate that the Nazis were a far-sighted elite fighting against a decadent culture. If the putsch had failed, it was not because of the weakness of the Nazis, but rather the decadence of Germany. The Nazis who were killed died not because they rushed into a foolhardy enterprise; they had died fighting against the evils of a dying culture. Hence, they became martyrs to a "lost cause," which fit nicely into the romanticism that enveloped the far right in the postwar years. In short, the time simply was not right, and the putsch was a "glorious defeat" that set the stage for later success. This was the message conveyed by the commemoration of 1935.

Conclusion

This chapter has examined the rise of fascist movements in Italy, Germany, and Hungary after the First World War. Picking up from the previous chapter, it has demonstrated how a war aesthetic came to characterize these movements. According to Michael Mann, the paramilitary character of fascism made it distinctive (Mann 2004). The war experience had permeated deeply into many of those who returned from the front, especially those who had served as officers. Feeling a sense of disempowerment brought on by demobilization and the return to civilian life, many of these men flocked to extremist politics where they could maintain a "warlike" footing. This meant either joining the revolutionary left or the extremist right. The profound postwar crisis experienced by all countries—but especially acutely in countries like Germany and Hungary, who had been on the losing side of the war, and Italy, which lost the peace—brought about a militarization of politics. Added to this was the threat of revolution from the left. This frightened the establishment, and many lost confidence in the postwar regimes.

All of this was part of a general and pervasive sense of crisis which overwhelmed many countries after the war. Although liberal democracy seemed to have won and became the system of choice in most postwar countries, there was a sense that something was profoundly broken in culture and society. Richard Evans has argued that the politicization of life after the war opened a "culture war" scenario that favored the rise of the extreme right (Evans 2004). Liberal democracy had opened the door to massive political mobilization with, in the case of Germany, huge voter turnouts in the post-1918 elections. While on the one hand these could have been seen as a success for democracy, in the case of Germany—but also Hungary and Italy—they became vehicles for the politicization of cultural issues. Politics became about culture and vice versa. In the spirit of wartime propaganda, internal cultural rivalries were contested politically. Cultural diversity spawned a battlefield. Those with differing worldviews became mortal enemies to be confronted on the streets.

Fascists viewed their opponents in cultural terms, attacking the press and the arts as arenas of the "enemy." Hitler's own obsession with the arts was, as we shall see, motivated by his hatred of the rising postwar avant-garde. Art and culture became battlefields— and they had to be confronted with violence. Antisemitism increased rapidly in this postwar context, since the Jews were seen as not only cultural but also economic and religious foes. Fascists in Italy saw socialists as degenerate and effeminate, leading to horrific acts of violence against them. The enemy was not simply a political opponent with a different point of view, but a castrated male ushering in a feminized world and all the horrors that entailed.

All of this emerged in an apocalyptic atmosphere best seen in places like Munich or Szeged, where violent fantasies purveyed by right-wing paramilitary groups were often played out. The war had convinced some that the battle between good and evil was about to reach a climax and that evil had to be destroyed at its roots. This explains the urge to violence which characterized these groups of men. None of this would have been possible without the massive dislocations and crises brought about by the war. The Bolshevik Revolution in Russia had instilled fear, especially in the middle classes, that a similar fate awaited them in Central Europe. The increasing support for socialism among the workers and peasants of the Po Valley in Italy, not to mention the left-wing revolutions in Bavaria and Hungary, played into these fears, which expressed themselves in a violent counterrevolution that felt no remorse for its actions.

The politicization of culture after the war benefited fascism. The lack of a precise and consistent ideological doctrine gave fascism a malleability that allowed it to absorb the diverse strands of the culture wars and appeal to different groups in society. Patriots, Christians, industrialists, and the middle classes could find something appealing in fascism's militarized call for order. Furthermore, a general and sustained sense of crisis made the otherwise extremist tactics of the fascists palatable. Much of this could have fizzled out with a return of "normality" in the 1920s. However, as the fascist movement came to power in Italy in 1922, violent fantasies could now become reality and usher in a new world.

CHAPTER 4
THE FASCIST SEIZURE OF POWER

The March on Rome

Fascism's first century officially began on October 31, 1922, when Benito Mussolini was sworn in as the prime minister of Italy by King Victor Emmanuel III. The ceremony, which took place at the king's residence in the Quirinal Palace, resembled other ceremonies held in the Italian Kingdom's short history. At thirty-nine years old, Mussolini had become Italy's youngest prime minister, and his appointment was accompanied by hundreds of fascist Blackshirts marching from the Borghese Gardens to the Victor Emmanuel Monument in the center of Rome. On the way to the Tomb of the Unknown Soldier, located at the monument, the Blackshirts passed under the balcony of the Quirinal Palace, where they were greeted by the new prime minister, the king, and the new Minister of War, General Armando Diaz. The squads were led by other generals Ceccherini, Fara, and Zamboni. In this unprecedented celebration of a new government, establishment Italy and the forces of political extremism came together. Only hours before, the Blackshirts were threatening to enter the Eternal City and take the government by force (Figure 4.1). Now, they were a peaceful invading force saluted by the leaders of the same Italian Army which had, only hours before, orders to stop the fascists by force, if necessary. What had happened? How did a subversive force come to power without having to resort to revolution? How was it that a movement founded on hatred of "politics as usual" now accepted this new government that had been appointed behind closed doors by the usual establishment?

Historians have always noted that the March on Rome, which began on October 27, was nothing but a side show, a work of elaborate political theater aimed at masquerading the reality of a change in government. It was a "palace revolution" and not a real seizure of power. Indeed, the fascist "seizure of power" did not occur in October 1922; rather, it happened over the next several years. The key for Mussolini was to get his foot into the door and *then* work out the details of the fascist revolution. Mussolini's pragmatic and opportunistic side, which had infuriated the *ras* in the previous years, suspected that for fascism to achieve power, it needed to be invited. So when Mussolini received a telegram from the Quirinal Palace on October 29, he got on the Number 17 overnight train in Milan and made his way to Rome. Stepping off the train at Termini Station the next morning, he immediately made his way to the king's residence, where he was given the appointment. Later that evening, Mussolini returned to the Quirinal Palace with a list of ministers for a so-called "National Government." This was a coalition government that included only four fascists. Far from a fascist revolution, the new government resembled the many other short-lived governments that had failed to solve Italy's grievous postwar

Figure 4.1 Blackshirts enter the Eternal City through the Porta del Popolo during the March on Rome, 1922. Credit: Alamy.

crises. Mussolini's attire of top hat and tails seemed to confirm that the wild man who had created the fascist movement in 1919 was, in the end, nothing more than a bourgeois politician on the make.

While Mussolini was sitting in Milan, waiting for a call from the king, thousands of Blackshirts had congregated around Rome, beginning October 27 when Blackshirts from around the country began making their way to the Eternal City. They were so ordered by the Quadrumvirs, the four men appointed by Mussolini to oversee the fascist insurrection and March on Rome. The men chosen were some of the more violent and intractable fascist leaders. Italo Balbo—the dynamic and violent *ras* of Ferrara who had led fiery attacks on socialists, including the paramilitary assault on Parma earlier that year—was joined by the former anarcho-syndicalist Michele Bianchi. Also included were the grizzled general, Emilio De Bono, and the Catholic fascist from Turin, Cesare Maria De Vecchi. All these men had served in the Great War, and all expressed the more militant side of fascism. They were appointed by Mussolini on the last day of the Fascist Congress in Naples. This congress was a show of force meant to introduce fascism to the otherwise indifferent Neapolitans, a part of Italy where fascism did not enjoy a great deal of success. The leaders set up headquarters in the Umbrian town of Perugia, after the local Blackshirts commandeered the City Hall.

Inspired by the Bolshevik coup in Russia in 1917, the fascists planned to take over the state by occupying public buildings in northern Italy, then marching columns of Blackshirts to Rome from three staging points: Santa Marinella, Monterotondo, and Tivoli. Ultimately, the squads would occupy the key ministries once they reached Rome and overcame military opposition.

The plan did not quite work out that way. The fascists were able to occupy several cities, including Florence, Siena, Cremona, and Bergamo, among others. They also could not meet at the three designated staging areas; bad weather and the closing of roads and railroads leading to Rome by the Italian military prevented this. Blackshirt morale and enthusiasm was dissipated by the incessant rain and lack of food, all the while waiting for the word to enter the Eternal City. They waited, as, unbeknownst to them, Mussolini sat in Milan waiting for the telegram from the king. When the call came, Mussolini was already in Rome with the government in his hand. All that was left was the parade and the quick demobilization ordered by Mussolini. All Blackshirts were to leave Rome as quickly as possible and go back to where they came from.

Thus ended the March on Rome, considered by many to have been an elaborate bluff that never had a chance of succeeding. However, Adrian Lyttelton has argued that calling the march a failure misses the point (Lyttelton 2004). In their approach to the march, fascists did manage to seize control of railway stations, telegraphs, and some municipal buildings in various cities. While it is true that the Blackshirts would have had no chance at resisting the military, their violent actions in northern and central Italy, especially in Tuscany, created what Lyttelton has called "an atmosphere of confusion and an impression of the widespread collapse of State power" (Lyttelton 2004, 89). Ultimately, the March on Rome was successful because it exposed the weakness and vacillation of the liberal state. The indecisiveness of the king— when asked by Luigi Facta, the outgoing prime minister, to declare a state of emergency—indicated the state's inability to act when faced with insurrection. While the Italian army was ready, with twelve thousand troops stationed in Rome, waiting for the command from General Pugliesi, and manifestos had been plastered in Rome declaring the government's intention to enact emergency powers, Victor Emmanuel decided, in the end, to reject the order and, instead, invite Mussolini to Rome to form a new government.

The king's decision came while fascist violence spread throughout the country. With the Mussolini government, this violence only increased, as Blackshirts destroyed socialist headquarters and the presses of anti-fascist newspapers. A Blackshirt column, led by Giuseppe Bottai, ravaged the San Lorenzo neighborhood in Rome, known for its socialist sympathies. Scores of people were killed throughout the country in a wave of fascist violence. This constant violence contrasts with the peaceful march of Blackshirts on October 31, and it demonstrates that a real insurrection did take place—albeit sporadically and in different locations. In many ways, this was a continuation of the violence unleashed by fascists since their founding in 1919. It came on the back of the brutal summer of 1922, when fascists assaulted socialist strikers in cities like Parma. While it is true that Mussolini was given power in the gilded halls of the Quirinal Palace with the approval of the liberal establishment, the bloodshed caused by fascists throughout the country must be considered a key element in the seizure of power in October 1922. The march was a demonstration of the sizeable force fascism had become in a short period of time. By 1922, there were over three hundred thousand fascists in Italy, and their influence was felt on a local level. To be sure, this membership was focused on certain regions—such as the Yugoslav frontier and the Po Valley—and they represented local interests more than an ideological force (Bosworth 2004, 153). However, they also represented an alternative to liberal politics. This was a politics of violence—and it allowed the transference of the war experience to politics (Mosse 1991).

Although the transfer of power happened behind closed doors, the March on Rome provided a mythos that was central to the fascist narrative in the future. It was central to the fascist ethos that power be seized by force and done outside of the normal parliamentary procedures. The fascist imagination exulted in the image of thousands of Blackshirts descending on Rome from all corners of the peninsula (Berezin 1997). A mythologized view of the March allowed fascism to place itself in a uniquely Italian tradition of marches on the Eternal City. Mussolini's call for a return to the Roman Empire (*Romanità*) mimicked the various marches undertaken by Roman generals. More recent examples included Garibaldi's marches during the Risorgimento, not to mention the Renaissance *condottieri*. That the March on Rome did not happen the way fascist myth makers related it is beside the point. Fascism relies on myth and legend much more than literal truth. The prosaic is never a substitute for the poetic in the fascist mind.

Indicative of the importance of the myth of the March on Rome was the designation of October 28 as the anniversary of the fascist seizure of power even though Mussolini was not officially made prime minister until October 31. On October 28, the fate of the March was still in flux. On that day, the Facta government was still resolved to introduce martial law, and Roman fascists had been given the green light to mobilize by the Quadrumvirs. That day marked the height of tension and highest possibility of conflict between the Blackshirts and the state. The anniversary of the fascist revolution became the most important date in the fascist calendar. It was marked as Year I in the calendar and became an occasion to celebrate the regime's achievements in the future. In 1932, during the celebrations of the *Decennale*, much effort was spent on expounding and expanding the meaning of the March on Rome (Morena 2015). In the service of "aura and mythmaking," that year saw the opening of the Exhibition of the Fascist Revolution in Rome. This was fascism's most concerted effort at making the March central to the fascist historic imagination (Fogu 2003). The exhibition was a spectacular example of fascism's exhibitionist culture, with its rooms curated by different architects and artists, many of them coming from a modernist perspective. The purpose of the exhibition was to demonstrate the dynamic nature of the fascist revolution and commemorate its martyrs (J. Schnapp 1992). The exhibition was open for two years and proved to be a great success, attracting some 2.8 million visitors, demonstrating that the public in the early 1930s were receptive to fascist mythmaking (Stone 1993).

The Exhibition of the Fascist Revolution tapped into the theatrical element of the March on Rome. This fascism was the self-appointed heir of D'Annunzio's March on Fiume in 1919. The success of D'Annunzio's march was just as dependent on the inaction of the authorities as was Mussolini's. However, that fact paled in comparison to the influence of D'Annunzio's Regency of Carnaro. The myth of Fiume was constructed after the occupation, and the legionnaires who marched with D'Annunzio were now heroes among Italian nationalists. The myth of the occupation and its narrative of national redemption is what mattered—even though D'Annunzio's reign ended under Italian bombs (Gumbrecht 1996). Indeed, one of the factors that convinced Mussolini that the time was right for the March on Rome was D'Annunzio's demobilization of his legionnaires in October. D'Annunzio's brief appearance on the balcony of Milan's City Hall during the insurrections of August gave some hope to those who hoped for the poet to lead a March on Rome—but his decision not to lead it opened the door for Mussolini's fascists. One thing that Mussolini had learned from the poet, however, was the importance of theatricality in politics. If the real transition of power happened in the halls of the Quirinale, the illusion of a march could still be useful. As with Fiume, the March was merely an opening act to, a curtain-raiser of, the real revolution that came after Mussolini's appointment as prime minister.

The "Liberal" Phase: 1922–4

In many respects, the first phase of Mussolini's ministry was a kind of theater. Dressed in a top hat, Mussolini played the part of the liberal prime minister after 1922. The first cabinet Mussolini presented to the king included ministers from different parties, such as the *Popolari*, the Social Democrats, and the Nationalist Association, along with independents and military figures. Only four ministers came from the PNF. One of those fascists was Alberto de' Stefani, the Minister of Finance, who would promote liberal economic policies. On the surface, the Mussolini government seemed nothing more than a center-right group of establishment interests (Bosworth 2004). In his famous essay on the portraits of Mussolini, the novelist Italo Calvino recalls that the first images he remembered of the fascist leader were those of him in "civilian clothes, with a stiff turned-up collar ... which was meant to emphasize a certain continuity and respectability in the man who had restored order" (Calvino 2003, 207).

Mussolini's "costume" as a defender of order must be understood in the context of the violence that had been unleashed by the fascists themselves. As an assurance to the establishment that order would be restored, but also as a means of institutionalizing fascist violence, Mussolini transformed the Blackshirts into the Voluntary Militia for National Security (MVSN) in February 1923. By bringing the anarchic violence of the *squadristi* under the control of the state, Mussolini was also putting it under his own control and thus curtailing the power of the local *ras*. With this move, Mussolini also quelled the concerns of the Italian military by placing generals in positions of command of the MVSN—despite resentment from the Militia commanders (Cannistraro 1982, 338). In truth, Mussolini was preparing the institutionalizing of fascism. While this may have upset some of the intransigents in the party, Mussolini was putting into effect an internal revolution of the existing liberal state. In December 1922, Mussolini created the Fascist Grand Council, a parallel body to the Cabinet in which prominent fascist leaders now became part of the State. All this rendered Mussolini's parliamentary coalition nothing more than a façade (Bosworth 2004, 188).

The Acerbo Law and the Election of 1924

Mussolini's intentions became even clearer with the major electoral reform of 1923, known as the Acerbo Law. Named after Giacomo Acerbo, a fascist deputy from Pescara, the legislation decreed that the candidate list with the most votes would get two thirds of the seats in the Chamber of Deputies. This electoral reform entailed the most radical change to the constitution since the founding of Italy. Indeed, as Adrian Lyttelton has noted, "it marked the first *legal* (the italics are his) alteration of the fundamental features of the representative state" (Lyttelton 2004, 126). Mussolini's decision to introduce the measure was in large part influenced by the intransigents within the Fascist Party, led by the *ras* of Cremona, Roberto Farinacci. In the campaign to get the bill passed, Mussolini used the violent elements within his party to threaten any opposition. In what had become standard fascist discourse, Mussolini both threatened violence and promised to end it if the bill was passed. This dual tactic of threatening violence and promising to restore order was now part of the fascist playbook. Furthermore, in his speech to parliament introducing the law, Mussolini claimed that the reform would reconcile parliament to the people of Italy by creating stable governments based on solid majorities. Undermining liberal democracy while outwardly seeming to respect parliamentary traditions became standard operating procedure.

The Acerbo Law passed, thanks largely to the abstention of most of the Popular Party deputies, who mistakenly believed that non-opposition would relieve some of the pressure put on Catholic institutions by the fascist government. None of these hopes—that violence would subside and that the PNF would become a normal conservative party—played out during the parliamentary elections of April 1924. The election campaign saw Mussolini benefit from the violence of the fascist militia and the repression of the national police, now controlled by the Ministry of the Interior. Rampant election fraud and a massive, state-directed campaign of propaganda further aided the government, not to mention the general apathy of Italians and weakness of the anti-fascist forces. While the government allowed harassment-free voting in the large northern cities, the polls in central and southern Italy were largely manipulated by the presence of fascist militia, the fraudulent practices of fascist election scrutineers, and promises of violent reprisals to anyone who voted against the government list.

The Matteotti Crisis

The election of 1924 returned, predictably, the desired result for Mussolini's government. The National List obtained 65 percent of the popular vote and thus gained an absolute majority in parliament. While the Acerbo reform was directly responsible for this, the methods used by the government in ensuring victory did not go unnoticed by fascism's opponents. The main figure here was the independent socialist leader Giacomo Matteotti. Born into a well-off family in the Po Valley, Matteotti obtained a law degree at the University of Bologna and then became a socialist organizer. First elected to parliament in 1919, Matteotti was the victim of several physical assaults from fascist *squadristi*. Undaunted, Matteotti continued his efforts to resist fascism. This included keeping a detailed diary of fascist violence in the Po Valley and elsewhere (Matteotti 1969). During the election campaign, Matteotti realized that a fair election was impossible, as the government mobilized both Blackshirts and police to intimidate opposition candidates and voters.

On May 30, in the presence of Mussolini, Matteotti stood up in the Chamber of Deputies and denounced fascist violence. Matteotti also claimed that he had evidence of government kickbacks from an American oil company that was benefiting Mussolini personally. On June 10, while walking to the Chamber along Rome's Lungotevere, Matteotti was kidnapped by a group of fascists. His mutilated body was not discovered until August in a shallow grave north of Rome. In the meantime, the Mussolini government found itself in a deep crisis. The car used for the kidnapping was traced back to the Ministry of the Interior, and the culprits were violent Blackshirts who now worked for the ministry. Their leader was Amerigo Dumini, a Tuscan *squadrista* who had won a reputation for his brutality. The subsequent crisis, which played out throughout the summer of 1924, very nearly toppled the Mussolini regime. Despite the absence of a direct order, the assailants were working on the assumption that Matteotti's elimination was favored by the Italian prime minister.

The imminent threat to the regime was triggered by the so-called Aventine Secession. Opposition deputies brilliantly used ancient Roman imagery against the regime, protesting Matteotti's assassination by declaring an "Aventine Secession." Mussolini attempted to placate criticism by firing the undersecretaries of the Ministry of the Interior, including the Quadrumvir Emilio De Bono and Aldo Finzi. He also replaced himself as Minister of the Interior with Luigi Federzoni, a member of the Italian Nationalist Association. In December, a memo written by Cesare Rossi, Mussolini's former press officer, implicated Mussolini directly in the murder. Faced with the possibility of removal by the king, Mussolini also came under pressure from the intransigents within the party, who demanded that the prime minister either attack the anti-fascists or face a party insurrection. This was the most severe threat to Mussolini since he became prime minister in 1922, and it took a toll on his health (Figure 4.2).

Faced with this threat, Mussolini stood up in the Chamber on January 3, 1925, and made the most important speech of his career. Taking responsibility for the murder, not because he ordered it but because the men responsible worked for him, Mussolini promised to resolve the crisis and deal with the opposition. The speech not only earned him the applause of the fascist-dominated Chamber but also the confidence of the king, who was more afraid of the potential left-wing uprising should the government topple. The speech was a brilliant display of Mussolini's ability to grab victory from the jaws of defeat. What should have been the end of the regime turned out, in fact, to be the start of the fascist revolution. Matteotti was presented as a kind of "sacrificial victim" needed

Figure 4.2 The body of Giacomo Matteotti is removed from the shallow grave he was buried in by his fascist assassins north of Rome. August 1924. Credit: Alamy.

to purify the national community. A recent rhetorical study on Mussolini's speech on January 3 has argued that Mussolini presented himself as both "poisoner" and "healer" at the same time (Ferrari 2013, 24). He had created the crisis and was now the only one who could resolve it.

Mussolini was able to play on the fears of the liberal establishment. Although the Aventine Secession was an alternative to a socialist uprising, the establishment was easily manipulated to believe that it was the beginning of a left-wing revolution. Conservative fears of disorder leading to Bolshevism went back to the events of the postwar period—and Mussolini knew how to take advantage of it. The crisis also revealed the fascist ability to take a defeat and turn it into victory. The weakness of the liberal forces and the inability of anti-fascists to take advantage of the situation further aided Mussolini's survival. The death of Matteotti would not be forgotten by anti-fascists, however, and though Mussolini came out on top in this crisis, Matteotti's death made Mussolini into a marked man. Assassination attempts and the eventual demise of the fascist leader in 1945 could be traced to this "original sin" of the fascist leader, as one cultural historian has argued (in a fascinating study of Mussolini's corpse) (Luzzatto 2005). In the short term, Matteotti's death was the occasion for the construction of the fascist state.

The Fascist Revolution

Mussolini's confirmation as prime minister had, then, opened the door to the fascist overthrow of the liberal state, nearly three years after Mussolini had first taken power. In the wake of the Matteotti Crisis, a new wave of fascist violence swept through Italy, led by extremists like Roberto Farinacci, who became the Secretary of the Fascist Party in February 1925. Farinacci's reign as party secretary was accompanied by a series of atrocities committed by fascist militia. In July, Giovanni Amendola, one of the leaders of the Aventine Secession, was brutally beaten by a group of fascists. He later died of his injuries in France. In September and October of that year, a wave of fascist violence descended on Florence, targeting anti-fascists. Many of these attacks occurred in broad daylight and were witnessed by horrified tourists, causing the government some embarrassment, forcing Mussolini's intervention. Farinacci, who Mussolini always viewed as a potential rival, was replaced as PNF secretary in 1926 by Augusto Turati, whose task was to "normalize" the party by purging it of its more violent members and incorporating it into the state. This did not mean that fascism renounced violence—far from it. *Squadrist* violence would now be sublimated into the state through the increasingly repressive policies starting in 1926.

In November 1925, Mussolini escaped what would be the first of four assassination attempts lasting until October 1926. A former socialist deputy attempted to shoot Mussolini at the Palazzo Chigi but was arrested before Mussolini appeared on the balcony of his office. In April 1926, Mussolini was grazed by a bullet fired by an Irish woman in Rome. In September, an attempt on his life came from an anarchist bomb that injured several people. The final attempt came in Bologna in October, which resulted in the lynching of a fifteen-year-old boy accused of trying to kill Mussolini. The horrific violence meted out to Anteo Zamboni on this occasion provided yet another example of the brutality of fascist methods. The wave of assassination attempts gave Mussolini the opportunity to pass a series of repressive laws, called the Exceptional Decrees, between November 1926 and January 1927. These laws were comprehensive in that they banned all political parties—except for the PNF—and all anti-fascist associations. Anti-fascist newspapers were suppressed, and political crimes could now be punished by death or internal exile (*confino*). Internal exile meant banishment to small, isolated villages in the south or to one of the many islands off the Tyrrhenian coast. Political criminals would also be tried by the newly created Special Tribunal for the Defense of the State. In September, Mussolini had appointed Arturo Bocchini as Italy's new Chief of Police, a job he held until his death in 1940. A career police officer, Bocchini was never a fascist, but he did his job effectively and Mussolini trusted him, especially as a counterweight to renegade fascists. In 1927, the national secret police called OVRA (*Organizzazione di Vigilanza Repressione dell'Antifascismo*) was created and overseen by Bocchini.

With the repressive apparatus in place, Mussolini also moved toward dismantling the liberal democratic state that had existed since 1861. This task was given to Mussolini's new Minister of Justice, Alfredo Rocco. A former member of the Italian Nationalist Association (INA), Rocco joined the PNF at the same time his association merged with fascism in 1923. Rocco was a legal scholar who taught at the University of Padua before he became active in politics. As a member of the INA, Rocco shared Enrico Corradini's critique of liberal Italy as weak, unable to turn Italy into a great power (Gregor 2005). For this to happen, it needed an authoritarian state capable of transcending particular or factional interests. His appointment as minister of justice placed him in a position where he could bring about the constitutional changes needed to bring such a state into being. Gaining Mussolini's trust, Rocco remained as minister until 1932, considerably longer than many of his fellow ministers. In that time, Rocco took charge of drafting several of the laws that transformed the liberal state into a fascist state. He also presided over constitutional changes that gave the executive branch greater powers over the legislature and codified the Fascist Grand Council as supreme organ of the state.

Rocco was also instrumental in drawing up the Corporative State. Influenced by Mussolini's background in syndicalism—and by the Regency of Carnaro created by D'Annunzio in Fiume—the corporative state replaced representative democracy. Italians would now be represented by an economic corporation, which itself stood under the authority of the state. The Rocco Law declared strikes illegal and recognized only one workers' association as legal. To placate industrial leaders, the fascists brokered the Vidoni Pact of October 1925, which ensured that workers would never be able to control factories. A further law passed in July 1926 created a Ministry of Corporations, and in 1929, the Chamber of Deputies was reformed so that representation was no longer based on geographical districts, but on corporations.

Touted as a "third way" between communism and capitalism, fascism's creation of the Corporative State went hand in hand with an increasingly nationalist and autarchic conception of the Italian economy. In July 1925, Alberto de' Stefani was dropped as finance minister—with him went the liberal economic policies of the early Mussolini administration. Economic nationalism now became the dominant philosophy behind fascism's economic vision, a vision geared toward transforming Italy into an imperial power (Morgan 2009). Like the March on Rome, corporatism worked on the level of myth rather than reality. As many have noted, the system was worth more in theory than in practice. In fact, the system was there to ensure the fascist regime's vision of an autarchic economy with the compliance of industry. Under fascism, economics became entirely political (Morgan 2009). In 1925, Mussolini launched his so-called Battle for Grain, which called for Italian self-sufficiency in grain production. In 1927 came the Quota 90, whereby the regime pegged the Italian lira at a fixed rate, going against the advice of financial and economic advisors. This move, too, was political, aimed at giving the Italian currency a nationalist and autarchic character despite the potential economic consequences.

The Cult of the Duce

The fascist revolution was fueled by two seemingly contradictory impulses: Rocco's constitutional legalism, on the one hand, and the violence of the Blackshirts, on the other. Cementing these together was a third critical component: Mussolini's personality cult. Christopher Duggan has argued that the Cult of the Duce was the "cornerstone on which the subsequent regime was built" (Duggan 2013, 27). Central to this was the publication, in 1926, of Margherita Sarfatti's biography of Mussolini, *Dux*. Duce, the Italian form of the Latin *dux*, was once the title of Roman frontier generals and would become the favorite title of Mussolini. Sarfatti, an Italian-Jewish intellectual from Venice and patron of the arts, became one of Mussolini's lovers in the 1920s. She played a predominant role in the arts in the 1920s, helping found the *Novecento* school. Mussolini approved this biography in 1926, which painted him as the charismatic leader that Italy needed. Extolling Mussolini as a youthful and energetic leader, Sarfatti portrayed Mussolini as a man who stood above the masses and represented the true Italian who would return Italy to the glory of the Roman Empire. The book is an example of the mythmaking so central to fascism—and, like some of fascism's other myths, it found a wide response. The book was a bestseller, going through seventeen editions and being translated into eighteen languages by 1938 (Storchi 2013, 53).

Sarfatti's book was a bestseller because it presented a fascinating figure in a messianic light. The postwar era was open to this kind of figure, a leader who appeared to be the solution to the myriads of problems caused by the Great War (Ben-Ghiat 2020, 21). This advent of strongman leaders was anticipated by the German sociologist Max Weber. Mussolini had encountered similar ideas in his reading of Friedrich Nietzsche and Gustave Le Bon. The notion that the masses would follow such a leader was something he often expressed. In his interview with the German journalist Emil Ludwig in the early 1930s, Mussolini talked about himself as an artist who shaped the masses. To be sure, this idea of "one man alone" served Mussolini in his efforts to keep the *ras* in line within the Fascist Party and govern without sharing power. However, the idea of the authoritarian leader was increasingly common in postwar Europe. Mussolini was one of the first to make it into an effective instrument of government. Sarfatti's biography merely popularized the notion.

Mussolini furthered the devotion of his own cult by modeling his own persona and image after those of movie stars. The 1920s was the era of film stars and Mussolini appropriated their image to construct his charismatic appeal. One of the most famous screen characters in Italy at the time was the strongman Maciste. Stephen Gundle has noted how Mussolini's self-representation paralleled Maciste's existing image (Gundle 2013, 44–5). Not only did Mussolini bear a striking resemblance to Maciste, but, as Gundle points out, he also personified many of Maciste's characters—particularly a willingness to use violence to restore order. Beginning in the mid-1920s, Mussolini was often photographed doing strongman things, such as playing with lion cubs, racing cars, and flying airplanes. He began to appear bare chested, as in the famous images of his threshing of grain during the Battle for Grain campaign (Antola Swan 2020). In the 1930s, as the demolition of major parts of Rome got underway, he was often pictured taking a pickaxe to a building. His movie star persona could be seen in kitschy items, such as women's bathing suits featuring his picture (Figure 4.3).

Mussolini's physical presence also became more visible. In 1923, while campaigning for the Acerbo Law, Mussolini visited several provinces of Italy. He became the first Italian prime minister to make an extensive tour of the country, which included the south (Gundle 2013, 112). Into the 1930s, and with the adoption of his "going toward the people" policy, Mussolini made frequent visits to different parts of the country, often with the intention of inaugurating some public works projects or announcing major policy initiatives. One famous example was his visit to the city of Trieste in 1938, where he announced the regime's Racial Laws (Baxa 2013). These visits gave the impression of a Mussolini who was ever present and physically proximate. It allowed him to play on his movie star, celebrity persona. At times, his image was that of a demigod graciously descending to the people (Gundle 2013, 122). His presence transformed the familiar public squares of the towns into sites of secular worship.

1929

On March 24, 1929, Italians went to the poll booths for the first time since 1924. This election was different, though, as it presented the voter with only one list, that of the PNF. All that was asked was a "Yes" or "No." Of the over 9 million voters who showed up, 8.6 million voted yes, with only 135,773 brave souls voting no. Over eight thousand ballots were invalid. The fascist list thus took over 98 percent of the vote and 100 percent of the seats in the Italian parliament. This was not an election, but a plebiscite, and the vote was based on a very restricted franchise. While the plebiscite lacked the overt threats and violence of the 1924 campaign, the secrecy of the ballot was questionable. The regime also had the campaigning field to itself. Oversized portraits of Mussolini's

The Fascist Seizure of Power

Figure 4.3 The Cult of the Duce goes to the beach. Anzio, July 1929. Credit: Alamy.

face alongside fascist slogans were plastered throughout Italy. The absence of opposition newspapers and parties meant no competition. Anti-fascists had been either silenced, exiled, or imprisoned, which suggested that the true will of the Italian electorate was not expressed.

While the plebiscite cannot be seen as an accurate barometer of the Fascist regime's popularity, there is evidence to suggest that Mussolini was riding a wave of popularity in 1929. Just over a month before the plebiscite, the regime signed the Lateran Accords with the Vatican, thus ending the Roman Question, which had bedeviled the Italian state since its founding. This seminal moment in the history of Vatican–Italian relations proved a major diplomatic and domestic coup for Mussolini. It recognized the Vatican as an independent state in return for the Vatican's recognition of the legitimacy of the Italian state. It also prompted Pope Pius XI to call Mussolini the man sent by Providence (Kertzer 2014). To be sure, the Vatican continued to be suspicious of the anticlericalism still present within fascism (especially with men like Farinacci) and would deride the "idolatry" of the state in fascist ideology (Pollard 2008, 91–2). There would also be clashes over youth education in the future. Still, the Vatican's acceptance of Mussolini's regime, like that of many Italians, benefited the regime enormously.

Mussolini marked the successes of 1929 with a move to the Palazzo Venezia in the summer of 1929. Since he had become prime minister, Mussolini's offices were in the Palazzo Chigi, not far from the Chamber of Deputies in the Palazzo Montecitorio. By 1929, Mussolini was no longer interested in parliament and sought a new location to reflect the grandeur of his office. The Palazzo Venezia is a fortress-like structure built in the fifteenth century as a papal residence. It sits at the foot of the Piazza del Campidoglio, right next to the imposing monument to King Victor Emmanuel II, the "father of Italy." In 1921, the Tomb of the Unknown Soldier was built on the monument, making it a site for nationalistic sentiment, the celebration of Italian unification, and commemoration of the Great War. It was only natural that Mussolini wished fascism to be celebrated in this site of memory. The other attraction was the very large piazza outside the building. Mussolini located his office in the massive Sala del Mappamondo on the building's second floor. Not only did the room take up the whole floor, but it also provided access to a balcony that overlooked the square. Here the cult of the Duce would achieve its highest expression in the next several years, allowing Mussolini to speak to the vast crowds, which he called "oceanic rallies." Ultimately, Mussolini was able to replicate D'Annunzio's famous balcony speeches in Fiume—only Mussolini had a vaster stage in a city that stood at the heart of Western Civilization. The Palazzo and the Piazza became the setting for Mussolini's one-man rule over Italy and the destination of the fascist revolution.

CHAPTER 5
WEIMAR AND THE RISE OF THE NAZI PARTY

Two Rallies

On a mid-August weekend in 1927, over twenty thousand Nazi Brownshirts descended on the medieval Bavarian town of Nuremberg. The occasion was the annual Nazi Party rally in a field outside the town. The star attraction was their leader, Adolf Hitler, who greeted the arriving Brownshirts from an open top Mercedes-Benz in the city's Market Square. A few feet from the statuesque Hitler stood a movie camera, run by the party's newly created film section. The film was directed by a Berlin party hack, Julius Lippert, working for his boss, Joseph Goebbels, the party's propaganda minister, who was also a film buff. The finished product was an approximately twenty-minute silent film with intertitles. The film, entitled *Eine Symphonie des Kampfwillens* ("A Symphony of the Will to Fight"), was a documentary that resembled the newsreels of the day with a largely stationary camera. The film recorded the scenes of arriving Brownshirts, the cheering crowds, close-ups of prominent personalities, and finally the rituals associated with the Nazi rallies (Figure 5.1).

As art, the film paled in comparison to the more famous *Triumph of the Will* made seven years later by the accomplished director and film actor, Leni Riefenstahl. As an historical document, however, the Lippert effort is invaluable, as it demonstrated the still small party's embrace of mass media, something that Goebbels's office would excel in. The title was also a nod to the burgeoning film culture of the Weimar Republic. By 1927, film in Weimar was heading in the same direction as the arts in general, that is, toward the *Neue Sachlichkeit* (the New Sobriety), a trend in the arts that moved away from Expressionism—which characterized the early 1920s—and toward an aesthetic focused on social reality (Willett 1978). The influence of newsreels and of film documentaries—pioneered by Dziga Vertov in the Soviet Union—also played a part in the Nazi approach to film. While Lippert's film cannot be compared on an artistic level with Vertov's work, nor with that of Walter Ruttmann's *Berlin: Symphony of a Great City*, also released in 1927, *Eine Symphonie* demonstrated that the Nazi Party was on the same wavelength of cinematic developments and, thus, miles ahead of its major political rivals in embracing the medium of film (Aufderheide 2007, 14–15).

Nor does the film compare to Riefenstahl's magnum opus. When Riefenstahl filmed the 1934 Nuremberg Party Rally, Hitler had already been in power for over a year, and the Nuremberg field had been transformed by Albert Speer into a vast stadium. The scale of the event felt and was much larger; this time round, rather than driving in a car, Hitler descended upon the crowds in an airplane. The regimented lines of soldiers contrasted with the more jovial, festive attitude of the young Nazis in 1927. Moreover, the newsreel

Figure 5.1 The first Nuremberg Party Rally, 1927. Credit: Alamy.

style of Lippert's film gave way to a more artistic approach undertaken by Riefenstahl. Although Riefenstahl would later claim that she was doing nothing more than filming an event that she had no hand in creating, the obvious presence of certain film techniques—such as dissolves and tracking shots—belied her claim that this was nothing more than a documentary (Bach 2007, 140).

For all their differences, there is a great deal that these two films have in common. The message is the same, but the two films are shot in different contexts. In 1927, the Nazi Party was still small but growing. It boasted some seventy thousand members but had no presence in the Reichstag, and any prospects it once had seemed diminished. Weimar was enjoying a period of relative stability due to the Dawes Plan and the Locarno Pacts, in contrast to the chaotic situation of the early 1920s, which helped groups like the Nazis grow. Despite this, the message of Riefenstahl's film can be seen already in *Eine Symphonie*: the hope for a united Germany with purpose. The intertitles of the film were replete with Nazi slogans like "Germany Awake," and it highlighted the main figures in the movement, like Gregor Strasser and Julius Streicher. It also quoted from German and foreign newspapers, indicating the NSDAP's desire to present itself as a growing and significant movement. One of the papers quoted was the Italian *Corriere della Sera*. Once a strong critic of Mussolini's regime, by 1927, the Milanese newspaper was firmly under the control of the fascist regime after its editor, Luigi Albertini, was forced out in 1925. The Italian newspaper noted that Hitler's movement was the closest thing to Italian fascism and related it as a predominantly youthful movement with an almost fanatical devotion to its leader.

Both films also focused on the mystical aura surrounding Hitler. Because Hitler arrived by plane in 1934, the first shot of Riefenstahl's film is that of a leader descending from the clouds. Erwin Leiser's classic study of Nazi film describes it this way: "He poses as the prophet of a new religion, as the grand master of a mystical order" (Leiser 1974, 27). Although not possessing the technical skill and equipment of Riefenstahl, Lippert's film presents Hitler in a similar fashion. He is the star of the show, and a lengthy take from a medium close-up position shows Hitler, arm outstretched, in his car with piles of flowers on the car's bonnet. Other parts of the film show Hitler giving a speech (a central feature of the Riefenstahl film) and performing the rituals of the rally, which involved consecrating the flags of local chapters by touching them with the blood-stained flag of the Beer Hall Putsch. In each case, intertitles tell us what region the flags are from.

In short, these are two very different documents of two rallies held in two very different eras. Each demonstrates, however, a continuity of purpose and a common message: Nazism was an unstoppable and dynamic force, and its destiny was to take control of Germany and lead it to a new age of dominance. In other words, Nazism was more than a political movement—it was a messianic force led by a new prophet. Both films give some credence to the idea that Nazism was a kind of "political religion." This is what gave it an edge compared to its political rivals. Hitler was no mere politician—rather, as Michael Burleigh describes him, he was a "revivalist huckster transplanted to Central Europe," a prophet who "came from nowhere" (Burleigh 2000, 115). Film was the ideal medium to bring out the divine character of Hitler's image. Presenting him as a god appealed to an emotional longing that politics, as usual, found impossible to reach. It also played on the film star attributes Mussolini had already incorporated into his persona. Offering something different proved necessary, as the Weimar Republic was enjoying a period of stability. The appeal of the Hitler-God, however, demonstrated clearly that there was nothing stable or peaceful about Germany in the mid-1920s. In this sense, Lippert's low-budget documentary proved more prophetic than the triumphalist masterpiece of Riefenstahl.

The Golden Years of Weimar

When the Brownshirts gathered in Nuremberg in August 1927, there was little to suggest that the rally would be anything more than a weekend of a small group of fanatics hoping for the unlikely demise of the Weimar Republic. It was hard times for political radicals on either side of the spectrum, as the Republic appeared to be holding despite its fraught beginnings. The period 1924–27 is often referred to as the "Golden Years of the Weimar Republic." In late 1923, with Germany experiencing hyperinflation and a continued French occupation of the Ruhr, a new Chancellor, Gustav Stresemann, who also served as foreign minister, began to work with the Allies to resolve the crisis. Along with Charles Dawes, the Director of the US Budget Office, Stresemann worked out a scheme in which US loans would flow into the country to help rebuild the economy and create a new German currency. The Dawes Plan also called for a new payment plan for reparations that satisfied the French enough to persuade them to pull out of the Ruhr. In 1925, Stresemann, now only foreign minister, signed Germany onto the Locarno Pact, where Germany agreed to accept the post-Versailles western borders (thus renouncing any return of Alsace-Lorraine to Germany). In return, Germany was brought into the League of Nations.

For these efforts, Stresemann was awarded the Nobel Peace Prize in 1926 and was given much of the credit for rehabilitating Germany in the eyes of the international community. American dollars, meanwhile, flooded into Germany in the form of loans given to the state, municipal governments, and even private enterprises. The stabilizing of the economy was accompanied by a boom in mass entertainment, most of which was concentrated in Berlin. According to Walter Laqueur, Berlin became the world's "entertainment capital" (Laqueur 1974). Germany's film industry, thanks to the UFA Studios, made the country into a film capital that rivaled Hollywood. None of this impressed the radicals like the Nazis, but it did trouble a few establishment conservatives. Many thought Stresemann's guaranteeing of the western frontiers was a cave-in and that his pact with the Soviet Union in 1926 opened the door to communism. The fact that Stresemann had made no similar guarantees about Germany's eastern frontiers was little consolation.

Hopes that Weimar would soon come to an end were stoked when Field Marshal Paul von Hindenburg was elected President of the Republic in April 1925. The Republic's first president, Friedrich Ebert, had died unexpectedly in February, just days before the election, and no obvious candidate emerged as favorite. The first vote was inconclusive, and when the runoffs were held in April, Hindenburg presented himself as a candidate. Hindenburg's pedigree strongly suggested that he would be an opponent of the Republic. He was presented as a new Napoleon whose prestige came from the battlefield, not the political arena. His refusal to represent a party gave the impression of a man who was above parties in a manner that Georges Boulanger would have appreciated. The seventy-seven-year-old Field Marshal's election was symbolic of the return of the Prussian establishment. His victory also appeared as a rebuke of the avant-garde cultural developments of the era, representing what Peter Gay has called the "revenge of the father" on the sons who wanted to overthrow the establishment (Gay 2001, 118). Hindenburg ended up being a disappointment for those who hoped for a restoration of the old Prussian order, however, as he ended up respecting the Weimar constitution.

While Hindenburg's election coincided with a decline in political radicalism, it did not mean that the Republic was safe in his hands. Hindenburg made it clear that as president he would never accept a government coalition led by the Social Democrats (SPD) even though they were the founding party of the Republic and the largest party in the Reichstag up until 1932. In addition, Hindenburg's intention to increase presidential power, while barely perceptible at first, became gradually apparent (Kolb 1988, 74). Hindenburg's insistence that the Conservative Party (DNVP) be included in any coalition belied his conservative sympathies. Furthermore, his support of the center-right governments of Brüning, von Papen, and von Schleicher after 1930—and their use of emergency decrees—reinforced Hindenburg's authoritarian instincts. Hindenburg became enamored with Article 48 of the Weimar Constitution, which gave emergency powers to the President in times of emergency. The inclusion of this provision was largely due to Max Weber, the sociologist who argued that only a charismatic leader could break the rationalized systems of modern governments and their inability to deal with emergencies. While it is doubtful that Hindenburg had any appreciation for the abstruse arguments of Weber, he certainly shared Weber's confidence in the need for a strong executive power. However, with Hindenburg, Article 48 was to be more than a temporary expedient. Nonetheless, until the emergency brought on the collapse of Wall Street in 1929 and the calling back of loans made by the United States to Germany, the Republic seemed to be enjoying a period of tranquility and peace, and this was a bad sign for radicals like Adolf Hitler.

The Rebuilding of the Nazi Party

The Brownshirts who marched jovially into Nuremberg in August 1927 represented a movement in a phase of reconstruction. When Hitler was sent to prison in 1924, his party fragmented, as many Nazis joined one of the many radically right groups that sprung up in the aftermath of the Beer Hall Putsch. One of these groups was led by Erich von Ludendorff, the general who marched with Hitler in the Beer Hall Putsch. Ludendorff's party, known as the National Socialist Freedom Movement, contested the May 1924 Reichstag elections, in which it picked up nearly two million votes and 32 seats in the 491-seat parliament. In the subsequent December elections, the party lost one million votes and ended up with a paltry 14 seats. The NSDAP did continue to exist, however, and while Hitler languished in prison after the putsch, the Strasser brothers, Gregor and Otto, kept the party going, focusing more and more on the movement's socialist aspects. The Strassers, influenced by Gottfried Feder, emphasized Nazism's economic platforms, adopting the "soldier's socialism" that had attracted Gregor Strasser to the movement in the first place.

Soldier socialism was informed by the grievances of returning veterans who found no work and came to despise the economic and financial elites, which they associated with Jews. The attack on department stores, found in the Nazi Party's first manifesto, was an expression of this economic antisemitism. The Strassers called for a breakup of large-scale economic enterprises and a return to small-scale enterprises run by Aryans. The socialism that informed the Strassers came from Arthur Moeller van den Bruck's book *The Third Reich* (1923), which called for a "Prussian socialism," defined as a state-driven socialism aimed at preventing the German working classes from falling into the clutches of Marxism. Equally influential was Oswald Spengler's *Decline of the West* (1918, 1922), which argued that the West was currently facing a phase of decadence and decline brought upon by excessive individualism and that only a strongman could save it. Spengler also claimed that there was a unique form of Prussian socialism and that this was demonstrated in August 1914, not in 1918–20, when the people of Germany came together to fight in the First World War. "War is the eternal form of higher human existence," claimed Spengler, "and states exist for war" (E. D. Weitz 2007, 336).

The rise of the Strassers within the NSDAP, with older brother Gregor becoming the most important figure of the movement after Hitler, revealed some fault lines within Nazi ideology. Ultimately, their project was to bring to the movement a materialist, anti-bourgeois, and anti-capitalist ideology, synthesizing it with the more "spiritual" *völkisch* ideas that had come out of the Munich beer halls in the days of the German Revolution (Mosse 1999). Part of the Strasser effect was to broaden the geographical range of Nazism by including material concerns that could challenge the Marxist influence in the larger industrial centers of the north. Antisemitism proved the link that held these two poles together. Out of this northern Nazi circle around the Strassers would come prominent figures like Joseph Goebbels.

While the Strassers were making this ideological link between northern and southern German Nazism, Hitler spent much of his prison putting together his vision of Nazism in *Mein Kampf*. With the help of Rudolf Hess, Hitler started working on his memoirs in Landsberg in the summer of 1924. The book was aimed at communicating his ideas to a wider public and giving Nazism a kind of catechism that the movement could use to revive itself in the mid-1920s. By the time he left prison in December of that year, he had completed most of the book. By the end of the 1930s, some ten million copies had been sold. Yet, as one historian has noted, it was barely read due to the difficult prose of its "pseudo educated" author (Fest 1974, 202–4). Since the book was published long before he came to power, and since it is unreliable and unreadable, many believe *Mein Kampf* is not much help when trying to understand Nazism's rise. Historians have debated the ideological coherence of the book and whether a consistent worldview (*weltanschauung*) can be discerned in this rambling text (Rosenbaum 1998, 288–9). To be sure, Hitler does not provide any consistent ideology, but it would be a mistake to dismiss the book, since it reveals a great deal about its author and, therefore, of National Socialism. According to one biographer of Hitler, *Mein Kampf* demonstrates "nationalism, anti-Bolshevism, and antisemitism, linked by a Darwinian theory of struggle" (Fest 1974, 206).

While the autobiographical elements of the book need to be taken with a grain of salt, Hitler's book made some important observations about Nazi tactics, and these prove the most valuable insights in the book for those searching for the why and how of Nazism. It also provides an account of some of the methods Hitler thought of as he went about rebuilding the movement after his release from prison. Great attention is paid to the importance of propaganda, which Hitler called an art. He also compared political propaganda to the techniques of advertising, that is, how it can reach the masses on a psychological level by appealing to their emotions. The best propaganda, according to Hitler, is one that presents its position as truth and does not make any accommodation to opposing positions. At one point, Hitler also mentions the efficacy of the "big lie" compared to "small lies." Although he was blaming the Jews for using the technique of the Big Lie, it was the Nazis who made good use of it through the Stab in the Back legend, along with the belief that the German Army had not actually lost the war. Of course,

Hitler's rants about Jews and about the need for Germany to attain *lebensraum* (living space) would all characterize the Nazi regime in the future.

In the short term, *Mein Kampf* was of limited importance in rebuilding the movement. More pressing was organizing the movement on the ground—and here the Nazis proved most effective. In the 1930s, a sociologist from Columbia University visited Nazi Germany and interviewed people who had supported the movement in its early years. His study revealed the crucial importance of local structures in the NSDAP known as the *Orstgruppen* (Abel 1996). While Hitler coordinated the party on the national level, it was the local cells that provided the driving force of the movement through personal contact, the spreading of leaflets and posters, and, crucially, the raising of money. Although Hitler was successful in raising money from industrialists and business leaders, little of this money made its way down to the local groups. William Sheridan Allen's study of a small town under Nazism confirmed the importance of local activism, to which was added the ability of the Nazis to offer a flexible propaganda that was responsive to local grievances. They demonstrated a "unified, purposeful, and vigorous alternative" to the other parties (Sheridan Allen 1984, 298).

Fighting the Culture Wars

While Weimar was experiencing a period of economic and political stability in the mid-1920s, Hitler's movement focused on the culture wars. The center of Germany's culture war was Berlin. The Nazis had difficulties in getting their message across in the capital partly due to the strength of working-class support behind the Communist Party (KPD), but also due to the city's cosmopolitan character, with its large Jewish population and many Polish immigrants. The size of Berlin also made it difficult for the Nazis to penetrate. By the end of the 1920s, Berlin was the second largest city in Europe with over four million inhabitants. Thus, the size and diversity of the population in the capital cut against the Nazi appeal in the small towns and rural centers of the country.

Berlin also posed another major challenge—and opportunity—for the Nazi movement, as the center of Weimar culture and mass entertainment. It became a meeting place for artists and intellectuals, as Munich had once been, much of it politically left, which raised the concerns of conservatives, who feared what was frequently called *kulturbolschewismus* (cultural bolshevism). The right-of-center governments that came to power in Germany after 1929 often attempted to attack this rising culture. The film *All Quiet on the Western Front*, for example, based on the novel by Erich Maria Remarque, was censored not only in Germany but in other countries as well. The film's anti-war message and its American pedigree—having been made in Hollywood but based on a German novel—angered German conservatives. It also mobilized the Nazi Party, who disrupted the film's premiere in Berlin in December 1930, where they set off smoke bombs and released mice in the theater.

The assault on the movie theaters was coordinated by the local Nazi leader, Joseph Goebbels, and his newspaper, *Der Angriff* ("The Attack"). Goebbels took over Nazi

Party operations in Berlin in 1926 partly due to his knowledge of modern art and mass culture. A self-proclaimed film enthusiast, Goebbels even expressed some sympathy for some modern artists like Vincent van Gogh (Spotts 2003). Goebbels's task was to counter the culture of "Red Berlin" with a Germanic aesthetic that suited not only Hitler's own tastes but also the cultural ideas of the conservative establishment of Berlin. Goebbels's strategy involved not only sending in the Brownshirts into working class districts to clash with communist supporters but also to attack the "decadent" culture of the city. Berlin was well known in the 1920s as a center for American jazz, modernist architecture, and expressionist art, which Goebbels attacked incessantly through his newspaper. Berlin also became known for its modern attitudes toward sex and the body. The city boasted the highest number of gay bars in the world. In 1919, Magnus Hirschfeld, an early advocate for gay rights, opened the Institute for Sexual Research in Berlin (E. D. Weitz 2007).

The Nazi opposition to Berlin's cultural scene made the movement palatable to conservatives in the city who did not see the other parties as actively engaged on that front. Indeed, Goebbels's abilities as an organizer and propagandist helped increase the Nazi presence within the city and gave them an in with upper-class districts of the city. Fighting the culture war in Berlin clearly paid off for the Nazis. By 1929, the party had increased its representation in the Berlin municipal elections threefold (Evans 2015). Using tactics that had served the party well in smaller communities, the Nazis made frequent shows of force, with marches through working class districts and impressive rallies, including one with Hitler speaking in the newly constructed Sports Palace. It was to Berlin that the SA took their beer hall brawl skills, fighting communist supporters on the streets. In March 1927, some seven hundred Brownshirts assaulted a group of communists in the railway station and then proceeded to attack Jewish shops on the Kurfürstendamm (Large 2000). Out of Berlin came Nazism's most important martyr: Horst Wessel. Wessel was killed in a dispute with the landlady of a prostitute he was frequenting. When he refused to pay, the landlady sent in a collector who also happened to be a communist. Goebbels turned Wessel's somewhat sordid death into something heroic, giving him a massive funeral surrounded by Nazi ritual. It so happened that the late Brownshirt was also a poet of sorts and had written a hymn to the Brownshirts, which the NSDAP made into the *Horst Wessel* song.

The Nazi Electoral Machine

For all his considerable efforts, Goebbels was never able to make the Nazis the largest party in Berlin, always playing second fiddle to the KPD. On a national level, however, the NSDAP did become the largest party in the Reichstag by 1932 due in part to the ineffectiveness of the traditional parties to deal effectively with the crisis. Hindenburg's reliance on center-right parties simply could not muster the votes needed in the Reichstag; so, beginning in 1930 with the Heinrich Brüning government, Germany was effectively ruled by decree through the implementation of Article 48.

The result was an increase in the electoral gains of the NSDAP on the right, and the Communist Party on the left in a series of Reichstag elections held between 1928 and 1932. These elections, both at the federal and state levels, witnessed the meteoric rise of the NSDAP. For a movement opposed to democracy, the Nazis proved effective at campaigning and getting the votes out.

Without a doubt, circumstances helped Nazi electoral success. In the Reichstag elections of 1928, the party hardly made an impression, garnering just over 800,000 votes and a paltry 12 seats in the parliament. The KPD, by contrast, boasted over 3 million votes and 54 seats. Things changed dramatically with the next elections in September 1930, where the Nazis skyrocketed to over 6 million votes and 107 seats, making them second only to the SPD. In between the two elections came the Wall Street Crash and the subsequent Great Depression, which, as mentioned, hit Germany very hard. The spike in unemployment aided in the rise of the extremist parties, with the Nazis on the right and the communists on the left. Hit hardest were the liberal-bourgeois parties, which were unable to offer concrete solutions to the economic crises. This was aggravated by the ineffective Brüning administration, installed in March 1930. A centrist politician, Brüning made liberal use of emergency powers to enact austere measures that were deeply unpopular. In 1931, Brüning used those powers against the radical parties, enacting various bans on meetings and the wearing of uniforms, not to mention restrictions of the press. The Brüning government fell in May 1932, but his successors, von Papen and von Schleicher, largely continued his policies. In the meantime, political polarization and radicalization increased in the Weimar Republic. Nazis and communists fought pitched battles in the streets of such brutality that they often left bystanders shaken.

The ineffectiveness of governments in the face of the deep crisis and their inability to offer solutions to alleviate the suffering of masses of Germans provided the context for the rise of Nazism. The increasing willingness of conservative elites to work with the Nazis was crucial. In 1931, Hitler entered an informal alliance with the National Conservative Party (DNVP), led by the media magnate Alfred Hugenberg, and the veterans' organization the *Stalhelm*, called the Harzburg Front. It also included the former President of the Reichsbank, Hjalmar Schacht. The alliance was aimed squarely at the Brüning government. The front did not last long, but it was one of the first signs of a willingness to bring Hitler into respectable circles.

The Nazis were also helped by the fear of "Marxism" that was gripping the German middle classes. On a local level, this fear was often directed not at the KPD, but the SPD, the party most associated with Weimar, and who continued to use Marxist language, despite their moderate socialism (Sheridan Allen 1984, 34–5). The continued strength of the Social Democrats in the large cities also fed into the culture wars, associated as they were with urban cosmopolitanism. Finally, the negotiations associated with the Young Plan in 1929 also helped the Nazi cause. This was a revision of the Dawes Plan, and it set up a schedule of reparation payments that would go into the 1980s. While the plan made financial sense, the length of the payment period gave the Nazis a chance to claim that the German people were being "enslaved." The fact that this plan was American, like its predecessor, only added fuel to the culture war fire.

All of this seems to confirm Robert Paxton's thesis that the Nazis succeeded because they exploited certain spaces—political and cultural—the existing regime left open. This is true, but it ignores the very real talents the Nazis demonstrated in their election campaigns. Hitler proved adept at gauging his audience and was willing to shift the focus onto different groups when needed. For example, after the 1928 elections, Hitler decided to start appealing to the German middle classes and less to the working classes (Sheridan Allen 1984). This shift was anticipated by the local Nazi organizations who discovered the importance of flexibility in messaging. William Sheridan Allen's study of the town of Northeim demonstrates how, in 1929, various meetings showcased different speakers who spoke on various topics, most of which were economic in nature. Only one of the speeches was overtly antisemitic (Sheridan Allen 1984). Fundraising efforts at these meetings allowed the Nazis to gauge what the local electorate wanted to hear, allowing them to tailor meetings according to these interests. Lists of speakers would be circulated by the local *Gau* (state leadership) from which the cells could choose.

The success of Nazis on a local level was aided by the abilities of Hitler at the national level. Through the help of his close friend and official photographer, Heinrich Hoffman, Hitler perfected the image he presented to the German electorate. Hoffman took the famous 1927 pictures of Hitler rehearsing his speech gestures. He also took the pictures used in the electoral posters for the 1932 Presidential elections. In April of that year, Hitler presented himself as a candidate against Paul von Hindenburg. Riding the wave of the Nazi success in the 1930 Reichstag elections, Hitler believed that his time had come to lead Germany. Although he picked up some 13 million votes, Hitler lost to the old Field Marshall after a runoff election. The posters used by the Nazis in this election are striking. One presents a portrait of Hitler's face surrounded by black. This was an imitation of the Mussolini portrait that appeared in Sarfatti's biography. Another image was that of *Hitler über Deutschland* ("Hitler over Germany"), showing the candidate in an airplane. These images became part of a book published by Hoffman and a film of the same name.

Hitler's use of the airplane was a masterstroke, although, once again, he was imitating Mussolini, who had already embraced the airplane for propaganda purposes. By 1932, Italo Balbo, the *ras* of Ferrara, had already completed his Transatlantic flight to Brazil, leading a squadron of twelve seaplanes (Segrè 1987, 220). Hitler had already shown his willingness to use modern transportation with his supercharged Mercedes Benz—now he moved up to the air, which allowed him to celebrate the "mythical modernity" that became a hallmark of fascism (Esposito 2015). On a practical level, the use of the airplane made it possible for Hitler to cover large distances and appear at several different rallies throughout the country. This embrace of modernity extended to Hitler's willingness to use media like the radio and to appear in large venues, thanks to the microphone, something that Mussolini generally shunned.

These devices and techniques transformed Hitler into a compelling figure that closely resembled the sense of vigor and purpose demonstrated by the Nazi movement in general. What was to become the cult of the *Führer* was worked out during these election campaigns, in a manner that not only won votes but also allowed Hitler to crush the internal revolt within the party. His abilities to transfix a crowd are well noted. Preferring to use enclosed spaces, like stadiums and arenas, Hitler was able to project an almost messianic presence that resembled a revivalist meeting. His proclivity for violent stabbing gestures and ability to modulate his voice to appeal to emotions was unmatched by his rivals.

With Hitler as the celebrity centerpiece, the Nazis became effective campaigners and by 1933 boasted the largest representation in the Reichstag. So who voted for them? The traditional view, usually put forward by Marxist historians, was that the Nazis drew on lower-middle-class support. In other words, that part of the so-called *mittelstand* that had the most to lose in economically precarious times. They had been hard hit in the hyperinflation of the early 1920s and were now faced with another economic shock in 1929. Later research has demonstrated, however, that the Nazis had a broader appeal and were able to get supporters from different socioeconomic groups, ranging from the upper middle classes in the larger cities, to some workers, and to farmers. Richard Hamilton's study of the elections of July 1932 demonstrated that while the Nazis generally lost in the larger cities to the left-wing parties, they received disproportionate support in the wealthier districts of those cities (Hamilton 1982). Outside the major cities, the Nazis were overwhelmingly popular in Protestant, rural districts and in smaller towns. While there have been no definitive conclusions about the Nazi electorate, there is general agreement that it was volatile and not restricted to any class. Hitler's appeal cut across class lines while, regionally, the Nazis were strongest in the Protestant areas of Germany. Although Nazism was born in predominantly Catholic Bavaria, the consistent strength of the Center Party prevented the Nazis from making any major breakthroughs in Catholic circles. Significantly, the Nazis won the Prussian Landtag elections in April 1932, taking 37 percent of the vote and supplanting the SPD. This included a strong showing in East Prussia, the traditional seat of the Prussian landed elite and of Paul von Hindenburg. It was Hindenburg and the former Catholic Center politician, Franz von Papen, who would orchestrate the entry of Hitler into government.

The Nazis Come to Power

In November 1932, Germans went to the polls again. It was the second Reichstag election in half a year and an indication that the increasingly unpopular measures by the federal government needed some parliamentary majority to back it. Once again, the Nazis came out on top, but they had lost some 2 million votes and 34 seats compared to July. This dip made Hindenburg more willing to take on Hitler in government. Hindenburg had been reluctant to accept the Nazis in government, especially when Hitler demanded to be Chancellor, rather than the Vice Chancellor position offered to him earlier in the year. Now that the Nazis seemed to be losing some of their popularity, Franz von Papen began the initiative of giving Hitler the Chancellorship, on the assumption that he could be checked. This proved to be a fatal miscalculation that resembled the mistake made by King Victor Emmanuel III in 1922 with respect to Mussolini. The increased votes behind the KPD added another element of urgency to find a workable, right-wing government. Ruhr industrialists, like August Thyssen, began lobbying for the Nazis to be given a position of power in a future government, fearing as they did an imminent communist takeover. Moreover, it was increasingly difficult to keep the Nazis out of the government, considering their strong representation in the Reichstag.

Hitler was appointed Chancellor of Germany on January 30, 1933. The appointment was greeted by a massive torchlight parade of Brownshirts in Berlin. Hitler watched from a window in the Reich Chancellery building, frequently saluting his Nazi followers. It was an impressive display, aimed at giving Berliners the impression of a unified and energetic movement. One of the conditions that Hitler demanded upon being nominated Chancellor was the calling of new elections, which was granted by Hindenburg only two days after Hitler's appointment. The elections were called for March 5, giving Germans their third federal election since the previous July. Unlike Mussolini, who made sure to reform the electoral system, Hitler made no attempt to change the system before the election. Instead, he resorted to Nazi muscle. On February 22, thousands of Brownshirts were drafted into an "auxiliary police." This injection of Nazi thugs into the police force was made possible by the two key Nazis in the Hitler cabinet: Wilhelm Frick and Hermann Göring. The former was the Reich Interior Minister, while the latter was Minister without Portfolio. Significantly, Göring was also made President of the Prussian State Council. Hitler owed this last appointment to the work of Franz von Papen. In July 1932, after the Nazi victory in the federal elections, von Papen, serving as Chancellor, effectively carried out a coup by illegally removing the Prussian government, run by Social Democrats, and replacing it with conservatives. The move was contested in court but was partially upheld.

The von Papen coup was yet another example of how the groundwork for the Nazi Revolution was partially laid by non-Nazi governments. Hitler inherited a situation in which the Reich government controlled the government of Germany's largest and most powerful state. Göring's police immediately got to work harassing and assaulting communist and socialist meetings throughout Germany during the election campaign. Centrist Catholic candidates were also harassed if they dared to criticize the Hitler government. Jews were also persecuted and left with little or no recourse to the authorities. As Richard Evans has noted, the Nazi opponents were woefully unprepared for this Brownshirt onslaught and police persecution (Evans 2004, 334–5). No one was prepared, however, for the events of February 27, when the Reichstag building went up in flames.

The burning of the Reichstag is one of the seminal events in the rise of the Nazi regime. Ever since the election was called, Hitler and the Nazis emphasized the Marxist threat, claiming that the communists were only waiting for the right moment to start a Bolshevik Revolution. That moment appeared to come when a Dutch communist, Marinus Van Der Lubbe, was arrested for starting the fire. Just as Mussolini used the Matteotti Crisis to raise the specter of communism, Hitler immediately pounced on the fire to get Hindenburg to sign an emergency decree giving the government extraordinary powers to crack down on the KPD. While Hitler did not ban the party, he had many of its members and leadership arrested, making it impossible for them to campaign in the election or to sit in the Reichstag. Over four thousand people were arrested in the police sweep that followed the fire. To this day, there are many mysteries surrounding the fire, but the Nazis were very quick to exploit it and were able to deliver a major blow to the party that had gained seats in the November 1932 election.

Hitler and the Nazis campaigned effectively in large part through control of the state apparatus and through the support from business circles. The money that flowed into the Nazi campaign allowed Goebbels to crank out propaganda while the police made sure that Nazi opponents were rendered ineffective. While socialists and communists struggled to get their message across due to Nazi violence, Hitler had at his disposal the radio which broadcast his rallies throughout the Reich. Not surprisingly, the Nazis made significant gains in the election, winning over 12 million votes and increasing their seats in the Reichstag from 192 to 288. Significantly, the Nazis did not win a majority, confirming Peter Fritzsche's point that Germany was a deeply divided nation. In other words, Germany was in a state of political paralysis—it had "checkmated itself" (Fritzsche 2020, 3). While this may have seemed a loss for the Nazi Party, in fact, it created an opportunity for Hitler to make a convincing case for the dismantling of the Weimar democracy. Just as appointment as Chancellor was an attempt to break the deadlock in the Reichstag, the results of the March elections opened the door to a Nazi, anti-democratic solution to Germany's political and economic problems. What better way to do this than at the opening of the new Reichstag.

The Day of Potsdam

The Nazi Revolution began in an atmosphere of nostalgia. On the first day of spring, 1933, the new Reichstag was formally opened in the sacred site of the Prussian Hohenzollern monarchy. Potsdam was the heart of Prussia. There, in the Garrison Church, lay the mortal remains of Frederick III, also known as Frederick the Great, the eighteenth-century monarch who turned Prussia into a European power. At 10:00 am, on a brisk March morning, a cavalcade of cars brought President Hindenburg, Chancellor Hitler, and the members of his government and the Reichstag to Potsdam. The first stop was a morning church service, one for Protestants and one for Catholics. Everyone then convened at the Garrison Church for the official ceremony. Built in the eighteenth century as the parish church of the Hohenzollerns and the Prussian army, the church was once graced by the music of J. S. Bach and visited by conquerors like Napoleon. As the resting place of the Prussian monarchs, it was a sacred site for the nostalgists of the Second Reich, a place of consolation for those who hated the Weimar Republic and longed for the return of the Kaiser.

With the Reichstag building still in tatters, Hitler decided to hold the opening ceremony of the Reichstag here, in the presence of Hindenburg and the Crown Prince, who appeared wearing the death's head insignia of the Hussars Regiment. With the famous carillon ringing, the participants made their way into the historic church.

Hindenburg sat in front of the altar; on either side of him, slightly set back, sat the Crown Prince, with two empty chairs for the absent Emperor and Empress. In front of a solemn assembly, Hindenburg and Hitler gave brief addresses. Hindenburg, dressed in full field marshal regalia with baton and spiked helmet, spoke first. The eighty-four-year-old president called for a return to the values of Old Prussia: fear of God, fidelity to work, love of country, and a willingness to sacrifice. In a not very subtle stab at the Weimar Republic, Hindenburg called for an end to the party politics, claiming this as the necessary precursor to spiritual revival. Hindenburg's remarks played to the desire for a return to Prussian military authoritarianism. It was a nostalgic call for a lost era buried by the Great War and the November Revolution. His was the voice of a generation that was passing (Figure 5.2).

Up next was the younger Chancellor. Not yet forty-three years of age, Hitler was dressed in coattails when he stood and faced Hindenburg. Taking account of the solemn occasion and site, Hitler gave a restrained speech "notable for its restrained moderation," according to Richard Evans (Evans 2004, 350). Hitler avoided the histrionics usually associated with his performances; however, the content of the speech made the point that while the old traditions had to be respected, something new was being born on that spring day. He began with an observation on German history, noting its cycles of rise and decline, usually caused by internal divisions that were then exploited by foreigners. Since

Figure 5.2 Adolf Hitler addresses members of the Reichstag at the Garrison Church during Potsdam Day, 1933. Opposite him sits Reich President Paul von Hindenburg. Credit: Alamy.

the November Revolution of 1918, Germany was in a period of decay that manifested itself in all aspects of German life. A breakdown caused by decay led Germany to accept the war guilt imposed on it by the Allies. Ultimately, the degradation of traditional values led to self-doubt, sending Germany into a spiral downward and a crisis without end. However, now Germany had an opportunity to rise again, thanks to the wisdom of the old president who extended a hand to the young generation represented by the Nazis.

Emphasizing this link between ancient and new, Hitler called for national unity as a necessary step toward the revival of Germany as a great power. Singleness of mind—all social groups working toward a single goal—was required if an era of peace was to descend on Germany—and for the wounds of war to be healed. To this end, Hitler pledged a new era where the cultivation of historical traditions and values would be led by an authoritative government committed to organizing the nation's life. The fractured and divided Germany was a thing of the past, a product of the degenerate and decaying Weimar Republic. The tomb of Frederick the Great and the living monument of Hindenburg were witnesses. Hitler's speech at Potsdam did not make any overt references to Nazi themes. Nothing was said explicitly about the Jews. But his reference to outsiders taking advantage of Germany's weakness was a clear antisemitic dog whistle. The speech was rich in references to Germany's Prussian past and served to emphasize some of the points made by Hindenburg.

There was little that was overtly revolutionary, and the speech and ceremony served to assuage the fears of German conservatives who wanted the Nazis to prevent a Marxist uprising and restore German authoritarianism. Hitler did not sell out Nazism to German conservativism, though. The speech demonstrated the growing convergence of Nazi ideology and National Conservatism that had been developing since the mid-1920s. Hitler understood the emotional appeal that Potsdam evoked in conservative Germans, especially Prussians. However, rather than simply calling for a return to tradition, as Hindenburg did, he presented tradition as a starting point for a new Germany, one where the youth of postwar Germany would look back to forge a revolutionary future. Hitler was not going to restore the Hohenzollerns or turn the clock back to the Second Reich.

While those inside the Garrison Church might fantasize about a return to the past, the thousands of torch-bearing Brownshirts who marched in Berlin and other German cities that evening evoked something different. Peter Fritzsche has noted how the Potsdam ceremony was one of four major celebrations held by the Nazis since Hitler came to power, representing the Third Reich's "pastoral myth" (Fritzsche 2020, 12). The Day of Potsdam followed the sophisticated choreography of January 30 and March 4 (Day of the Awakening of the Nation) and preceded the May 1 Day of National Labor. Each event, designed by Goebbels's propaganda team, promised a national reawakening fulfilling the Nazi slogan, "Germany, Awake!" Hitler's speech, therefore, was not just a call to return home or a cynical appeal to tradition to placate conservatives, but a key moment in expressing palingenesis: a reach back to the past to bring about a new dawn. Hitler was not simply making the old Hindenburg happy, waiting for him to die, but introducing one of the key elements of fascism, an emotional appeal to those who believe that they live in an era of decline and decadence and desire a return to national greatness. This reawakening was not given to the old guard, but rather a young generation of militants inspired by some mythical past glory. Both Hindenburg's spiked helmet and Hitler's coattails would soon be shelved for the jackboot and Brownshirt.

The Nazi Revolution Begins

A key appeal of Nazism was its energetic and decisive action. Hitler did not wait long to begin his takeover of the Weimar state once he left the "sacred grounds" of Potsdam. That same evening, while Brownshirts marched and celebrated in the streets of Berlin, the new Reichstag met in the Kroll Opera House, the temporary seat of the German parliament. The session was presided over by Hermann Göring, who had been the President of the Reichstag since July 1932. Göring made it clear that a new era was beginning when he dispatched with the usual formalities and rules associated with the opening of parliament. The correspondent for the *New York Times*, noting this and the Potsdam ceremony earlier in the day, prophetically claimed that Weimar democracy was now in the "dustbin."[1] In his opening address, Göring repeatedly referenced the Potsdam spirit that now united Germany. The Crown Prince, still in his Hussars uniform, was given an honored seat in the meeting. The Communist and Social Democratic deputies, meanwhile, were notable for their absence. The KPD deputies were either in detention or in hiding, while the SPD deputies protested the Potsdam trappings of the event. In the streets, outside the Opera House, Brownshirts marched and nationalist slogans were plastered everywhere.

The Kroll Opera House was the scene of Weimar's demise. On March 23, two days after the Potsdam ceremony, the government introduced the Enabling Act for ratification. This law would give the Chancellor and his government emergency powers that only the president could use through Article 48. According to the Weimar constitution, such an act required two-thirds approval. The Nazis did not have that many votes in the Reichstag, even with the votes of the DNVP. Thus, Hitler needed to rely on the Catholic Center Party to get the measure passed. Notably, at Potsdam, neither Hitler nor Goebbels attended the Catholic service, deciding instead to visit the graves of Nazi martyrs. The decision by German bishops to withhold the sacraments from Nazi leaders contributed to this snub. However, with the Center Party votes needed, Hitler began to reach out to the Catholic Church in speeches, appealing to the importance of religion in the same way that he appealed to Prussian tradition at Potsdam. It helped that some prominent Catholic bishops proved receptive to a détente with the NSDAP (Broszat 1981).

Hitler's ability to exploit the desire for law and order and the latent authoritarian tendencies within the Center Party and other bourgeois parties aided in the passage of the law. However, there was one other key fascist technique needed to secure its passage— the threat of violence. The thin line between legal and illegal methods, skillfully wielded

---

[1] N.A., "Empire Setting is Revived in New Reichstag Meeting," *New York Times*, March 22, 1933, p. 1.

by the Nazis, was on display on March 23, when hundreds of Brownshirts packed the Reichstag and milled around the entrance. Deputies that were known to be opposed to the bill, particularly those of the SPD, were jostled and harassed as they tried to enter the building. Speeches against the bill, especially that of Otto Wels, who made a heroic defense of constitutional freedoms in the presence of Hitler, were shouted down forcefully by the Nazi deputies and those in the galleries. The passing of the Enabling Act demonstrated the full arsenal of weapons at Hitler's disposal. This was legalism backed up with the threat of violence. It was also a legal means of effectively destroying the Republic.

The act had an expiry date of April 1, 1937. Its very title reflected the emotional appeal to order and security desired by many Germans. It was called the "Law to Remedy the Distress of the People and the Reich." It was a concise law, made up of only five articles, and it gave the Chancellor the power to enact laws without the Reichstag's approval. It could also make laws outside the constitution so long as it did not impact the Reichstag and the Office of President. In other words, it gave Hitler the right to appoint state governors and detain political opponents as well as ban political parties. The German Supreme Court upheld the law—even though none of the communist deputies were present, nor were several Social Democrats who had been detained. Technically, quorum was not reached—but this did not stop Göring from declaring quorum by discounting the KPD representation. With the Enabling Act, Hitler's dictatorship was firmly established. One day before the bill's passage, some two hundred political prisoners, most of them communist, were taken to a new prison in Bavaria near the town of Dachau. The first concentration camp was now operational, and the Third Reich was firmly established.

The Enabling Act gave Hitler the power he needed to eliminate all political opponents and establish a dictatorship. The final act of this consolidation of personal power had to wait until the summer of 1934, however, when Hitler decided to move against internal rivals within the NSDAP. Like Mussolini, Hitler realized that his authority within Nazism depended on keeping his personal authority within the party safe. Hitler's methods proved more ruthless than Mussolini's, but they amounted to the same thing: the reduction of fascism to the charisma and power of one individual. On June 29, Hitler moved to purge the party of its more leftist elements. Gregor Strasser was arrested and executed. So too was Ernst Röhm, Hitler's old comrade and the head of the Brownshirts. Röhm was associated loosely with the Strasser faction and there were fears that he wanted to use the SA to create a socialist revolution. Moreover, Röhm had designs to replace the Reichswehr (the regular German army) with the SA, something that concerned the Prussian elite that dominated the military. Pressure from Hitler's conservative allies along with pressure from Röhm's rivals within the party, like Göring and Heinrich Himmler, convinced Hitler to move against his old friend.

The purge itself was an act of choreography. Hitler had ordered the SA leadership to meet at a resort in Bavaria. Accompanied by his personal bodyguard, Himmler's SS, Hitler burst in on the sleeping SA men, had them arrested, and summarily shot. Röhm was arrested and jailed before being shot a few days later. Hitler took advantage of that night to have other opponents executed, like his predecessor as Chancellor, Kurt von Schleicher. Estimates of how many were killed vary, but most agree it was in the hundreds. Hitler publicly announced the purge in mid-July, claiming that sixty-one men had been executed. Crucially, he mentioned that no trials had been held but that he had taken it upon himself to be judge and executioner. The parallels to Mussolini's Matteotti speech in 1925 are striking. Like the Duce, Hitler used this murderous episode to establish his undisputed leadership—and it was done by taking responsibility.

The Night of the Long Knives, as Hitler himself called it, revealed much about the dynamics of Nazism and, by extension, fascism. It also revealed the depth of Nazi collusion with conservatives. Hitler's actions were applauded by the conservative establishment, beginning with Hindenburg. Even though Hitler had the Enabling Act in his pocket, the fact that he still needed to placate the conservative elite of the country demonstrated how deeply involved that establishment was with the Hitler movement. Hitler used the power of the state to illegally arrest and execute hundreds of men without due process, without objection. The acceptance of violence by the mainstream proved fertile ground for fascism. An important element was the highlighting of homosexual activities among SA men, which Goebbels' propaganda machine played up in the ensuing days, knowing that it played to conservative prejudices against gay men. The movement also demonstrated that it needed one all-powerful charismatic leader to be truly fascist. The *Führer* principle was to be established later that year as the cornerstone of the Nazi state. The NSDAP was not to be a party run on democratic principles, just as fascism was not to be a democratic movement. Unity under one leader was all that mattered.

Conclusion

The rise of the Nazis in Germany was neither inevitable nor accidental. It was helped along by a conservative establishment that, like in Italy, was afraid of Marxism and suspicious of liberal democracy. The massive shocks of war, inflation, and economic depression made the survival of the Weimar democracy tenuous, even in times of relative stability, as in the mid-1920s. Political deadlock and polarization contributed to a desire to search for radical solutions in the face of economic distress. Hitler, like Mussolini, proved adept at exploiting these crises and was able to present Nazism as a viable solution. However, whereas Mussolini never enjoyed success at the ballot box, the Nazis proved capable of garnering support in elections. The irony of the Nazi rise to power was that this fundamentally antidemocratic movement was made possible by democracy. In fact, Weimar democracy proved to be the handmaiden of Nazism. An authoritarian establishment required the mass support of the Nazi Party. This was the realization made by von Papen and Hindenburg in 1933, despite their inherent mistrust and dislike of Hitler and his movement.

While Weimar had opened the door for the Nazis to step in, the appeal of Nazism itself must not be discounted. Hitler understood the cultural pull of National Conservatism and the hatred toward any progressive, liberal, and leftist cultural manifestations. What made Nazism's rise to power possible was the increasing acceptance of Nazi radicalism by conservative bourgeois elements mistrustful of the cultural revolution happening in the cities like Berlin. The seminal moment arrived with the release of the film *All Quiet on the Western Front* in December 1930. Joseph Goebbels's campaign against the film, which involved violent disruptions of screenings, endeared the Nazis to conservatives who might not have reacted with such violence on their own. The energy and decisiveness demonstrated by the Nazis in events such as these, not to mention their willingness to take on communists in the streets, may have caused some disorder; conservatives, however, proved willing to look the other way if the victims were on the left. This pattern of tolerating violence depending on the target had already been established in the early years of the Weimar Republic when right-wing assassins often got away with their crimes due to indulgent conservative judges.

Hitler's abilities as a speaker and an organizer, united to a ruthless suppression of internal dissent and willingness to call for violence, made him an appealing figure to those looking for a charismatic personality who had an air of destiny about him. This sense of destiny, of a rising, irresistible force was carefully cultivated by Goebbels and could already be seen in the early Nuremberg Rally of 1927. When Leni Riefenstahl presented the 1934 rally in *Triumph of the Will*, she captured Nazism's most powerful image. Whether she was merely pointing a camera or carefully crafting a cinematic masterpiece, the result was a film that endorsed the Nazi image of a movement destined to rule. Riefenstahl understood that film appealed powerfully to the emotions—and this is just what Hitler used to appeal to a cross section of the German population. Nazism understood and capitalized on the emotional appeal of unity especially in times of profound crisis. This Hitler learned from Mussolini, and this was the image projected at Nuremberg.

CHAPTER 6
FASCISM AND THE STATE

The New Caesar

They came from all corners of the Eternal City. On a gray autumnal day in 1932, thousands of Romans flocked to the city center to watch the spectacle of the *Decennale*, the ten-year anniversary of the March on Rome. On October 28, the Fascist state choreographed what it called an "epic day," on which Mussolini, riding a horse and wearing the uniform of the fascist militia, capped off with a steel helmet, rode from Piazza Esedra to the Coliseum. As thousands watched on the side of the road and on balconies and out windows, the Duce moved through the new part of the city built by the liberal regime in the nineteenth century, past the Exhibition of the Fascist Revolution on the Via Nazionale, and down to Piazza Venezia, where his headquarters in the Palazzo of the same name was based and where the Unknown Soldier lay in the Victor Emmanuel II monument. Known as the Altare della Patria, the monument, commonly called the Vittoriano, was the focal point of celebrations marking the founding of the Kingdom of Italy—and of commemorations for those who died in the Great War (Figure 6.1).

From this site of memory of the liberal era, Mussolini moved onto the new stage offered by the Via dell'Impero, the new seven-hundred-meter boulevard built by the regime and inaugurated by Mussolini during the ceremony. Still sitting on his horse, Mussolini cut the tape and proceeded to ride down the new boulevard. The road was built as part of Rome's Master Plan of 1931, which called for a reconfiguration of the Roman landscape to facilitate, in Mussolini's words, "grandeur and necessity" (Painter Jr. 2005). It had the virtue of making a direct link between Piazza Venezia and the Coliseum and cut straight through the Imperial Fora built by Rome's emperors. The flat and wide boulevard opened out onto a wide vista on the Coliseum, the Palazzo Venezia, and the Vittoriano, surrounded by the isolated ruins of the Roman Fora. When Mussolini reached the Coliseum, he stopped and waited for the parade.

With arm outstretched in a Fascist salute, Mussolini watched as thousands of war-wounded and Blackshirt militia paraded on the boulevard in an impressive display that would resemble the Nazi parade captured by Riefenstahl in *Triumph of the Will*. Once completed, Mussolini traded his horse for an Alfa Romeo sports car, which took him back along the Via dell'Impero to the Palazzo Venezia. While planes flew over in V-formation, thousands of school children sang the fascist anthem *Giovinezza* in front of the Tomb of the Unknown Soldier. When finished, Mussolini stepped out onto the balcony of the Palazzo, where he addressed the "oceanic crowd" assembled in the square. There, he gave a brief address noting that of all the great celebrations held in Rome over the centuries, this was surely the greatest of all. He concluded by mentioning the

Figure 6.1 Mussolini addresses the "oceanic crowd" of supporters from the balcony of Rome's Palazzo Venezia during the year of the Decennale, 1932. Credit: Getty Images.

new road he had just inaugurated and called for a renewed fascist faith to carry over to the next ten years. He finished with an exhortation to the fascist revolution and then returned to his office.

While Mussolini was clearly indulging in hyperbole, there was no doubt that the *Decennale* celebration was an impressive piece of fascist choreography. It capped what had been a series of celebrations throughout the country, which included the inauguration of hundreds of public works projects up and down the peninsula. It also came a few months after the regime finally published a definitive definition of fascist "doctrine." The occasion was the publication of the Treccani Dictionary and Encyclopedia the previous summer. On August 5, the front page of Italy's newspaper of record, the *Corriere della Sera*, published Mussolini's definition of fascism in its entirety. Its coauthor, the neo-Hegelian philosopher Giovanni Gentile was not mentioned. It took ten years for Mussolini to get the official definition of fascism down on paper, just in time for the celebrations of the regime's anniversary. It is not known how many of the thousands of Romans who turned out on October 28 had bothered to read the doctrine, but even if they had not, they were given a visual display of its contents.

Historians have sometimes claimed that fascist spectacle, like the one on display in 1932, was an elaborate smoke and mirrors ceremony that masked the reality of fascist power. Richard Bosworth has frequently argued that what fascists did was more revealing than what they said (Bosworth 1998). The assumption here is that fascist deeds never actually lived up to their claims. In "The Doctrine of Fascism," Mussolini introduced the word "totalitarian" to describe the fascist state, whereby nothing existed outside the state. Even Hannah Arendt recognized that for all its talk of totalitarianism, Italian fascism proved woefully inadequate, since the monarchy and the Church continued to wield great influence outside fascism (Arendt 1968). In the end, according to Arendt, Italian fascism was nothing more than an "ordinary nationalist dictatorship." Arguments like this downplay the significance of fascist ideology and disregard the claims made by Mussolini and his admirers. They also relegate spectacles like the *Decennale* to nothing more than elaborate side shows designed to distract Italians.

Cultural historians, starting with George Mosse in the 1960s, suggest otherwise. Specifically, many argue that while fascism may not have been totalitarian, that does not mean that a distinctive fascist ideology, or doctrine, was not present in Mussolini's or Hitler's regimes for that matter. The concept of totalitarianism as discussed by Arendt no longer holds the same conceptual power it once had during the Cold War, and new approaches to fascism have replaced it with a close study of rituals and spectacles. Such is the case with the ten-year celebrations of 1932, an event destined to become one of the three major spectacles put on by the fascist regime in Rome. The second came in May 1936 when the regime announced the Italian Empire after the conquest of Abyssinia, and the third came in May 1938 during Adolf Hitler's state visit to Italy. The celebrations of October 28, 1932, revealed a great deal about the fascist state, especially in light of Mussolini and Gentile's doctrine. It also shed a great deal of light on other fascist regimes, like that of Nazi Germany, which relied on similar spectacles.

The ceremony gave the usual impression of unity and force, a successful recipe that helped the rise of Nazism in Germany, as we have seen. In the case of Mussolini's Italy, it offered the advantage of linking the fascist present with the past. Starting at the Piazza Esedra and making its way down the Via Nazionale, Mussolini appropriated the legacy of Liberal Italy, since this area of the city had been built in the years following Italian unification. The Piazza Esedra was the site of the Church of Santa Maria degli

Angeli. Sculpted out of ancient Roman baths by Michelangelo, the church was the official state church of the Italian monarchy. It was in this church that the body of the Unknown Soldier lay in state in 1921 after being transported from the battlefields in northeastern Italy. The Via Nazionale was Liberal Italy's major thoroughfare, linking this neighborhood with the ancient city center. It was here, at the Palazzo delle Esposizioni (the state exhibition gallery), that the regime chose to hold its exhibition. Thus, the procession allowed the fascist regime to make an important link to the preceding liberal order that it undermined while still respecting the monarchy.

This link between fascism and the liberal monarchy was further reinforced by the Piazza Venezia and the Altare della Patria. Once on the Via dell'Impero, however, Mussolini made the more significant connection to Imperial Rome. Here, Mussolini became the new Caesar, surrounded by the Imperial Fora. To review the parade, Mussolini set himself up next to the Coliseum facing the Basilica of Maxentius. These two imposing relics of ancient Rome framed Mussolini's presence and made clear that Italian fascism entailed the rise of a new emperor. Passing in front of this new leader was the Italy of past, present, and future. Here were the wounded of the Great War, with blinded and lame war veterans in the front row. Behind them came the Blackshirts of the fascist militia, most of them young. After this there were the children singing fascist songs. All of this on a stage provided by that most modern of settings, the broad boulevard designed for speed and unobstructed passage through the ancient ruins (Baxa 2010, 82–5).

Of course, this scenario played into Mussolini's policy of *Romanità*—a policy unique to Fascist Italy—but it also focused on the most important element of the fascist state: the leader. This chapter examines the fascist state as it developed in Fascist Italy and Nazi Germany in the 1930s. To be sure, Mussolini and Hitler had different approaches to the state. While Mussolini placed the state at the apex of the regime, Hitler largely ignored it in his writings and speeches and focused instead on the idea of a "racial community." While these two regimes were different in many ways, they both believed that a true totalitarianism could remedy the deficiencies of the liberal state they had dismantled. They also were centered upon a cult of personality, a cult of a charismatic leader. This was the main message of the *Decennale* celebrations and of the fascist doctrine laid out by Mussolini that same year.

A "Fascist Century"

Mussolini's "Foundations of the Doctrine of Fascism" was the necessary precursor to the events of the *Decennale*. For anyone still questioning the purpose and meaning of fascism, this was the guide to help them. Its primary author, of course, was Mussolini—but the actual writer was Giovanni Gentile. A neo-idealist philosopher who had once collaborated with Benedetto Croce, Gentile eventually went his own way after a fallout with Croce over politics. Gentile became an enthusiastic supporter of fascism after the First World War. He characterized Mussolini's movement as an example of "actualism," a philosophy that explored the nexus between thought and action, which proved appropriate for the atavistic side of fascism.

In 1922, Gentile became the Minister of National Education in Mussolini's first government, in which he authored the regime's first major piece of legislation, a thorough reform of the educational system named after him. In 1925, Gentile launched the Treccani Encyclopedia funded by the wealthy industrialist Giovanni Treccani. With this project, Gentile hoped to give Italians a resource of knowledge on a par with those of other countries in the West. Significantly, Gentile used a wide range of intellectuals known for their expertise, and not their politics, thus allowing anti-fascist intellectuals to participate (Cannistraro 1982, 183). This fact has led some to argue that Italian fascism had little control over culture in Italy and that this was more evidence of the regime's inability to be truly totalitarian. The first edition of the encyclopedia came out in 1929. The revised version of 1932 included the famous definition of fascism, which first appeared on the front page of the *Corriere della Sera* in August.

Gentile's influence is stated clearly in the first sentence of the introduction: "Like all sound political conceptions, fascism is action, and it is thought" (Mussolini and Gentile 2000). Beginning with this premise, Gentile/Mussolini go on to explain that this action and thought come together in a state that is "totalitarian," outside of which nothing exists. Reflecting Gentile's neo-idealist philosophy, the fascist state was primarily a spiritual entity reflecting fascism's rejection of the materialist philosophies of the nineteenth century, such as liberalism, Marxism, and socialism, not to mention positivism. The fascist state is a "living, ethical entity to the degree that it is evolving … A higher, more powerful expression of personality, the fascist state embodies a spiritual force encompassing all manifestations of the moral and intellectual life of man" (Mussolini and Gentile 2000). The "ethical state" has a will of its own; it is a product of thought and action. It is organic, a unique and original creation and is, therefore, revolutionary.

Despite its newness, the fascist state did not come out of nowhere. It was, rather, the product of development and a force of history. Mussolini-Gentile note on a couple of occasions that the twentieth century promises to be a "fascist century," leaving in the dust the materialist belief systems that had dominated the previous century. If it took this long to hammer out a "fascist doctrine," it was because fascism started as a movement of all action. In the years of struggle against the materialist forces, fascism did not have the luxury to work out a systematic set of beliefs. "Discussions there were," argued Mussolini-Gentile, "but something more sacred and more important was occurring: death. Fascists knew how to die" (Mussolini and Gentile 2000). Mussolini-Gentile presented fascism as a religion, sustained by faith and by martyrs. This point was driven home by the Exhibition of the Fascist Revolution, which included a *sacrario* where the fascist martyrs were exalted. To be sure, this new religion was not replacing Roman Catholicism, which fascism supports and protects. Rather, Mussolini-Gentile presented fascism in spiritual terms: it has no theology, but does have a moral code, one that does not wish to become its own god or to erase God altogether, even though fascism is a faith with its own doctrine.

Significantly, little or nothing is said about a leader. The "doctrine" presents the state as a spiritual force supported by the masses, but where is the Duce? Although there is no explicit theory on the cult of the leader in the doctrine, a close reading suggests that it is permeated by the need for an all-powerful leader. The need for the state to be vital and active needs a prime mover, and if the party is not that mover, then it must be the dictator.

The doctrine's concluding section turned to the need for the state to expand territorially. Imperialism was a necessity for a country like Italy, which had endured centuries of "servitude." Italy's Roman tradition demanded that imperialism be a moral and spiritual force, not just territorial, and that this be an expression of a nation's vitality. Mussolini-Gentile's reference to the Roman heritage and to the concept of *imperium* clearly required a strong leader, someone like Mussolini who could "crystallize this moment in the history of human thought" (Mussolini and Gentile 2000). An *imperium* requires an emperor. The choreography of the *Decennale* brought the Mussolini-Gentile doctrine to life, showing how Italy represented that thirst for "authority, direction, and order" that fascism delivered through the "ethical state."

None of this would matter without the man on the horse, though. Mussolini was the central figure around which the fascist state revolved. Fascism was first and foremost about a leader who was the head of a state that "expresses the will to exercise power and command" (Mussolini and Gentile 2000, 60). Only this kind of state represents a new departure in history, one that is illiberal and finds inspiration not just in the ancient emperors but in more recent figures like Napoleon III and Otto von Bismarck.

State, Party, and Economy in Fascist Italy

The doctrine combined with the ceremonies of the *Decennale* gave the impression of a strong, united fascist state. However, this did not seem to fit the actual picture of the state in 1932. For one thing, the monarchy was still present, and King Victor Emmanuel III, as the Head of State, stood above Mussolini. Additionally, the trappings of the liberal state remained in place, with the Chamber of Deputies and Senate still operating, albeit no longer as properly representative institutions. Finally, the Fascist Party did not appear to have much in the way of authority. Since Augusto Turati was forced out of his position as party secretary in 1930, following some scandalous rumors spread by his many enemies, the PNF had lost whatever initiative it previously possessed. For those looking at the corporative state as an example of fascism, it had not lived up to the high expectations its framers, like Alfredo Rocco, had hoped for. The National Council of Corporations had been formally created in 1930, and by 1934 it encompassed twenty-two corporations covering the entire productive force of the country. However, it possessed little authority or initiative in economic policy, and although it formally replaced the Chamber of Deputies in 1939, it never amounted to much, at least not for labor. Economic initiatives remained in the hands of the state and industry, as the former became stronger into the mid-1930s.

All of this suggests that the "ethical state" promoted in Mussolini-Gentile's doctrine did not actually exist and that the fascist state was nothing more than, in the words of Alexander De Grand, a cracked façade (De Grand, 1991). Mussolini's limited power was seen in the way he was eventually removed by King Victor Emmanuel III in July 1943, after the Fascist Grand Council voted for Mussolini's removal. Mussolini's inability to control the military as Hitler did make him more vulnerable, as evidenced by his replacement, Marshal Badoglio, a man staunchly loyal to the monarchy and the man Mussolini removed as military Chief of Staff in 1940. Fascism's compromised state was also evident in Mussolini's inability to eliminate the Church's influence in education and check the influence of Catholic Action after the pope had protested fascist incursions in these areas.

Despite these obvious flaws, it is possible to see some glimpses of a fascist order emerge in Italy in the 1930s. This is evident in the numerous activities of the party, the encroaching state control over the economy, and in the Cult of the Duce. To be sure, the PNF did not enjoy any real power within the state, but it was a presence in Italian life, and membership became a necessity for anyone who wanted to have any kind of meaningful place in Italian society. Under the leadership of Achille Starace, who became Party Secretary in 1931, membership was opened to the masses. By 1942, the PNF boasted nearly five million members. In the words of one historian, the PNF was a kind of "transmission belt" whose function was to transmit Mussolini's orders to the country (Laqueur 1996, 35). Starace made sure that this "belt" functioned when he overhauled the party statutes in 1932 to give Mussolini absolute authority over party matters.

Starace's major contribution to the party—which he led until 1939, becoming the PNF's longest serving secretary—was to make it subservient to Mussolini and the state. Starace's faithfulness to Mussolini's wishes meant that the party always played second fiddle to the state. Mussolini largely maintained the structures of the liberal state with its network of prefects overseen by the Ministry of the Interior. In a PNF circular issued in 1927, prefects were declared to be the highest authority of the state in the provinces, even higher than the party representatives (*federali*) (De Grand 1989). Mussolini maintained authority over the prefects, often choosing them from among experienced administrators and not from the ranks of the party, an example of the Duce's pragmatism—and his distrust of ambitious party leaders.

Despite this diminution of the party within the state, the party was able to carve out some influence. In the late 1920s, thanks to the work of Augusto Turati, the PNF was given control over the *Dopolavoro*, an organization that provided leisure and travel for workers as a means of making up for their lost labor rights. The party also gained influence over youth organizations, such as the *Opera Nazionale Balilla*. Their influence extended to the world of sport. At one point, Turati headed both the party and the Italian Olympic Committee, which had sweeping authority over sport, both professional and amateur. Under Starace, the party's rituals and appearance were turned into something sacred. Through a flurry of circulars, catechisms, and orders, Starace gave the party a militant and disciplined image that often bordered on the ridiculous. Indeed, Starace was often ridiculed for his exaggerated mannerisms and demonstrations of fascist virility, such as jumping through hoops of fire on his horse. Despite this, the image he gave of the party in the 1930s was that of unity, order, and discipline. His fanatical interest in uniforms provided fascism one of its most important aesthetic qualities.

With respect to the economy, while the project of a "third way" through corporatism did not work out as envisioned, the fascist state did ultimately wield a great deal of authority not only because of the debilitating effects of the Great Depression; the state was also motivated by fascism's emphasis on an autarchic national economy directed by the state. Assessing Italian fascism's ideas on economics is hampered by the relatively little scholarship on the topic, but the consensus is generally negative (Carter 2010). The key question is whether a distinctly fascist idea of economics existed in the first place beyond the "third way" policy.

During Mussolini's first years as prime minister, the regime's policy was distinctly liberal under the guidance of De' Stefani. After the installation of the dictatorship, the regime's policies moved toward state interventionism. Mussolini's pegging of the Italian lira to the gold standard at an artificially high value in 1927 was clearly a political move. Economically it made little sense, and it had the effect of arousing opposition from industry and business. It also sent the Italian economy into a recession after a period of growth. The fixing of the currency was one of several "battles" that the regime initiated in the mid- to late 1920s. The so-called Battle for Grain started to limit the amount of wheat that Italy imported, a fact that had negatively impacted Italy's balance of trade. In 1928, the regime initiated its "battle" against the marshlands surrounding Rome and elsewhere with a massive land reclamation project called the *Bonifica Integrale* (land reclamation). This initiative, too, was aimed at increasing the amount of arable land and fit with the regime's call for the "ruralization" of Italy. In the early 1930s, suffering under the impact of the Great Depression, the regime moved to save Italy's banks and failing industries with the creation of the Institute for Industrial Recovery (IRI) in 1933. Finally, in 1936 came the policy of autarchy, a move to make Italy entirely self-sufficient as a response to the sanctions levied by the League of Nations after Mussolini's invasion of Abyssinia in 1935.

In all the above initiatives, it is possible to argue that the regime was responding to internal and external pressures to save the Italian economy in the face of market volatility and weak economic structures inherited from the liberal era. The regime's economic interventions indicate a fascist stamp. The purely political decision to revalue the lira and the use of military nomenclature betrayed a distinctly fascist tone, as did the increasingly interventionist approach of the economy into the 1930s. The regime's economic policies were driven by status, prestige, and military concerns, rather than sound economic thinking. The moderate, short-term uptick in the economy and drop in unemployment in the 1930s was due to massive state intervention in the economy, which aimed not so much to put people to work but to construct massive public works projects, most of which, like the demolitions and urban planning, had a propagandistic aim. Even the draining of the Pontine Marshes was presented as an example of *Romanità* since the Romans had tried the same thing along with road building.

The fascist element was mainly seen, though, in the repressive nature of the economy. Workers' wages were kept low, one of the policies enacted in the corporative structure.

Meanwhile, those workers who moved to the cities to work on public works schemes were made to live in hastily built shantytowns on the outskirts of the cities called *borgate*. Autarchy, announced in 1936, demanded further sacrifices from workers and consumers. The drive for economic self-sufficiency was motivated by foreign policy initiatives and international prestige. It was an economic nationalism that aimed not at improving the lives of Italians but asserting fascism's power in the world. It rejected the economic ideas of liberalism and Marxism by relegating economic needs to national interest. While autarchy did lead to the fostering of new economic initiatives and the development of synthetic materials, it was ultimately a failure economically. The Second World War forced Italy to see just how economically fragile the fascist agenda had rendered them.

Finally, a fascist tone was also evident in the regime's increasing presence in the economy, especially in industry. That the IRI bailed out several companies indicates this. Ultimately, this allowed the state to have a controlling interest in major sectors of heavy industry (De Grand 1989, 81–5). The state's increasing footprint in the economy encouraged cartelization and monopolies, economic structures that paralleled the totalitarian drive in politics. While this did not reflect the utopian aspects of corporatism, it demonstrated fascism's state-driven economic policies aimed at increasing national prestige and the desire to foster a war economy. Workers lost their right to organize and have any say in their wages, while industry fell under the sway of the state through bailouts. In the end, the regime came to dominate all aspects of the economy: labor, industry, and trade. While some highly touted fascist goals—such as ruralization—never worked out, the ideologically driven decision-making gave the economy a distinctively fascist look and more. The initiative always came from Mussolini, who had long since given up consulting advisors on the economy.

"Shapeless" Totalitarianism in Nazi Germany

President Paul von Hindenburg died on August 2, 1934, after slipping into a coma. He was eighty-six years old and just two years into his second term as president. Hindenburg had been ill for at least two months before succumbing to his illness at his estate in Neudeck. One of his last visitors was Adolf Hitler, who assured the fading president of the nation's prayers. After a few days of official mourning, Hindenburg was laid to rest in a lavish state funeral on the site of the Tannenberg Memorial in East Prussia. The memorial marked the German Army's great victory over the Russians in the opening months of the First World War, for which Hindenburg was given credit. Opened in 1924 by Hindenburg himself, the memorial was in the shape of an octagon and included eight towers. The style was a tribute to Emperor Frederick II's Castel del Monte in Italy, thus making a direct link between the German Army in the First World War and the First Reich. The funeral was yet another instance of Nazi spectacle, with torches lighting the sixty-five-mile route from Hindenburg's estate to the mausoleum. Some two hundred thousand people watched as the field marshal's coffin was carried on an open carriage to the burial site, located right in the center of the octagon. In a manner befitting the masculinist ethos of Nazism and Prussian militarism, no women were allowed in the funeral cortège.

This was not a place for republicans. Indeed, as soon as Hindenburg's tomb was sealed, and after Hitler delivered the eulogy, the last nail was driven into the coffin of the Weimar Republic. Ten days after the funeral, Hitler held a national referendum, asking Germans to approve the unification of the offices of Chancellor and president. Ninety percent said yes. The plebiscite was accompanied by a massive propaganda campaign urging voters to say, "Yes to the *Führer*!" While it is always difficult to assess the true feelings of voters in such a climate, historians like Ian Kershaw argued that much of the support was genuine and enthusiastic (Kershaw, 1998, 526). However, Richard Evans has pointed out that intimidation by Nazi stormtroopers and the lack of a secret ballot in places suggest otherwise (Evans 2015, 106).

Either way, the plebiscite was the last act in the destruction of the republic. This process had started as soon as Hitler became Chancellor in 1933 with the Enabling Act and with the concentration of police powers in the hands of the Nazis. In April 1933 came the Law for the Restoration of the Civil Service, which allowed the Nazis to purge the civil service of political opponents and Jews. Significantly, the law was extended to cover all professionals, including judges, teachers, and university professors. This law was part of a process the Nazis called Co-ordination (*Gleichschaltung*), which implied the dismantling of the multiparty republic and the creation of the one-party dictatorship. In July, all parties except the NSDAP were banned. With the Enabling Act, Hitler also dissolved all existing state governments in the Reich. They were replaced with a Reich governor appointed by the Chancellor who reported directly to the Ministry of the Interior.

As in Italy, party membership was required for state civil servants. More than eight million Germans belonged to the NSDAP by the end of the 1930s, making it a mass party like the PNF; the Nazi party, however, enjoyed more influence on power than its Italian counterpart (Laqueur 1996, 38). The NSDAP maintained its local character from its years of campaigning and continued to mobilize the masses at the grassroots level. However, like the PNF, the NSDAP did not have the power that many of its more radical members had hoped for. The Night of the Long Knives made clear that the Nazi Party was subordinate to Hitler. This included the Stormtroopers. The new leader of the Brownshirts after the purge, Viktor Lutze, made sure that the SA never posed a challenge to the German Army.

Whereas in Fascist Italy, the subordination of the party to the state was clear, the situation in Germany was somewhat different. In many ways, the party was parallel to the organs of state and its jurisdiction was never effectively demarcated, creating some degree of confusion and conflict between party and state. In a system that Martin Broszat has called an "organizational jungle," the Nazi state was designed in a haphazard way that allowed different centers of power to jostle with each other to attain influence (Broszat 1981, 358). The rather chaotic and "shapeless" nature of the Nazi state stands in stark contrast to the image of unity and order expressed in party rallies. The dualism was there from the beginning, and Hitler did little to fix the situation, thus leaving the "boundaries between state and party fluid" (Broszat 1981, 348). Despite this situation, which created a great deal of friction, Martin Broszat has argued that the system worked since the Nazis were able to bring together the state and the mass movements. Not only did it work, but when Hitler made major changes to the government in 1938 by eliminating many of the old state functionaries and replacing them with convinced Nazis, the chaotic structure of the regime served to further radicalize decision-making within the Reich.

The polycratic nature of the Nazi regime differed greatly from the regime established by Mussolini in Italy. While Mussolini governed alone, and made sure to neutralize any potential rival, Hitler allowed individuals to carve out enormous spheres of influence within the state. Men like Heinrich Himmler, head of the SS, Martin Bormann, head of the party, Hermann Göring, Joseph Goebbels, and Albert Speer were able to construct power centers of their own. This kind of structure has led some historians to liken the Hitler state to a feudal monarchy (Koehl 2003, 274). Hitler was able to check their power by encouraging rivalry among them, creating conflicts that often required his mediation. In many cases, though, he was content to let the conflicts simmer. This competition and rivalry within the system gave it momentum as each leader attempted to interpret Hitler's will. While Hitler did not always make clear his intentions, his "will" shaped the climate in which these men worked (Kershaw 2000, 91–2). The tendency known as "working towards the *Führer*" seems to have guided decision makers in the Third Reich and directed the multiple rivalries within the state. The workings of this system were a key element, as we shall see, in the planning and execution of the Final Solution during the war.

Nazi economic policies were part and parcel of this polycratic structure. The Nazi regime made no significant changes to the German economy, largely keeping intact the economic structure inherited from the Weimar Republic (Bracher 1970, 330–1). None of the left-wing ideas found in the early Nazi movement or in the Strasser wing of the party saw the light of day in the Third Reich. Nor was there any attempt to create a corporatist system like that in Fascist Italy. This is not to say that Nazi economic policies were simply an extension of German capitalism, as some Marxist historians have claimed, nor that the Nazis operated a kind of command economy, as liberal historians have claimed. Instead, as Ian Kershaw has argued, Nazi economic policies were the product of a "power cartel" system, in which the Nazi state, "big business," and the army worked together to advance each other's interests (Kershaw 2000, 58). In some ways, this was like the kind of "total war" arrangement that functioned in Germany during the First World War. As in Mussolini's Italy, labor lost all political influence when unions were banned—except for the Nazi Labor Front. Attempts to deal with the unemployment crisis resulted in public works initiatives, such as the construction of the *Autobahn*, Germany's highway network.

This raises the question of what, exactly, made all of this fascist. As Kershaw has argued, in the early years of the Reich, the "power cartel" clearly favored the interests of big business and the army. After 1936, however, the Nazi state began taking the initiative. This was due to the Four-Year Plan, announced at the Nuremberg Party Rally and guided by a secret memorandum written by Hitler and sent to Hermann Göring, who was put in charge of the plan. The plan was Hitler's resolution to create a major rift in the "power cartel" between those who wanted to maintain Germany's international contacts and those who called for a policy of autarchy. The key issue was rearmament. The latter group argued in favor of a massive rearmament campaign that would take priority over consumer goods. Notably, several large-scale enterprises like the chemical giant, IG Farben, favored autarchy and rearmament, and was even involved in putting the plan together in cooperation with Nazi officials (Kershaw 2000). The Four-Year Plan put wage and price controls in place as well as restrictions on labor mobility. It also put the Third Reich on a clear war footing. In a famous conference with the heads of the armed services in 1937, Hitler informed them that the only way to keep rearmament sustainable was to seize raw materials through expansion. All of this gave the Nazi state increasing initiative in economic policy in the late 1930s and was reflected in the gradual pushing out of conservative elements in the state after 1938. At no point did the regime lose the support of the industrial sector; in fact, the situation trended toward cartelization and the concentration of capital, as smaller and medium businesses were not able to keep up with the demands of rearmament (Bracher 1970).

Skeptics have argued that the economic policies in Germany and Italy do not show a distinctly fascist approach to economics. Rather, they merely continued the policies of previous regimes. While there was no "command economy"—as might be argued by the totalitarian school—the fascist state increasingly held the initiative in driving policy toward an autarchic model. If there was anything that was distinctly fascist, it was autarchy and the creation of a military–industrial complex. These policies also revealed that big business found fascist authoritarianism acceptable, even if fascism was not necessarily an attractive ideology. If not the ideology, then it was fascist leadership that industrialists could work with. This leads us to the central element that characterizes the fascist state: the charismatic leader.

The Cult of the Leader and the Leadership Principle

The Nazi German state and the Italian fascist state were clearly very different in many respects. In Italy, many of the trappings of the liberal state were maintained, and important non-fascist institutions continued to exercise power throughout the *Ventennio* (1922–43). Hitler was more thorough in wiping away the Weimar Republic, but he did not eliminate its economic structures, nor did he create a rational constitutional order to replace what had been destroyed. In both cases, the party was kept in check, but the NSDAP had a great deal more influence in Germany than the PNF had in Italy. While the Fascist Party was made subordinate to the state, the Nazi Party became a parallel institution with unclear boundaries between it and the state. Mussolini did not allow prominent party figures to carve out any influence within the state. Farinacci was kept at arm's length, and Italo Balbo and Giuseppe Bottai were exiled once they became too influential and popular. In contrast, Nazi Party figures like Goebbels, Göring, Himmler, and Bormann became immensely powerful within the Third Reich. Finally—as will be discussed later–a remaining key factor in Nazi Germany was race. In Italy, race was virtually a nonfactor until Mussolini introduced the Racial Laws in 1938.

These differences have led prominent historians like Renzo De Felice to argue that Italian fascism and German Nazism had nothing in common and that they were, in fact, two very different movements (De Felice 1976, 94–6). According to De Felice, who became one of Italy's leading, albeit controversial, authorities on fascism in Italy, the two movements had only "negative" similarities—that is, they merely opposed the same things. The very different states they constructed was evidence that Italian fascism and German Nazism did not envision the same kind of society. De Felice's influence on contemporary historiography has been strong but has not gone unchallenged, notably through the work of Roger Griffin and the journal *Fascism* (though this challenge has focused more on culture than politics).

If they had something in common, it was the cult of the leader, and the leadership principle more generally. In Nazi Germany, the *Führer* was given institutional shape with the fusion of the offices of Chancellor and president in 1934. It was also confirmed through loyalty oaths given to Hitler by civil servants, judges, and, in 1935, by the military. Rituals and propaganda propped up Hitler's institutional status, insulating him from a period of economic crisis in 1934. During the Saar plebiscite, held after the Nazis remilitarized the Rhineland in March of 1936, the propaganda campaign focused exclusively on Hitler and his role in reversing the Treaty of Versailles (Kershaw 1989). Goebbels's propaganda ministry exploited Hitler's charismatic leadership, but it is important to note the institutional basis for this principle.

Mussolini did not enjoy the same kind of institutional protection. He remained officially the *Capo del Governo* (prime minister) while the king remained head of state. The term Duce was never formalized. However, a cult of the Duce was repeatedly emphasized by the regime and its supporters. In 1926, the former nationalist turned fascist, Leo Longanesi, coined the phrase *Mussolini ha sempre ragione* (Mussolini is always right), which was repeated in slogans and in schools. Like Hitler, Mussolini was surrounded by an aura. He was called the "man sent by Providence" by Pope Pius XI after the signing of the Lateran Accords, and the regime was quick to use this during the referendum of March 1929. Significantly, however, when Pius XI denounced Italian "state idolatry" in his 1931 encyclical *Non Abbiamo Bisogno* ("We Have No Need"), over the question of education, nothing was said about the cult of the leader. One of Achille Starace's main responsibilities as party secretary was to introduce Mussolini on the balcony of Palazzo Venezia with his *saluto al Duce* cry. Under his leadership, the PNF became the instrument to reinforce the cult of the Duce.

The cults that surrounded these leaders thus served to insulate them from criticism of their regimes; the cult of the leader also became the organizing principle around which an otherwise chaotic and confusing state structure revolved. In other words, fascism was most clearly expressed through the charismatic leader and less so in the institutional arrangements of their respective governments. In fact, the leadership principle permeated those governmental systems. Everything went back to the national leader through intermediary leaders. All organizations were organized around a leader, creating a system of "little Duces and Führers" up and down the system. Ironically, this contributed to the infighting and chaos within the system, as individuals carved out little fiefdoms that clashed with other fiefdoms. This was especially notable in the Third Reich, where the proliferation of leadership positions created a system of overlapping and antagonistic jurisdictions (Bracher 1970, 346). Paradoxically, this confusion only increased the power of the national leader and contributed to the radicalization of policy initiatives.

In both cases, the cult of the leader required that an "aura" be constructed around Hitler and Mussolini. In his famous essay on the "Work of Art in the Age of Mechanical Reproduction," Walter Benjamin argued that one of the essential mechanisms of fascism was the aestheticization of politics, and this involved restoring the "aura" that had once existed around works of art (Benjamin 1968). The "sacralization" of the state involved constructing such an "aura" around the leader that elevated him above the masses—and above the state, even. This came out clearly in the ways the leaders were publicly presented. Portraits of Mussolini and Hitler were hung in every public office and in many private homes. Their images could be seen in public spaces along with the slogans they coined. Portraits abounded and personality cults were diffused. The key moments in both regimes revolved around public appearances, whether it be on balconies (Mussolini) or arenas (Hitler). Other key moments included trips to states and provinces. Mussolini made the regional visit a central plank of his rule, especially when important public works projects were inaugurated or major policy initiatives introduced. For example, Mussolini announced the Racial Laws in September 1938 during a visit to Trieste, a former Habsburg city with a large Jewish population.

The Headquarters

The architecture of the leaders' headquarters defined the fascist cult of the leader in an unmistakable way. For Mussolini, it was the Palazzo Venezia in the center of Rome; for Hitler, it was the new Reich Chancellery building, and the Berghof, his mountain estate in Bavaria. In both cases, the headquarters of the leaders reflected their status and set them above their people and their state. A study of their architecture and special arrangements reveals a great deal about the fascist state and the leadership principle.

As mentioned in Chapter 4, Mussolini moved his office from the traditional palace of the prime minister to the massive Palazzo Venezia in the square of the same name in 1929. The palace was built in the fifteenth century as the residence of Cardinal Pietro Barbo. When he became Pope Paul II in 1464, the palazzo became one of the official residences of the papacy. In the sixteenth century, the palace was gifted to the Republic of Venice and became the ambassador's residence. In 1797, it became the embassy of the Austrian Empire and was subsequently confiscated by the Italian state in 1916 as war booty. In the 1920s, before Mussolini moved in, the interior was restored. When Mussolini installed himself in the first floor Sala del Mappamondo, he was placing himself in a medieval building with a Renaissance interior.

One of the most famous descriptions of Mussolini's new office came from the German Jewish journalist Emil Ludwig, who interviewed him for a book (*Talks with Mussolini*) in March and April 1932, the year of the *Decennale*. Ludwig remarked on the treasures found in the palazzo and the massive size of the rooms, which he claimed outdid all the other palazzi in Rome. The most spacious of all was the sixty-foot-long Map Room. The massive room was mostly empty, with Mussolini's desk placed at the furthest end of the room from where guests entered. Ludwig described the first time he entered the room: "When the doors are flung open it is to disclose that which makes us feel we are contemplating a landscape rather than the interior of a room" (Ludwig 1933, 11). Ludwig remarked also on the floor mosaics and the paintings on the wall, with portraits of Doctors of the Church and painted columns. Next to Mussolini's desk was a massive marble fireplace. On the opposite side of the room were the large windows looking out onto Piazza Venezia, with the center window providing access to the famous balcony where Mussolini harangued the crowds.

What surprised Ludwig the most was the proximity Mussolini's office gave him to the people of the city. He noted that the Archaeological Library on the third floor was open to the public, thus giving them access to the same building, a potential opening for an assassin. He remarked that one such person had been caught after he had gained access to the building with a library card. The central location of the palazzo in Rome was also notable. The palace was located next to the ancient ruins of the Roman Forum and the Victor Emmanuel II monument. As Medina Lasansky has pointed out, this placed the center of the Fascist regime near former governments and allowed the Renaissance-style building to act as a "buffer" between the Ancient city (desired by the regime) and the more problematic post-unification liberal state (Lasansky 2004, 13).

Despite this central location and its proximity to Rome, Mussolini was an isolated figure. Ludwig remarked on the thick walls and fortress-like appearance of the Palazzo. The vast room made Mussolini seem small and distant, an impression augmented by the long walk a visitor had to make before reaching Mussolini's desk. In an early chapter of *Talks*, Ludwig relates watching Mussolini give a speech to the crowds in the Piazza Venezia. Before stepping out onto the balcony, Mussolini was alone. In the book's concluding chapter, Ludwig deals directly with the "loneliness" of the dictator who admits that he is a "prisoner" and the palazzo a "prison" (Ludwig 1933, 223). Mussolini's isolation as leader was reinforced by his tendency to keep everyone at arm's length. Whereas Hitler allowed other Nazi officials to attain great power, Mussolini did not and was always careful to put others in their place. When the question of succession came up, as it often did during the Grand Council meetings, Mussolini tended to put it off.

Unlike Mussolini, who isolated himself in the Palazzo Venezia, Hitler surrounded himself with courtiers daily. He was notoriously lazy when it came to work and would spend hours sitting around with other Nazis, usually engaging in long monologues on any given topic. Many of these took place in the cavernous Reich Chancellery building in Berlin, designed by Albert Speer. Opened in January 1939, the new building sat next to its smaller predecessor on the Wilhelmstrasse. Unhappy with the small size of the Hohenzollern Chancellery, Hitler needed something more grandiose. Speer obliged with

Figure 6.2 The "Long Hall" of Hitler's Reich Chancellery Building. Part of the long trek visitors had to make before reaching Hitler's office. Credit: Getty Images.

an oblong building that covered over two blocks and forced any visitor to walk over seven hundred feet up and down stairs and through a four hundred and eighty foot gallery before reaching Hitler's large office. According to Speer, Hitler was delighted by the effect this would have on people. "On the long walk from the entrance to the reception hall," exclaimed Hitler, "they'll get a taste of the power and grandeur of the German Reich!" (Speer 1970, 103). In truth, Hitler spent little time in the office, preferring his private dining area where he had lengthy lunches with other Nazis (Figure 6.2).

The Reich Chancellery was not Hitler's most important site of power, though. Rather, it was the Berghof, his mountain top chalet in Bavaria. Hitler purchased the chalet in the early 1930s. In 1935, Martin Bormann began the process of buying the land around the Berghof and creating a large compound of buildings that included residences for himself, Hermann Göring, and Joseph Goebbels. The site also included barracks for the SS and a large hotel intended for "pilgrims" who hoped to catch a glimpse of the *Führer*. The chalet was expanded and included a large picture window that gave a panoramic view of the surrounding mountains. This included the mythical Untersberg mountain where it was said Frederick Barbarossa, the twelfth century Holy Roman Emperor who built the First Reich, slept, along with nymphs, dwarves, and other magical creatures. It was in this chalet that Hitler held court for much of the year, and while it gave the impression of solitude among the mountains and forests, in truth Hitler was never alone, surrounded always by courtiers, SS guards, and, at a distance, thousands of Germans hoping to catch a glimpse of the man. Hitler often obliged by waving at them but never really encountered them closely (Geiss 1980).

Both Hitler and Mussolini benefited from the celebrity culture that had been growing in the West since the First World War, and their leadership styles required them to be in proximity to their people—at the same time, however, their status as the head of the fascist state required that they project an aura of Olympian detachment. Mussolini had his medieval fortress in central Rome, while Hitler had his cavernous Reich Chancellery and mountain top chalet. Although the two men had different styles of governing, they promoted the leadership principle as essentially fascist. The buildings and their interior spaces made this clear to any visitor, as they entailed long journeys before reaching the leader. In the case of the Obersalzberg, the mountain where Hitler's Berghof was located, a visitor had to take a steep and winding road before reaching the first of two perimeter fences staffed by SS guards. These long journeys were not accidental: they were purposely designed to give architectural and spatial expression to the idea of working up toward the leader, a central feature of the fascist state.

Conclusion

The fascist state proved to be something amorphous. For all Nazi and fascist calls to order, very little order could be seen in the constitutional arrangements of the respective regimes. In Italy, much of the apparatus of the liberal state remained and the corporatist experiment never got very far. Nazi Germany proved to be more active and expeditious in making sweeping constitutional reforms, but the result was less a clear structure and more a series of overlapping jurisdictions that made little rational sense. For this reason, it is difficult to subscribe to Hannah Arendt's totalitarian thesis when considering Hitler's and Mussolini's regimes, at least not in the sense of some monolithic state structure. Even in the case of Nazi Germany—which was more totalitarian than Fascist Italy— significant pockets of conservatism continued to exist within the state, at least until 1938.

Similarly, the position of the parties suggested something less than all powerful. Both the PNF and the NSDAP became bloated, mass institutions that one had to join to get ahead professionally. They became parties for opportunists and less for true believers. In both cases, the militants in the party had to take back seats to seasoned government administrators. However, it would be a mistake to argue that party militancy disappeared in a process that the famous Italian historian Renzo De Felice described as "movement to regime" (De Felice 1976, 51). Despite their mass membership, both parties retained their intransigent and dynamic elements, which contributed to the increased radicalization both regimes experienced into the late 1930s. The unclear boundaries between party and state were particularly important in the case of Nazi Germany, but also in Italy, where the Farinacci-led intransigents enjoyed a return to influence during the war. In the case of Germany, party leader Martin Bormann became arguably the most powerful individual in the regime due to his proximity to Hitler. Even though the parties may not have enjoyed institutional prominence, they would have an impact in the realm of culture and society, as we shall see in the next two chapters.

Ultimately, the key characteristic of the fascist state must be found in the leader principle, and this represented a continuum from the party to the state. Both Hitler and Mussolini fought for undisputed leader status within their parties before they came to power. Once in power, they affirmed their status within the state, as demonstrated by the respective cults that surrounded them and, by extension of the leader principle, throughout state and society. The fascist state was one where unquestioned obedience to a leader—whether it be at the national or local level—became the norm. The charisma of Mussolini and Hitler proved crucial in shaping the otherwise bewildering state structures, especially in Germany. This did not mean that Nazi Germany and Fascist Italy can be reduced to Hitlerism and Mussolinianism. However, personalism is a key element of fascism, and the centralizing figure of the leader has become a key identifying feature of fascism.

Does this mean that fascism is just another form of authoritarianism? No, since the personal rule of the leaders did not rely exclusively on pragmatism and conservatism. Rather, the dynamic element of the movements remained within the regimes, and this was often reflected in the violence of the movements, which continued throughout the regime years. Indeed, as Ruth Ben-Ghiat has noted, violence in both regimes became normalized (Ben-Ghiat 2020). The combination of the cult of the leader, violence, and the continuation of ideological fundamentalism—a combination which characterized fascism in the interwar years—came together at the expense of a rationally ordered political system. In fact, such a system would have hindered the radicalization of the regimes in the years leading up to the war. The organizational jungle looked different in each country, but in both cases, they served the power of the leaders. It can be argued that the essential elements of fascism are to be found, not in state structures, but in their impact on culture and society. This is where we now turn.

CHAPTER 7
FASCISM AND SOCIETY

The Nazi Olympics

The flame was lit. On July 20, 1936, a scantily clad youth took the Olympic torch from the Olympia site in Greece and began the 3,000-kilometer trek to Berlin. The final runner arrived on August 1 at a stadium filled with 110,000 spectators. There was only one spectator that mattered there, however—Adolf Hitler, who officially declared the twelfth Olympiad opened. The pageantry that surrounded the Berlin Olympics went above and beyond those of previous games. The German organizer of the games, Carl Diem, came up with the idea to have the Olympic flame run from Greece to Berlin, a ritual still followed today. The run involved more than 3,000 runners in one-kilometer stages. The flame crossed several frontiers, traversing Greece, Bulgaria, Yugoslavia, Hungary, Czechoslovakia, and finally Germany. It was promoted as an epic voyage, and it appealed to Hitler's Philo-Hellenism. The torches were constructed by the Krupp factory, and the final sixteen kilometers of the run were on the newly built Via Triumphalis, a grand boulevard that stretched from the Alexander Platz, through the Brandenburg Gate, to the stadium on the city's western outskirts. Like Mussolini, Hitler appreciated the straight, wide boulevards as a symbol of fascism (Figure 7.1).

All this, despite Hitler's lack of enthusiasm for the games, which were awarded to Berlin in 1931, when the Weimar Republic was still in existence. Troubled by the thought of "inferior races" competing in the games, Hitler was convinced that the games could be a positive public relations exercise. The attacks on the Jews which began almost as soon as Hitler came to power had made Germany the object of criticism. In fact, a large boycott movement grew in the United States, but the American Olympic Committee rejected their demands that the US athletes stay home. Hitler proved sensitive to international opinion in the early years of the Nazi regime. Indeed, the regime went to great lengths to make sure that antisemitic signs and actions were put away for the duration of the games. Joseph Goebbels's newspaper, *Der Angriff*, wrote, "we must be more charming than the Parisians, more easygoing than the Viennese, more vivacious than the Romans, more cosmopolitan than London, and more practical than New York" (Mandell 1971). This was certainly a shock—coming from such a source—but it indicated how strongly the regime wanted to promote a certain image.

The Olympics gave the Nazis an opportunity to promote the accomplishments of the regime. While the world was languishing amid the Great Depression, Germans were happy, and they were working. This carefully constructed scenario aimed at showing the *Volksgemeinschaft*, the Nazi vision of a harmonious, unified society, directed toward prosperity and peace. The trappings of peace, symbolized by the thousands of doves

Figure 7.1 Opening of the Summer Olympics in Berlin, 1936. Credit: Alamy.

released in the stadium, were products of Nazi propaganda. Yet, in the same month that the games were being held, the regime was drafting the Four-Year Plan, to be announced at the party rally in September. The pleasant picture of order was heavily propped up by a strong police presence. The regime also detained many Roma people and other "undesirables." In case there was any doubt as to who was responsible for this new Germany, swastika flags flew in abundance throughout the city next to the Olympic flags.

The Olympics also gave the regime an opportunity to display the Aryan body. The last runner into the stadium was a perfect example of the blond, blue-eyed youth the Nazis valorized. The Nazi Cult of Beauty, a central pillar of the *Volksgemeinschaft*, was first promoted in the documentary Leni Riefenstahl produced, directed, and wrote for the Nazi Olympics. *Olympia* was released as a two-part film in April 1938 on Hitler's birthday. Using the skills and techniques on display in *Triumph of the Will*, Riefenstahl opened the documentary with a close study of naked bodies engaged in athletic contests. Riefenstahl also used different camera angles and close-ups of the athletes in the games, often in slow motion, heightening the aesthetic qualities of the athletes, giving them a god-like appearance, an impression emphasized by low-positioned cameras. Young, athletic bodies were the template of the Fascist New Man, the product of a unified *volk*, which was tapping into classical sources yet remained modern and forward looking. In short, the Berlin Olympics provided a glimpse into the ideal society and culture of fascism.

What was not on display was the violence needed to create such a society. When Riefenstahl visited the United States in November 1938 to promote the film, she was met with boycotts and protests—especially after the news came out that thousands of German Jews had been arrested and synagogues burned during the Night of Broken Glass. Behind the beautiful bodies that graced Riefenstahl's film lay the shattered glass and blood of Nazi violence. This too was the *Volksgemeinschaft*.

Building the Fascist Utopia

This chapter will examine the policies and initiatives undertaken by the Italian fascists and the German Nazis to build a fascist utopia. Unlike the fascist government, a more consistent approach characterized fascist culture, and it can be argued that fascism's true nature is best seen through a cultural and societal lens. Here too, there were important differences between Mussolini and Hitler in constructing this perfect fascist world, which reflected the movement's origins and the national context. There were, however, key similarities, and among the most prominent was the ideal of the perfect fascist man—and a society unified behind its leader. Both leaders advocated for a youthful, physically powerful specimen who became part of the collective in a mass-organized society.

The cultural initiatives of the regimes have received a great deal of attention from scholars and, in the case of Fascist Italy, has raised controversy. A major reason for this involves the effectiveness of fascist culture and its role in garnering domestic consensus behind the regimes. Since the 1960s, scholars like Renzo De Felice and George Mosse have argued that fascist culture is worth studying, not as a set of empty phrases, but as an effective instrument in getting Germans and Italians to support their respective regimes. This school of interpretation, benefiting from the cultural turn in historical studies, has been resisted vigorously by other scholars, who have accused the culturalists of undermining anti-fascism, an important pillar of postwar democracy (Bosworth 1998). Despite this, social and cultural histories of Nazi Germany and Fascist Italy have increased, especially in the pages of the *Journal of Contemporary History*, founded by George Mosse and Walter Laqueur in 1966. The interest in Nazi and fascist culture has not abated and has produced a rich collection of articles and books that have given us insight into the nature of fascism. The centrality of culture in fascism can be seen in fascism's engagement in culture wars and the emotional connections it made with its disciples. Thus, it is not surprising that the fascistization of society and culture was a priority for both Mussolini and Hitler. Critics of these studies have pointed out that most of these initiatives failed—but this does not take away their value in gaining insight into the fascist mind.

Although cultural and social policies are crucial to understanding fascism, here too some contradictions and ambiguity are found. Historians debate whether fascist culture was conservative or revolutionary. They also note a heterogeneity within Italian fascism—which tolerated very different forms of art—in contrast to Nazi Germany. Finally, to what extent this created domestic consensus behind these regimes remains an open question, as it is difficult to determine consensus in a regime that did not allow democratic mechanisms like elections. Still, historians like Robert Gellately and Detlev Peukert have used sophisticated methods of historical scholarship to argue that Hitler enjoyed a great degree of popularity in the late 1930s. As in the case of the fascist state, social and cultural policies and consensus thus hinged on the figure of the leader. Both Hitler and Mussolini were central in fashioning the fascist utopia.

What follows is a study of social policies, policies that idealized a rural vision combined with advanced technology in what Jeffrey Herf called "reactionary modernism" (Herf 1986). The mix of traditional and revolutionary can be seen in all areas of fascist culture and society. Women, for example, were expected to fill traditional roles as mothers and homemakers, but both regimes mobilized women in unprecedented ways. Demographic policies called for an increase in population that reflected traditional values, but also expressed the Social Darwinism of fascism. In culture and the arts, there was a call for classical revivals in both regimes, but it was a modernized classicism, one that challenged the ideas of harmony and proportionality that informed classical art. Similarly, Nazi and fascist culture aimed at forging a Nietzschean elite while at the same time forging a mass, collective society of obedient fascists. Thus, fascist culture exhibited the same kinds of contradictions and overlaps with conservatism seen in other areas. There was, however, a clear vision cutting through these and that was the forging of a perfect fascist society, where citizens were not coerced but convinced of their country's destiny under Hitler and Mussolini.

Mussolini's Vision of Fascist Italy: The Ascension Day Speech

What the Berlin Olympics tried to demonstrate in visuals, Mussolini aspired to in words in his famous Ascension Day Speech of May 1927. On that day, Mussolini strode into the Chamber of Deputies, now filled only with fascists. Mussolini was given a standing ovation from the black-shirted deputies, and he began by warning them that, contrary to his usual style, he was going to give a longer address than normal. He also promised that it would be his last appearance in the chamber until the next year, when he would give the same speech with "inserts" denoting updates. This was greeted with laughter and acclamation—the deputies knew that Mussolini was insulting parliament and liberal democratic politicians who mastered the art of "putting men to sleep" with their long orations.

After this shot at liberal democracy, which he now declared to be as distant as the Middle Ages, Mussolini gave what was effectively a state of the nation address. He declared to his enraptured audience that he was placing Italy in front of the mirror. Using statistics, he was going to demonstrate how Italy was in a period of decadence and what the Fascist regime, now that it had abolished all opposition and brought the state under its control, was going to do about it. The speech was divided into three parts. The first part of the speech dealt with the social situation in Italy; part two discussed the administrative changes made by the regime at a local level; and part three introduced future political initiatives at home and abroad. It was the first part of the speech that was the most significant and reveals much about fascism—regarding social issues, at least. Mussolini declared that while Italy had managed to get control over some diseases and social problems that had plagued Italy since unification, there were others that were getting worse. These were tuberculosis, alcoholism, and suicide. Public health, declared Mussolini, was of primary concern to the state and should not simply be left to its own devices. While he was not promoting prohibition, he was calling for Italians to drink less, and to that end the regime set about shutting down 25,000 saloons. We could do that, proclaimed Mussolini, because the regime no longer needs the vote of publicans and their clients. This elicited much laughter, but it was yet another reminder of the totalitarian ambitions of the regime.

The need for greater state control was reemphasized with the question of crime. Mussolini boasted of how he increased the number of police officers in Italy, especially on the frontiers. As far as crime went, there were three major "battles" fascism had to fight. There was the battle against fraud, the battle against the criminality in the Pontine Marshes, and the battle against the Mafia in Sicily, which Mussolini called the Black Hand. In all three cases, Mussolini outlined how the state was dealing with this, and it involved police officers and prefects who were given carte blanche to do whatever was needed to fight crime. In the case of Sicily, Mussolini read from Prefect Cesare Mori's account, which related how the effort to squash the Mafia was costing many *Carabinieri* lives (Italy's national police force). Mussolini read the death toll as if it had come from the fields of the Great War. The deputies cheered wildly. Although Mussolini promised that the state would eradicate the Mafia—and the romantic notions that surrounded it—the Mafia survived the fall of fascism (Dickie 2005).

The Ascension Day speech is most famous, though, for what Mussolini had to say about the nation's demographics. Since 1886, Mussolini claimed, Italy had been suffering a steady decline in the birth rate. At just over forty million Italians in 1927, Mussolini called for that number to increase to sixty million by 1950. The reason, said Mussolini, was national strength. Comparing Italy to other European nations, Mussolini noted that Italy would not possess the manpower needed to fight another war—which would be necessary if Italy was to fulfill its historical mission. That mission was like that of the Roman Empire: to become masters over the Mediterranean. With the declining birth rate, however, Italy was fated to become someone else's colony. To fight this demographic winter, Mussolini proposed active state policies to encourage Italians to have babies. This naturally implied that women had to rediscover their vocation as mothers and homemakers and that married couples had to have several children. Government organizations, already set up, were there to help promote nativity and maternity. To fund this National Foundation for the Protection of Maternity and Infancy, Mussolini proposed a tax on bachelors—and even suggested a future tax on sterile couples.

As it turned out, these policies would fail in the long run. Mussolini's long speech, though, gives one of the best glimpses into the fascist mind regarding society and the state. Fecundity was something that conservatives and the Catholic Church had always promoted, but for Mussolini this "moral issue" was about national strength. He called for an army of five million men by 1940, driven by the sound of engines and the sky darkened by thousands of airplanes. This was Social Darwinism, of course, and it was one of the key elements that fueled fascism as it developed in the early twentieth century. Mussolini also looked ahead to an Italy filled with young men who would one day succeed him, although due to the immense work that still needed to be done, Mussolini told the Chamber that he would need to rule for another ten to fifteen years. His successor had not been born yet, he famously said. This, no doubt, was a shot at any current *gerarchi* who had designs on his leadership, like Farinacci. In ten years, promised Mussolini, Italy would be unrecognizable to Italians and to foreigners.

The Ascension Day speech is a landmark in fascist social thinking. It revealed the agrarian fantasies Mussolini harbored for Italy. He pointed out that the industrial cities of the north were the most sterile places in Italy, proof that industrial urbanism caused a nation's decadence. He was determined to stop Italians who flocked to the cities to chase their "stupid pleasures." The future of Italy was on the land and the sea, not the city. Of course, this policy was never achieved, as the idealistic ruralism was undermined both by the need to mechanize agriculture and by the emigration of thousands of Italians to work on the public building sites in the cities. It was precisely in the cities that the fascist imprint is mostly seen today. Ultimately, fascism was to prove itself as a moral force for the regeneration of society. According to Mussolini, "we carry the idea of order, obedience, and discipline against the suicidal idea of disorder, indiscipline, and irresponsibility."[1]

Mussolini's vision of a healthy, fecund, and powerful Italy was not much different than that of conservative nationalists and Catholics, but it did differ in its Social Darwinism

---

[1] "Full Text of Mussolini's Speech Outlining his Plans for a Greater Italy," *New York Times*, May 27, 1927, https://www.nytimes.com/1927/05/29/archives/full-text-of-mussolinis-speech-outlining-his-plans-for-a-greater.html.

and its call for an ever-youthful fascism. The goal was to foster the new fascist elite and reverse the decadence in which Italy found itself. It was a prelude to the New Roman Empire and the creation of the New Italian, free from the disease and moral afflictions that characterized liberal Italy. The draining of the Pontine Marshes was destined to become one of Fascist Italy's most famous achievements, but its importance was also symbolic of a society and culture that needed *bonifica integrale* (Ben-Ghiat 2001). With this speech, Mussolini laid down the fascist manifesto on society and culture. Public health became a metaphor for racial health. Disease was identified with undesirable elements in society. The cult of youth implied the sweeping away of the liberal democratic order. Eliminating criminality preceded the widening of the definition of "criminal." Fascism presented itself as the only option for reversing the moral and physical decadence of the nation. In both Italy and Germany, fascism was the cure for degeneration—and this began with a call for a return to the land.

Fascism's Rural Fantasies

The draining of the Pontine Marshes began not long after the speech. Part of a vaster project called the *Bonifica Integrale*, the swampy area around Rome was the most famous bit of marshland in Italy. It provided a link to the other two Romes: that of the Ancient Romans and that of the Papacy. Both had attempted to drain the swamp but with little success. Not accidentally, Mussolini identified this site as "evil" and plagued with crime. He saw the Pontine Marshes as a diseased, crime-ridden region inhabited by beasts and subhumans. During his rise to power, Mussolini often described Italy's parliament and Rome as a "swamp" that needed to be drained. He had already done this, now it was time to drain the real swamp.

Not long after the speech, the regime drafted a new law that paved the way for the land reclamation scheme. Passed by the all-Fascist Chamber of Deputies, the law was drafted by Arrigo Serpieri, former undersecretary of Ministry of Agriculture in the first Mussolini cabinet. Now a deputy, Serpieri drafted a bill that required massive government spending and some degree of coercion of private property owners. In short, it reflected the statist and repressive turn that the Mussolini regime was now engineering. The plan also called for thousands of Italians from the north—specifically from the Veneto and the region around Ferrara—to come and work on the project and, afterwards, settle in the area to farm the land. In his Ascension Day speech, Mussolini discussed the need to Italianize the Alto Adige region acquired after the war—and the only way to do this, according to Mussolini, was to colonize the ethnically German region with ethnic Italians. This deliberate movement of internal populations was later used to plan the emigration of Italians to the African colonies (Pergher 2017).

The draining of the Pontine Marshes stands as one of Italian Fascism's successes, even though the project was not completed due to the financial constraints imposed by the Great Depression. Draining the marshes was also symbolic of what fascism claimed to have done for Italy as a whole. Moreover, the project was part of a massive social

Figure 7.2 Mussolini rides a Fiat tractor at the foundation of Aprilia, one of the new towns on the Agro Pontino, 1936. Credit: Getty Images.

engineering vision to re-ruralize Italy according to the vision laid out by Mussolini in 1927. The translocation of people from one part of the country to the other required settlements, a process overseen by the official veterans' organization, the *Opera Nazionale Combattenti*. This organization divided the reclaimed lands into plots of about twenty hectares and proceeded to settle some sixty thousand people. The settlements were named after First World War sites and were positioned to serve as model towns that reflected the regime's vision of a ruralized society. In 1932 and 1933, Mussolini inaugurated the towns of Littoria and Sabaudia. They were followed in later years by Pontinia, Aprilia, and Pomezia (Figure 7.2). These towns reflected the classicized modernity that became characteristic of fascist era architecture (see Chapter 8). They were designed using rectilinear roads centered around a large piazza, which included a church and the *Casa del Fascio* (local PNF headquarters), which included a tower and a speaker's balcony.

Mussolini's agrarian fantasies had only limited impact as more people moved into the major cities than moved out of them, often to work on the massive public works projects that transformed many of Italy's cities. This obvious contradiction should not take away from the power of the agrarian vision in fascism. Furthermore, fascism's agrarianism was intimately bound up with modernization aimed at a "socially engineered existence" that included a dialectic between urbanity and rurality (Caprotti 2007, 63). The vision of the transformed Pontine Marshes made its way into fascist propaganda and became a setting for films. In 1933, the Istituto LUCE, the regime's official newsreel and filmmaking arm, produced a feature film called *Camicia Nera* ("Black Shirt"), which opens in the pre-reclaimed marshes. It opens with a woman lamenting life in a malaria-infested swamp who desires to emigrate overseas. The film recounts the history of the Fascist Revolution, intercutting the chaos of socialism with the peace and order brought on by fascist ruralism. Mussolini had a hand in the film's production, but it proved to be a box office failure. Nonetheless, the direction by Giovacchino Forzano, one of Italy's leading directors, is a slick example of fascist propaganda. Fittingly, the film's final scene shows footage of Mussolini inaugurating the town of Littoria.

Blood and Soil

German Nazism shared Italian fascism's fantasy of ruralization to an even greater degree. Blood and Soil ideology permeated Nazism. A product of Romanticism, the Blood and Soil movement saw a deep connection between race and the land. It became part of the *völkisch* stream within the early Nazi Party and butted up against the proletarian urbanism advocated by the Strasser brothers. Its most eloquent advocate was Richard Walther Darré, the Reich Minister of Food and Agriculture, who published several pamphlets and books idealizing the Aryan peasant and his attachment to the land. He was also appointed chief of the SS's Race and Resettlement Office (RuSHA) by Heinrich Himmler, a position he held from 1932 until 1938. As Reich Minister, he oversaw the application of laws guaranteeing the inheritance rights of small farmers and supervised the creation of food estates which brought together small food-producing businesses.

Blood and Soil ideology played a dominant role in Nazi Germany because it connected to other crucial Nazi initiatives. For example, RuSHA's main goal was to protect Germany's racial purity, and the back to the land movement was, to the Nazis, essential in accomplishing this goal. The cities were associated with "race chaos" and Jews—only the countryside was considered *Judenrein* (Jew-free zone). In the Nazi imagination, the Jews had been responsible for the decline of the peasantry and the countryside. According to Nazi propaganda, it was the Jews who had made the cities into places of decadence, crime, and sin and had thus encouraged Germans to leave the land for the factories. Darré's laws forbade Jews from owning and working land. Blood and Soil also became an integral part of Nazi Youth movements. Boys and girls were encouraged to volunteer in the countryside as much as possible, and incentives were given for them to do so.

The ideology also connected with important elements of Nazi foreign policy. A key figure here was Alfred Rosenberg, a Nazi ideologue who published one of Nazism's most infamous antisemitic texts, *The Myth of the Twentieth Century*. Rosenberg embodied the link between Blood and Soil, *völkisch* ideology, and racism. In 1933, he was appointed the leader of the party's foreign policy office, oversaw the education of the NSDAP membership, and then, in 1941, was appointed Reich Minister for the Occupied Eastern Territories. In this last position, he attempted to influence the administrative reorganization of previously Soviet-controlled territories. His influence was blunted by his rivalry with Ribbentrop's foreign office and with the SS. His esoteric religious theories also alienated him from Hitler, but he remained in his position to the end of the war.

Blood and Soil ideology infused Nazi foreign policy in several ways. First was the idea of *Lebensraum*, the Nazi drive to seek living space for Germans through military conquest. This living space, found in the east, was to serve as land for German farmers, not the building of cities. The Nazi Empire was designed to be a primarily agrarian empire where ethnic Germans would rediscover the virtues of living off the land. The new settlements were designed to mimic traditional German villages where blond, blue-eyed Aryans would live a healthy existence close to nature. Both involved the shifting of populations, organized by the Nazi government. The annihilation of the Jews was one consequence of these Blood and Soil initiatives.

As in the case of Fascist Italy, the back to the land movement in Nazi Germany was not successful. In fact, the number of people who made a living off the land continued to plummet throughout the 1930s (Peukert 1987, 88). Undoubtedly, this was exacerbated by the number of workers who made their way into the armaments factories in the cities or were involved in public works projects. The Nazi love of modern technology also limited the regime's rural fantasies. The German countryside was increasingly crisscrossed by the highway network named the *autobahn*. Hitler opened the first stretch of this network in May 1935 with the Frankfurt-to-Darmstadt section. By 1939, the network managed to cover most of the country. These roads were meant as parkways, designed to harmonize with the landscape. However, like all motorways, they involved a radical transformation of that landscape, as hills were leveled and embankments were created. These were engineering marvels, first and foremost, and the bridges and service stations became rare instances of architectural modernism in the Third Reich (Evans 2005, 325). Moreover, Hitler spent most of his time dreaming of the cities he was *going* to rebuild, like Berlin and Linz, and the new cities he planned in the conquered territories. Ultimately, despite the ruralism at the heart of fascist thinking, it was the urban populations who would occupy much of the interest of fascist social engineers.

Strength through Joy

Hitler loved fast cars. When he was released from Landsberg Prison in 1924, he was picked up by his new Mercedes-Benz, driven by a car dealer who became an ardent Nazi supporter. Throughout the years of the Third Reich, if he wasn't flying from one city to another, he could be found in the latest sporty model of the Mercedes. Hitler also made it a point to visit the annual motor show in Berlin. At the 1934 show, Hitler announced the Reich's intention to increase the number of cars on the roads of Germany from half a million to twelve million (Evans 2015). To that end, Hitler set about encouraging the construction of a car most Germans could afford. This turned out to be the "Strength through Joy" car, more commonly known as the Volkswagen (People's Car). Sponsored by the German Labor Front, the car was designed by Dr. Ferdinand Porsche, the chief designer of the successful Auto Union Grand Prix race cars. The prototype of the car was rolled out in 1938, and Hitler was the first to occupy the car that in future would be called the "Beetle."

Getting Germans mobile on the new *autobahn* was one part of the Nazi regime's desire to mobilize mass leisure. That the car was officially named after the mass leisure organization was no accident. *Kraft durch Freude*, Strength through Joy (KdF) was created in 1933 for workers and was run by the Labor Front. Subsidized by money seized from the now-banned trade unions, the KdF used the money to invest in ocean liners and Volkswagen cars. It sponsored package tours and built sports facilities. It ultimately proved one of the most successful Nazi ventures, providing millions of Germans with holidays. Its leader was Robert Ley, an early Nazi activist who became the head of the Labor Front in 1933. A favorite of Hitler's, Ley was the embodiment of the vulgar antisemite who proliferated through the ranks of the NSDAP. It was Ley who made mass leisure into an instrument of Nazi totalitarianism. KdF excursions were planned so that no one was ever left alone. It was Ley who famously said that "the only people who still have a private life in Germany are those who are asleep" (Peukert 1987, 237). KdF would not have been possible, however, without the example set by Mussolini.

The *Opera Nazionale Dopolavoro* (OND) was created in 1925, just as Mussolini was establishing his dictatorship. Like its Nazi counterpart, the OND was partly created to compensate workers for the loss of their political rights and right to organize in labor unions. Its main purpose, however, was to direct leisure activities under the guidance of the state. First set up as a standalone organization under the authority of the Duke of Aosta, the OND came under the control of the PNF in 1927, where it served as an instrument of fascist indoctrination. To this end, the organization was structured according to hierarchy and all activities were closely monitored, lest they lead to possibly subversive ends. The organizing of new mass-consumer activities, such as visits to the cinema or attending sporting events, allowed the regime to give consumers what they wanted without having to increase wages. All of this was designed to get Italian workers to forget their old socialist associations. The OND also aided the regime in fostering consent behind the regime even from those who did not necessarily sympathize with fascism (De Grazia 1981).

Importantly, when it came to social associations, Fascist Italy, unlike Nazi Germany, was willing to absorb existing institutions into fascist organizations. The OND swallowed some of these earlier associations. Associations like the Touring Club Italiano (TCI) and the Royal Automobile Club of Italy (RACI) continued under the regime, but they, like every other organization were fascistized, coming under the authority of the state, their directors appointed rather than elected by members. The Italian Olympic Committee (CONI) also continued to exist, but it became an organ of the PNF in 1925 under Lando

Ferretti (Martin, 2011). Sport and leisure went hand in hand in the fascist state, and here, both Mussolini and Hitler both exerted massive influence.

Fascist Sport

The Berlin games demonstrated the close attention paid to sport and athleticism in Nazi Germany. Fascist Italy also took the Olympics seriously. In the previous games, held in Los Angeles in 1932, athletes from Fascist Italy had excelled, coming second in the medal count to the host country. These results came after the disappointments of the 1928 games, which led to the Italian Olympic Committee being taken over by the PNF. In 1928, the release of the Charter of Sport by the Fascist Party announced the regime's intentions of fascistizing sport, both as a mass activity and in the professional arena. The Charter of Sport committed the regime to building sporting facilities throughout the country. These included stadiums and training grounds, which proliferated in large and small communities. Large stadiums, like the Stadio Littoriale in Bologna in 1927, were already opened. This stadium was built with the support of Leandro Arpinati, the Fascist *podestà* of Bologna and future head of CONI. The stadium seated sixty thousand spectators and boasted a tower with a statue of Mussolini on horseback (Martin 2004). This was one of the venues for the 1934 World Cup of soccer, won by Italy.

Success in sport on the international stage proved important for Italian fascism. Mussolini's regime strongly encouraged maximum results in the Olympics and in soccer. Italy's soccer team won World Cups in 1934 in Italy and 1938 in France, where the national team faced hostility when giving the fascist salute during the Italian anthem. In cycling, the regime encouraged success in the Tour de France more than it did in the *Giro d'Italia*, Italy's great national cycling epic. In 1938, Gino Bartali was ordered by the cycling association not to participate in the Giro in May so that he would be in maximum shape for the Tour in July. Bartali duly won the Tour but let it be known that he had not been happy about the decision to stay out of the Giro, as he had won the race in the previous two years. For the regime, the Tour de France carried greater prestige, and only one other Italian had won it previously. Italian achievements in these areas boasted an enormous audience, as attested by the proliferation of sporting magazines in newspapers.

Boxing and motorsport proved particularly influential within the regime. These blood sports enjoyed support precisely because they promoted militaristic values and showcased the ideal of the New Man as a powerful physical specimen not afraid to risk his life for a cause. In Germany, Max Schmeling became a national hero after he knocked out the American boxer Joe Louis in 1936. His stature was diminished when he lost the rematch in 1938. In Fascist Italy, Primo Carnera enjoyed a similar status after becoming World Heavyweight Champion in 1933.

Perhaps no sport better represented fascism, however, than motorsport. In Italy, motor racing benefited from the promotion of the fascist regime. The national autodrome at Monza, near Milan, hosted the Italian Grand Prix, where Italian nationalism was supported by the Italian automakers, Alfa Romeo, Fiat, and Maserati. Italian racing drivers dominated the 1920s, and they quickly became national heroes. After Antonio Ascari was killed at the French Grand Prix in 1925, he was given an elaborate state funeral after his body was returned with great ceremony from Paris. The martyred racecar driver was placed on a level with those who died in the war and in the cause of fascism. Race car drivers were often represented in the same way as aviators during the First World War. Several drivers had been fighter pilots. In 1923, the parents of the war hero Francesco Baracca gave a young Enzo Ferrari permission to use his symbol on Ferrari's cars. The symbol—prancing horse—is now world famous as the symbol for Ferrari automobiles. The regime's support for motor racing was seen in the construction of a second autodrome in Libya and in the promotion of several Grand Prix races on public roads.

Perhaps the most famous motorsport artifact to come out of Fascist Italy was the *Mille Miglia*, a one-thousand-mile race that covered half of the peninsula. Starting and ending in the northern city of Brescia, an industrial town important in Italy's automobile industry, the race went through Italy's major cities, including Rome. Advanced sports cars raced on open roads in an event that took several lives, including those of spectators. The race was exploited by fascist propaganda to demonstrate the technological advancement of the auto industry and the military discipline of a nation that was able to open its public roads to a high-speed automobile race. Popularizing motorsport helped the Mussolini regime promote the automobile industry–especially when it came to producing specialized sports cars. This demonstrated the main strands of fascist ideology. Motor racing represented a synthesis between the decadent ideas of Gabriele D'Annunzio, who celebrated speed and death, and the ideas of Futurism, with its celebration of the race car as a new form of beauty, and speed as a new morality-religion (Baxa 2022).

Motorsport took on an even greater significance in Nazi Germany. The regime devoted a minister to the sport, and he oversaw the disbursement of government funds to Germany's two Grand Prix teams: Mercedes-Benz and Auto Union (Figure 7.3). From 1934 to 1939, the two Germans dominated the race circuits of Europe, thanks to new materials used for their bodywork and the use of highly advanced engines. When they won races in Germany, the victors gave Nazi salutes, including non-German drivers who won in German cars, like Dick Seaman from Great Britain. Some of the German drivers, like Bernd Rosemeyer, came to embody the Aryan myth. Blond and blue-eyed, the immensely talented Rosemeyer conquered motorsport for two years until he was killed attempting a land speed record on the Frankfurt-Darmstadt Autobahn in January 1938. Rosemeyer's life was immortalized in a memoir written by his wife, Elly Beinhorn, who was a famous aviator. In his study of language under the Third Reich, Victor Klemperer analyzed Beinhorn's book, noting how the "masked figure of the racing driver, his crash helmet, his goggles, his thick gloves" represented the "second uniform of Nazi heroism" (Klemperer, 2006, 4).

Figure 7.3 Hitler examines a Mercedes-Benz Grand Prix car. This was one of the "Silver Arrows" cars that dominated Grand Prix racing under the Nazi banner in the 1930s. Credit: Getty Images.

Women

Fascist hypermasculinity did not permit women to see themselves as anything other than homemakers and mothers. The masculine ethos of the war veterans put paid to any early notions in Italian fascism that women should be given the right to vote (De Grand 1989). The regime's pro-natal policies put women at the forefront of the Battle for Births, with medals given to women with many children. The fascist policy towards women proved contradictory, however, as motherhood became a civic duty, giving women new roles and opportunities (Stone 2013). Although women were pushed out of the workforce by the regime, Mussolini's regime required them to be mobilized to the cause, thus getting women involved in the state in a way that had not existed previously. Thus, women experienced Italian fascism in different ways as the regime attempted to "nationalize" them (De Grazia 1992).

Women played a role in both movements. Claudia Koonz's classic study published in 1986 argued that, in Germany, women even played a part in Nazi terror (Koonz 1987). As in Fascist Italy, the Nazi Party provided organizations for women, like the *NS-Frauenschaft* (NSF), but women were, ultimately, expected to play traditional roles. Women were involved in some of the more experimental areas of the Third Reich, such as the SS's *Lebensborn* program. This program encouraged SS men to sire children whether in or out of wedlock. Single mothers of Aryan descent were sheltered in *Lebensborn* homes. One of the more troubling images of women was their involvement in the

Holocaust. Several thousand served as guards in the concentration camps, while others worked in the euthanasia programs.

Youth and Education

A cult of youth was central to the fascist mystique. Fascism's obsession with avoiding decay and degeneracy made a focus on youth imperative. They would be the regeneration and rebirth of the nation. The cult of youth was not original to fascism. It went back to the Romanticism of the eighteenth and nineteenth centuries, but fascism viewed youth as the new elite that would propel the Fascist Revolution. Mussolini's desire to cultivate a new generation of young fascists began before he even came to power, with the establishment of the *Gioventù Universitaria Fascista* (GUF) in 1920. Once Mussolini was in power, organizing youth became a central initiative in the regime with the *Opera Nazionale Balilla* (ONB) in 1926, later reorganized into the *Gioventù Italiana del Littorio* (GIL) in 1937. Both fell under the jurisdiction of the PNF. By 1940, the GIL encompassed nearly five million youth from ages six to eighteen.

Indoctrination was the order of the day. Mussolini would often appear to the groups holding a rifle in one hand and a book in the other. On Saturdays, the groups would gather in the main squares of the towns, where they indulged in war games, parades, and other activities heavy in rituals and singing. The goal was to create the future fascist ruling class and future soldiers. Like other mass mobilization efforts, the results were limited, and even the regime recognized that the efforts to create a future ruling class failed (Koon 1985, 250). In fact, it may have even led to anti-fascist attitudes, especially in the university groups. The regime's emphasis on youth also caused conflict with the Church. Even before the ink was dry on the Lateran Accords, the regime and the Vatican were at odds over Catholic youth organizations. The conflict unleashed a wave of violence from fascist Blackshirts against churches before the dispute was finally settled. Such was the intensity of the clash that the Vatican issued the encyclical *Non Abbiamo Bisogno* (We Have No Need) in 1931, which denounced the "idolatry" of the State practiced under fascism.

In Germany, the Nazis drew upon the tradition of *fin-de-siècle* youth movements. These nationalist groups were inspired by an anti-industrial, Romantic love for the German forests. Founded in 1926 as a part of the SA, the Hitler Youth was led by Baldur von Schirach from 1928 to 1940. By 1940, the movement included 3.5 million youth. The Hitler Youth (HY) was compulsory for all boys between ages fifteen and eighteen, where they were put through military drills and were expected to compete in athletic contests. They also took excursions throughout the Reich, where they were given lessons in the history and geography of the country.

In the latter stages of the war, the HY were pressed into combat, where they manned air defense systems in the German cities. Others joined SS Panzer units. It was the HY who acted as the last line of defense in Berlin in the final days of the war. One of the last photographs of Hitler shows him reviewing these children amid the rubble of the Reich

Chancellery building. As in the case of Fascist Italy, youth organizations provided an opportunity to promote an unadulterated ideology, free of compromise with traditional groups. The Hitler Youth were given a steady diet of anti-Christian ideas. Hitler was substituted for Christ, as is shown in the lyrics of a song sung by the HY at the 1934 Party Rally. "We are the jolly Hitler Youth," went the song, "We don't need any Christian truth for our leader Adolf Hitler, our Leader always is our interceder" (Evans 2005, 250–1).

The cultivation of youth as the future of fascism depended a great deal on education. The very first piece of legislation from Mussolini's government was a reform of the educational system, designed by Giovanni Gentile, who served as Mussolini's first Minister of National Education. The Gentile Reform of 1923 was called the "most fascist of reforms" by Mussolini himself, as it dealt with the education and training of youth. The reform itself was more traditional than fascist, as it emphasized a liberal arts training regimen designed to form a young elite. There was nothing specifically fascist about it in terms of content, as it was more of a challenge against positivist practices of teaching than anything political. It did, however, result in the centralization of the educational system, with leadership principle informing the entire system, from the minister in Rome right down to the principal of local schools (Koon 1985, 250). Fascism's increasing imposition on the educational system was gradual. In 1929 the regime decreed a single textbook (*libro unico*) for all students across the country. This textbook was government approved and injected fascist values into all lessons, regardless of subject matter. The book presented Mussolini as savior of the nation and showcased the regime's public works. It was written so as to transform children into future warriors. Traditional gender roles were, of course, drilled into the students, as was the future greatness of Italy they would lead.

That same year all teachers were required to provide an oath of loyalty to the regime. In 1931, university professors were required to do the same. The professoriate proved a difficult problem for Mussolini. In 1925, a group of intellectuals produced the Manifesto of Fascist Intellectuals, led by Giovanni Gentile. Not long after, though, another group produced the Manifesto of Anti-Fascist Intellectuals, led by Gentile's mentor, Benedetto Croce, Italy's most important living philosopher, who taught at the University of Naples. Croce had once supported the regime but eventually came to oppose it as Mussolini began to construct his dictatorship and dismantle the liberal institutions that Croce supported. Many anti-fascist intellectuals left Italy after this, but not all professors who stayed supported the oath of loyalty. Twelve out of more than a thousand refused. These ended up losing their jobs, causing an international outcry. Some of these faculty members endured harassment and even beatings from fascist youth as a result (Koon 1985, 66–7).

Mobilizing universities became a key element for Nazism long before Hitler came to power. The National Socialist German Student League had been founded as early as 1926 and it immediately found a receptive audience. In fact, the universities proved fertile soil for Nazi activism. Professors and students had engaged in Nazi electoral mobilization, and the universities were the site of the notorious book burnings of May 1933. These burnings saw professors give speeches. There was little or no resistance to the Law for the Restoration of the Civil Service of 1933 that dismissed Jewish professors. The regime also attempted to limit the number of students who attended university with the Law against Overcrowding in Schools and Universities. Restrictions were placed on women attending. Helping the Nazi cause were prominent intellectuals, like the philosopher Martin Heidegger. In 1933, Heidegger became rector of Freiburg University. His inaugural address in May celebrated the new regime and called upon students and faculty to rally to the Nazi cultural revolution, referring to "blood and soil" *völkisch* ideology. Later that summer, Heidegger oversaw the application of the leadership principle in his university; this meant that the Rector would, henceforth, be appointed by the Reich Minister of Education. Other prominent philosophers and legal experts like Carl Schmitt would also rally to the Nazi cause.

Ultimately, the Nazification of education proved limited, as there was little substance to Nazi claims of an intellectual revolution. Nazi education remained largely focused on training future warriors, and physical education more than any other discipline was emphasized. In the lower grades, education remained largely traditional, despite being infused with Nazi ideology. The regime created special schools designed specifically to train the future Nazi elite called the Adolf Hitler schools, but these did not have the chance to create anything of lasting value. Moreover, by the 1940s, the universities became the site of a bourgeoning anti-Nazi movement. Resistance groups, like the White Rose and *Edelweiss*, were evidence of growing dissent in the universities, although it is impossible to know how widespread such resistance was.

Race

Racial purity preoccupied many fascists. Scholars have noted how Italian Fascism did not have race as an ideological plank until later in the 1930s—even then, so the argument goes, Mussolini was merely imitating Hitler, as the two regimes moved closer together. Some argue that Mussolini had no animosity toward Jews, pointing out that the early fascist movement had Jewish supporters and the fact that Mussolini's Jewish mistress Margherita Sarfatti had a major influence in the regime's art policies. Mussolini's interview with Emil Ludwig in 1932 is often cited. In it, Mussolini condemned the racism preached by the Nazi movement. Renzo De Felice has been a major proponent of the view that Italian fascism was not racist, at least not in the biological sense. If anything, Mussolini's racism was of a "spiritual" nature (De Felice 1976, 95-6). All of this ties into a general view of Italians as *brava gente* ("good people") who needed to be distinguished from German Nazis. Apologists for this thesis often cite the low number of Italian Jews who perished in the Holocaust and the general lack of antisemitic sentiment in Italy.

Historians have increasingly challenged this orthodoxy, noting the persistence of an antisemitic strain within the PNF, led by men like Roberto Farinacci. Figures like the former priest Giovanni Preziosi and the journalist Telesio Interlandi were vocal antisemites who were allowed to communicate their ideas throughout the *Ventennio*.

Preziosi's antisemitism derived from Catholic traditionalism, Interlandi's, from biological racism, while the philosopher Julius Evola—who became a significant figure in Italian neofascism after the war—promoted antisemitism of a "spiritual" variety. Racism became especially prominent within Fascist Italy after the conquest of Ethiopia when the colonial authorities enforced racial laws against intermarriage and segregation. In 1938, Interlandi became the publisher of the journal *Difesa della Razza* ("Defense of the Race") where he wrote about "scientific racism" to justify measures taken against native Africans and Jews.

In the summer of 1938, the fascist regime decreed the Racial Laws, which stripped Italian Jews of all civil rights and removed them from the professions. Jewish children could no longer attend schools with gentiles, and Jews who obtained their Italian citizenship after 1918 had them stripped. Furthermore, foreign Jews were invited to leave the country. Exemptions were granted for Jews who had distinguished themselves in the Great War, been early members of the PNF, or had served the regime in some way. This led some of the more rabid antisemites to denounce the laws as weak. Despite these loopholes, the laws had a very real impact on Italian Jews. The laws were bolstered by the Manifesto of Race, released in July 1938. The Manifesto claimed that Italians were Aryans and therefore superior to Africans and Jews. Mixed in with this was the regime's growing friendship with the Nazi regime, which began in 1936 with the Axis pact and continued in 1938 when Hitler made a famous visit to Italy in May.

Ambivalence towards race was never an issue in Nazi Germany. Racism was a major plank in Nazi ideology and informed the Third Reich's social and cultural policies from the beginning. It was left to Heinrich Himmler's SS to craft Nazi Germany's Aryan future by breeding an elite of men and women with proven Aryan bloodlines. The "health" of the Aryan race was seen in the SS's selection process and the Lebensborn program. The *Aktion T4* euthanasia program, meanwhile, was entrusted to the Reich Chancellery Office in 1939. The program, designed to murder the mentally and physically disabled, was discontinued in 1941 after international protests. Domestic outcry, led by prelates of the Catholic Church, played a role as well. The program recommenced in 1942. Meanwhile, propaganda films and instructional materials proliferated throughout the Reich, educating Germans on the defining features of an Aryan.

The most persistent part of the Nazi racial program was the persecution of the Jews. Antisemitism was a consistent element in the Third Reich, and the so-called Jewish Problem permeated all levels of the regime. The persecution of German Jews began immediately upon the rise of Hitler to Chancellor. Jews were subjected to daily harassment and often beatings administered by Stormtroopers and SS men. Victor Klemperer's diaries are replete with such incidents (Klemperer 1999). Some of these incidents were stopped by Nazi leaders, due to the Nazi fear of international outcry. On a national level, the campaign against the Jews began early. On April 1, 1933, the regime called for a day of boycott against Jewish businesses. That same month came the Law for the Restoration of the Professional Civil Service, excluding Jews and all political opponents from the civil service. The economic and professional attacks on German

Jews was followed by legal restrictions, as the Nuremberg Race Laws were issued at the 1935 Party Rally. These laws declared that anyone with three or four Jewish grandparents was considered Jewish, regardless of whether they practiced Judaism or even converted to another religion. Jews were stripped of citizenship and intermarriage was forbidden. The Nuremberg laws became the basis for subsequent legal restrictions on Jews and were even applied to the Roma people.

Hitler's regime had made it clear that Germany was to be *Judenrein* in the future. Alon Confino has argued that central to the Nazi imagination was a "world without Jews" (Confino 2014). The question was not if but when and how this was to be achieved. In the early years of the Third Reich, the aim was to encourage Jews to leave Germany. Jews made up only 1 percent of Germany's population in 1933. There was an early wave of emigration, but this tapered off in the mid-1930s, due partly to immigration restrictions imposed in the United States but also due to the stabilization in Germany. Many Jews chose not to leave, believing that the Nuremberg Laws would be the furthest extent of persecution while others did not want to give up their property to the Reich.

This changed in November 1938 with the events of *Kristallnacht*. The pogrom unleashed by the Nazi regime, led by Goebbels, raised persecution to a new level. The incitement to violence was the Nazi response to the assassination of a German diplomat in Paris by a Polish Jew, angered by the government's treatment of Polish Jews living in Germany. The Night of Broken Glass on November 9–10 was led by Stormtroopers and Nazi Youth, who smashed Jewish property and burned down synagogues. Thousands of German Jews were arrested and incarcerated in the growing concentration camp system. To add insult to injury, Germany's Jewish community was then ordered to pay for the damages. The Nazi leadership's response to the violence indicated the still confused policy of the regime toward Jews. Hermann Göring called an emergency meeting a few days later and made it known to Goebbels that such violence could cause international rebuke that would lead to financial hardship for German insurance companies. Restraint was called for in future. Still, the aftermath of the event led to further legal measures against the Jews, and a new wave of refugees, many from the recently annexed Austria. The fate of the Jews was still an open question, though, and as the Second World War loomed, different agencies within the Reich were tasked with proposing alternatives. It was the war that provided the scenario needed to "solve" the Jewish Problem as we will see in a later chapter.

Conclusion

The image of a happy and prosperous Germany during the 1936 Olympic Games led some foreigners to believe that Germans were united behind their *Führer*. Visitors to Italy, especially Italian immigrants returning to their homeland, thought the same about Mussolini and fascism. Of course, others realized that, despite the elaborate masquerade of the Olympics, both regimes were constructed on repression and murder, along with the dismantling of liberal democracy. Leni Riefenstahl was on her way to New York

City to promote *Olympia* when the news came out about the anti-Jewish pogrom in Germany. A planned visit to Hollywood was canceled after a protest was planned against her. The debate centered on the question of just what made these regimes tick: was it coercion or consensus? Had Italians and Germans become true believers in fascism—or were the respective regimes held in place by terror and repression?

In the decades following the Second World War, the general view among scholars was that Nazism and Italian fascism depended primarily on repression. However, beginning in the 1980s, this has changed, as some historians began to suggest that both regimes enjoyed a degree of consensus. In Italy, Renzo De Felice led this revisionism, arguing that, at least between 1929 and 1936, Mussolini's regime enjoyed a degree of popularity that went beyond any coercion. De Felice argued that the consensus behind the regime was not so much a recognition of what fascism had given Italy but rather of what it managed to avoid—namely, economic crisis and social instability (De Felice 1976, 64–5). De Felice's thesis sparked a major historiographical reaction led by British historians Denis Mack Smith and Richard Bosworth among others. Other historians have accepted De Felice's thesis and explored how this consensus might have been achieved and, more importantly, how it was squandered after 1936.

The Nazi experience has produced a similar debate among historians. In his book, *Inside Nazi Germany*, Peukert argued that the economic prosperity caused by the rearmament program appealed to a middle-class longing for "normality" after the turbulence of the Weimar years (Peukert 1987, 246–7). For Peukert, Nazism offered new answers to the challenges of the postwar era many Germans found convincing. The electoral successes carried over into the years of the regime, even though Nazism's increasingly radical policies entailed more brutal responses to modern problems and resulted in an atomized society. Robert Gellately argues that Nazism's plebiscitary dictatorship aimed at building consensus and that such a consensus was achieved by succeeding where Weimar failed (Gellately 2001). Terror was limited and directed at specific groups, and the knowledge that political dissidents and other undesirables were put in camps was met with general approval.

There has been a reaction to what historians have called the "voluntarist turn" in Nazi historiography. This claim that most Germans voluntarily supported the Nazi regime has been criticized for downplaying the real impact of Nazi terror on German society. Consent requires a degree of freedom to be valid, and Germans had essentially lost that freedom of consent. Moreover, there is evidence to suggest that most Germans were not in favor of the persecution of German Jews and had to resign themselves to the increasing radicalization of Nazi policy, a radicalization which further eroded any consensus that might have existed (Evans 2007). Of course, it is difficult to prove something like consensus in a dictatorship. However, the fact that Mussolini and Hitler may have enjoyed a degree of popularity over and beyond their respective ideologies holds some validity in an era when the cult of the leader was crucial to fascist operations. Moreover, consensus and coercion need not be viewed as mutually exclusive. As Gellately suggests, Germans would not have necessarily been repelled by the violence perpetrated by the regime. The same applies to Italy, where the call for a restoration of law and order had a certain emotional appeal even to those who were not true believers. For convinced fascists, this restoration and rebirth required the purificatory power of violence. In any case, the true test of whether Italy and Germany were fascistized to any real extent is to be found in the regime's cultural policies and the formation of the New Fascist Man. For that, we turn to the next chapter.

CHAPTER 8
FASCISM AND CULTURE

Two Exhibitions in Munich

In July 1937, Hitler made one of his frequent visits to Munich, the Capital of the Movement and the Capital of German Art. On this occasion, Hitler arrived to open the House of German Art, and the exhibition held within it was called the Great Exhibition of German Art. Not on the public agenda was a private visit that Hitler would make to the Degenerate Art Exhibition, slated to open the day after the Great Exhibition of German Art. The concurrent running of these exhibitions—just a few blocks away from each other—spoke volumes about the Third Reich's cultural policies. In one exhibit, a promotion of what Hitler considered true, German art; in the other, a show designed to define the "other" of German art—namely, modernist art. The thousands of Germans who visited Munich on that July weekend had a chance to see both and, in doing so, to understand the crucial role played by Nazism in purifying art as a means of working toward the Aryan utopia fixed in the Nazi imagination.

Holding the two exhibitions at the same time was an innovative Nazi technique. This weekend demonstrated art's importance in the Nazi worldview. One of the events held on July 19 after the inauguration of the Great Exhibition of German Art was a massive parade dedicated to 2000 Years of German Art. In this parade, over 3000 costumed participants forming a line some four kilometers long marched through Munich, celebrating German contributions to world culture. Following the different historical floats came marching groups of SA and SS men in the formation in a Nuremberg Party Rally style (Hagen 2008). If anyone had any doubts about the connection between art and Nazi violence, the parade—which took over two hours to complete—laid these doubts to rest. Munich was the stage on which Hitler made clear his vision for the role of art in the Third Reich. Art, too, was part of the Nazi regime's revolutionary agenda to transform Germany and create the Fascist New Man. What this New Man looked like could be seen in the Great Exhibition of German Art, where massive sculptures by Josef Thorak and Arno Breker displayed muscular and chiseled men brandishing swords and shields. The ideal German women could be viewed in the numerous nudes painted by Adolf Ziegler, the man in charge of the entire pageant. These figures embodied what George Mosse called Nazism's cult of beauty which lacked sensuality (Mosse 1999). The Degenerate Art Exhibition, on the other hand, demonstrated what the Aryan ideal was not, with distorted and abstracted human figures as seen in the work of the German Expressionists. There was no room for this art in the new Germany.

The connection between the cult of beauty and the violence needed to uphold it was made clear in the long speech Hitler gave at the inauguration of the Great Exhibition.

Hitler gave a speech on art and culture at every Nuremberg Party Rally, but those familiar with these earlier speeches noted he surpassed himself on this occasion. Observers noted that "his manner of speaking became more agitated, to a degree that had never been heard even in a political tirade. He foamed with rage as though out of his mind, his mouth slavering, so that even his entourage stared at him in horror" (Spotts 2003, 162). Although he was inaugurating the exhibition of German Art and the new House of German Art, the speech seemed to have the Degenerate Art Exhibition as its focus. In the speech, Hitler gave a clear exposition of what he viewed as authentic German art and its opposite. In doing so, he provided a manifesto on the Third Reich's view of art and its place in the Nazi Aryan utopia.

Underpinning Hitler's thesis was the role of art in shaping the moral and racial perfection of society. German art was one of "eternal value," and the new building was a "temple for a true and everlasting art" (Hitler 1992). For Hitler, true art expressed the essence of a race's being, standing as an "eternal monument." The true artist is one who creates for the people, not for other artists. Hitler was obsessed with the idea of art as something timeless, rejecting any historicizing approaches that viewed art as primarily a product of its time. Art could never be fashion, according to Hitler. Since the character and blood of a people never changes, so too art's values are not subject to change. False art is driven by the times and arbitrated by art critics.

Hitler saved his rage for modern art. This was a product of Judaism, and its ascendancy was due to the Jewish control of the press and art criticism. This was an art produced by those with no talent. It was an art supported by "claptrap and jabbery," which undermines the "wholesome feeling" produced by authentic art. In imagery typical of the Nazis, Hitler equated this art to a "diseased body" afflicted by "inner decomposition." Modernism's ascendancy was a product of the "slime and ordure … belched forth" by the Revolution of 1918. In this way, Hitler linked the rise of the Nazis with the culture wars ushered in by the Weimar Republic. The identification of modernism with disease referred to the *fin-de-siècle*'s preoccupation with degeneracy and decline. The Third Reich's exaltation of German Art was the antidote to this decline.

Hitler's speech was not simply a rant against modern art—a rant that, in many ways, reflected mainstream, bourgeois attitudes. Rather, it was a declaration of war on modernism. Hitler pledged to "clean house" and suggested that penal measures might be inflicted on modern artists. At one point, he used the word "liquidation," promising to rid Germany of all the pernicious influences caused by modern art. The "end of the destruction of German culture," claimed Hitler, began with the inauguration of the House of German Art. Hitler concluded that "from now on we will wage an unrelenting war of purification against the last elements of putrefaction in our culture." Hitler's aggression against modern art took on even more strident tones as the years went on. In July 1942, he called for modern artists to be either sent to an asylum or to a concentration camp (Grosshans 1983). Hitler's language of purification and liquidation resembled closely the language used to justify genocide. He was not introducing something new here; this purification was already present in the book burnings of 1933 and in the purging of museum directors and managers since then.

The Nazi Revolution required the elimination of all that was considered unclean in the world of art, and before this happened, Hitler was determined to display this so-called degenerate art. This was the purpose behind the *Entartete Kunst* exhibition, which opened on July 19 in the Municipal Archaeological Institute in Munich, not far from the new House of German Art. Narrow and confined, compared to the spacious Greek-style building of the House, the Institute provided a deliberately claustrophobic space aimed at discomforting the viewer. There were over six hundred paintings and sculptures crammed into small rooms. They were haphazardly hung and in broadly thematic rooms. Themes included "Distortion of Form," "Mocking of Religious Feeling," "Art that Simulates Political Anarchy," and "Ridiculing of Military Virtue and Courage." These insulting themes were illustrated by equally insulting comments made on individual works. "Nature as Seen by Sick Minds" read one. "Crazy at any Price" read another, making references to the high monetary value the art world placed on modernist art (Barron 1991).

The exhibition was organized by Adolf Ziegler under the aegis of Goebbels's Propaganda Ministry. Most, but not all, of the over one hundred artists represented were German Expressionists, many of whom were part of the avant-garde scene in Munich in the years leading up to the First World War. Artists included Kirchner, Nolde, Dix, Grosz, Beckmann, Kandinsky, Klee, and others who were central to the Expressionist movement. Ironically, Expressionism and Nazism were not necessarily mutually exclusive for some. Emil Nolde had joined the Nazi Party as early as 1920, and Josef Goebbels was known to be sympathetic to some of the artists. In fact, he had lobbied Hitler to accept the art form as uniquely German to no avail. The discussion over Expressionism's suitability had set off a typical Nazi internal rivalry between Goebbels and Hans Rosenberg, who shared Hitler's hatred of modern art (Spotts 2003). By 1937, Goebbels had learned to keep his sympathies to himself and became the leading advocate for the exhibition within the regime. Photographs show him accompanying Hitler during the latter's private tour of the exhibition the night before it opened.

The Degenerate Art Exhibition was a stunning example of Nazism's assault on modernist art and represented a novel way of expressing this hostility. Rather than simply hiding the artwork or destroying it, the regime felt it was best to expose it to a German audience in a way that would provoke ridicule from patrons. Admission to the exhibit was free, and Hitler encouraged Germans to visit the show. When patrons entered the institute, they were first greeted by a massive head sculpted by the German Expressionist Otto Freundlich titled the *New Man*. Drawing upon primitivist influences, the size and distorted features of the work made it the representative image of the exhibition. It even adorned the cover of the guidebook. The prominence given to this work was not accidental, as it served as a counterpoint to the Nazi examples of the New Man in the German Art Exhibition.

The Degenerate Art Exhibition began on the first floor. Visitors had to ascend a narrow staircase to reach it. As they went up the staircase, they had to be careful not to hit their heads on Ludwig Gies's *Crucified Christ*, a large wooden crucifix which had previously hung in the Lübeck Cathedral. Once in the rooms, visitors took in the haphazardly hung paintings and the numerous writings on the wall. They included the insulting epitaphs mentioned earlier, but also had quotes from Hitler and Rosenberg. Cleverly, the Nazis also cherry-picked quotes from the artists themselves to show their degeneracy.

By the time the exhibition wrapped up, it had attracted some three million visitors, compared to the paltry four hundred thousand who went to the exhibition at the House of German Art. It was a smashing success, and it raises the question as to why. What was the appeal? Some have argued that Germans simply preferred to see this art compared to the official art and that this may have been a subtle act of resistance to Nazism. The more likely explanation, however, was the show's lurid appeal. It was designed as a kind of Chamber of Horrors where respectable Germans could be shocked and horrified in a safe space. The fact that it was free helped, of course, but so did the appeal of horror so common in Nazi discourse. W. Scott Poole has argued that "both Hitler and Mussolini successfully made a politics of horror out of both their own terror and the terror of their generation" (Poole 2018, 170). In his famous study of Weimar cinema, Siegfried Kracauer argued that the monsters who frequently appeared in Expressionist films like *The Cabinet of Dr. Caligari*, *The Testament of Dr. Mabuse*, and *Nosferatu* tapped into the German fear of outsiders, thus strengthening their longing for authoritarianism. These "monsters," Poole argues, eventually made their way into Nazi antisemitic films.

This chapter will explore the relationship between fascism and culture. It will argue that uniquely fascist forms of culture existed and that, while they drew upon existing cultural traditions, they also added new techniques and new forms (like the Degenerate Art Exhibition). Both Mussolini's and Hitler's regimes harnessed culture to revolutionary ends, designed to purify and transform Italy and Germany into ideal fascist utopias. Although the regimes certainly differed in their approaches, the chapter will conclude by identifying important points of convergence between Italian fascism and German Nazism. Since fascism was in many ways the product of culture wars that had raged in Europe since the late nineteenth century, culture was central to the fascist revolutionary project (Figure 8.1).

Is There a Fascist Culture?

Hitler's Degenerate Art Exhibition and the neoclassicism and neoromanticism of official Nazi culture suggests that there was little difference between Nazism and mainstream bourgeois tastes. With its rectangular design and monumental columns on all four sides of the building, the House for German Culture was nothing more than an updated Classical Greek temple. The puzzlement and derision thrown at German Expressionism was not unique to Nazis. What was different was the method and the role that art played in the Nazi Revolution. In other words, the packaging was new, but the contents were not. If this is the case, then why has so much attention been devoted to culture under fascism in scholarship since the 1960s? As mentioned in Chapter 7, the so-called cultural turn in fascist studies, which began with the first issue of the *Journal of Contemporary*

Figure 8.1 Hitler and Goebbels visit the Degenerate Art Exhibition in Munich, 1937. Credit: Getty Images.

History in 1966, continues to inform critical studies of fascism. In the 1970s, Susan Sontag's famous essay "Fascinating Fascism" argued that fascism continues to captivate the Western imagination, even in the most unlikely places, such as gay culture. In 1996, the *Journal*, in honor of the thirtieth anniversary of its first issue, took Sontag's title as the theme for a collection of articles on the subject.

The continued fascination for fascism suggests that Mussolini's and Hitler's regimes must have made some original contribution to culture that was uniquely fascist and not just warmed-over bourgeois sentiments. This chapter will explore those contributions aimed at creating a mass culture centered on the New Fascist Man which both regimes claimed to create. Norberto Bobbio has forcefully argued that fascism had no culture—that it was, in fact, anti-culture (Bosworth 1998, 155). Fascist scholars today—such as those who trace back their intellectual lineage to Denis Mack Smith—continue to be critical of any study of fascist culture, arguing that whatever fascist cultural ideals existed ultimately failed to make any impact on society and that ultimately fascism was a continuation of anti-liberal and antidemocratic elite culture that long predated fascism.

The culturalist turn in fascist studies raises the question of its nature: was fascist culture modern or traditionalist? With respect to Nazism, the latter may seem the obvious answer. However, this is not necessarily the case, as historians like Peter Fritzsche, Fernando Esposito, Jeffrey Herf, Mark Antliff, and Roger Griffin have noted modernist elements in Nazi culture. Although Hitler personally despised Futurism, there certainly was an element of Futurism in the cult of technology that thrived in Nazi Germany. As we have seen, Hitler indulged in airplanes and automobiles. The sleek, modernist lines of Panzers, Stukas, and uniforms has resulted in a veritable cult of German military machinery. While Hitler insisted that public buildings be monumentally neoclassical, factories and other functional buildings were firmly modernist. Two examples of this modernist-functional architecture include the grandstand and tower built for the AVUS autodrome in Berlin and the resort built for the Strength through Joy program on the island of Rügen in the Baltic.

The traditionalist versus modernist debate is especially prevalent when it comes to Italian fascism. Unlike Hitler's Germany, where traditionalism dominated with a few exceptions, Mussolini's regime did not have any favorites. In fact, the regime tolerated an aesthetic pluralism that cultivated both classical and modern art (Stone 1998, 5). Mussolini never set an official art for the regime. Artists of varying persuasions had the freedom to create as long as they did not make explicitly anti-fascist art. Mussolini's lack of interest in the arts partially explains this situation, in sharp contrast to Hitler's art fixation. Development in the arts largely continued along the nonpolitical lines the fascist regime had inherited from the prefascist era. However, Italian Fascism's *laissez-faire* approach to the arts created a situation where artists from various backgrounds competed for the attention and patronage of the regime, something Mussolini deliberately promoted. For example, in 1926, he spoke at the inauguration of an exhibit on *Novecento* art in Milan, a form of classicized modernism promoted by his mistress, Margherita Sarfatti. At other times he gave audiences to modernist architects, but he also relied on Marcello Piacentini, who more than anyone pioneered the *Stile Littorio*, the monumentalized classicism that came to characterize fascist architecture by the late 1930s.

The dissimilar approaches to culture between Nazi Germany and Fascist Italy should not deflect from what they had in common. Nor should it suggest that culture was secondary to fascism in general. Far from it. In fact, culture was central to fascism. This chapter will also show that both Italian fascism and Nazism shared four common approaches to the arts that went beyond strictly aesthetic styles. The first was the search for an authentic, national style of art, which reflected fascism's militant nationalism. The second was the condition that the state was the artist's sole patron. Artists in both countries had to accept what Marla Stone has called a "Faustian bargain" with the regime to continue as working artists (Stone 1998, 6). Third, art had to be considered a part of the Fascist Revolution in both countries. As Hitler pointed out in his inauguration speech for the Great Exhibition, there was to be no more art for art's sake in Nazi Germany. The artist had to be part of the new order of things. Finally, both Nazism and Italian fascism came to express their ideologies in the monumental, whether in architecture or sculpture. Tellingly, when the fascist regime in Italy became increasingly radicalized in the later 1930s, a sort of official style in the arts did emerge, resembling that of Nazi Germany. In architecture, at least, an identifiable fascist style did emerge, albeit one that drew heavily on the classical tradition. Along with the style of architecture, fascism emphasized monumental spaces and remade entire cities while at the same time celebrating rural values and vernacular styles. These seemingly contradictory tendencies did not prevent fascism from producing a distinctive cultural style aimed at cultural revolution.

Stracittà/Strapaese

Although Mussolini never decreed any official style, culture and the arts held an important place in Italian fascism due to its culture war origins. Having said this, a very real debate over culture characterized Italian fascism from its beginning, and it followed the same fault lines as the debate over the political character of the PNF. The tension between intransigents and revisionists that marked the party in the mid-1920s had its cultural corollary in the *Strapaese* and *Stracittà* factions. The former celebrated traditional rural values, finding authentic fascism in the peasant villages, while the latter looked to urban cosmopolitanism as the fascist ideal. Together, they reflected the political debate, with intransigents like Roberto Farinacci supporting rural *squadrismo*, while revisionists like Giuseppe Bottai were open to cultural influences from the rest of Europe, and sought a fascist identity in the large, industrial cities. Both sides agreed that fascism was to bring about a cultural revolution; they simply disagreed as to the nature of that revolution. The debate between these views continued until the end of the regime. In 1939, Farinacci instituted the Premio Cremona, a prize given to the artist who produced a work of art that best exemplified traditional values. That same year, his rival Bottai started the Premio Bergamo, which opened the door to modernist artists like Renato Guttuso, who won the first prize. Significantly, it was Bottai, then serving as the Minister of National Education, who inaugurated the Farinacci exhibition, a clear sign that, though they represented two distinct visions of art, both agreed on the common project of finding an authentic fascist art (Stone 1998, 180–6).

As with the political conflict, the cultural conflict was never definitively settled, not least because Mussolini found this to be in his interest. In fact, the tension and debate between the cultural factions became a means for having open discussions over the nature of fascism in a regime that no longer allowed political discussion. The arts became the arena where alternative visions of fascism could be presented. Subtle anti-fascist narratives could even emerge from artistic debates, such as those produced by modernist painters like Fortunato Depero and Scipione (White 2020, 162). One of the best examples of this came with the competition to design the Fascist Party headquarters in Rome. Announced in 1934, the competition to build the Palazzo Littorio solicited over one hundred proposals from Italy's leading and lesser-known architects. The submissions included a wide range of styles, from modernism to neoclassicism. Such was the diversity that the competition caused a fierce debate in the Chamber of Deputies between the defenders of modernism, like Alberto Calza Bini, and traditionalists like Roberto Farinacci. The fierce tone of the debate made it seem as if Fascist Italy had gone back to the parliamentary debates of the prefascist era. Other flashpoints of disagreement came with the construction of the new train station in Florence, designed by a team of architects called the Gruppo Toscano. The clearly modernist lines of the station caused outrage among traditionalists who felt that the station did not reflect Italian values. Significantly, Mussolini granted an audience to the Gruppo Toscano in Rome, a move that cut short the opposition and demonstrated that Mussolini preferred not to take sides in artistic debates.

That fascism took culture seriously can be seen in the regime's patronage of the arts and the institutionalization of culture. In 1925, Giovanni Gentile founded the Institute of Fascist Culture, which aimed at integrating the masses into an authentic Italian culture. In 1935, the Ministry of Popular Culture was created from what was once the Press Office. Its first minister was Mussolini's son-in-law, Galeazzo Ciano, before he became foreign minister. The ministry's task was to promote the regime's initiatives and guide the arts through state patronage. One of its most well-known activities was to oversee Italy's film industry. In 1937, Mussolini inaugurated *Cinecittà* ("Film City"), a massive state-run movie studio on the outskirts of Rome. Across the street from the studio, a film school was created to produce Italy's future filmmakers. Mussolini hoped to combat the popularity of American films by producing films that exemplified Italian and fascist values. Overseen by Luigi Freddi, the fascist film industry's most famous production was *Scipio Africanus*, a sword-and-sandals epic that portrayed the Roman conqueror of the Carthaginians as a proto-fascist. During the war, the studios produced a series of films celebrating the Italian Empire and the war effort (Ben-Ghiat 2015). The regime also sponsored traveling theater troupes and even promoted radically experimental productions such as *18BL*, an example of "theater for the masses" that centered on the Fiat truck made famous by the *squadristi*. The stage for the play was a massive outdoor set in Florence (J. Schnapp 1996).

Institutionally, the most important initiative taken by the regime was in its exhibition culture. The regime sponsored numerous exhibitions, both locally and nationally, throughout the *Ventennio*. Some of these were held regularly, such as the *Biennale* in Venice, the *Triennale* in Milan, and the *Quadriennale* in Rome. The *Biennale* included a film prize as well as an international art exhibition. The Roman event focused on Italian artists from various schools, while the Milanese exhibition was devoted to the industrial and decorative arts. These exhibitions were joined by those which were more specific to fascist ideology, the most famous being the Exhibition of the Fascist Revolution, which opened in 1932. The exhibitions proved crucial in the promotion of the arts under fascism. According to Marla Stone, they "played a central role in the regime's anesthetized politics" (Stone 1998, 17). These exhibitions became pilgrimage sites, they exposed artists to the masses, and they provided a forum for cultural producers and influencers. The exhibitions allowed artists of all styles to exhibit their work, sometimes in the same space.

Film and Music in Nazi Germany

Nazi German culture presented a more coherent vision than that of Fascist Italy. Tensions did exist, however, as seen above, between those who rejected modernist art completely and those who, like Goebbels, saw some value in it. Whereas the visual arts remained a point of contention, a seamless synthesis between the modern and the traditional presented itself in film and music. While the content of film and music remained staunchly traditional, the Nazi regime did not hesitate to use the most modern methods at their disposal to promote traditional culture. The use of film to promote Nazi values has already been seen in the work of Leni Riefenstahl. As in Mussolini's Italy, the film industry had the regime's backing. However, Hitler and Goebbels were more successful in producing German films that promoted ideological goals. Not surprisingly, Nazi film favored historical dramas, showcasing themes that exalted German history, authority, and destiny (Leiser 1974). However, these themes were not always overt, and the high quality of the film productions—along with the sentimental and melodramatic tone of the films—are still popular today (Rentschler 1996). Thanks to film buffs like Goebbels, the Nazis understood that successful films put entertainment first and indoctrination second (O'Brien 2004). In Fascist Italy, many of the feature films became depoliticized middle-class melodramas and screwball comedies called "white telephones" due to the seemingly ubiquitous telephones on the Art Deco–inspired film sets (Hay 1987; Landy 1986).

Whereas fascism's highly visual style could find a place in film, music was a different matter. Despite Hitler's passion for music, this was a question that was never settled. The Nazis appropriated classical music for their own ends. Not surprisingly, Hitler's favorite composer, Richard Wagner, was given pride of place in Nazi Germany. His close friendship with the Wagner family preceded his rise to power. The result was the continued success of the Bayreuth Festival, founded by the composer himself. Hitler was a regular attendee and patron of the event. Wagnerian overtures saturated Nazi events like the Nuremberg Rallies and other celebrations. However, not all Nazis were comfortable with the Wagner Cult. For example, Alfred Rosenberg, Goebbels's hated rival as culture czar and a fanatical *völkisch* devotee, found the Wagnerian festival decadent (Ross 2022). Next to Wagner, the Nazis favored composers like the Austrian Anton Bruckner and Ludwig van Beethoven. The latter enjoyed a special place in the Nazi regime, especially his Ninth Symphony. Many Beethoven enthusiasts to this day claim that the greatest performance of the Ninth came in 1942, conducted by Wilhelm Furtwängler in the presence of Goebbels and other Nazi officials.

The heavy appropriation of the German classical tradition made things difficult for contemporary German composers who, if they wanted to remain in the regime's favor and patronage, had to find a distinctly "German" style. Michael Kater has argued that finding such a sound proved difficult and was rendered even more complicated by the inconsistent directives laid down by Hitler, Goebbels, Rosenberg, and other cultural mandarins (Kater 1997). The regime also allowed a great variety of music to be played, despite Hitler's narrow tastes. One of the most successful pieces produced under the regime was Carl Orff's *Carmina Burana*. The piece premiered to general praise in 1937 despite its clearly modernist influences. This was not without controversy, however, as Orff had to deal with constant harassment and suspicion, especially from Rosenberg's Culture Office (Kater 1997).

Nazi Germany was literally immersed in music. It was played at all Nazi events. It was on the radio. Orchestras even performed in factories during the Second World War. Popular songs like the *Horst Wessel* song and military marches also enjoyed significant airplay. Composers and conductors petitioned for the state's patronage. These included famous conductors Herbert von Karajan and Furtwängler. Richard Strauss, whose fame predated Nazism, was also a key supporter of the regime, though the love affair was not always reciprocated. In 1936, he composed music for the Olympic Games and was on hand to conduct the orchestra at the opening ceremonies. Still, all this failed to create a distinctive Nazi sound. Instead, the long-dead Wagner became the "official composer" of the regime, an appropriation which has spawned numerous controversies since the end of the war. Ironically, Italian opera enjoyed greater popularity among German audiences at the end of the 1930s and had lesser enthusiasm for Wagner (Evans 2005).

Italy's musical heritage naturally played an important role in Fascist Italy, but it too faced the problem of finding a fascist sound. Popular songs with fascist lyrics were played incessantly, especially in Fascist Youth events. These ranged from a celebration of fascist values to blatantly racist songs like *Faccetta Nera* ("Little Black Face"), inspired by the regime's conquests in Africa. Italy's operatic tradition was celebrated, especially with the patriotic operas of Verdi and Rossini. As in Nazi Germany, contemporary composers and conductors jockeyed for the regime's patronage regardless of their ideological adhesion. This competition began to fade, however, as the regime exerted strong centralizing pressures upon musical institutions (Sachs 1987). One famous example of this can be found in the internationally renowned conductor, Arturo Toscanini. An early fascist enthusiast, Mussolini placed Toscanini on the electoral slate for the 1919 elections. Toscanini also performed for D'Annunzio during the poet's occupation of Fiume. Toscanini's support of fascism faded quickly, however, in the face of Blackshirt violence. He eventually became an outspoken critic of the regime and Mussolini in particular. In the 1920s, Toscanini was lead conductor of La Scala Opera House in Milan, a position that gave him international recognition. This made it difficult for the regime to sanction him, especially after his categorical refusals to play the fascist anthem, *Giovinezza!* He was eventually forced out of the position and left Italy altogether in the 1930s.

As in Germany, it became difficult for contemporary composers to thrive and search for a distinctly fascist sound. Ottorino Respighi came closest with his neoromantic symphonic poems dedicated to Rome. The final section of his "Pines of Rome" ominously conveys, through heavy use of brass, the march of Roman Legions on the Appian Way. However, Fascist Italy's more tolerant cultural climate allowed for a group of self-proclaimed modernist composers. In a manner that resembled the aspirations of modernist architects (discussed later in this chapter), modernist or avant-garde composers saw an opportunity to craft the fascist sound. This was the case with Alfredo Casella and Gianfrancesco Malipiero, who in 1923 created the Corporation of New Music under the patronage of Gabriele D'Annunzio. Both composers attempted to craft a fascist musical aesthetic, especially through operas and other vocal works. Casella's opera, *Il Deserto Tentato*, was an homage to fascist aviators and their role in pacifying the "barbarians" of Africa, while Malipiero's opera *Giulio Cesare* exalted the regime's obsession with the Roman Empire. Another modern composer associated with this group, Luigi Dallapiccola, composed an opera set to Antoine de Saint-Exupéry's *Vol de Nuit*, whose main character can be read as a fictional Mussolini (Earle 2004).

While the themes and subjects of these operas were dedicated to fascism, it is difficult to find a specifically fascist sound in these works. Musicians like Casella and Malipiero aimed to find an authentically Italian music that harmonized with Italian fascism's project of national regeneration. Part of this project was to explore a neglected part of Italy's musical heritage, namely the seventeenth-century composers Antonio Vivaldi and Claudio Monteverdi. Artists took their cue from fascist politics, appropriating the romantic past in the service of a revolutionary project, these composers hoped to fuse a style from Italy's past with a modern aesthetic, in a process that resembled the Novecento style in literature (Ben-Ghiat 2001, 27). Whether a distinctly fascist sound resulted is a matter of debate, but in both Italy and Germany the search for a distinctive national music that could be appropriated for the fascist revolution resembled fascism's influence on other areas of culture—most significantly of all, in architecture.

Architecture: Fascism's Signature Art

Fascism's most visible legacy in the arts is found in its architecture and sculpture. In both Germany and Italy architects achieved a certain degree of fame, especially those considered closest to the dictators. Albert Speer in Germany and Marcello Piacentini in Italy came to embody the fascist style of architecture—specifically, a monumentalized classicism. Both leaders took a keen interest in architecture. Mussolini's many trips around Italy usually consisted in the inauguration of buildings and towns. He surrounded himself with architects at these sites and was famously photographed wielding a pickaxe in propaganda images with the title "His Majesty the Pickaxe." These scenes were intended to promote fascism's public works programs, programs that often involved some degree of demolition to make way for new buildings and spaces. Adolf Hitler reveled in architecture. They not only constituted the main subjects of his watercolors but seemed to preoccupy much of his waking hours. Massive scale models of the future Linz (his hometown in Austria) and Berlin were found in his bunker (in his last days). Hitler was the self-styled "master builder" of Germany, and all Speer's architecture was ultimately attributable to his inspiration (Spotts 2003, 311–12).

Architecture was, then, prominent in the fascist imagination. It can be argued that it was the most important activity next to war. In Fascist Italy, architects became prominent public figures, and their writings often appeared in major newspapers and journals. Their debates became public too. In a country where public debate over politics and policy had become stifled, architects enjoyed a great deal of freedom in discussing and arguing their positions. Each tendency had their own journals. In the 1920s, a group of modernists, called rationalists in Italy, challenged the dominant Novecento group. Calling themselves *Gruppo 7*, these young architects promoted the international modernist style against the neoclassicists in the Novecento group. The debate was at times intense and even personal. One of the leading promoters of the Novecento group, Ugo Ojetti, was called "Mr. Arches and Columns" by his opponents. Satirical cartoons in the respective side's journals mocked their rivals mercilessly.

Regardless of their personal rivalries, both sides thrived in Fascist Italy where Mussolini refused to baptize either one as an official style. Novecento-style buildings designed by Giovanni Muzio and Gio Ponti can be seen throughout Italy, though most of their work was confined to Lombardy. The rationalists, on the other hand, were also rewarded with important commissions. Perhaps the most famous was Giuseppe Terragni's Casa del Fascio in Como. The Casa was one of many examples of local PNF headquarters built in Italy. Terragni's was striking because of its obvious Bauhaus influence. The building was rectangular, with prominent windows giving the structure an element of transparency, inspired by a quote from Mussolini, exhorting the PNF to be a "home of glass into which all can look" (Etlin 1991, 439). Rationalist architecture can be found in the design of the new towns like Sabaudia in the Agro Pontino.

These two factions competed fiercely for favor of the regime. To do so, both claimed that they were drawing upon authentically Italian sources. Neoclassicists like Ojetti argued that fascism's policy of *Romanità* clearly called for classical motifs like arches and columns and the abundant use of marble. Rationalists, like Giuseppe Pagano, on the other hand, argued that the modernist style was, in fact, an updated version of Italian vernacular architecture found in the rural villages (Sabatino 2010). Reconciling the two sides was the work of Marcello Piacentini. A member of the Royal Academy and head of the Fascist Union of Architects, Piacentini became Fascist Italy's most influential architect by the end of the 1930s. He promoted the monumental Imperial style that eventually became the regime's unofficial style. Calling it the *Stile Littorio*, Piacentini attempted to synthesize the neoclassicism of the *Novecentisti*, with the modernist lines of the rationalists.

Apart from pioneering the new fascist style, Piacentini's most important contribution was his leadership on major projects designed to create fascist spaces. He was a leading spokesperson for the urban renewal schemes and master plans for various cities. The most famous was the master plan for Rome in 1931, which led to the demolition of much of the city center to make way for the boulevards and open spaces around the ancient ruins. He was also put in charge of designing the new campus for the University of Rome called the Città Universitaria. He also led the E42 project, the site of the Universal Exposition of 1942, and the subsequent "Third Rome" decreed by Mussolini. In all these projects, Piacentini worked with both neoclassicists and modernists, but in every case a clearly distinctive *Stile Littorio* emerged. The best-preserved examples of this today are the EUR district of Rome (the former E42), the massive Piazza Vittoria in Brescia, and the University of Rome. These fascist spaces came to resemble metaphysical sites depicted in Giorgio De Chirico's paintings and Mario Sironi's murals; these two artists prefigured the monumentalism of fascist architecture and were patronized by the Fascist state.

Italian fascist culture, like that of Nazism, filled its spaces with monumental sculptures demonstrating the idealized New Man. One of the most obvious examples, still standing today, is the Foro Mussolini in Rome (now called the Foro Italico). The site on the Tiber River in the northern part of the city was reserved for the offices and sports facilities of the ONB (Fascist Youth). The massive site at the foot of Monte Mario was secured by the President of the ONB, Corrado Ricci, in 1926. The project was headed by Enrico Del Debbio, who put together a team of architects of the modernist school to design functional buildings (Kallis, 2014). A close associate of Piacentini, Del Debbio was an architect who tried to synthesize the classical with the modern. In 1934, he was succeeded by Luigi Moretti, who was closer to the rationalists.

Despite the change in master architects, the Foro Mussolini demonstrated a unity of style that harmonized the classical and the modern. More than the buildings, however, the site became famous for its statuary and totems, like the massive sixty-foot obelisk dedicated to Mussolini at the entrance to the facility. The obelisk, with *Mussolini Dux* carved into it, still stands. Behind the obelisk is a broad plaza called the Piazzale dell'Impero surrounded by large tablets marking important moments in the history of Italian fascism. The pavement is made up of mosaics imitating an ancient Roman style depicting the events of the March on Rome. The most spectacular landmark in the Foro Mussolini is the Stadium of Marbles. Designed as a classical stadium, with marble benches, the complex was ringed with sixty large statues representing the Italian provinces. The statues, designed by twenty-four different sculptors, embodied Roman virtues and were clearly based on classical styles. The stadium sat next to the larger Olympic Stadium built for the 1944 Olympic Games (which were never held). Taken as a whole, the Foro Mussolini represented the ideal of the New Fascist Man as young, male, virile, and athletic. The synthesis of classical and modern on a monumental scale came to shape the *Stile Littorio*, later reproduced in the E42. Moreover, the site was designed to immerse the individual in the grandeur of the Fascist Revolution and its transformation of Italy (Figure 8.2).

Conclusion

The crucial role of architecture in the fascist imagination is best seen in the plans Hitler and Mussolini had for their respective capitals. In both cases, the plan was to build a new Rome and new Berlin on a giant, megalomaniacal scale. Mussolini's Rome, the E42, was to be filled with Piacentini's *Stile Littorio*, while Hitler's Berlin, which he called *Germania*, was dominated by massive, neoclassical structures. The centerpiece of the E42 was to be a gigantic triumphal arch designed by the rationalist architect Adalberto Libera. The new Berlin's centerpiece was a domed hall that rose to a height of over six hundred feet. His inspiration was the Pantheon in Rome, a building he gazed at longingly during his visit to Rome in 1938. In both cases, a wide, straight boulevard would serve as the main axis, allowing for military parades and other processions.

In neither case was the capital to be on a merely human scale. This contradicted fascism's celebration of rural values and suspicion of cities, but these cities were not meant to be functional, nor were they to be metropolises. They were stages built for the glorification of the movement and its leader. While they gave a nod to tradition, they also represented radical departures and thus represented the revolutionary appropriation of tradition typical of fascism. Hitler's Berlin, while paying homage to classical architecture, would supersede that architecture in scale. The Great Hall was designed to overwhelm the dome of St. Peter's in Rome. Mussolini had to be more circumspect in challenging

Figure 8.2 The Palazzo della Civiltà Italiana in Rome as it looks today in Rome's EUR Quarter. The building is an example of the *Stile Littorio*, a monumental mix of classicism and modernism that characterized Italian Fascist architecture. Credit: Alamy.

the Vatican, but one of the buildings in the E42 was a basilica, dedicated to St. Peter and St. Paul, whose dome was second only to that of St. Peter's in Rome. In neither case was the new capital to be a modern, functioning city. It is telling that the "Third Rome" was to be inaugurated as the site of the World's Fair. Typically, these sites were made up of temporary structures, but the E42 would have all permanent buildings. In his memoirs, Albert Speer writes how Hitler's new Berlin paid no attention to the city's needs, saying that the city's grand boulevard was nothing more than a "display piece and an end in itself" (Speer 1970, 77).

The rebuilding of the capitals encapsulates fascism's approach to culture by both claiming and going beyond tradition. These cities were designed to satisfy conservative cultural tastes with their classical inspirations. Even though Marcello Piacentini's team of architects included rationalists like Adalberto Libera and Giuseppe Pagano, the E42 came down firmly on the classical side of the *Stile LIttorio*. The buildings that came closest to modernist styles, like the Palazzo della Civiltà (known popularly as the "square Coliseum"), were dominated by arched windows and clad in marble. A similar classical dressing was given to Libera's Palazzo dei Congressi, ringed by a columned portico beneath the modern design. Libera hoped to modernize these columns by not giving them capitals, but the overall effect was that of a classical structure (Etlin 1991).

At the same time, the look and function of the sites went beyond any traditional notions of city building. They resembled works of art, and the art was political, putting in marble and concrete the sense of unstoppable destiny demonstrated by the Blackshirts and the Brownshirts during fascism's rise to power. The effect of the buildings and wide open spaces was one of intimidation, aimed at browbeating the individual and destroying any hope of privacy and anonymity. Reminders of who had built these and why were ubiquitous. A large, sculpted relief demonstrating Mussolini as the culmination of Roman history can still be seen in one of the administrative buildings of the EUR (Painter Jr. 2005, 158). The New Berlin, meanwhile, was going to include a massive palace for Hitler.

These fascist spaces, only partially built, are eloquent testimonies to the fascist project of palingenesis and purification. These cities would attest to a New Order of purity and destiny. They were designed to last and become a testimony for future generations of the greatness once Italian fascism and German Nazism passed away, according to their builders. They were representative of cultural revival, a "draining of the swamps" of the old, liberal, democratic order. Culturally, they embodied the return to a healthy culture which would reinvigorate their respective nations.

Fascism and art were inseparable. Mussolini's and Hitler's regimes can be understood as essentially aesthetic enterprises. Modris Eksteins has described fascism as primarily a "cultural eruption" where "existence becomes a matter of aesthetics, a matter of turning life into a thing of beauty, not of right, or of good, but of beauty" (Eksteins, 1989). The new cities best expressed what Eksteins has called the "monumental egocentrism that excluded compromise, debate, and conciliation" (Eksteins, 1989, 314). Both Hitler and Mussolini viewed themselves as artists. Fascism's "fascination" with art has come down to an aesthetic enterprise of uniforms, parades, and buildings, of vast open spaces where the Fascist New Man was celebrated in oversized sculptures, of communication networks shaped by speed and modernity. Fascist culture ultimately aimed at reconciling the traditional with the modern, as seen in artistic movements like the Novecento. Fascist culture was an alternative modernity that would purify culture, exalting the ancient while making room for the modern. This was best expressed with the Italian word *bonifica* (reclamation), a reclamation of culture that would retrieve the best of the past and project it into a fascist utopian future (Ben-Ghiat 2001). Meanwhile, the culture wars that opened a space for Mussolini and Hitler were still raging elsewhere, providing an opportunity for fascisms to spring up outside of Germany and Italy.

CHAPTER 9
FASCISM AND ITS IMITATORS

A Meeting in Montreux

The town of Montreux sits at the western edge of Lake Geneva, part of the so-called Swiss Riviera. Since the publication of Jean-Jacques Rousseau's *La Nouvelle Heloïse* in 1761, this sleepy enclave nestled between the lake and the foothills of the Swiss Alps has become a site of pilgrimage for European romantics. The medieval castle on the shores of the lake was the setting for Lord Byron's "The Prisoner of Chillon," based on the true story of a Genevan monk chained in the tower during the Wars of Religion. In 1906, to cater to tourists who found Montreux a place of escape, one of Europe's great grand hotels, the Palace, opened not far from the castle. It was there, in this massive, two hundred and thirty room Art Nouveau resort that a group of men, representing thirteen countries descended on December 17, 1934, to take part in a singular conference held in one of the hotel's fifteen meeting rooms.

The occasion was a meeting of the *Comitati d'Azione per l'Universalità di Roma* (CAUR), an organization founded in Mussolini's Rome to foster a "universal fascism," aimed at bringing together fascist parties and movements from European countries and beyond. Created in 1932, on the occasion of the fascist regime's *Decennale*, the CAUR hoped to create links between fascist movements via the myth of Rome, a better option than the idea of a Fascist International first floated in the 1920s (Kallis 2016). The organization's statutes called for a "spiritual alliance that will give the world, still tormented and full of discord, its political restoration and civic and social salvation" (Kallis 2016). To this congress came fascist leaders from all parts of Europe. These included representatives from Austria, Belgium, Denmark, France, Greece, Ireland, the Netherlands, Norway, Portugal, Romania, Sweden, Spain, Lithuania, and Switzerland (Ledeen 1972, 114–15).

That CAUR should hold its congress in the swanky Palace Hotel in Montreux seemed a curious location to forge a "spiritual alliance." The hotel reflected the crass materialism that many of these movements rejected. The Palace Hotel and the Swiss Riviera were haute bourgeois, which contradicted the social and moral revolution hoped for by the fascists. One Italian fascist, writing to Galeazzo Ciano, the Minister of Press and Propaganda, complained of the locale as an underhanded means of getting people to come to the congress (Ledeen 2002, 124). For those who looked deeper, the location reflected some of the deeper aspirations of fascism. Lake Geneva and its surroundings had long pandered to fantasies of making a new world. From the "New Jerusalem" of Jean Calvin's Geneva, to Mary Shelley's *Frankenstein*, the lake and its surrounding mountains and densely wooded slopes appealed to those who hoped for a new world and a New Fascist Man instead of the materialist cities of the West. Montreux, in contrast to the austerity of Geneva, attracted those who longed for escape. The Palace Hotel was a refuge for Russian emigres fleeing Bolshevism, as well as other exiles who dreamed of a different world. The violence and terror that lurked under the surface of these dreams was not lost on fascists. The theocratic repression of Geneva and the murderous actions of the "victim" created by Dr. Frankenstein stood against the horror of castle Chillon's torture chambers as told in Byron's sonnet.

The men who convened at Montreux were in the thrall of fantasy and horror suggested by the "deep" lake and the severe mountains. Moreover, the Art Nouveau and neobaroque surroundings of the hotel reminded them of the decadent Belle Époque that originally gave rise to fascist longings. The combination of cruelty and Romanticism was not lost on the man Mussolini appointed to lead CAUR, Eugenio Coselschi. A follower of Gabriele D'Annunzio, Coselschi was a man of letters, holding degrees in law and French literature. He had been with D'Annunzio at Fiume and had been a founding member of Fascism's Institute of Culture. Coselschi possessed a poetic sensibility, something his predecessor, Asvero Gravelli, who had led the Fascist International, did not have. Michael Ledeen has pointed out how Coselschi's poetry closely imitated the rhetorical style of D'Annunzio (Ledeen 1972, 109). It is thus no surprise that Coselschi would find the settings of the Palace Hotel congenial, as it reflected the tastes of D'Annunzio, who lived in similar surroundings on the shores of Lake Garda.

Like D'Annunzio, Coselschi reveled in fantasy. This was typical of the men who convened in December 1934 at Montreux. The Universality of Rome, eloquently captured by Coselschi in a poem he penned for CAUR in 1933, was a fantasy that Coselschi hoped would bring together European fascists under the banner of Mussolini's Rome. Unfortunately for Coselschi and Gravelli, fantasy met reality at the Palace Hotel. Any hopes that a Universal Fascism would be forged at Montreux quickly dissipated under the weight of definition. Similarly, to future historians, the fascists in 1934 could not agree on what it meant to be fascist. At Montreux, this was reflected in the division between Latin and Nordic fascisms, which, in turn, revolved on the perceived differences between supporters of Italy's corporatist model and those who identified with Nazism's racial ideology. Hitler did not send any representatives to the meeting, so the Nordic version was instead advocated by Vidkun Quisling and his *Nasjonal Samling* party. The Nordic side found support from the representative of Romania's Iron Guard, Ion Moța, who demanded that the congress recognize the Jews as the world's greatest threat.

In the end, the congress rejected racism as fascism's defining attribute, although it recognized that the Jews presented a problem in many countries and that fascist movements could deal with them as they saw fit. All could agree that communism and liberal democracy constituted fascism's two main enemies. The congress's statement proved a pyrrhic victory for Coselschi, as the CAUR lost a great deal of momentum and ultimately failed to present a united and clear definition of fascism. Aristotle Kallis has pointed out that many of the attendees who had been sympathetic to Mussolini's fascism ultimately gravitated to the more dynamic Nazi model (Kallis 2016). Behind this lack of unity was the tension in 1934 between Fascist Italy and Nazi Germany, a tension reflected in the events of the summer, when Austrian Nazis assassinated the Austrian dictator Engelbert Dollfuss, a close friend and admirer of Mussolini. Tellingly, one of the resolutions of the congress was the condemnation of any interference in the affairs of other countries.

This resolution, and the conflict over antisemitism, clearly showed the inherent contradictions in trying to construct a Universal Fascism. How could movements founded on nationalism and the peculiarities of individual countries possibly be universal? The ultimate failure of CAUR, which became increasingly meaningless after 1936, ironically due to the rapprochement between Fascist Italy and Nazi Germany, is seen as evidence that no such thing as pan-fascism existed and that any attempts to find a common definition of fascism that could describe all fascist movements was futile. This was not lost on international observers. *TIME* magazine, in its report on the congress, wrote that the "conference amply demonstrated that no one thing yet exists which can be called fascism with any precision of idea."[1]

The search for definition continues to haunt scholars, a fact that is complicated when considering the various movements that called themselves fascists—or were called fascist—in Europe and the Americas in the interwar period. As Roberta Pergher has argued, the problem of definition renders the study of transnational fascism in the 1920s and 1930s problematic (Pergher 2022). This chapter will examine the rise of fascist parties in Europe and Latin America without falling into the definitional hairsplitting or ideological essentialism seen in the classic studies of Stanley Payne and Roger Griffin among others. Instead, it will emphasize what those authors downplay—namely, the importance of style. A survey of the fascist movements in the interwar era reveals the fault lines and differences that were on display at Montreux, but they also reveal shared values and shared fantasies of a New Europe founded on the fascist style. Whether Latin or Nordic, corporatist or racist, the varieties of fascisms that mushroomed in the era after the First World War came about due to fascism's decidedly fashionable nature. The perceived success and dynamism of the Mussolini and Hitler regimes made fascism appealing, even if one was not a convinced fascist. In short, many wanted to be at Montreux even if only to take it all in.

Fashionable Fascism

A study of the fascist phenomenon after the war must consider what Kallis and Pergher have called the hybridization and exchange that occurred not just between fascists but also between fascists, authoritarians, and conservatives in the interwar period. This goes against much of the scholarship of the last several decades. Stanley Payne's influential taxonomy of fascist, radical right, and conservative movements in his landmark work, *A History of Fascism, 1914–1945*, argued that distinctions must be made between the

---

[1] N.A., "Pax Romanizing," *TIME*, December 31, 1934, p. 16.

three traditions, and such distinctions reveal that actual fascist movements, based on social revolution, were quite small and isolated. A similar school emerged among French historians, who argued that the various leagues and paramilitary movements that sprung up in France in the 1920s and 1930s were not actually fascist, despite their outer trappings. More recently, Roger Griffin has insisted that fascism properly understood required a desire for revolutionary ultranationalist palingenesis, which leaves out many movements that might have imitated fascist styles without being fascist. Even the two most successful fascist regimes—Italy and Germany—are seen as distinct, having little in common, thanks to the influential work of Renzo De Felice. However, while it is true that the two regimes had many differences, and that the various fascist movements fell into one of these two groups, they had more in common than it may have seemed at Montreux.

Interwar fascism demonstrated great variety, yet all instances had in common a certain style. This chapter will study them from a chronological and thematic perspective showing that what they had in common—style—was their most important attribute and what made them attractive even to committed non-fascists. The fascist style worked on an emotional level, drawing in people who found the gestures, words, and actions of fascism appealing. These gestures and practices seeped into more conservative elements on the right to the point where the distinctions between conservative right, radical right, and fascism became blurred. As Aristotle Kallis and António Costa Pinto have demonstrated, this cross-fertilization created political hybrids or parafascisms, in which conservative elites adopted fascistic practices in their challenge to liberal democracy (Kallis 2014). During the interwar period, fascism became fashionable, so much so that non-fascists often adopted fascist practices and style to the point of ironically deflating the fascist movements while radicalizing conservatives (Vincent 2009).

A survey of the fascist phenomenon in interwar Europe can be divided into two distinct periods. The first is the 1920s, when fascist movements emerged in predominantly Latin or Mediterranean countries following the model of Mussolini's Italy. This phase of European fascism emphasized the struggle against Bolshevism, the rejection of liberal democracy, and a focus on more traditional approaches to society, culture, and economy, led by a strongman of Latin masculinity. This was a variety of fascism that could and did work with traditional elites including the Catholic Church. Using Italian fascism as their template, these movements emphasized corporatism, youth, uniforms, and rituals and gestures often borrowed from traditional religion. Portugal, Spain, France (in the 1920s), Austria, and Greece saw these movements, as did the early British Union of Fascists (BUF) in Great Britain.

The second period, the 1930s, witnessed new varieties of fascism that modeled themselves on Nazi Germany. This "Nordic" form of fascism focused less on economic issues like corporatism and more on race and antisemitism. They were more dynamic than the Italian model and less willing to work with traditional elites. Like the Latin variety, this fascism exalted violence and militarism and shared a hatred of communism and liberal democracy. It also promoted a cult of the leader but preferred a more "mystical" type of leader than the image of the virile Mussolinian type. It was also marked by a more aggressive, expansionist attitude and militarism. To be sure, Italian fascism harbored the same expansionist desire, but Latin fascism tended to be more insular than its Nordic counterparts. Included in this Nordic school were the fascisms that sprouted up in Central and Eastern Europe, movements marked by xenophobic attitudes against neighbors and grievances traced back to the Paris Peace Conference settlements of 1919. In all cases, fascism was a response to circumstances and events within each country. They also adopted the distinctive fascist style of uniforms, gestures, rituals, and violence. Antisemitism was also a constant, albeit expressed in different forms and with different degrees of importance.

These fault lines were evident at Montreux in 1934 and at the second Montreux Congress in 1935. However, the developing friendship between Italian fascism and German Nazism blurred the boundaries further. The two types of fascism could also be seen in the same country such as France and Austria. At times they were antagonists; at other times they could work together. What they all had in common was their lack of success. None of the fascist movements in Europe was able to achieve power in the 1930s. Their fantasies of a panfascist Europe had to wait for the Second World War. Despite the cleavages, what the attendees all had in common was a belief that they were living in a period of decadence and that their mission was to renew Europe through a spiritual revolution and a war of purification. This can be seen in all fascist movements that emerged in Europe after the Great War.

Fascism in France—Back to Where It Started

What Robert Soucy has called "first wave fascism" began in the 1920s, immediately following the First World War; still, as in the case of Italy, the seeds of the movement could be seen before then (Soucy 1986). The first postwar fascist movement in France emerged in the wake of the *Cartel des Gauches* victory in the 1924 national elections, led by Georges Valois (R. Paxton 2004, 69). Once an anarchist, like Mussolini, Valois (real name Alfred Georges Gressant) experienced a political and religious conversion at the turn of the century when he became a monarchist and devout Catholic. He also became a confirmed antisemite and anti-parliamentarian. Valois served with distinction in the First World War and returned from the trenches committed to transforming France via war veterans. This was the group that formed the nucleus of *Le Faisceau*, which he founded in 1925. Like Mussolini's idea of trenchocracy, Valois saw war veterans as the future elite of France. He also supported corporatism on the Italian model. His supporters wore distinctive blue shirts.

Valois's *Faisceau* clearly demonstrated the influential pull of Italian fascism. Valois, like Mussolini, retained a devotion to the work of Georges Sorel, the anarchist philosopher who preached the positive value of violence. In the 1930s, Valois turned back to the left, opposed Nazism, and eventually joined the French Resistance during the Second World War. He would die in a German concentration camp in 1945.

Out of Valois's movement came Marcel Bucard, French fascism's representative at Montreux. A wounded war veteran, Bucard shared Valois's devotion to the idea of war veterans as a new spiritual elite, destined to replace the corrupt parliamentary system and lead France to future glory. In 1933, Bucard helped found the *Parti Franciste* (PF), one of several right-wing "leagues" that began to emerge in France. The PF adopted the Blueshirts' look and quickly became known for its dynamic and violent actions against political opponents. Images of Bucard and his followers show them giving the Roman salute in uniform. The movement's principles closely followed those of Italian fascism in its opposition to liberal democracy, communism, and the Jews. At Montreux, Bucard supported the resolution, downplaying antisemitism; however, after 1936, when his group was suppressed by the Popular Front government, he openly espoused a hatred for Jews (Payne 1995, 296–7).

Bucard's idealization of veterans led by a strongman was typical of the so-called "leagues" that emerged in France in the 1930s. The rise of veterans' movements on the right have been the subject of debate among French historians. The main point of contention has been over the question of whether they were fascist or not. Robert Soucy has pointed out how the so-called "Consensus School" rejects the label of fascist for movements like the *Croix de Feu* (CdF) led by Colonel François de La Rocque, because they were mostly conservative. These historians accept Zeev Sternhell's thesis that French fascism was an ideology of the left, founded in the anarchist movement of the prewar era. Thus, Georges Valois was fascist, whereas De La Rocque and the CdF were not (Soucy 1995). Stanley Payne places the CdF among conservative right-wing movements, while the *Faisceau* and the *Francistes* were clearly fascist (Payne 1995). Soucy and Bill Irvine argued, on the contrary, that De La Rocque's group was clearly fascist, thanks to De La Rocque's ability to create a mass movement, something that Valois and Bucard failed to do (Irvine 1991).

The debate among French historians suggests the difficulty in defining fascism and is largely determined by whether one views fascism as a phenomenon of the left or of the right. In the case of the CdF, the fascist trappings were obvious. The movement celebrated war veterans, wore uniforms, practiced a cult of the leader, and reveled in wartime camaraderie as an antidote to liberal society. Founded in 1927 around veterans who had been awarded the *Croix de Guerre* in the First World War, the movement broadened its base under Colonel De La Rocque, who became the movement's leader in 1930. By 1936, the league boasted some six hundred thousand members. Its ideology was ultranationalist, xenophobic, and anti-parliamentarian. Although antisemitism was common among its members, it was never an official policy of the movement. Only in Algeria did the CdF openly express its antisemitic and anti-Islamic ideas. Part of the reason for this suppression of antisemitism was the desire not to copy Nazi Germany, for the league was strongly anti-German.

The growing membership of the CdF, especially after the events of February 1934 (discussed later in the chapter) put it in the sights of the new Popular Front government after the election of May 1936. This coalition of left-wing movements, led by the new prime minister, the Léon Blum, outlawed the leagues in June. To keep the momentum going and taking advantage of the fear on the right of an imminent socialist revolution, De La Rocque reinvented the CdF into a political party called the *Parti Social Français* (PSF) in 1937. The new party proved remarkably successful in gaining membership. Irvine argues that the PSF could boast some three million members by 1938—the year the Popular Front collapsed. There was some drop off after that, but the party managed to retain solid membership numbers and could have been a force in future elections had not the Second World War intervened (Irvine 1991).

The severity of the economic crisis, the perceived threat of the left, and political scandals—not to mention the foreign threat of Nazi Germany and the Spanish Civil War—spurred a rise in right-wing extremism in France. The leagues promoted an authoritarian solution to the problems of interwar France, a solution driven by war veterans and the success of the Fascist regime in Italy. After the victory of the Popular Front in 1936 and the subsequent gains made by organized labor, the perceived danger of the left galvanized the right. The leagues seemed best placed to counter this danger. Blum's crackdown on the leagues further strengthened the determination of extremists on the right to bring down the Popular Front and bring about a right-wing authoritarian regime. Added to this was the culture war that a Popular Front victory seemed to presage.

Unique to French fascism was its intellectual and cultural character. The Montreux Congress's call for a spiritual renewal of Europe found echoes in the French right. Robert Soucy has noted the important place held by writers like Pierre Drieu La Rochelle, Robert Brasillach, Bertrand De Jouvenel, and Louis-Ferdinand Céline. Although they differed in many important respects, these men shared a common concern with decadence (Soucy 1995, 281). According to Soucy, French far-right intellectuals shared six essential beliefs: a distaste for democracy, a rejection of class conflict, a passionate nationalism, a call for spiritual renewal (as opposed to a materialistic culture), a hatred of cultural decadence, and a belief in violence as something positive. Additionally, they identified this growing decadence with feminism and the Jews. All four were Social Darwinists who believed militarism and authoritarianism could successfully counter Europe's decline. Some of them openly admired German Nazism, like Drieu La Rochelle, who wrote an ode to "Hitlerian Man" (Soucy 1995, 287).

Of the four, Céline proved the most significant as a literary figure. He also embodied many of the contradictions typical of fascism. A war veteran, Céline emerged from the Great War hating war, becoming a committed pacifist. A trained medical doctor, he often worked pro bono in some of the poorest districts of Paris. He later traveled to Africa and America, working for the League of Nations. These experiences became fodder for his first and most successful novel, *Voyage au bout de la Nuit*, published in 1932. In this celebrated work, written in a modernist style, Céline presented a rather pessimistic image of the human body and revealed his general distaste for humanity (Poole 2018, 189). He shared with his fascist contemporaries a diagnosis of the degeneracy and decadence of contemporary society and culture; he did not, however, share their enthusiasm for war, nor did he offer any utopian solutions. While his pacifism seemed out of step with militant fascism, his reasons for that pacifism were all too familiar to the extreme right.

This hatred was compounded by his belief that it was, in fact, the Jews who wanted war to destroy Aryanism.

These ideas came out in three pamphlets he published between 1937 and 1941. In these incendiary works, Céline did not hold back on his antisemitism, which he presented in crude and vulgar terms. The Jews were associated with vermin and disease and the soulless nature of modern civilization. Moreover, the Jews represented a sexual threat and were behind every conspiracy that sought to destroy Western civilization (Soucy 1995, 302). These works place Céline firmly in line with Nazi ideology, which he openly supported, calling for France to ally itself with Hitler's Germany. Showing little inclination toward politics, Céline was galvanized by the election of the Popular Front government in 1936, deepening a hatred of communism that began when he visited the Soviet Union. Likening the Popular Front to a Jewish-Masonic conspiracy, Céline became a fervent fascist. Though he did not officially join any of the far-right movements in France, he did become critical of some of the traditional movements like the Action Française.

Although Céline never subscribed to nor presented a specific fascist ideology, his attitude and worldview made him a natural fascist. He remained convicted of this to his death in 1961. In a television interview given later in his life, Céline described his passion for style and outer forms in writing. He also discussed his lifelong fascination with disease and suffering and how he wanted to be, above all, a healer. Rejecting a belief in God, Céline declared himself a mystic who, using Nietzschean imagery, admired only those who "create" and not those who simply "destroy." Although he did not mention the Jews, this last point could easily become a classic antisemitic trope, which viewed the Jews as destroyers of culture.[2] These sentiments demonstrated an affinity with the fascist fantasy of healing a culture under attack from disease—namely the Jews.

Cultural decadence became a leading anti-theme of French fascism, one of the few elements that the various movements had in common. This was especially prevalent in the *Parti Populaire Français* (PPF) founded in 1936 by Jacques Doriot, a former communist mayor of the Parisian suburb Saint-Denis. A laborer, Doriot became a socialist during active service in the First World War. His disillusionment with communism came with the rise of Stalinism and his rejection of the Popular Front. His new party, viscerally anti-communist, attracted intellectuals like Drieu La Rochelle and De Jouvenel. Doriot founded a newspaper, *L'Emancipation Nationale,* which made "cultural antisemitism" a main feature. It enjoyed a circulation of two hundred thousand copies (Griffin 1991, 134). Although not given to violence, the PPF stylistically resembled other fascist movements, donning blue shirts, berets, and arm bands.

Also affiliated with Fascist Italy—and more open to violence—was Eugene Deloncle's *Comité Secrète d'Action Révolutionnaire* (CSAR), more famously known as *La Cagoule* (hooded cape). A former Maurrassien, Deloncle, a naval engineer and war hero, believed that France was on the verge of a Bolshevik revolution in 1936 after the election of the

---

[2]Louis-Ferdinand Céline, "Interview avec Louis Pauwels," www.youtube.com/watch?v=4hjtjZYXXic (accessed December 27, 2022).

Popular Front. Inspired by events in Spain, where a Popular Front victory sparked a counterrevolution led by Francisco Franco, Deloncle organized a secret army aimed at committing terrorist acts. Convinced that the French Army would support a far-right uprising, Deloncle cultivated contacts not only within the military, such as retired General Edmond Duseigneur, but also with members of the secret service. Deloncle also contacted Benito Mussolini in Rome, and money received from Mussolini's regime helped fund the purchase of weapons, stashed in various parts of France (Soucy 1995, 48–9). These funds supplemented money coming from industrialists who feared an impending communist revolution.

Using these arms and Italian money, Deloncle's organization kidnapped and murdered the Rosselli brothers, Carlo and Nello, leaders of the Italian anti-fascists in exile in June 1937 (Pugliese 1997). In September of that year, the Cagoulards bombed the National Confederation of French Charities, causing extensive damage. The goal of the bombing was to frame the communists. These, and other acts of terrorism, failed to ignite an anti-communist uprising and, instead, led to the arrest of several Cagoulards, including Deloncle, who was subsequently imprisoned. The defeat of France in 1940 and the establishment of the Vichy regime gave Deloncle and other Cagoulards a second life, though some of them would eventually join the French Resistance. In the meantime, the Cagoulards' clandestine activities would influence a later generation of militant neofascists.

Part of Deloncle's frustrations with the traditional far right arose from the failures of the February 1934 uprising in Paris. This event was the closest French fascism came to overthrowing the Third Republic. The riot that involved many of the far-right fascist leagues was the spark that helped the anti-fascist Popular Front win the national election in 1936. Historians have debated the nature of the riot, as some argue that it was not a coordinated coup attempt, while others suggest that its goal was to overthrow the leftist government and not the Third Republic. This debate overlaps with the general discussion over the fascist character of groups like the CdF. Some see Colonel De La Rocque's refusal to lead the coup as evidence of his non-fascism. Whatever the intentions of the rioters, the events of February 6 had a profound impact on French politics, not only because it rallied anti-fascist forces, but also because it affected fascists like Deloncle, who began to look for more direct and violent methods to overthrow the Republic.

Leaving aside the specific intentions and failures of the rioters, the participants in the demonstration were motivated by a worldview common to the fascist sensibility. The immediate cause of the riot was the Stavisky Scandal and the firing of Paris's police chief, Jean Chaippe, seen as too lenient with respect to the violent actions of far-right groups like the *Camelots du Roi*. This was hardly the first scandal to hit the Third Republic, but it involved a Jewish financier and government corruption, a mix that triggered the far-right already susceptible to antisemitic conspiracy theories. Alexandre Stavisky was an embezzler who was known to have friends among the Radical Republicans who were then governing France. When this was revealed in December 1933, it confirmed for critics that the government was corrupt and incapable of dealing with France's economic crisis. Moreover, Stavisky was a Ukrainian Jew, and several members of the government were Freemasons, facts which only fed into the multiple prejudices of the far right. For those who remembered the Dreyfus Affair at the turn of the century, the Stavisky Scandal seemed to raise the same issues of a Republic in thrall to a Judeo-Masonic conspiracy. Not surprisingly, Charles Maurras and the *Action Française* turned out as one of the more visible participants in the February 6 demonstration.

It was the Maurrassians who ended up taking the brunt of the casualties when the demonstrators, filtering in from all parts of the city toward the National Assembly in the Palais Bourbon, were met by the police. Since some of the demonstrators were armed, the police opened fire. Sixteen were killed and thousands injured. De La Rocque's men managed to surround the assembly, having come from a different direction, but the leader of the Croix de Feu decided not to storm the building, thus ending the riot. If the goal of the demonstration was to force the government to resign, it succeeded: the government led by Édouard Daladier stepped down the following day. If the goal was to upend the Third Republic, however, the demonstration was a failure. As it stood, the demonstrators had different goals that day, which reflected the variegated nature of the extreme right in France. It also demonstrated the lack of charismatic leadership needed to bring the groups together. What brought them together in the first place, though, mattered more than their ultimate failure—namely, a shared vision and belief that France was decadent, corrupt, and in need of spiritual renewal.

It was fantasy, not realism, that drove fascism, and this fantasy needed circumstance to touch it off. The lack of planning and coordination in the February 6 riots shows that the political fantasies of fascism could only react to specific circumstances, which seemed to confirm their worldviews. This gamble and leap into the unknown, typical of all fascist movements, clearly betrays a movement driven by fantasy. Failure also fed into the myth of victimization Hitler and the Nazis used in the aftermath of the Beer Hall Putsch. The terrorist activities of Deloncle's Cagoule were driven by a mixture of victimization and fear (Figure 9.1). On the other hand, it led other fascists to think a more pragmatic and realistic approach was needed—but this, too, was based on fantasy.

Mosley and the BUF

Bucard, who was present on February 6 and later at Montreux, represented a fascism that tried to promote a hard realism with corporatism as the solution to France's economic problems. A similarly hard-nosed pragmatic approach to fascism came from Oswald Mosley's British Union of Fascists (BUF) in Great Britain. Mosley came to fascism through economics. Descended from minor nobility, Mosley had a brief stint with the RAF in the First World War. Sensing a vocation in politics, Mosley was elected to parliament in 1918 on the Conservative ticket. In 1924, he left the Conservatives to join the Labor Party. Party loyalty was not his calling card: Mosley eventually left the Labor Party in 1930 after failing to convince his party of radical economic proposals loosely based on the corporative model espoused in Mussolini's Italy. In 1931, Mosley traveled

Figure 9.1 Masked members of the Cagoule celebrating, 1937, Credit: Getty Images.

to Italy where he met with the fascist leader. Inspired by Mussolini's vision, Mosley returned home and subsequently created the BUF.

Throughout his peregrinations from conservative, to labor, to fascist, Mosley remained committed to his economic proposals first produced in the late 1920s in a tract known as the *Mosley Memorandum*. Mosley's preoccupation with economics formed what Stanley Payne has called the "most thoroughly programmatic of all fascist movements" (Payne 1995, 305). Mosley did not seem preoccupied with social revolution nor with overthrowing the British parliamentary system, though he did express a dislike of politics as usual and hoped for a corporative system (Carsten 1967, 221). He expressed these ideas in his book, *The Greater Britain*, published in 1932 on the founding of the BUF. The book laid out Mosley's plans for a corporative state and for an economy that would benefit all British citizens through profit sharing and employment that would be reserved for whites and not colonials. Mosley called for Great Britain to remove itself from the international economic system and replace its democracy with corporatism. Mosley adopted the term "Greater Britain" from previous authors who exalted the role of the British Empire in the world. Significantly, Mosley's economic proposals were not simply materialist. Rather, they reflected an organic and spiritual view of society that contrasted with his earlier proposals, before he had become a fascist (Love 2007, 450). This "spiritual" conception of economic corporatism was very much in tune with the attendees at Montreux and was distinctly fascist.

Undergirding this concern with economics was a general worldview that fit in with fascists anywhere. Drawing on his military experience, Mosley called for an interventionist state to solve the country's economic and social problems on the model of the total war governments as seen during the Great War. The war experience fed the fantasy Mosley promoted of a country in the throes of cultural decadence. Only the common purpose found during the war years could help British society return to greatness. To bring this about, Mosley crafted his BUF into a distinctly fascist-looking entity, complete with Roman salutes and black shirts. Slogans and eye-catching symbols were on display at his large rallies. Antisemitism and violence soon followed. BUF rallies became notoriously riotous affairs, with Mosley often getting directly involved in physical altercations with opponents. Mosley adopted Mussolini's rhetorical style, and, like all fascists, he often evoked the glories of the British past to rally his supporters.

In October 1936, Mosley decided to lead his troops in a fascist march in London's East End, a neighborhood with a large working-class Jewish population. On the BUF's anniversary, Mosley brought some two thousand of his supporters to Whitechapel, where they were met by hundreds of thousands of anti-fascists and several thousand police officers. The ensuing clashes have since become known as the Battle of Cable Street to go along other "battles" that often erupted at BUF gatherings. This resulted in several injuries and arrests and was a "defeat" for Mosley's forces, who were forced to leave the area before completing the march (Figure 9.2). The ensuing crackdown by the British government, which included banning military-style uniforms at political events, was the beginning of the end for the BUF. The government rightly perceived that a fascist style contributed to the increasingly violent atmosphere of the meetings. Such a measure may have also contributed to the BUF's poor performance in London City Council elections the following year.

Significantly, the loss at Cable Street also coincided with Mosley's increasing move toward the Nazi orbit. A firm supporter of Mussolini in the early years, Mosley, no doubt influenced by his second wife Nancy Mitford, began to see in Hitler the future of fascism. Like other fascists who had been at Montreux, Mosley found Nazi Germany the more dynamic of the two fascist nations. After 1937, he joined other British voices in calling for a rapprochement with Hitler's Germany, a position that caught him out after 1939 and eventually led to his imprisonment. Throughout, Mosley remained convinced that he was a man of destiny and attempted to revive the BUF after the Second World War, as he inspired a new generation of British fascists (Skidelsky 1968, 237). More than any other fascist movement, the BUF exalted the cult of personality: Mosley was the charismatic figure who completely dominated the movement, leaving no successor. More importantly, however, the circumstances in Great Britain did not give the BUF the room to fully take root. This was not the case in Central and Eastern Europe.

Central and Eastern European Fascism

As in the Mediterranean countries, the Central and Eastern European states, many of which were founded after the war, were swept by authoritarianism. The rise of fascist

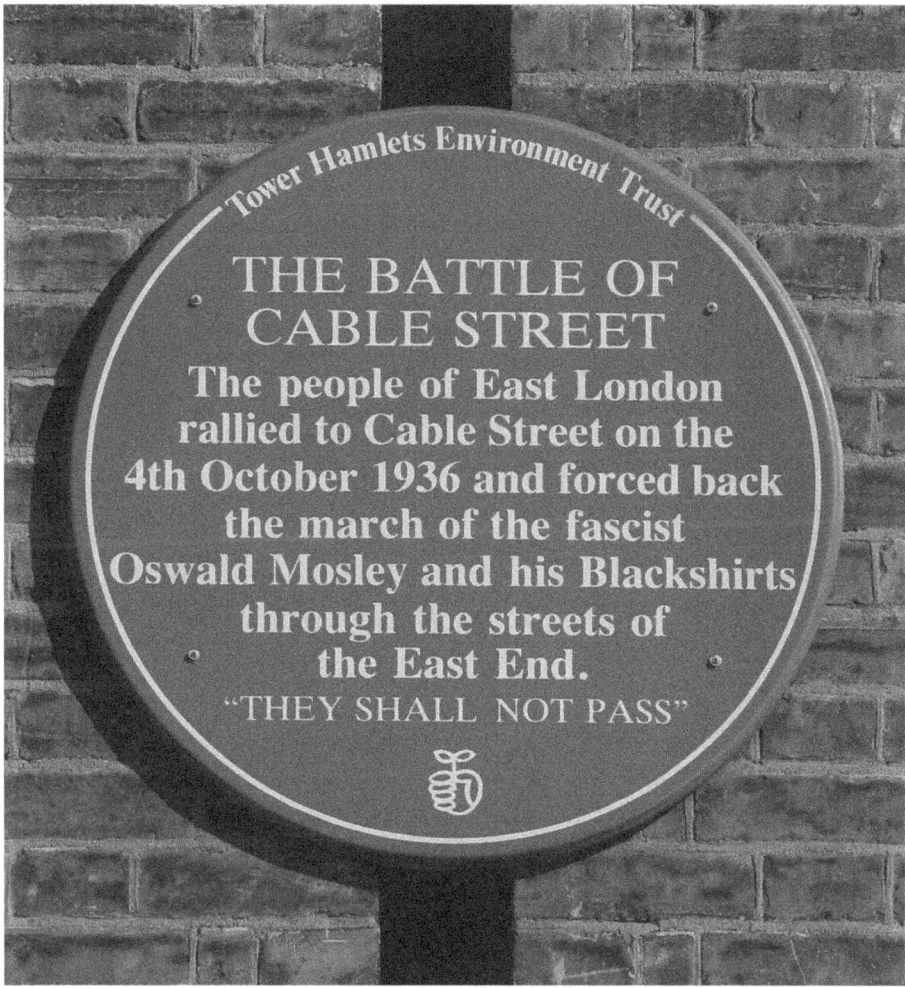

Figure 9.2 Plaque commemorating the Battle of Cable Street in London's East End. Credit: Getty Images.

movements thus swooped in in a context in which liberal democracy was undermined by conservative forces. This was further aggravated by ethnic disputes and disputed boundaries, dilemmas France, Spain, and Portugal did not have to face. In short, this region was fertile ground for a movement like fascism. The entire region lent itself to fantasy, given the radical and unprecedented changes that followed the Great War (Eksteins 1999). The three empires that dominated most of East and Central Europe, the Russian, Austro-Hungarian, and Prussian, disappeared and new states came into being. The region proved remarkably fluid and heterogeneous during the interwar period. This historical moment was accentuated by the influence of foreign powers, like Fascist Italy and Nazi Germany, who helped foster fascist movements as a function of foreign policy.

In such circumstances, the liberal democratic regimes that emerged in these countries were all on shaky ground. Nostalgia for the empires and their authoritarian approaches to government abounded, as did the conservative forces that motivated agrarian parties fighting against the industrial and commercial elites found in the cities. In some cases, these overlapped with ethnic disputes and inflamed antisemitism, as foreigners and Jews were frequently pegged as promoters of modern, industrial, and liberal democratic institutions. This was compounded by the economic displacements caused by the end of empires. What were once hinterlands now became independent economic regions. The difficulty in adjusting to this new reality was made worse by the economic crises of the postwar era. Economic insecurity, xenophobia, and antisemitism inevitably found expression in the fear of Bolshevism. Not surprisingly, liberal democracy largely fell apart in all the successor states, with the notable exception of Czechoslovakia.

Austria

No country better exemplified the split at Montreux than Austria. Once the center of the Austro-Hungarian Empire, Austria was left a rump state with an uncertain future because of the Paris Peace Conference. Given a liberal democratic government, the country was divided between a large capital city dominated by socialists and a very conservative countryside. Border and ethnic disputes and severe economic problems contributed to a volatile postwar period during which paramilitary units abounded. Despite a short period of stability in the mid-1920s, nostalgia for the old Habsburg empire mixed in with a fear of the "red tide" produced a far-right movement called the *Heimwehr*. This group of war veterans formed in the wake of a general strike in Vienna, which seemed to presage a socialist takeover of Austria. This group was hardly the only force on the right, as they were joined by Austrian Nazis, calling for Austria to join with Germany, and by Catholic corporatists (Peniston-Bird 2009).

Out of the three groups, the *Heimwehr* would prove the most successful in the late 1920s and early 1930s. After a period of intragroup rivalries and a failed putsch attempt in 1931, the movement gained a new leader, Prince Ernst Rüdiger Starhemberg, who joined forces with the Christian Social Party in 1933 to form the Fatherland Front. Led by Engelbert Dollfuss, who became Austrian Chancellor in 1932, the Fatherland Front joined the Catholic conservative Christian Social Party with the *Heimwehr*. The Front had the blessing of Benito Mussolini, who had been funneling money and arms to Starhemberg's group. Mussolini hoped to transform Austria into a fascist regime like that of his own and, in doing so, get Austria to drop any claims to the South Tyrol, which was given to Italy after the war (Carsten 1967).

In February 1934, claiming the imminence of a socialist uprising, Dollfuss suspended the Austrian constitution, banned all parties except his own, and created a new authoritarian regime. This state abolished parliament and replaced it with an assembly on the corporatist model. This model resembled the model established in Portugal and was based on the principles of Pope Pius XI's 1931 encyclical, *Quadragesimo Anno* (Payne 1995, 249). Starhemberg was named vice chancellor, a move that clearly demonstrated the importance of the *Heimwehr*. It also demonstrated the significance of foreign influence, as Mussolini's pressure on Dollfuss to adopt an authoritarian-corporatist state became clear. Unfortunately for Dollfuss, he did not live long enough to develop his new regime—he was assassinated by Austrian Nazis in the attempted putsch of July 1934.

The Dollfuss assassination made it clear that Austrian fascists were divided. It also revealed the rivalry between Fascist Italy and Nazi Germany in 1934. Historians like Stanley Payne believe this proves that neither the *Heimwehr* nor the Dollfuss regime were fascist. According to Payne, only the Austrian NSDAP could fit neatly into this category. Added to this was, on the one hand, the clearly conservative character of the Christian Socialists and, on the other hand, the lack of any radical social agenda from the *Heimwehr*. Furthermore, Stahremberg and his group would be kicked out of government by Dollfuss's successor, Kurt von Schuschnigg. In its place, Schuschnigg created a new paramilitary force that aped fascist rituals and behaviors without being fascist. Its focus on corporatism also suggested that this was a reality centered movement aimed at dealing with concrete economic issues and not some political fantasy.

However, the "trappings" adopted by the Fatherland Front should not be casually dismissed. The symbolism of the movement, beginning with its crutch cross—based on the symbol of the Teutonic Knights—its emphasis on youth, the wearing of militarized uniforms, and the large party rallies, revealed a fascist-like style. In 1930, the *Heimwehr* leaders took the Korneuburg Oath, which bore a striking resemblance to fascist ideas (Carsten 1967, 225–6). In the oath, the leaders of the movement swore to bring down the liberal democratic state and replace it with a corporatist state that would resemble the old, decentralized Holy Roman Empire from the Middle Ages. In September 1933, the union of the *Heimwehr* with the Dollfuss regime was consecrated with a celebration of the 250th anniversary of Vienna's liberation from the Turks in 1683. It helped that Stahremberg was a descendant of Vienna's "liberator" in the seventeenth century (Botz 2014).

The Fatherland Front was thus forged on fantasy based on returning to a lost and glorious past, which starkly contrasted with the present. Rather than being simply a conservative regime, which used and then discarded the *Heimwehr*, Dollfuss's regime was a hybrid or parafascist state (Griffin 1991, 124). Although the Schuschnigg regime disbanded the *Heimwehr*, this marked not a lessening of the regime's fascism, but a turn to the more radical Austrian NSDAP. This represented a turn toward Nazi Germany, as the Austrian Nazis were largely directed by Germany. As a result, two Austrian Nazis became part of the government, including Arthur Seyss-Inquart, who attempted to forge a closer bond between his party and the Fatherland Front by introducing Catholic ideas among the otherwise pagan Austrian Nazis. Thus, the Fatherland Front became more fascist after the death of Dollfuss, not less. The final act in this play came in March 1938, when Hitler's troops marched into Vienna and effaced Austria from the map.

Romania

Another country that fell into the Nazi orbit and possessed a radically fascist movement was Romania. This was not a successor state (i.e., one of the new nations that emerged after 1918), but it did profit from the postwar settlement with the acquisition of Transylvania, Banat, Bukovina, and Bessarabia, doubling Romania's territory. These acquisitions included a significant number of Jews, as well as Germans, Hungarians, Ukrainians, and Bulgarians. At Montreux, the representative of the Iron Guard, Ion Moța, unleashed a vitriolic defense of antisemitism, attempting to persuade the congress that hatred of the Jew should be the most important element of fascism. Fearful of losing these territories to neighboring countries like Hungary and Russia, Romanian fascism was marked by extreme nationalism and xenophobia.

These security issues—as well as economic insecurities—helped fuel Romanian fascism. Added to this, however, was a Christian, mystical component that celebrated anti-modern peasant virtues. The movement that promoted these ideas was called the Iron Guard and its leader was Corneliu Codreanu. If fantasy was a key characteristic of fascism, then the Iron Guard was clearly fascist. Founded in 1930, the Iron Guard idealized a deeply religious, peasant society. The Guard rejected modernity and was anti-communist and antisemitic. The movement originated in the mid-1920s at the University of Iași in Moldova, one of Romania's prewar regions. Ironically, for a movement that idealized peasant life, Codreanu's ideas found fertile ground among urban students and intellectuals (Figure 9.3). Codreanu's Legion of the Archangel Michael, founded in 1927, accommodated this elite. The attempt to harmonize an elite with a populist movement, a distinctly fascist trait, was a central tenet of Romanian fascism.

Romanian fascism was unique compared to other movements discussed in this chapter because it was an indigenous movement that did not copy the style of Italian or German fascism (Mann 2004, Ch. 8). That Romanian fascism would take on many of the characteristics of the more famous movements was a result of the postwar situation in Romania. The Romanian context after the First World War had a great deal to do with this, as it resembled in some ways the situation in Italy and Germany. On the winning side of the war, Romania benefited from a doubling of its size, a fact that brought a substantial non-Romanian population into the country. This population ended up having a disproportionate number of Jews, Hungarians, and Germans represented in commerce and the liberal professions (Mann 2004, 261). Furthermore, these non-Romanians mostly lived in the cities.

Iași was a university town with a significant German and Jewish population. It was while attending this university that Codreanu became radicalized, largely under the influence of A. C. Cuza, a professor of Political Economy at the university. Cuza was a Romanian nationalist and virulent antisemite. In 1923, Codreanu joined Cuza in a new party called the League of National Christian Defense (LANC). Codreanu did not stay in the party long, however, as he got tired of endless discussion with no action. For Codreanu, direct action meant killing the movement's liberal opponents in government—especially Jews. Arrested for preparing a list of targets in 1924, he was

Figure 9.3 Corneliu Codreanu gives the fascist salute in peasant costume. Credit: Getty Images.

found not guilty and upon his release promptly shot Iași's police prefect. Put on trial for this crime, he was acquitted, thanks to a jury filled with supporters.

It was during his brief stay in prison that Codreanu outlined the new movement he would call the Legion of the Archangel Michael. Codreanu claimed the organization came to him in a vision. This was the beginning of Codreanu's mystical fascism, one deeply connected to Orthodox Christianity. He trained the Legion to be a spiritual elite that combined monasticism with the militarism of medieval crusaders. His followers, mostly made up of students and young people, would hold processions in the agricultural towns along the Moldavian border. They carried sacks around their necks filled with soil and led open air religious services, often blessed by the local priests. Indeed, priests would become a large group within the Iron Guard. In the 1937 elections, thirty-three of the one hundred and three Iron Guard candidates elected to parliament were priests (Ioanid 2009, 406).

The religiosity of Codreanu's movement made it distinct from most other fascisms. But it shared with them the idea of a spiritual revolution and the desire to create a new man— in this case an idealized peasant—a desire not much different than the Nazi fantasy of the ideal Aryan, or even Mussolini's ruralism. It shared with these movements a dislike of foreigners, communism, and Jews. Codreanu, too, fashioned around himself a cult of personality. He was called "the captain" by his followers, and he was viewed as a kind of prophet who had a direct connection to God. His murder in 1938 only increased this devotion by elevating him to the status of martyr. Romanian fascists, too, had a propensity for violence. However, rather than getting into street brawls with opponents, Codreanu's followers preferred assassinations. Ion Moța, Codreanu's representative at Montreux, had already served time for murdering an Iron Guard member suspected of being a spy. When the Guard was dissolved in 1937–38 by the Romanian king, it had already assassinated four sitting and former prime ministers. Some three thousand Iron Guard members claimed membership in the movement's "death squads" (Mann 2004, 281). Not simply violent, the Iron Guard proved adept at elections. Their processions helped gain the rural vote, as did their promises for land reform and the elimination of the banking and commercial elites, which many peasants saw as enemies. At the national level, the Iron Guard's high point came in 1937 when it came third after winning nearly 16% of the national vote.

The success of the Iron Guard in 1937 spelled the end of the party. Unlike other countries in Europe, the authoritarian impulse in Romania, led by King Carol, led to the suppression of liberalism and fascism. Carol had no desire to work with Codreanu's group, as he was not interested in its revolutionary ideas of land reform. Codreanu and other Iron Guards were arrested after the king suspended the constitution and instituted an authoritarian regime. Just after being arrested, Codreanu and hundreds of others were hanged. (The official story is that Codreanu was shot while trying to escape.) The Iron Guard was not the only fascist movement to be suppressed by right-wing authoritarian regimes. It had already happened in Austria and Portugal. Unlike those movements, however, the Iron Guard would be resurrected and even given a share of power in 1940, when Ion Antonescu, an authoritarian general, led a successful coup against the king. Codreanu's successor as leader of the Iron Guard, Horia Sima, became vice premier of what was called the National Legionary State. As we shall see in a later chapter, the marriage between Antonescu and the Iron Guard was short-lived; in the meantime, however, the conservative-authoritarian regime of the general had taken on a fascist character (Iordachi 2014, 263).

Like French fascism, a striking characteristic of the Romanian variety was the support of the intelligentsia. This is not surprising, given the importance of universities in the movement's foundation. The mystical, Christian exaltation of the peasantry and rural life traced its origins back to Romanian Romanticism. This literary ideal found adherents in both Codreanu and his successor Sima, as both fancied themselves writers. Romanian fascism found more substantial intellectuals in figures like Mircea Eliade, Mihai Maniolescu, and Emil Cioran. Eliade, the philosopher of religion who would find a second life in the United States after the Second World War, was a devoted follower of Codreanu. In 1936, he wrote that Codreanu would be the savior of Romania and how the Legionnaires would "create a *new man* attuned to a new *type of life* in Europe" (italics are Eliade's) (Mann 2004, 278). Cioran, a philosopher of decadentism, believed terror would stem the decay of modern society. "Romania needs exaltation reaching fanaticism," claimed Cioran, "the fanaticization of Romania is the transfiguration of Romania" (Mann 2004, 279).

Eugene Ionesco, the absurdist playwright, resisted Romanian fascism, but did comment on the seemingly irresistible pull of the movement on the country's intellectuals. After the war, he wrote: "They were very few who opposed the fascist dementia, few who took the side of democracy. So few that we were asking ourselves if the truth is on our side, if a lonely individual could be right, despite the majority" (Ioanid 2009, 410). Romanian fascism attracted those intellectuals who were most interested in the culture wars. Modernist writers and artists came under attack, as they did in Nazi Germany. Not surprisingly, these intellectuals led the call for a closer friendship with Hitler. The purification of culture and the desire to Romanianize the country was a powerful stimulant to radical right intellectuals who believed Romanian culture threatened by the influx of non-Romanians after the war. It allowed them to fantasize about a pure Romanian culture rooted in the soil, exemplified in the decidedly non-intellectual peasantry.

Hungary

In contrast to Romania, Hungary lost territory after the First World War and was subsequently engulfed in a Bolshevik Revolution followed by the White Terror. The result was the emergence of an authoritarian regime under Admiral Miklos Horthy, who maintained a semi-pluralistic state that allowed for some liberal practices throughout the 1920s and into the early 1930s. As in Spain, Horthy's quasi-authoritarian regime, which banned the Communist Party, kept fascism, for the most part, at bay. However, the *völkisch* movements that formed in Hungary after the war, combined with the persistent anger over the Trianon Treaty—which had ceded significant territory—kept fascist sympathies simmering below the surface. These sympathies were kept alive as well by Hungary's persistent economic problems, aggravated by the Great Depression. Robert Paxton has argued that few countries provided more fertile ground for fascism after the war (R. Paxton 2004, 24). In 1932, the former White Terror leader and fascist, Gyula Gömbös, was appointed prime minister by Horthy, in a move that signaled a significant shift to the radical right.

In Hungary, fascist ideas found support among military officers and civil servants who had been displaced by the war and the reduction of Hungary. By the 1930s, radical right ideas continued to remain popular among the ranks of junior officers who were anxious to regain Hungary's lost territories. The so-called Government Party, which held power since the end of the war, did not satisfy these desires. When Gömbös was appointed prime minister, hopes of a Hungarian revival ignited, as Gömbös was a product of the postwar Szeged Idea, which called for revanche against Hungary's neighbors. Gömbös ended up a disappointment for Hungary's fascists, though. He made no significant structural changes and did little to foster mass mobilization, preferring instead to maintain the landowning elite's influence on the governing party. An admirer of Mussolini, Gömbös dreamed of creating a corporatist state, but a "top down" corporatism that did not include the land reform many Hungarian fascists demanded (Mann 2004, 243). Ultimately, Gömbös's leadership did not indulge in the fantasies that stoked fascism, despite his background and activities in the immediate postwar years. He had gone to the establishment.

Gömbös did, however, manage to accelerate the fascistization of the Horthy regime, even though he was not able to make it completely fascist. The development of the Regency as a "hybrid" regime owed much to Gömbös's four years in office before his untimely death in October 1936. Crucially, he aided in getting the influence of international fascism into Hungary by fostering closer relations with Mussolini's Italy and Hitler's Germany. Although he could not get the establishment behind the ruling Unity Party to fully accept fascist ideas, his relations with the two fascist powers made the Horthy regime more open to influences from Italy and Germany, which sparked the birth of various domestic fascist movements. According to Stanley Payne, in the mid-1930s, Hungary had the "largest assortment per capita of fascist-type, semifascist, or radical right movements" (Payne 1995, 267).

The flowering of fascist-style movements in Hungary was due to several factors, not least of which was the crushing economic crisis. However, Hungarian fascism already had roots going back to the *völkisch* movements in the immediate postwar era. It had lain dormant for a while, but the rise of Fascist Italy and Nazi Germany inspired a new generation of fascists. The most important figure was Ferenc Szálasi, a professional soldier and veteran of the First World War attached to the General Staff. Szálasi embodied the ambitions and far-right feelings of many officers in the Hungarian Army. In the 1930s, he served in counterespionage until he found a political vocation, creating the Party of National Will in 1935. A true believer in Hungarianism, Szálasi opposed the Horthy regime, getting involved in anti-government conspiracies. These got him arrested on a couple of occasions. In 1939, Szálasi helped found the Arrow Cross Party, which participated in that year's elections. Stunningly, the Arrow Cross won the second highest number of seats in the Hungarian Diet and collected over five hundred thousand votes thanks, in part, to the votes of communists, who, not allowed to vote for their own party, voted Arrow Cross because Szálasi's advocated for industrial workers and miners.

The proletarian appeal of the Arrow Cross made this fascist movement different from those in Italy and Germany. Szálasi called for land reform, which gained the party significant support in the countryside. He also supported labor and miners' strikes in 1939 and 1940 as attacks on the landowning, conservative elites of Hungary. Yes, the Arrow Cross was a fully fascist party, whose ideas contrasted significantly with the left in many ways. From the moment he entered politics, Szálasi called for a Carpathio-Danubian Great Fatherland led by Hungarians but allowing for a degree of autonomy for non-Hungarians in areas where Hungarians were not present. Everywhere else, Magyarization was the order of the day. For Szálasi, Hungarians occupied a unique place between Western Europeans, the Slavic peoples of Eastern Europe, and the Greco-Latins of the Mediterranean. He believed Hungary could, thanks to its geography and location, prove uniquely useful to the Rome–Berlin Axis. For Szálasi, Arrow Cross offered Hungarians a movement based on three principles: The moral principle came from Christianity, the spiritual from Hungarianism, and the material from National Socialism (Mann 2004).

As with all fascist movements, Arrow Cross was based on a belief that modern society was decadent and needed rescuing from shadowy forces outside the home country. Antisemitism became a major platform in the Arrow Cross even though Szálasi claimed to be "a-Semitic" (as opposed to antisemitic). In truth, Szálasi's view of the Jews was like that found in other fascist (and non-fascist) movements. He identified the Jews with capitalism and Marxism, associated them with Freemasonry, and saw them as foreigners who were exploiting Hungarians. In this case, Szálasi's prejudice was confirmed by the fact that Hungarian Jews were overrepresented in commerce, finance, and the liberal professions. Some eighty percent of those employed in banking were Jewish, thus feeding into antisemitic stereotypes (Payne 1995, 271). Furthermore, Jews were overrepresented also in universities, where fascism appealed greatly to students (as in Romania, but without the level of intellectual leadership) (Wittenberg 2014).

Since there was no immediate communist threat—since the party was banned—and the socialist presence in Hungary was weak, the Jews became the "enemies" Hungarian fascists needed. Although Szálasi was not given to violence personally, his Greenshirts did make it a habit of attacking Jews and their property. In 1944, when the occupying Nazis put the Arrow Cross into power, they became enthusiastic helpers in shipping Hungarian Jews to the concentration camps. Antisemitism was the glue that cemented the alliance between the Arrow Cross and the more traditional authoritarian groups in Hungary, even though their antisemitism took on the racial aspects of Nazism. Even though Hungary had not been known to be antisemitic before the war, after the war it became the first country to adopt antisemitic laws. These were the *Numerus Clausus* law, which restricted Jews from universities. In 1938 and 1939, even stricter laws were put in place by the Horthy regime, which used explicitly racial language (Wittenberg 2014).

Arrow Cross also proved effective in gaining memberships, boasting some five hundred thousand members at its peak (Griffin 1991, 128). As with other fascist movements, the Arrow Cross drew support from a cross section of society, as workers and peasants comprised anywhere between 8 and 13 percent, while army officers made up 17 percent of its membership (Mann 2004, 248). The movement's goals proved vague, however, and as with other fascisms, it was fueled by fantasy and the conviction of cultural decay. This was augmented by the circumstances of Hungary, a rump state with fantasies of reuniting all Magyars under one ethno-state. Like the movements in Austria, the Hungarian fascists felt the pull of foreign fascisms and ultimately relied on Nazi Germany to come near power. Although Szálasi lacked the charisma of a Hitler or Mussolini (and his writings were somewhat turgid), an effective cult of personality was built around him, helping the Arrow Cross survive his stints in prison. Like Codreanu, he had the air of a mystic or visionary without the overt references to Christianity of the former. Additionally, he, like Codreanu and other fascists, could claim they were persecuted and victimized by the state. Horthy never trusted him, however, and it was only after the Regent was deposed by the Nazis in 1944 did Szálasi and his Arrow Cross finally achieve power—it did not, however, last very long.

Conclusion

This chapter has not provided an exhaustive study of interwar fascism. Nor has it attempted to make fine distinctions between fascists, quasi-fascists, and authoritarians. Rather, it has argued that fascism became fashionable in the interwar years, largely because of its perceived success in Germany and Italy. The shared experience of war, economic distress, and distrust of unstable liberal democracies contributed to fascism's popularity. Added to this were the ethnic and border disputes in East and Central Europe resulting from the haphazard nature of the postwar peace settlements.

Ultimately, though, it was the style and panache of fascism that made it enticing for many on the right. The shirts, the charismatic leaders, the gestures, the rituals, and the violence appealed to those who were rejecting more conventional ideologies and were looking for something new. It was, as Kallis and Costa Pinto have pointed out, a truly transnational movement that was at the same time deeply nationalist. The ability to bring these two seemingly antithetical ideas together was not easy and caused a great deal of tension within the movements. The two models proposed by Fascist Italy and Nazi Germany also caused difficulties, as could be seen in the failed experiment of Universal Fascism driven by CAUR.

It is tempting to argue that these disparities—and the failure of Coselschi's movement—are evidence that little held the various fascisms together apart from style. Yet, it was the style and the fantasies promoted by these movements that made transnational fascism possible. Notably, none of these movements succeeded in taking power, and they were often suppressed by right-wing authoritarian regimes, but only after these regimes themselves adopted many of the characteristics of fascism, notably in their styles, rituals, and gestures. Though the Montreux conference could not agree on the question of antisemitism, none of the movements rejected it outright—they merely disagreed as to its degree and nature.

National circumstances played a large role in keeping these movements away from ultimate power. Robert Paxton has argued that fascism relied on an open field to give them the space needed to reach power. What they lacked was a war. Although the fascist movements varied in their national aims—some were expansionists, while others wanted to defend what the nation already had—they all agreed that war was necessary for life. War also created the conditions in which fascist fantasy had a chance at becoming reality. That war came in 1939, and it is to that context that we now turn.

CHAPTER 10
THE SECOND WORLD WAR: FASCISM'S PLAYGROUND

Palladian Settings

A few miles west of the Austrian city of Salzburg is a casino. Named after the city, the casino was opened in 1993 in a building that was originally owned by the Archbishop of Salzburg and built for him in the eighteenth century, when the prelates of the Catholic Church enjoyed great power in the Austrian Empire. This symbol of power was taken over by the Nazis soon after the Anschluss in 1938, and in 1940, it was converted into Hitler's Guesthouse. Not far from Hitler's Alpine residence in Berchtesgaden, the Baroque-style Schloss (castle) Klessheim would host some of the key Axis summits during the Second World War. Here, in April 1942, with the German armies deep in Soviet territory and much of Europe under the direct and indirect control of the Axis, Hitler hosted Mussolini in one of the dictators' thirteen wartime summits (Schieder 2022).

The spectacular setting of the Hitler–Mussolini summit was not lost on the Italian delegation. Italy's foreign minister and Mussolini's son-in-law, Galeazzo Ciano, wrote in his diary about the "grandiose building" that hosted the summit (Ciano 1947, 461). The castle seemed an appropriate venue for an Axis alliance that was dominating Europe and witnessing Japanese successes in the Pacific. It appeared as if the fascist vision of remaking the world was succeeding. By 1942, Hitler and Mussolini had taken turns using elaborate gestures to impress one another and the world (Goeschel 2018). It began with their first meeting in Venice in 1934, where the two men spoke in the elaborate setting of the Villa Strà and the Piazza San Marco, a site that "intoxicated Hitler" (Schieder 2022, 94). The meetings continued with Mussolini's visit to the Nuremberg Party Rally in 1937, a visit he topped when he invited Hitler for a one-week stay in Italy in 1938. The grandiosity of those visits was only matched by the success of the Axis war machine after 1939 and by the Schloss Klessheim, where Axis fantasy was becoming a reality.

Before the outbreak of the Second World War, fascist dreams were restricted to only two countries: Italy and Germany. After the German invasion of Poland in 1939, and the subsequent successes of the German armies in Western Europe, Scandinavia, and the Balkans, followed by deep penetration into the Soviet Union, the fascist dream of a New Order was being imposed on millions of Europeans. The seemingly imminent collapse of fascism's nemesis, Bolshevism in Russia, only made those dreams more intoxicating. It was precisely in the "euphoria" of the summer of 1941, that the Final Solution of the so-called "Jewish Problem" presented itself to Hitler and the Nazis (Browning 2007). When Hitler and Mussolini and their retinue convened at Salzburg in April 1942, the trains were well on their way to the newly built extermination camps in Poland. Hitler's fantasy of a world without Jews was becoming reality, and Schloss Klessheim represented the ideal of European culture uncorrupted by the influence of the Jews, the so-called "destroyers of culture."

There would be three Mussolini–Hitler summits at the Schloss in 1942–4. In those years, the Axis's situation would dramatically change, and when a gaunt and defeated Mussolini traveled to Salzburg for the last time in the spring of 1944, Axis defeat seemed imminent. Indeed, in the words of F. W. Deakin, the 1944 meeting would be "the last of a series held in such a world" (Deakin 1962, 681). In reality, fascist dreams seemed unattainable as early as the 1942 summit. The setting of the conference, however, not to mention the Berghof, Hitler's chalet on the nearby Obersalzberg, provided the stage for this dream seemingly brought to life by the drama of the Second World War.

The former salt mining area near Salzburg had become the Nazi idyll during the Third Reich. Here, Hitler purchased a chalet, the Berghof, and eventually developed a compound around it that housed other Nazi leaders. This was done through at times ruthless land expropriation methods. These efforts were led by Martin Bormann and entailed the elimination of the village of Obersalzberg (Feiber and Schlemmer 2022, 186–7). The Berghof became Hitler's favorite retreat, a place to which he would return before and during the war. It also became a site of pilgrimage for Germans who wanted to see their *Führer*. The expanded chalet included a large picture window, measuring 60 x 50 feet, out of which Hitler could gaze on the Bavarian landscape and specifically on the Untersberg mountain, awaiting the rise of a new Reich (Speer 1970, 102–3). The window was used to impress visitors, especially foreign dignitaries, whom Hitler hosted on several occasions, none more so than the Italians. Although Mussolini did not visit the Berghof until 1941, Ciano had already visited on several occasions, as did Italo Balbo. In many ways, the Obersalzberg meeting was the site on which the Axis alliance was forged (Feiber and Schlemmer 2022) (Figure 10.1).

The Schloss Klessheim and the Berghof were the sites of the April 1942 summit, and the Nazi propaganda machine made a great deal out of it. Indeed, it was one of the "last large-scale diplomatic events" held by the Axis (Feiber and Schlemmer 2022). The Italian Ministry of Popular Culture, too, was directed by Mussolini to publicize the meeting, especially the Schloss Klessheim.[1] The task was given to the LUCE Institute, the state-run newsreel service, which produced a 10-minute film of the summit. The newsreel, directed by one of LUCE's most important directors, focused on the surroundings with a series of jump cut stills showing the richly furnished rooms.[2] It also showed the two dictators admiring the halls with Hitler pointing out some of the key features to his guest. Similar images of the Berghof were shown in the newsreel with the more spartan

---

[1] Archivio Centrale dello Stato (ACS), Ministero della Cultura Popolare (MCP), busta 36: "Viaggio a Salisburgo: Appunto per il Capo di Gabinetto."
[2] Archivio LUCE, Cinegiornale, GL C0245: "L'incontro del Duce con il Fuhrer." (May 11, 1942): https://patrimonio.archivioluce.com/luce-web/detail/IL5000016730/2/l-incontro-del-duce-fuehrer-3.html?startPage=0&jsonVal={%22jsonVal%22:{%22query%22:[%22convegno%20di%20salisburgo%22],%22fieldDate%22:%22dataNormal%22,%22_perPage%22:20}} (accessed July 4, 2023).

The Second World War: Fascism's Playground

Figure 10.1 Hitler's Berghof with the massive picture window in full display. Credit: Getty Images.

décor of Hitler's chalet contrasting with the opulence of the Schloss. Despite these contrasts, both locations had the same goal—to exalt the vision of the New European Order pursued by the two leaders.

The surroundings of the Schloss Klessheim, the Berghof, and the alpine scenery combined to promote the vision of the Axis and its connection to an Italian tradition. The description of the Schloss by the Italian Ministry of Popular Culture noted the "quasi-Palladian" lines of the villa, which is reminiscent of the Villa Strà near Venice, where the two leaders held their first meeting in 1934.

The link to the Italian Renaissance architect Andrea Palladio was not accidental. Palladio was Italy's most influential architect, inspiring classical-style villas throughout Europe and the Americas since the sixteenth century. Palladio was the favorite architect of the noble Venetian families during the late Renaissance. His villas were known for their porticoes, pillars, windows, and grand staircases. They served as backdrops to demonstrate the power and wealth of the Venetian aristocracy who desired to create a new Rome (Cosgrove 1993, 41). Palladio's villas were designed as performative spaces for the elite of Venice. In these houses, the Venetian nobility could display their power and wealth. The villas were designed to embody messages to those who entered them (Ackerman 1990, 32). They presented an agrarian vision, which suited the ideals that fascism wanted to convey in the twentieth century. At the heart of the villa stood the image of the Renaissance man, or prince, who used the décor and the space of the main hall to demonstrate his power (Stern 1989). Hitler and Mussolini, in the surroundings of the Schloss Klessheim, were presented as Renaissance *condottieri*. They were war lords, diplomats, and men of culture. The stately interiors and exteriors of the palace and chalet underscored this. The windows of the buildings, especially the massive picture window of the Berghof, allowed the dictators to survey the Alpine landscape. This too was a function of the Palladian villas, where both interiors and exteriors communicated power, and the prince could keep an eye on his domain outside the windows.

The Baroque surroundings of the villa played into the fantasy world of fascism. The Baroque style was developed during the Catholic Counter-Reformation era and emphasized spectacle and illusion. Jesuit architects designed churches to draw observers into the dramatic play of the religious conflicts of the sixteenth and seventeenth centuries. Hitler admired the domes of these churches and wanted to design a domed arena in Berlin that would outsize St. Peter's Basilica in Rome. These structures of illusion and spectacle provided by the Schloss, the Berghof, and the Bavarian Alps served to remind Europeans of the New Order the Axis wanted to construct. Galeazzo Ciano noted in his diary how these settings encouraged Hitler to pretend that he was a Renaissance prince who could discuss any topic. "Hitler talks, talks, talks, talks … He omitted absolutely no argument: war and peace, religion and philosophy, art and history" (Ciano 1947, 462). The fascist New Order as a return to the condottieri of the Renaissance was performed by other Nazi leaders as well. The Italian writer Curzio Malaparte noted the same tendency in Hans Frank, the leader of the General Government in Poland, who behaved like a Renaissance prince in the opulent surroundings of the Wawel Castle in Krakow. "Don't forget to tell Frank," advised Malaparte, "that he is a prince of the Italian Renaissance" (Malaparte 2005, 67).

It is tempting to dismiss these settings as mere refuges, places where the reality of war could be escaped and forgotten—but they were more than that. They embodied the Europe Mussolini and Hitler were attempting to construct. It was a Europe of Italianate settings, a return to the ruthless and cultured world of the Renaissance, places where the fascist New Man was at home. It was here, in these settings, that the Second World War's fascist playground was best represented. During the war, Hitler invited all his allies to meet him at the Schloss. Between 1943 and 1944, as the war turned against the Axis, the baroque palace at Klessheim hosted Ion Antonescu, Miklós Horthy, Ante Pavelić, and Jozef Tiso (Feiber and Schlemmer 2022). The Schloss thus became the stage where the fascist vision of Europe was expressed even as that vision was collapsing. Palladian settings backdropped the Wagnerian drama that came to mark the final months of the Second World War.

Hitler's War, Fascism's Dream

It is more than a quirk of biography that Hitler viewed the war in Wagnerian terms. When German troops invaded Poland on the morning of September 1, 1939, Hitler was not only avenging the Treaty of Versailles—he was also unleashing the fascist vision of the world. This vision, which entailed the destruction of the Jews, was laid out at the Kroll Opera House on January 30, 1939, the sixth anniversary of Hitler's rise to the Chancellorship. Built in the 1840s, the opera house became the temporary home of the Reichstag after the fire of 1933. The opera house stood across the square from the old Reichstag and its theater was large enough to hold the members of the German parliament. Despite these more pragmatic reasons, the building suited Hitler's Wagnerian fantasies: its design, in the neoclassical style, echoed the Renaissance image cultivated at Schloss Klessheim.

In that setting, Hitler opened the new year with a fiery speech that foretold Germany's search for more living space and promised a final reckoning for the Jews. The speech was belligerent but also promised peace, a contradiction typical of fascist thought (Longerich 2019, 605). In the Hitlerian fantasy, peace could only be achieved after a destructive war rid the world of the Reich's enemies—and the main enemies were the Jews. A sizable portion of the speech dealt with the Jews, whom Hitler pegged as Bolshevists and warmongers. "If," claimed Hitler, "international finance Jewry inside and outside Europe should succeed in plunging the nations once more into war, the result will be not the Bolshevization of the earth and thereby the victory of Jewry, but the annihilation of the Jewish race in Europe" (Herf 2006, 52).

As the war went on and the Final Solution became a reality, Hitler and his followers would often refer to this speech as "Hitler's Prophecy Speech." Indeed, the Nazi fantasy started to become reality only during the Second World War. The conquest of living space (*Lebensraum*), the building of a Greater Germany made up of Aryans unsullied by inferior races—and the complete annihilation of the Jews—was made possible by war.

Fascism in Europe and Beyond

The idea of struggle and conquest was part of the fascist fever dream that the Second World War made possible. This chapter will demonstrate how the Second World War set the stage for the fascist conquest of the world. The experiment that was to be the New Order, with its Palladian and neo-Renaissance settings, Wagnerian soundtrack, and bucolic villages of racial purity could only find expression in a war setting. The idea of fascist peace required apocalyptic destruction; order required violence. The "joy" proposed by Nazi leisure organizations could only be achieved at the expense of genocide. When Hitler promised that war would mean the annihilation of the Jewish people, he was setting the scene for the atrocities that followed. Just four days before Hitler's speech, Hermann Göring issued a directive to Reinhard Heydrich, the number two man in the SS, to create a Jewish Emigration Bureau (Krausnick and Broszat 1970, 63–4). Heydrich eventually became the point man for getting the Final Solution underway in 1941. Fantasy—a world free of Jews—was about to become reality.

Blitzkrieg

The German invasion of Poland on September 1, 1939, was presented as another stage in the revision of the Treaty of Versailles. The pretext was the liberation of the free city of Danzig, an ethnically German city surrounded by Polish territory taken from Germany after the First World War. To ensure that an invasion would keep the Soviet Union out of the fray, Hitler shocked the world by signing a nonaggression pact in late August. The negotiations were so secret that not even Mussolini was aware of it. Hitler was not too concerned about Mussolini's reaction. He had already locked up Italian support with the signing of the Pact of Steel in May, in which the two powers pledged to help each other in the event of war. This pact was more legally binding than the Rome–Berlin Axis signed in 1936, and it represented Mussolini's greater willingness to a closer union in the Axis.

By the summer of 1939, the Axis war machine was well and truly underway. Hitler had taken what was left of Czechoslovakia in March without firing a single shot, leaving a rump Slovakian state run by a Roman Catholic priest and fascist sympathizer, Monsignor Tiso. In April, Mussolini sent troops to Albania and took the country relatively easily. The Axis desire to remake Europe in a New Order was thus underway long before German troops entered Poland. The fact that Great Britain and France were no longer willing to appease Hitler no longer seemed so important. He was only concerned with the Soviet Union's response to an invasion, hence the signing of the non-aggression pact. Publicly, the pact pledged that the two ideological enemies would not fight a war. What was not shared with the public, however, was a provision to divide Poland among themselves in what became a new Polish Partition.

That Hitler would make an agreement with the "Judeo-Bolshevik" Soviet Union seemed to imply that he was a pragmatic diplomat and that Nazi ideology did not really dictate German foreign policy. Hitler's desire for Lebensraum, however, meant that this was only a temporary measure, as was the nonaggression pact Germany signed with Poland in the mid-1930s. In the fascist mind, treaties and pacts are only ever for expediency and rarely get in the way of broader ideological goals. If anything, they are meant to distract and even sow confusion. They are part of what Jason Stanley calls the fascist ability to "destroy information spaces and break down reality" (Stanley 2018, 57–8). The war opened the door to the lying endemic to fascism and would provide a cover for the "unreality" Nazism wished to construct.

The war launched in 1939 introduced the world to the tactic of blitzkrieg (lightning war). This combined land and air attacks, using infantry, tanks, and airplanes. The declaration of war came only after the Germans had invaded. It was designed to disorient and shock opponents and lead to a swift conclusion, thus avoiding a protracted conflict like the First World War. Once again, the Nazism marriage of pragmatism and ideology was on display here. The "lightning war" tactic was designed to manifest fascist practices of a swift and violent campaign that would disorient its victims in a manner that resembled the way Hitler dismantled liberal democracy in Germany. The military tactic of blitzkrieg paralleled Nazism's political tactic. The Reichstag Fire in 1933 and the subsequent imprisonment of his political opponents, not to mention the Night of the Long Knives in 1934 are but two examples of how Hitler used similar shock tactics on his domestic opponents. Blitzkrieg was meant to terrorize not only opposing militaries but also civilians, as Hitler's instructions to his generals on the eve of the Polish invasion confirmed.

The German victories of 1939 and 1940 were spectacular. Poland was eliminated within a month, and, in the spring of 1940, Denmark, Norway, Luxembourg, Holland, Belgium, and France fell quickly under the wheels of the Panzers. In the invasion against France, launched in May, Hitler had to choose between alternative strategies presented to him by his generals. The more cautious option advocated engaging the Allied forces in Belgium; the more brazen option would send Panzers through the Ardennes Forest. The latter, devised by Erich von Manstein, was chosen by Hitler. The speed with which France was vanquished contrasted sharply with the slogging campaigns of 1914–18 and seemed to prove the effectiveness of Blitzkrieg. Of course, France was not prepared militarily or otherwise to deal with the German invasion, partially due to the political polarization experienced in the 1930s when those on the far right preferred Hitler to Blum. Marc Bloch's eloquent analysis of the French defeat in 1940 remains poignant. Amid the many failures of the French military and political establishment in 1940, there was the inability of the French to understand the speed and flexibility of the Nazi military mind. Only the Germans, it seemed, understood the needs of the "new war" (Bloch 1949, 36).

The new psychology of war unleashed by the Nazis can be seen in the methods utilized in 1939–40. The heavy use of Panzers and the Junkers Ju 87 aircraft, popularly known as the Stuka dive bomber, showcased the Nazi approach to war. These tools were not designed merely as effective weapons; they were to leave a psychological impression upon those who faced them. The Stuka was equipped with sirens meant to instill fear in soldiers and civilians. These were used to good effect in the Polish Campaign (Boyne 1994). The large-scale bombing of civilian targets summed up Nazi Germany's military strategy in the early years of the war. Warsaw was pounded for several days in September 1939, as was Rotterdam in June 1940. The Germans would employ similar tactics in the Battle of Britain, targeting British cities, especially London, with massive bombing raids that killed thousands of civilians. To be sure, the Allies would use similar strategic bombing initiatives in the war, but only after the Germans introduced them in the early campaigns.

In the Nazi mind, the war was not just a military affair—it was also political and cultural. In the Polish campaign, special action squads (*Einsatzgruppen*) run by SS through Heydrich's Reich Security Main Office (RSHA) were sent to identify and execute civilians who were deemed to pose a threat to the Germans. These units had already been used during the Anschluss and the dismantling of Czechoslovakia. Now, in Poland, they were motorized units trained to fight the war from a "world philosophy point of view" (Krausnick and Broszat 1970, 67–8). In this task, the special squads, helped by the Order Police and the *Waffen-SS*, rounded up and shot Polish intellectuals, priests, and anyone else seen as a threat to German control of Poland. On September 21, an order from Heydrich tasked the *Einsatzgruppen* with rounding up Jews and deporting them to what would be called the General Government, a colonial state run by Hans Frank, where they would be concentrated into ghettos. The *Einsatzgruppen* would next be called upon to operate in Hitler's most important campaign in Russia.

Operation Barbarossa, or the invasion of the Soviet Union, launched on June 22, 1941, was the fulcrum of that "world philosophy" which guided Hitler's war. Unable to bring Great Britain to heel in 1940, Hitler turned his attention to the Soviet Union, the key target for Hitler's Lebensraum ambitions in the east. After more swift campaigns to bail out Mussolini in Greece and the Balkans in early 1941, the Germans prepared for the massive blitzkrieg operation along a vast front stretching from the Baltic to the Black Sea. In the lead-up to the invasion, Hitler told his military that this was to be a War of Annihilation between not just two countries, but two ideologies and worldviews. The early weeks of the campaign seemed to bear out Hitler's belief that one needed only to kick in the door and the whole rotten structure would collapse. The German armies plunged deep into Russian territory, surrounding Leningrad and knocking at the gates of Moscow.

The dizzying advance of the Wehrmacht in the summer of 1941 brought on the "euphoria" discussed earlier in the chapter. Armed with the so-called "Commissar Order" issued by the German Army High Command, the special squads that trailed the army were told to shoot communist leaders and any civilians that threatened the Germans. Guided by Nazi ideology, which equated Bolsheviks and Jews, the *Einsatzgruppen* began rounding up Jews and shooting them en masse. In one operation, known as the Babi Yar Massacre, the SS murdered over thirty-three thousand Jews in Kiev. Similar executions took place in the Baltics, Belarus, and elsewhere in Ukraine. While the mass of this killing was done by SS units, the responsibility of the Wehrmacht needs to be considered. Long considered innocent of these operations, historians like Omer Bartov have demonstrated the active participation of the regular German Army, especially in their campaigns against partisans (Bartov 1992). Field commanders like von Manstein called for Jews and Bolsheviks to be cleared from their military jurisdictions on the Eastern Front (Förster 1986).

In the meantime, Hitler's plans to create a Greater Germany in the east continued with the evacuation of Poles and Jews, who were sent to the General Government, and their replacement with ethnic Germans from the Baltics. They were to settle in the Polish territory incorporated into the Reich. As the German armies advanced, Hitler gave wide powers to the party's chief ideologue, Alfred Rosenberg, as Reich Commissar of the east. In a move typical of the administrative chaos of the Nazi regime, Hitler also authorized Rosenberg's enemy, Heinrich Himmler, to implement a revised *Generalplan Ost*, which called for a massive campaign of Germanization of the east. Himmler, for his part, planned the eventual annihilation of the Slavs through mass starvation.

Thus, the war became the opportunity for Hitler to implement his vision of the Third Reich. To what extent can these measures be considered fascist? Historians like Mark Mazower have argued that these plans closely resembled the colonial policies practiced by the European powers in Africa and Asia and that their only novelty under the Nazis was their implementation in Europe (Mazower 2009). Timothy Snyder, in his monumental work, *Bloodlands*, also downplays the uniquely fascist character of the Nazi vision, demonstrating how the Soviets equally ravaged this swath of territory in the east (Snyder, Bloodlands: Europe Between Hitler and Stalin 2010). It can also be argued that Germany's land grab in the east resembled to some extent Imperial Germany's expansion after the Treaty of Brest-Litovsk in 1918, thus suggesting a continuity between the *Kaiserreich* and the Third Reich—an argument famously made by Fritz Fischer's controversial book in 1961 (Fischer 1968).

These arguments ignore or downplay the centrality of Nazi ideology in the Second World War, especially in the drive to the east. Nazi fantasies were played out in Eastern Europe. There, the millions of Jews who came under German control were to be eliminated either through forced emigration, or, ultimately, through mass murder. There, too, the new Germany as an Aryan paradise would be constructed, whether in the way conceived by Rosenberg (who called for some autonomy for Ukrainians) or Himmler (who envisioned the disappearance of non-Aryan groups). Essential to these plans was the war, which provided the cover and opportunity for these plans to be implemented. The war was essential for the Nazi vision, not just as a cover but also because war was a fundamental pillar in the Nazi worldview. It provided not only an opportunity to enact Hitler's antisemitic fantasies, but it also allowed for the annihilation of other groups the Nazis wished to eliminate, such as homosexuals, the Roma and Sinti, and other undesirables, such as Poles, Afro-Germans, and Jehovah's Witnesses (Bergen 2016).

The war was the occasion for the Nazi experiment in vast social engineering. In the early days of the war, Hitler authorized a euthanasia campaign to eliminate the disabled, an extension of the sterilization policies already carried out earlier in the 1930s. Known as the T-4 program, this campaign laid the groundwork for the Final Solution, when the Nazis decided to exterminate the Jews in gas chambers instead of shooting them. Many of those who worked in the T-4 program, such as Christian Wirth, eventually were conscripted into Operation Reinhard, the systematic murder of Polish Jews via gas begun in the General Government during the spring of 1942. The building of extermination camps, such as Auschwitz, Treblinka, and Sobibor, among others, began under the cover of war. Camps like Auschwitz also served as labor camps. In his famous memoir, Primo Levi, an Auschwitz survivor, came to identify Auschwitz as an example of a "gigantic biological and social experiment" meant to see what happens to human beings under extreme privation (Levi, Survival in Auschwitz 1996, 86). The concentration camp "universe" the Nazis had begun as soon as Hitler came to power in 1933 had, by the 1940s, become a vast industrial killing complex run by the SS. It became its own economy and an integral part of Germany's war effort since it provided slave labor for the war; it was also a vast thieving operation, stealing the goods brought by the Jews to the camps. The camp system was, in the words of Nikolaus Wachsmann, "a transformer of values" (Wachsmann 2015, 626). As such, the camp system was central to the world the Axis was bringing into being and part of fascism's crusade on the Eastern Front.

The Fascist Crusade

The Nazi campaign on the Eastern Front almost immediately became a crusade that involved other Axis states and fascist sympathizers. The war was promoted as one of defense against the Judeo-Bolshevik hordes on which the fate of the West depended. To be sure, the Germans were always more concerned about immediate war needs and tended to downplay the crusade analogy. Still, it proved useful in persuading its allies to commit to the war against the Soviet Union (Hanebrink 2018). Such was the power of this view, that, after the war, the Eastern Front became a kind of "lost cause" mythology that would prove influential during the Cold War (Smelser and Davies II).

The Axis allies who sent troops to the Eastern Front were similarly motivated by a mixture of territorial and ideological ambitions. Romania, for example, wanted Bessarabia and Bukovina back. In Italy, ideology clearly played a role, as it had little to gain from Operation Barbarossa. Mussolini's petition to Hitler to join the campaign claimed that Italian fascists were longing to fight Judeo-Bolshevism (Bosworth 2004).

The crusade analogy proved especially persuasive among the Spanish volunteers in the Blue Division. The "euphoria" of the war against the Soviet Union emboldened the Falange Party in Spain, as Franco insisted a force be sent to the Eastern Front (Payne 1995). In a speech to the National Council of the Falange in July 1941, Franco declared that Barbarossa was the "battle which Europe and Christianity have for so many years awaited" (Trythall 1970, 179). Even though Franco had resisted Hitler's advances to officially join the Axis, the possibility of fighting a Spanish Civil War redux against fascism's ideological opponents proved irresistible to the Falange, and Franco approved the sending of the Blue Division. By 1943, when the canny Franco withdrew the division, some twenty thousand Spaniards had fought on the Eastern Front. Some volunteers remained and fought to the bitter end in Berlin. A recent study on the Blue Division has argued that these volunteers' motives were varied—some simply desired adventure, others, money (Núñez Seixas 2022). Most joined, however, because of a sense of ideological mission and a belief that the future of European Civilization was at stake.

Those who volunteered for the *Waffen-SS* were similarly spurred on by a crusading spirit. The military arm of the SS originated in 1934 when a paramilitary branch of Hitler's bodyguard was formed. In 1939, this unit merged with the Deaths' Head units to become the *Waffen-SS*. The so-called "fourth branch of the Wehrmacht" was immediately pressed into service during the invasion of Poland (Stein 1966, 27–8). Despite the strict racial requirements for membership in the SS, the decision was made in 1940 to create volunteer units from other nations. Beginning with Danes, Norwegians, and Finns in 1940, membership was eventually opened to volunteers from over twenty countries, including auxiliary groups from the Soviet Union. By the end of the war, the *Waffen-SS* had some twenty-five divisions of foreign volunteers. They were named in a way that linked the Third Reich to national historical traditions. For example, one division of French volunteers was named after Charlemagne. The Scandinavian units were called Viking divisions, and one of the Belgian divisions was named after Langemarck, the Flemish town that contained a large German military cemetery from the First World War.

Like the Blue Divisions, the reasons foreign volunteers had for joining the SS varied. Early studies dismissed them as criminals, misfits, and outsiders in their own countries. A recent study, however, which focuses on volunteers from Denmark, Switzerland, and Sweden, suggests that many who joined the officer corps were well integrated in their societies and often came from professional backgrounds (Gutmann 2013). What motivated them to join the *Waffen-SS* was not only a sense of adventure, but also a pan-European ideal and a sympathy for fascism. Moreover, the voluntarism of the *Waffen-SS* members was driven by the political soldier idea that traced its heritage back to the French Revolution and to the "myth of the war experience" that fed into the origins of Nazism and Italian Fascism (Mosse 1991). In some ways, the *Waffen-SS* foreign divisions can be seen as a development of the International Fascism of CAUR in the 1930s. While there were obvious differences in the makeup and purpose of these organizations, they both point to a fascist and pan-European, transnational identity that Mussolini attempted to foster in the 1930s. While not all the five hundred thousand or so volunteers could be characterized as pan-Europeanists, or even Nazi sympathizers, the divisions contributed to the belief that fascism could realize the transnational ideal as envisioned before the war and become a myth that could outlive the Second World War—as proven by postwar neofascists who found inspiration in the *Waffen-SS*. If nothing else, the volunteers demonstrated that the Nazi conquests had the power to attract non-Germans, as seen in the overlap between the *Waffen-SS* and the various political fascisms that came to the fore during the war.

Fascism and the Nazi Empire

The quick successes of the Nazi armies and the subjection of much of Europe to Hitler's empire not only inspired individuals to join the crusade on the Eastern Front, but it also opened the door for fascist movements to finally come to power in their respective countries. Outside of Nazi Germany and Fascist Italy, fascist movements had not been able to take over any other European power. In short, interwar fascism was a failure (R. Paxton 2004, 73–6). To be sure, the Second World War did not prove universal fascism a success. The record is decidedly mixed. As Paxton has demonstrated, conservative authoritarians would often use fascist movements—but just as quickly discard them when they were no longer needed. Moreover, the Nazis were not always enthusiastic about lifting fascist movements into power and would often work with more conservative elites to rule their empire. Ultimately, the Germans put their own imperial interests first when it came to governing the conquered countries—and this meant keeping them in line (Mazower 2009).

Attempts by radical right leaders to get involved in governance were curtailed by the Nazis, who did not trust the more radical fascists to hold power. A case in point was the Norwegian Nazi Vidkun Quisling, who was used and then quickly eliminated by the Hitler regime when he proved to be massively unpopular with the Norwegians, though his party, the *Nasjonal Samling* (NS) retained representation on the state council that governed Nazi-occupied Norway. In Hungary, Hitler was content to work with Admiral Horthy rather than the Arrow Cross. In Romania, Hitler developed a strong relationship with Marshal Ion Antonescu and sided with the marshal when he came into conflict with the Iron Guard. In France, the Nazis preferred Marshal Pétain and Pierre Laval to govern Vichy rather than the myriads of French fascists who came out of the woodwork with the German victory in 1940.

On the face of it, fascists did not necessarily enjoy access to power in the wake of the Nazi armies. However, as the war dragged on, the radicalization of Nazi policies—especially with respect to the Final Solution—opened the door to the radical right. In 1942, Quisling was restored to power, while French fascists like Marcel Déat found their way into power after the Germans occupied Vichy. In 1944, with the Soviets advancing on the Eastern Front, the Germans occupied Hungary and immediately started the deportation of Hungarian Jews to Auschwitz. That summer, Horthy opened secret negotiations with the Allies. When the Germans caught wind of this, Horthy was deposed and replaced by Ferenc Szálasi, the Arrow Cross leader. In the short time the Arrow Cross was in power, it instituted a reign of terror in Budapest, hunting out Jews, murdering them, and dumping their bodies in the Danube River. Tens of thousands of others were sent on death marches to Austria.

The *Ustaše* in Croatia

The success of fascist movements in Europe during the Second World War was mixed and depended on the good graces of the Nazi regime. In Croatia, though, a powerful fascist movement came to power in the wake of the German invasion of Yugoslavia in 1941. A key role in this development was played by the Italian fascists. Mussolini had sent a military detachment to take part in the German invasion in May. The Italians jumped off from Istria and moved into Dalmatia and Slovenia. They had a hand in installing Ante Pavelić as the ruler of the Independent Croatian State (NDH). Pavelić, a longtime Croatian nationalist, had spent years in exile in Fascist Italy after being tried *in absentia* by the Yugoslavian state for terrorist activities. While in Italy, Pavelić founded the *Ustaše* ("Intransigents") movement. Not surprisingly, the new regime imitated Fascist Italy's corporate model, at least in theory. The peasantry, meanwhile, were called the "foundation and source of all life" (Hoare 2009, 422). Furthermore, a strong cult of personality around Pavelić—and a willingness to carry out extreme violence against his opponents—made the *Ustaše* a firmly fascist movement.

Violence and antisemitism were, like nearly every fascist movement, two key planks of the new movement, not to mention a hatred of Serbs. Once in power, Pavelić began a campaign of terror against his enemies that even shocked the Nazis (R. Paxton 2004, 113–14). Without being told, the Pavelić regime immediately began to round up Jews and placed them in concentration camps The Jews were joined by Serbs, Roma, and other minorities and political opponents where tens of thousands were murdered between 1941 and 1945. These were only a part of the hundreds of thousands killed by the regime during the war. The most notorious of these camps was at Jasenovac and was run by a Franciscan friar, Miroslav Filipović.

The involvement of a Franciscan friar in the killing apparatus of the *Ustaše* indicates the involvement of the Catholic clergy in Croatian fascism. Catholic mysticism played a role in some of the fascist imagination; we saw this in Hungary and in the Romanian Legion of the Archangel Michael. Clerical fascism could also be seen clearly in the Slovakian regime of Jozef Tiso and in the Hlinka Movement. In Croatia, the *Ustaše* was welcomed by the Catholic hierarchy, including the Archbishop of Zagreb, Alojzije Stepinac, and was recognized by the Vatican. However, the *Ustaše* policy of forced conversions caused friction between the Church and the new regime before too long (Biondich 2005, 82). In the case of Croatia, Catholicism was not considered an end in itself but a vehicle for destroying Serbian identity since the Serbs were closely associated with Orthodox Christianity (Biondich 2005, 113). The brutality of the *Ustaše* regime and its sadistic leader showed that the war opened space for indigenous fascist movements to emerge within the Nazi sphere of influence. Thanks to the war, the *Ustaše* could attempt to make the fantasy of an independent Croatian state come alive.

The war cannot be said to have allowed European fascism to flourish, however, since these movements were often divided. For example, in Belgium, competing fascist movements reflected the ethnic Flemish and Walloon divide of the country. In other countries, the Nazis simply did not trust fascist parties to govern. In Romania, for instance, the Iron Guard was placed under the authority of the military general Antonescu; however, the Guard was quickly discarded when it tried to overthrow Antonescu in 1941. Clearly, the Germans preferred more conservative, traditional elites where possible, desiring, as they did, stability and predictability. Movements like the Iron Guard proved too unruly for the Nazis' tastes. However, this should not lead us to conclude that these fascisms had little impact—far from it. As seen in Hungary and Croatia, as the war progressed, more radical measures were taken that reflected the visions of the radical right. Even though Antonescu suppressed the Iron Guard, that did not prevent bloody pogroms in Bessarabia, Bukovina, and Ukraine carried out by Romanian troops fighting alongside the Germans. What the course of the war demonstrated—with respect to fascism, at least—is that the radical right increasingly came to the fore. Some more traditional elites either split with them or combined with the fascists in the process known as "parafascism," discussed earlier in the book. This process of radicalization developed clearly in France and Italy. In the case of the former, conservatives began a National Revolution that increasingly moved them closer to fascism; in the latter, the deposing of Mussolini in 1943 led to the creation of a "back to origins" fascism in the form of the Italian Social Republic.

Vichy France

The fantasy of a national revolution—made possible by the Nazi conquests—nearly became a reality in France. Vichy France, the collaborationist regime set up after the French fell to Germany in 1940, is rarely viewed as a fascist state by historians (Tumblety 2009, 520). Vichy was not established by the Germans but by the outgoing Third Republic when it voted to give Philippe Pétain, the so-called Hero of Verdun, full powers as President and Prime Minister. Not long after, Pierre Laval became Prime Minister of Vichy. A former socialist who then became an independent member of the National Assembly, first served as Prime Minister of the Third Republic in 1935, during which his most significant achievement was the signing of the Franco-Soviet Pact. He also helped broker the Stresa Front against Nazi Germany. None of these suggested that Laval would become a Nazi collaborator or even a fascist after 1940. As for Pétain, though he was connected to some far-right groups, he was seen as someone defending French interests in the face of German demands. His status as a hero of the First World War seemed to suggest that he would never be a German puppet.

All this strongly suggested that Vichy was going to be a "shield" aimed at resisting German demands. The famous "shield theory" became popular with Pétain's defenders after the war. The early historiography of the Vichy period, dominated by Raymond Aron's famous book, argued that any atrocities committed under Vichy were either carried out by the Germans or under heavy duress from the Nazis. Aron's work had become a kind of orthodoxy until the groundbreaking work of Robert Paxton, who argued in 1972 that Vichy was not pressured by the Germans to adopt anti-Jewish legislation in 1940 (R. O. Paxton 1972). While the Vichy regime may have kept some fascists at arm's length— like Jacques Doriot and his *Parti Populaire Français*—and refused to create a one-party state, its policies and actions could be traced back to the far-right ideologies that had percolated in France since at least the 1930s. The backlash against the Popular Front, the events of February 6, 1934, and the accusations against the Third Republic as decadent found expression in Vichy. Similarly, the Vichy regime did not need much arm twisting when deporting Jews to their deaths (Marrus and Paxton 2019).

The impact of the Paxton thesis was augmented by the controversy surrounding Marcel Ophuls's documentary, *The Sorrow and the Pity*. Released in 1969, the documentary was banned in France until 1981, since the film suggested a much higher degree of collaboration and even indifference toward German occupation. One of the most striking parts of the film is an interview with the aristocratic Christian de La Mazière, a supporter of Vichy who joined the Charlemagne Division of the *Waffen-SS*. De La Mazière expressed concisely the reasons why someone like him would join the Nazi cause, noting especially the events of February 6 and the rise of the Popular Front. These events demonstrated the weakness and the decadence of the Third Republic. He noted that Pétain expressed the "subconscious" feelings of many Frenchmen when he scapegoated the "democratic politicians" and a "certain kind of alien shop owner— shady, foreign, cosmopolitan; and of course, the Communist Party, which was the cause of all misfortunes" (Hoffmann 1972, 53–4). De La Mazière's comments reflected the conservative authoritarian basis for Vichy and its hatred of liberal democracy; his decision to join the *Waffen-SS*, however, brought out a more overtly fascist sentiment. He said he was attracted to the *Waffen-SS* after their triumphant successes early in the war. "I must say that the German Army at that time made a great impression on young people," he told Ophuls, "the sight of those German soldiers, stripped to the waist ... For the first time we saw an army which was all we had dreamed ours might be" (Hoffmann 1972, 49–50).

De La Mazière's comments in *Sorrow and the Pity* captured the essence of the Vichy Regime. It was a regime that both channeled a traditional, authoritarian hatred of liberal democracy—especially the republican tradition going back to the French Revolution— and the desire to build a reborn, dynamic France that would contribute to the Nazi New Order. These visions were embodied in Vichy's National Revolution. Julian Jackson, in his authoritative history of Vichy, has demonstrated that this collaborationism was fueled by different motives that ranged from "fanaticism, opportunism, and fanaticism" (Jackson 2001, 190). To be sure, it is impossible to isolate one common motive for the myriad of individual stories that drove people to collaborate (or resist) the German occupation. While collaboration was often presented as a shield, or a necessary evil, to prevent France from suffering more harm, most were enchanted by the idea of a remade France by collaborators, whether it be those who stayed in Paris or those who worked for Vichy (Figure 10.2).

The Parisian collaborators, those who chose to remain in the capital and under direct German occupation up until 1942, were the most obviously fascist. These included individuals like Jacques Doriot, Marcel Déat, and Eugène Deloncle, all figures from the prewar far right who tended to dislike the more "moderate" tone in Vichy. This collection of "fanatics, criminals, and adventurers" were kept at arm's length by the more conservative atmosphere of the Pétainists, but as Paxton, Jackson, and others have argued, this should not be overstated. When the Germans occupied the entirety of France in 1942 following the Allied invasion of North Africa, the Vichy regime stayed in place, but it opened the door to some of these more radical figures. Yet, before 1942, the Vichy regime had instituted antisemitic laws without pressure from the Germans and had helped round up thousands of (mostly foreign) Jews in the summer of 1942. They were then shipped east. These actions made it difficult to distinguish the "conservative" Vichyites from the fanatical fascists in Paris.

Figure 10.2 *Waffen-SS* recruitment poster for the Charlemagne Division in France. Credit: Getty Images.

The Second World War: Fascism's Playground

Besides the Jewish Codes of 1940, there was much else to suggest that the Vichy regime had taken on parafascist ideals and forms in the pursuit of its National Revolution. These included the cult of personality developed around Pétain, the creation of a police state, and the propaganda of a National Revolution that promised to turn back the clock on French history by eliminating all traces of the French Revolution, the great dream of French fascists from Maurras to De La Rocque. Not all collaborators were enthusiastic about the National Revolution (Laval) and not all adherents of the revolution supported collaboration (Weygand), but it is true that the German victory in 1940 made the revolution possible (Jackson 2001, 139–41). In its attempt to start the National Revolution, Vichy revealed its fascist pedigree.

The cult of personality which developed around Marshal Pétain proved to be the cement that held Vichy together. Vichy propaganda made liberal use of the marshal's image, claiming he embodied France's aspirations. That his legend was stoked by the fight against German aggression in the First World War helped frame him as the man who would once again defend the French against German demands during the Second World War. This shield theory was revived after the war when the marshal stood trial for collaboration. To be sure, this idea of Pétain as shield was promoted during the war, but so too was the idea that the old marshal would help France rediscover its true self. Although Pétain tried to present himself as someone who was above politics (in the Bonapartist tradition), his connections to far-right groups before the war were well known. Furthermore, he consistently presented himself in military uniform and became known as the savior of his country, a figure who embodied France like no other. One poster asked anyone who doubted this: "Are you more French than him?" Defenders of Pétain will point to the fact that he refused to create a one-party state and that he consistently relied on figures like Laval for governing Vichy. Still, the aura constructed around the person of Pétain and the way it was communicated borrowed heavily from similar practices in Nazi Germany and Fascist Italy.

While Vichy never became a one-party state, it did implement a police state that closely resembled that of its German masters. Through this police apparatus Vichy not only aided the Germans but also practiced the daily violence that characterizes all fascist regimes. The Germans did not have enough personnel to keep France under control and to carry out its Final Solution. They needed the French police—and they found, in Vichy, willing collaborators. Judges, prefects, and police commissioners working under the auspices of the Vichy regime, including in the occupied zone before 1942, helped keep order. Much of this became known in the various trials of the 1990s, when the roles of figures like René Bousquet, Maurice Papon, and others in the war became clear.

It was claimed that some of these figures were not fascist but simply collaborators doing their duties as *fonctionnaires* in the Vichy bureaucracy. Such an excuse cannot be made for Joseph Darnand, however. In January 1943, two months after the Germans occupied Vichy, Pierre Laval tapped Darnand to create a state militia known as the *Milice*. Anxious to eliminate his rivals on the far right (like Jacques Doriot), Laval decided to appoint a man who was even further to the right. In many ways, Joseph Darnand was the prototypical fascist man. Of working-class origins, not highly educated, Darnand found his calling in the trenches of the First World War, where he became a decorated war hero. Like many fascists who had been war veterans, Darnand found it difficult to adjust to peacetime and eventually gravitated to extreme right politics, where he became an inveterate opponent of the Third Republic and everything it stood for. His prewar activism found him participating in many of the different groups that made up the far right. He joined the *Action Française* and the *Camelots du Roi* until he was expelled for criticizing Charles Maurras, whom he accused of being too soft. After a brief flirtation with the Croix de Feu, he eventually joined Doriot's PPF and served in the *Cagoule*.

It was in Deloncle's *Cagoule* that Darnand felt most at home, given its emphasis on action and terror. When the Second World War broke out, Darnand served in the French Army again. He had little sympathy for the Germans, preferred Italian fascism, and was fiercely loyal to Pétain. However, this changed in 1941 with the German invasion of the Soviet Union, which Darnand viewed as a crusade against Bolshevism. In January 1942, Darnand organized a group of far-right war veterans into the *Service d'ordre Légionnaire* (SOL) to fight the Resistance. The SOL was the basis for the *Milice*, which Darnand put together in January 1943 at the request of Laval. While Laval viewed the *Milice* as nothing more than a police force, Darnand aimed to make it the basis of a political movement. He imitated the Romanian Legion of the Archangel Michael, a chivalric elite sworn to fight Bolshevism, Freemasonry, and the Jews (Jackson 2001, 230–1). The *Milice* would eventually grow to a force of twenty-five to thirty thousand men engaged in a war against the French Resistance. Its members joined for various reasons, most often to avoid being conscripted to Germany as labor. Still, the movement retained a strong ideological character that recalled the paramilitary forces of interwar fascism. While they helped Germans keep order in France, they also espoused the values of Vichy's National Revolution.

Vichy's National Revolution was a fantasy. It aimed at restoring a pure France, devoid of foreigners, Jews, Freemasons, and anything to do with the heritage of the French Revolution. This had long been the dream that characterized protofascists and interwar fascists. It also allowed these groups to connect with traditionalists, Catholic integralists, and other more conservative elements who had come together in February 1934 and then again in opposition to the Popular Front in the late 1930s. As soon as the Pétain regime was installed in 1940, the French slogan—"Liberty, Equality, and Fraternity"—was replaced by "Fatherland, Family, and Work." Vichy propaganda associated the slogans of the French Revolution with everything that had undermined traditional France, such as international capitalism, individualism, and socialism. All of these were promoted by anti-national groups like Jews and Freemasons. They were also associated with abominations, like urbanism and secularism.

On the surface, the ideals that replaced the French Revolution did not seem fascist; they would, though, be formulated in a way that appealed to both traditionalists and fascists. Under Vichy, France would return to an ideology of the soil, similar in some ways to the *völkisch* ideals of the Nazis but found in French protofascist movements like the *Action Française*. Furthermore, Vichy and its bureaucracy of technocrats, known as *la synerchie*, aimed at reorganizing the French economy along the lines of the corporatism espoused by Mussolini, but also according to the social encyclicals of the Catholic Church. The new France was to be a country of artisans and peasants, and Pétain was often portrayed as the "marshal-peasant" of the country, as Mussolini was portrayed as Italy's first farmer (Jackson 2001, 149).

The Second World War thus provided the opportunity for those on the French far right to build the France they longed for. Although there was rivalry between the different fascist groups, with tensions between traditionalists, conservatives, and fascists, all these groups found common cause under the banner of the National Revolution and in the person of Pétain. Several intellectuals found something in Vichy they could support. French fascism's "trinity" of literary figures, Robert Brasillach, Drieu la Rochelle, and Louis-Ferdinand Céline, despite their differences and vacillations, came to identify with the National Revolution. In 1941, both Brasillach and Drieu represented France at a writer's conference in Weimar, where they were impressed by Nazi Germany. Brasillach was the editor of *Je Suis Partout*, a literary journal that supported collaboration with the Germans. Like many others, Brasillach's original hesitation about the Germans was eventually overcome by their success in the war and the crusade against Bolshevism. Similarly, Drieu remained loyal to Vichy and the Germans despite his eventual disillusionment. Céline followed the Vichy government-in-exile to the bitter end of the war. All three men—along with many other literary and cultural figures—believed in both the National Revolution and in the New Order the Germans were building; they would contribute to the myth of Vichy among neofascists after the war.

The Italian Social Republic: Return to Origins

Mussolini's Italian Social Republic (RSI) was a collaborationist state that emerged from the circumstances of the Second World War. Italy was the home of fascism, of course, but the regime founded by Mussolini in 1922 abruptly came to an end in July 1943 after the dictator was deposed by his own Grand Council and subsequently arrested by Victor Emmanuel III. Mussolini's downfall was caused by failures in the war and massive supply shortages at home. When, in July 1943, the Allies landed in Sicily and Rome was bombed for the first time, the desperation within Italy's war effort became clear. It was a group of fascists—including Mussolini's son-in-law, Galeazzo Ciano—who moved that Mussolini should be removed from leadership. After his arrest, Mussolini was imprisoned on a mountaintop retreat in the Apennine Mountains, while power was given to Pietro Badoglio, a former military leader who Mussolini had fired in 1940. On September 8, 1943, the Badoglio government surrendered to the Allies, making Italy the first Axis power to fall in the war.

Days after the surrender, German forces flooded into Italy, while the king and Badoglio set up their government in the south in the area occupied by the Allies. In a daring action, German special forces, led by Otto Skorzeny, rescued Mussolini from his prison and brought him to Germany. There, Mussolini was greeted by a small group of pro-German fascists, led by Roberto Farinacci, his old rival and intransigent from the

1920s. The group also included the ex-priest and rabid antisemite, Giovanni Preziosi, former *Balilla* leader Renato Ricci, and former Minister of Popular Culture, Alessandro Pavolini, who was destined to become the most powerful figure after Mussolini in the new collaborationist regime Hitler planned to set up. These men became the nucleus of the collaborationist state Mussolini governed from September 1943 to April 1945.

The RSI, commonly referred to as the Republic of Salò, named after the town on Lake Garda that became the new regime's capital, was carved out in northern Italy. It governed the territory occupied by the Germans, save for some areas incorporated directly into the Reich. In total, the new state boasted a population of around twelve million people and a military of some four hundred thousand men, most of whom had been captured by the Germans when Italy surrendered (Morgan 2007, 165–6). The newly constituted fascist party, under the leadership of Pavolini, claimed nearly four hundred ninety thousand adherents, while the renamed fascist militia, the *Guardia Nazionale Repubblicana* (GNR), led by Ricci, had one hundred thousand men. Despite the numbers, Salò, like Vichy, was completely dependent on the Germans for its existence and for its survival. Like Vichy, however, its leaders saw this as an opportunity to rebuild the country, this time on pure fascist lines uncontaminated by compromise with the Italian monarchy and its institutions. It was this fantasy that engaged the delegates to a congress in Verona in November 1943 to hash out the goals and the character of this new state.

The Congress of Verona aimed at recreating the fascist state on a "back to origins" platform. Mussolini expressed a desire to bring fascism back to its radical, syndicalist days of 1919–21, when it called for a republic with a social program aimed at drawing workers away from communism. The manifesto produced at Verona was made up of eighteen points, calling for a plebiscitary regime in which the leader would be acclaimed by the people every five years. The manifesto included some elements of democracy such as an elected assembly and even workers councils in industry. The head of government, however, maintained total control over ministerial appointments. The state would control armaments industries, but private property was respected. The Catholic faith was respected as the true faith, but other faiths would be allowed if they did not threaten Catholicism. A corporate economy was to be established in which technicians and workers would cooperate and some degree of profit sharing would be practiced. Furthermore, unions would come under the umbrella of one general union. Public housing was to be constructed, and workers were given the opportunity to one day own their homes.

These left-of-center policies, harking back to the syndicalist origins of the early movement, were counterbalanced by continuity in foreign policy, which called for the protection of Italy's natural borders, and the search for *spazio vitale* (living space), along with colonialism in Africa. Article seven was devoted entirely to the Jews, who were defined as "foreigners" and as an enemy nation in the current war. Article 5 defined a pure fascist party. Echoing the definitional wars of the 1920s, when fascists debated whether the party should be made up of a select group of true believers or opened to the masses, the new Republican Fascist Party called for a party made up exclusively of "fighters and believers." Attempting to distance fascism from the compromises of the *Ventennio*, party membership was not required to get jobs.

The Second World War: Fascism's Playground

The manifesto was thus a mixture of elements from left and right, typical of the fascist movements of the interwar era and reflective of the group of people around Mussolini. The social elements were largely influenced by Nicola Bombacci, a one-time communist, while the more right-wing elements were inspired by Pavolini (Deakin 1962, 625). Thrown in, too, were elements of the Axis New Order mixed in with Mazzinian principles; these included bringing down Anglo-American plutocracies and creating a federal European Community in their stead. However, as with all fascist manifestos, such as those from 1919 to 1921, the fascist character of the new state was found not so much on paper as in practice.

It was on the ground, in the final months of the Second World War, that republican fascism's true character was on display. Salò was a regime based on brute violence, revenge, and civil war. Much of Salò was designed to exact revenge on the traitors of July 25, 1943. In January 1944, in the same place where the Verona Congress was held, in the ballroom of the Castelvecchio Palace, the six members of the Fascist Grand Council who had voted for the deposing of Mussolini were brought to trial. The most famous defendant was Mussolini's son-in-law, Ciano. In a trial whose outcome was clear from the beginning, Ciano and the others (with one exception) were condemned to death and shot the day after their conviction. The executions did not simply exact revenge. In the case of Ciano, they also demonstrated that the new fascism of the republic was not like the regime that had preceded it. Richard Bosworth has pointed out that Ciano's upper-middle-class lifestyle did not jive with the proletarian ethic Mussolini was attempting to build at Salò. This new regime was no longer bourgeois—it was, instead, a "switch towards the purity, efficiency, dedication, fanaticism, and blood lust of the Nazis" (Bosworth 2004, 515).

Even before the Congress of Verona drafted its manifesto, special tribunals, like those created in 1926, had been set up throughout the territory. However, much of the reckoning would happen outside these courts in the streets and towns of northern Italy. Alongside the militia of Ricci, there existed a group of freelance gangs reminiscent of the *Freikorps* in postwar Germany who took it upon themselves to hunt out partisans and political enemies in the territory controlled by Salò. These brigades, like the one named after fascist martyr Ettore Muti, or the group of paramilitaries organized by Junio Valerio Borghese called *Decima Mas*, terrorized communities suspected of harboring partisans thought to have killed fascists. One poster in the Veneto promised "terror and blood" to anyone who "at any time help[s] (the partisans) in even the smallest way, even if only putting them up, or only keeping quiet about their whereabouts" (Morgan 2007, 176–7).

Not to be outdone by these quasi-official groups, Pavolini created his own militia called the Black Brigades in 1944. Although the Black Brigades modeled themselves on the Blackshirts of the 1920s (often being led by now middle-aged veterans of those groups), the ferocity of their violence often made those earlier crimes seem tame by comparison. Gone was the *olio di ricino* (castor oil) and the club. Submachine guns were now the order of the day. Like their Nazi masters, the Black Brigades would leave the bodies of their enemies exposed for days in public spaces as a warning to others. This kind of violence began with the regime itself. Indeed, the Congress of Verona was interrupted so that fascists could travel to Ferrara to exact revenge for the assassination of a local fascist. In a scene that was later made into a film, eleven men were executed in front of the Este Castle and their bodies left there until the next day. In August 1944, fifteen partisans were shot by the Muti Brigade and dumped in Milan's Piazzale Loreto and left there for a day. Sadism and torture, meanwhile, were practiced by other such groups, like the group around Pietro Koch. The so-called Banda Koch plied their trade in Rome, Florence, and Milan. In various villas in these cities, Koch and his men set up torture chambers where they killed hundreds of people. Koch's brutality was such that Mussolini finally ordered his arrest in late 1944. The Koch Gang, like other gangs working for the RSI, gladly participated in the roundup of Italian Jews as well.

The motivations of those who served in these groups varied, as elsewhere in Nazi-dominated Europe. Some were motivated by self-interest, others by opportunism, crime, sadism, and ideological fervor. Bosworth has argued that these men were ultimately "thugs" driven by crime and violence and that not many were interested in any "political religion" (Bosworth 2004, 525). These motives were not mutually exclusive, however. Fascism, in all its contradictions, easily combined thuggery with idealism—and the fascism seen in Salò was a good example of what fantasy in politics could do. In their brutality, the RSI gangs were manifesting fascist dreams of purging and purification. Their collaboration with the Nazis was not just out of convenience but reflected a desire to create the New Europe claimed by the Axis. Philip Morgan has argued that these fascists were not interested in creating a mass consensus, unlike the previous fascist regime, but lived in small communities where they imagined themselves besieged by enemies and where they had to be the instruments of vengeance on an ungrateful nation. The republican fascists invoked a "civil war mentality" at the center of which was an imagined nation "peopled not by the living Italians around them, but by the dead, the fallen comrades of the Fascist and Axis war" (Morgan 2007, 177). The dream of the Rome–Berlin Axis inspired some, like the future historian Roberto Vivarelli, a committed fascist angered by the surrender of September 8 and inspired by the radio broadcasts of Alessandro Pavolini, to enroll in the Black Brigades (Duggan 2013).

Conclusion

On March 1, 1945, Benito Mussolini made his final visit to Gabriele D'Annunzio's Vittoriale on the shores of Lake Garda. The estate, declared a national monument by Mussolini in the 1920s, was only a few miles from Mussolini's residence at Gargnano and near the capital of the Italian Social Republic at Salò. The visit was to commemorate the seventh anniversary of the poet-soldier's death, and it was the first visit by Mussolini since D'Annunzio's funeral. Up until this moment, D'Annunzio had become a somewhat forgotten figure in Fascist Italy; however, as the war worsened for the Axis, and the Allies stood poised to cross the Rhine in Germany and advance onto the Po River Valley, the time had come to recall the hero of fascism's origins (even though D'Annunzio had never officially joined the Fascist Party). Remembering the poet who had taken Fiume with his

The Second World War: Fascism's Playground

legionnaires after the First World War suited Mussolini's desire to return fascism to its origins. D'Annunzio had been the prototype of the fascist style—a style Mussolini had copied.

When he arrived at the Vittoriale, Mussolini was greeted by Pavolini and several other ministers in his republican regime. In the courtyard of the main house, Mussolini reviewed troops from the Black Brigades and the *Decima Mas* units. These were men who were on the front lines, combating the Italian partisans. They had committed some of the most brutal acts of violence seen in the war. After paying his respects at D'Annunzio's tomb, Mussolini made his way to the newly constructed mausoleum, where D'Annunzio and several of his legionnaires were ultimately laid to rest. Located on the highest point of the property, this mausoleum could be seen from a distance overlooking the lake. At this spot, Mussolini was joined by the Japanese ambassador to Salò, Hatsuo Hidaka, and the German plenipotentiary Rudolf Rahn, making this the last time in the Second World War that representatives from the three main Axis powers stood together. There, Mussolini gave one of the last speeches of his career.

In his short address, Mussolini invoked the spirit of D'Annunzio, claiming the poet was not dead but very much alive in the hearts of true fascists and that his spirit would oversee the rebirth of Italy. Furthermore, D'Annunzio would have supported the republic had he witnessed the actions of the traitor-king, and Mussolini reminded his audience that it was D'Annunzio who wanted to lead a March on Rome in 1920 to overthrow the monarchy. Mussolini, who had always had a diffident relationship with D'Annunzio when he was alive, now celebrated the poet as the precursor to Salò.

For the small crowd listening to him on that cold March day, it was easy to connect the memory of D'Annunzio with the Italian Social Republic due to the geography. Gardone Riviera, where the Vittoriale was situated, was almost in the center of Mussolini's collaborationist regime. The idyllic location also came to symbolize the Italian German Axis. Many of the villas in and around Gardone, now used by the officials of Salò and the Germans, were built by and for wealthy Germans as holiday retreats. The Vittoriale had once been Villa Cargnacco. It was previously owned by the German art historian Henry Thode, whose ideas on art had laid the groundwork for Hitler's views on Degenerate Art. Thode had also been married to the stepdaughter of Richard Wagner (Hughes-Hallett 2013, 483). Down the hill from the Vittoriale on the shoreline road was the Villa Alba, a neoclassical, Palladian structure, designed by a German architect as a summer retreat for the Emperor of Austria. This building, known as the Acropolis of Gardone, even had a series of caryatid statues like those found on the real Acropolis in Athens. Across the road from the Villa Alba, which now served as a radio and transmission center used by the Germans, was the Torre San Marco. This structure was built by a wealthy German industrialist in the neogothic style and purchased by D'Annunzio, who changed it to a Venetian style building. In this tower, Mussolini would have his romantic trysts with Claretta Petacci, his mistress who would die with him in April. Petacci was living in the Villa Fiordaliso next to the tower.

Up the road from Gardone Rivera was Gargnano, where Mussolini lived with his wife Rachele. Contrary to the villas around Gardone, Mussolini lived in a villa built by the Italian industrialist Feltrinelli. A neogothic structure built in the 1890s, the house resembled a medieval castle, complete with a turreted tower and situated right on the lake. This gaudy castle was Mussolini's "gilded cage" from October 1943 to April 1945. Surrounded day and night by SS officers, Mussolini reigned over a fantasy world far removed from the war swirling around him. Both he and his entourage engaged in political and romantic intrigues in a style that D'Annunzio, the decadent poet and seducer, would have recognized. Like D'Annunzio's final years, the Republic of Salò played itself out in an atmosphere of illusion and fantasy, on a site where Germans and Italians met and continued to believe in their New Order. All around them, however, the fascist dream was crumbling and Mussolini, in a last-ditch effort to escape to Switzerland, comically dressed in a German uniform, was caught and executed on the shores of Lake Como, another resort area.

While Mussolini was visiting the Vittoriale, Hitler was already in the bunker deep under the Reich Chancellery building in Berlin, one of the few monolithic structures built by Albert Speer for the future Germania. Made up of two levels, the bunker was reached via a stairwell in the gardens. Hitler had moved into the bunker in January, and there he would remain until he took his own life on April 30. While, architecturally, the bunker had nothing in common with the opulent surroundings of Salò, the bunker allowed Hitler to live in the same dreamworld as Mussolini. In these dark, air-conditioned rooms 28 feet (8.5 meters) below the ground, Hitler could fantasize about the great cities that he would build once the war was over. He spent a great deal of time studying the scale model of Linz, his hometown in Austria.

While Hitler dreamed of Linz, the Reich was collapsing around him. In April, the Red Army had crossed the Oder River and advanced into Berlin, where some vicious street-by-street fighting ensued. The previous month, Hitler had issued the Decree Concerning Demolitions on Reich Territory, otherwise known as the Nero Decree. This decree ordered that all infrastructure in the Reich had to be destroyed in a scorched-earth policy. Although it was never fully carried out, the decree clearly expressed the Darwinian belief at the heart of Nazism—specifically, that the stronger should always annihilate the weaker. It also demonstrated fascism's predilection for destruction. In the fascist mind, victory could also be achieved via destruction and self-immolation. This was the crux of Mussolini's oration at D'Annunzio's tomb, a poet who had also fantasized about creative destruction.

For the Nazis, defeat and destruction served fascist fantasy just as well as victory. When the German Sixth Army was defeated at Stalingrad, the Nazi regime publicized the defeat and marked it with several days of mourning, accompanied by the Adagio from Bruckner's Symphony Number 7, which played on a loop on state radio. As the Allies advanced into Germany from the west and the east, the Germans provided stiffer defense; the Nazis eventually drafted children and the elderly into their civilian defense corps. One of the last photographs of Hitler shows him reviewing a group of teenagers in uniform. The destruction that rained on Berlin and other German cities from Allied bombing only confirmed Hitler's view that he was living a Wagnerian fantasy. The cataclysmic war zone that was Central Europe in March and April of 1945 confirmed the Nazi worldview that a true rebirth (palingenesis) could only occur when the present world was destroyed. Joseph Goebbels expressed this often both in his diary and in public broadcasts toward the end. "Under the debris of our shattered cities," he wrote in 1945, "the last so-called achievements of the middle-class nineteenth century have been buried … Now that everything is in ruins, we are forced to rebuild Europe" (Eksteins 1989, 328–9). Near the end he wrote, "A world is going down but we all retain faith that a new world will arise from the ashes" (Eksteins 1989, 329).

The upshot of these statements is that the defeat of the Axis did not mean the failure of the fascist dream, nor did it mean its end. When the war finally ended in Europe with the surrender of Germany on May 7, 1945, the continent was in ruins, millions of refugees were left homeless, and millions of others had died. Fascism had delivered the most destructive human-made event in European history. After he was forced out of Fiume in 1920, D'Annunzio announced it as the "City of the Holocaust," implying that defeat was temporary and that a greater victory lay in the future. Furthermore, the fascist war drew in conservatives, radicals, and other fellow travelers into constructing the European New Order. The "National Socialist sphere of influence," according to a recent study, "refers to a cognitive sphere of discourse between National Socialists, fascists, and conservatives of an ethno-nationalist disposition who agreed on basic principles of this new European order" (Dafinger and Pohl 2019, 2). The Second World War can be seen as a grand project to actualize the fascist dream of a purified Europe, a New Order with a racial hierarchy and the elimination of the forces that had made the West decadent, such as Jews, communists, and Freemasons.

All of this was to be achieved in Palladian settings where a past culture of triumph and power could once again serve to rebirth the West. In the villas of Lake Garda, or the palaces of Central Europe, a fascist fantasy played out while the destruction they created reduced Europe to rubble. The image left by fascism in the Year Zero of 1945 was of a fever dream accompanied by classical music and opulent settings. The juxtaposition of beauty, culture, and death was found in the poetry and prose of Gabriele D'Annunzio long before fascism came into existence. It is he and his villa that thus serve to close out this final phase of historic, interwar fascism. Significantly, D'Annunzio was never actually a fascist, but he helped construct the fantasy that fueled the fascist imagination. He, like millions of others who never adhered to fascism or Nazism, made it possible and cooperated in a process in which myth would give rebirth to a New European Order. This myth, like the house on the shores of Lake Garda, would not die but lie dormant while the world faced a new, even more potentially catastrophic future during the Cold War. While Mussolini and Hitler were dead and their regimes destroyed, fascist fantasy remained and waited for an opportunity to rise again in Europe. In the meantime, surviving fascists looked for new shores.

CHAPTER 11
COLD WAR FASCISM

The Valley of the Fallen

It can be seen for miles around. It is a massive cross standing nearly five hundred feet high on a promontory that also rises nearly five hundred feet. Thirty-three miles northwest of Spain's capital, Madrid, in the Cuelgamuros Valley, lies a massive complex topped by the cross known as the Valle de los Caídos (Valley of the Fallen). Underneath this granite cross, bored into the mountain, is a church, declared a minor basilica in the late 1950s; on the other side of the mountain is a massive Benedictine Monastery. Its cavernous interior is dark, and its nave stretches for nine hundred feet (two thirds longer than St. Peter's Basilica) from its porticoed entrance to the sanctuary, behind which are interred over thirty thousand dead from the Spanish Civil War. Until 2019, two more illustrious bodies lay beneath the altar: the remains of Jose Antonio Primo de Rivera, the founder of Spain's Falange Party, and the body of General Francisco Franco, victor of the Civil War and dictator of Spain from 1939 to 1975 (Figure 11.1).

Franco's burial in the basilica is not surprising. The monument was his project, and he played a central role in its development when the first stone was laid in 1940 to its official inauguration in 1959 (Bueno 2014, 52). It was Franco who decided to move Primo de Rivera's body from its original resting place in the Escorial Palace to the Valle, days before the monument's inauguration. The movement of the body was accompanied by thousands of fellow Falangists, the Spanish fascist party that was the only party allowed to exist in Franco's Spain. The proximity of the two bodies was fitting, as they represented the changes that had occurred in Spain. In 1940, Franco's Spain was riding the wave of triumphant fascism in Europe. In 1959, Franco's Spain was a faithful partner of the West in the Cold War. The secret of the Valley is that it could represent both eras. What held them together was the crusade against communism, a feature that allowed regimes like that of Franco, but also like that of Salazar in Portugal, to make a seamless transition from the era of fascism to the postwar, pro-NATO era.

It is nothing more than a giant work of fantasy. The cross, the basilica, and the monastery make it a destination for Catholic pilgrims. It is a monument to Spanish Catholicism, and it echoes the sixteenth-century baroque palace of the Habsburgs, which similarly made a close identification between church, state, and the concept of *Hispanidad* (Bueno 2014, 77). The appeal to Catholicism makes the Valle a link between Spanish nationalism and anti-communism, a fact which expressed important values in the fascist and the post-fascist eras. It links Franco's regime to the Spanish Golden Age but also expresses the fight against communism in the Cold War. Furthermore, the monument claims to unite the dead from both sides of the Civil War, as the remains of

Figure 11.1 Francisco Franco's tomb under the altar in the monastery of the Valley of the Fallen. Franco's body was exhumed in 2019 and moved to a family plot in Madrid. Credit: Getty Images.

Nationalist and Republican fighters are interred in the basilica. It proclaims national unity, but in doing so, it creates further division. "By fusing both sides into one," argues Alex Bueno, "the monument thus presents the illusion of unity on the surface while in fact highlighting the disunity" (Bueno 2014, 99).

The Valle is all about illusion and masquerade. It appears as a colossal tribute to Catholicism, but it is really a monument to fascist fantasy. It proclaims national reconciliation, but much of the labor came from prisoners of war. The bodies of the Republican dead were moved without permission of the families. Moreover, these bodies are in a complex that is saturated with the rhetoric of crusade, with chapels dedicated to the military yet overseen by armed stone angels. José Antonio Primo de Rivera, himself a victim of the war, was given a place of honor under the altar because, in the words of Franco, he was the spiritual leader of the fallen (Bueno 2014, 94). Not surprisingly, the complex became a site of pilgrimage for Falangists who would congregate every year on the anniversary of Primo de Rivera's death in the cavernous surroundings of the basilica, a structure that echoed the monumental structures of Franco's Civil War allies, Nazi Germany and Fascist Italy. These acts of celebration were finally put to an end by a center-left government in 2007.

The defenders of the Valle de los Caídos argue that it represents the overcoming of the Spanish Civil War disputes and enshrines Spain's fight against communism in the Cold War. They also point out that it is primarily a religious site, not a political one. The Cold War context, however, served as a mask to hide the obvious fascist overtones of the complex. Since the end of the Cold War, Spanish governments have attempted to neutralize its fascist character. In 2019, Franco's body was exhumed. Four years later, it was De Rivera's turn. The monumental structures remain, as do the bodies of the fallen, although attempts are being made to exhume the bodies of Republicans who died at the hands of the Franco regime. This effort to dispel the fantasy of the valley is not without its critics. Despite this, no attempts are being made to destroy the complex, whose monumentality continues to dominate the landscape. It is a testament to the continuity of fascism long after the end of the Second World War. The valley is an excellent example of how fascism not only survived the war but developed into a new movement called neofascism. In the guise of fighting the Cold War against communism, old fascists continued to find a *raison d'etre* after 1945 and became the mentors for new generations of neofascists. Like Franco's monumental complex, fascism hid behind other political movements and institutions, and its ghosts stalked the West in disguise. In short, fascist fantasy became sublimated into the struggle between communism and democracy.

Cold War fascism, or neofascism, found expression after 1945 in several ways. It became a clandestine movement made up of fascists unwilling to give up the struggle of the Second World War. In Italy, many supporters of Mussolini's Republic of Salò formed a party, while in Germany former Nazis joined "brotherhoods" and other networks, waiting for a day when they could influence politics again. Others, mostly war criminals, went on the run, using the infamous Ratline networks that helped war criminals to escape to other continents. Some of these men became influential in Latin American and the Middle East as technical advisors to authoritarian regimes. In all cases, the Cold War provided the context that shaped these different groups of former fascists. This chapter will examine how the Cold War allowed fascism and neofascism to continue to exist and to play a role, albeit minor, in the struggle between the United States and the Soviet Union. More importantly, the Cold War allowed fascism to mask itself and thus continue long after the "fascist moment" ended in 1945 and gave it an opportunity to reemerge in the twenty-first century. The politics of the Cold War opened a space where fascism and its heirs could keep the flame alive.

Ratlines

In the years following the Second World War, Franco went to great lengths to appease the Western democracies without ever giving up his dictatorship. A closer identification with the Catholic Church, which the Valle de los Caídos helped promote, fit in with the Papacy of Pius XII, who made the Vatican a close ally in the fight against communism. While Spain became a partner of the West in this fight, it also became a refuge for Nazis and fascists. Madrid was a meeting place where war criminals and other fugitives could mingle with younger neofascists and neo-Nazis. Some of them, like Otto Skorzeny, the special forces paratrooper who sprung Mussolini out of prison in 1943, and the Belgian leader of the *Rex* movement, Léon Degrelle, helped found an association called Spanish Circle of Friends of Europe (CEDADE) in 1966. Set up as an intellectual circle, which held meetings and lectures, the CEDADE aimed to bring Nazis and fascists together to foster a Europeanist network (Cento Bull 2010, 594). Other Nazi fugitives used Spain as a transit point on the way to South America, like Adolf Eichmann, the "Architect of the Holocaust." Was it a contradiction that Spain served as a place of refuge and transit point for war criminals while at the same time supporting the American side of the Cold War? Perhaps, but as the rest of this chapter demonstrates, Cold War exigencies allowed some former Nazis and fascists to not only escape justice, but also collaborate with the democracies in the fight against communism. In doing so, they allowed many of these former Nazis and fascists, most of whom were true believers, to continue promoting their ideals to a new generation of far-right activists. This chapter will also explore how some of these war criminals got involved with Middle Eastern politics and how neofascists helped with counterintelligence and security forces in their own countries, activities that at times involved terrorism.

Spain was a key stop on one of the Ratlines, most of which ran through Italy. Many Nazis escaped through these lines, helped by secret service agents and by individuals in the Vatican. The need to bring war criminals to justice was universally recognized as the fascist regimes crumbled in 1945. It did not take long, however, for a shift in priorities as the Allied countries turned their attention to the looming Cold War between the United States and the Soviet Union. Fearful of the spread of communism in Western Europe, the United States began to turn a blind eye to the presence of Nazis and fascists in Europe, content to bring only the "big fish" to the Nuremberg War Crimes Trials. As the trials wound down in 1946 and the need to reconstruct Europe took precedence, denazification efforts in the Allied zones were quietly shelved. In Italy, the "purgation" of fascists never fully achieved its aims, leaving thousands of fascists in place in government, while an amnesty, supported by the communist leader Palmiro Togliatti, allowed fascist criminals to elude justice. Moreover, many former Nazis and fascists proved useful to gather intelligence on communist networks throughout Europe, while in the Soviet Bloc some former fascists provided technical assistance in espionage and repression. In short, many former fascists, Nazis, and war criminals were able to escape justice after the war under the cover of the emerging Cold War. This was facilitated by the notorious Ratlines.

The reality of these escape routes has often been sensationalized, leading some to speculate about secret networks of SS men stashing gold and waiting to create a "Fourth Reich" (Sanfilippo 2003). The exaggerated accounts of these so-called Ratlines should not obscure the fact that they did exist and that they involved prominent individuals in the intelligence services, the Vatican, and the Red Cross (Steinacher 2011). In 1947, the infamous Butcher of Lyon, Klaus Barbie, was helped to escape by American Counter Intelligence (CIC) after the war in return for his help in tracking down communist networks in France and Germany (Breitman and Goda 2010, 40). Using the Ratlines, Barbie made his way to South America, where he became a businessman, arms dealer, and technical advisor to far-right paramilitary movements in the service of the Barrientos regime. Others, like Franz Rademacher and Wilhelm Beisner made their way to Syria and Egypt, respectively, where they helped pro-Arab and pro-Palestinian causes against Israel. Not only did they provide technical expertise to Arab nationalists like Abdel Nasser, but they also spread antisemitic propaganda.

Aid was given to fugitives by those who either believed in Nazism or in the cause of anti-communism. This was clearly the case with two clergymen in the Vatican, the Austrian bishop Alois Hudal and the Croatian priest Krunoslav Draganovic. Hudal was known for his pro-Nazi sympathies, and he used his position as rector of the Teutonic College in Rome to hide Nazi fugitives and procure them false documents from the Red Cross. Draganovic, a sympathizer of the *Ustaše* movement, helped Croatian war criminals escape through the northern port city of Genoa. In both cases, this so-called "monastery route"—named after the various monasteries and religious houses used by the fugitives—was unwittingly helped by the Vatican Relief Commission and a charity run by the American Cardinal Spellman. The latter was designed to help anti-communists and Catholics flee from the Soviet Bloc, while the former was overseen by Monsignor Montini, the future Pope Paul VI (Steinacher 2011, 102–4). While Hudal and Draganovich were aware of who they were helping, these agencies did not, nor did the International Red Cross, which issued some one hundred and twenty thousand travel documents by 1951, many of which fell into the hands of fugitives.

Latin America

Many of these Nazi and fascist fugitives did not have too much difficulty inserting themselves into other countries, thanks to their ability to render services to their host countries and the United States' (and their allies') inability to bring them to justice. This was especially the case in Latin America, where authoritarian states—some of which could both be defined as parafascist and allied to the American cause in the Cold War—gave them work. It helped, too, that Latin America had a large German diaspora into which these fugitives could assimilate and which they could influence. This was especially the case in Argentina and Brazil. Both countries had their own fascist movements that predated the war, and both had been influenced by the movements in Germany and Italy. After the war, some forty thousand Germans immigrated to Argentina. Among them were several hundred Nazis who blended into the mass migration (Sanfilippo 2003). They also found some political cultures akin to the fascism they left behind in Europe.

In Brazil, a fascist party known as the Integralists nearly came to power in the 1930s. Officially called the Brazilian Integralist Action (AIB), the movement was founded by Plínio Salgado, a writer who was inspired by Marinetti's Futurism and Mussolini's fascism. AIB's growth was explosive. Two years after the party was founded, in 1932, it boasted some sixty thousand members (Rees 1990). Led by the slogan, "God, Country, and Family," Salgado's party promoted a corporatist economy on the model of Italian fascism. Like Mussolini's movement, the AIB aimed for mass mobilization and used paramilitary tactics to attack their opponents on the left. Instead of black shirts, they wore green. Brazilian politics in the 1930s resembled to some extent the situation in Europe: a Popular Front coalition was gaining popularity among the working classes, while Salgado's party had great middle-class appeal. Significantly, the AIB attempted to bring together Roman Catholic traditionalism with some indigenous Brazilian linguistic expressions from the pagan Tupi people. Secret funding for the party came from Italy (Skidmore and Smith 2005).

Salgado's admiration of the military helped make his party an ally of order in Brazil; thus, the violence was tolerated—to a point. In 1930, the newly founded Liberal Alliance proposed Getúlio Vargas as candidate for president. A former army officer, Vargas represented middle-class interests and hoped to modernize Brazil's economy by breaking the power of the coffee plantation owning class. The coalition proposed liberal reforms, such as the secret vote and freedom of the press, while also calling for protectionist trade policies to foster the growth of national industry. In the 1930 election, Vargas lost but claimed that there was widespread fraud, which resulted in a revolution where the Liberal Alliance overthrew the duly elected government. This event in the still young Brazilian nation has been rightly called a major turning point in its history (Quiggins Tiller 1965).

The overthrow of a democratically elected government ushered in the Vargas dictatorship, which was formalized in 1937 with the declaration of the Estado Novo (the name of his new regime), inspired by Salazar's regime in Portugal. Vargas made use of Salgado's Greenshirts—until his new authoritarian constitution banned all paramilitary forces. As had happened in Austria and Hungary, right-wing authoritarian forces exploited the more radical fascist elements for their own purposes before turning against them. While Vargas's regime was not, strictly speaking, fascist, it did copy many fascist ideas, thus making it a parafascist regime (Costa Pinto 2020). While the regime was initially sympathetic to Nazi Germany's overtures, Vargas eventually accepted the Allied invitation to jump into the power against the Axis powers in 1943. This move foreshadowed the future neofascist tendency to side with the United States in the Cold War despite their own ideological inclinations against democracy.

A similarly parafascist regime, closely allied to the United States during the Cold War, was led by Juan Perón in Argentina. Perón was part of a group of military nationalists who came to power via a coup in 1943. Although officially neutral, Argentina's government was sympathetic to the Axis cause and remained so until 1945 as the war was coming to an end. Already home to a significant German colony, Argentina, like some other South American countries, like Brazil and Bolivia, was open to Nazi German economic involvement via the German embassy and the establishment of companies like Condor Airlines (Skidmore and Smith 2005).

In 1949, a new constitution set up an authoritarian state with a corporatist economic set-up that resembled in some ways that of Fascist Italy, a regime Perón admired after visiting in the late 1930s. While Perón promoted a nationalist economy, he eventually opened the country to foreign investment in the 1950s in line with Argentina's pro-American stance during the Cold War. Perón's movement also differed from classical fascism, as he promoted some socialist policies and worked closely with labor unions.

While the Perón regime differed significantly from interwar fascism in substance, in other ways his regime aped fascist practices. This included a cult of personality around Perón and his wife, Evita (Figure 11.2). When she died of illness in 1952, the nation went into mourning; Perón even planned to build a massive mausoleum that would have made it taller than the Statue of Liberty (Skidmore and Smith 2005, 88). The Perónist regime also exalted modernity. In the late 1940s, Perón's government actively sponsored a motorsport program that launched some of Grand Prix racing's greatest champions, like Juan Manuel Fangio. In 1952, on the suggestion of Fangio, Perón's government built an autodrome in Buenos Aires and named it after the date October 17, which marked Perón's release from prison in 1945, a year before he was elected president. Further mimicking Mussolini's regime, the Péron regime began an extensive public works program, aimed at transforming Argentina into an industrial powerhouse. These included building several hydroelectric stations, iron and steel plants, and the extraction of coal. A significant project was teaming up with the American company Standard Oil to conduct oil exploration in Patagonia (Gerassi 1963).

While Perón's regime—which lasted until 1955, when he was ousted by a coup—presented a more ambivalent form of fascism, it had no qualms about encouraging former Nazis to emigrate to Argentina. Through its embassy in Spain, Argentina issued visas to men like Adolf Eichmann, Josef Mengele, and Eduard Roschmann. From Argentina, many Nazis went to other South American countries, such as Bolivia and Paraguay. In effect, South America became a refuge for Nazis, where they were protected by countries that supported the United States in the Cold War. Melting into the German diaspora, these men could live freely and indulge in their nostalgia for the Third Reich; some, like Klaus Barbie, engaged in clandestine activities, supporting far-right authoritarianism. Even neofascists, like the Italian radical Stefano Delle Chiaie, found their way to South

Figure 11.2 A massive crowd greets President Juan Perón in Buenos Aires in 1948. Credit: Getty Images

America to help the cause of authoritarianism. Delle Chiaie, a terrorist and founder of *Avanguardia Nazionale*, was hired by the regime of Augusto Pinochet in Chile after making connections in Madrid, where Delle Chiaie sought refuge under Franco (Ben-Ghiat 2020).

It is best not to overestimate the importance of these fugitives in South America, nor to overstate the fascist character of these regimes. However, the rise of authoritarianism during the Cold War provided a home for ex-Nazis and fascists; it also allowed them to use the American alliance as a cover to keep the fascist flame alive, especially among immigrant communities. To be sure, there was much exaggeration and even conspiracy fantasies about the ex-Nazis in South America. Keeping the fascist flame alive in South America was mostly a fantasy, one that even inspired writers and filmmakers to make films like *The Boys from Brazil* (1978). Recently released FBI files show that the agency kept reports on rumors about Hitler escaping to Argentina (US Federal Bureau of Investigation 1945–7). Despite these fictions, the Cold War also provided continuity for interwar authoritarian movements, as figures like Vargas, Salgado, and Perón demonstrate. All these men began their careers before the Second World War, and their influence and presence continued into the Cold War era. This fascism-in-exile, however, was not just found in Latin America. It was also to be found in the heart of fascism—Europe.

Neofascism in Europe

Not all Nazis and fascists left Europe after the war. Many stayed. Some were in hiding for a time, but many others simply continued with their jobs. In fact, there was a great deal of continuity in Italy and Germany as they transitioned to democracy. Institutions founded by the Fascist regime, like the Institute for Industrial Reconstruction (IRI), were kept in place and, in the case of the IRI, written into the constitution (J. T. Schnapp 1998). Although attempts were made to identity and purge fascists from both Italy and Germany, the general amnesty granted by the provisional government in 1946 allowed most to simply carry on in the economy, state, and culture. Similarly, in Germany, the much-publicized denazification policies carried out by the Allies were inconsistent and incomplete and soon gave way to the more urgent need to rebuild Germany in a Cold War context.

This context not only favored fascists on the run; it also allowed for the emergence of the only neofascist movement that came close to entering the political mainstream, the *Movimento Sociale Italiano* (MSI), founded by ex-supporters of Mussolini's Italian Social Republic. It is fitting that the country that created fascism should also be the one that gave rise to neofascism after the war. The MSI was established in December 1946 by a group of men who had been hiding in convents and monasteries in Rome. It was led by Pino Romualdi, Giorgio Almirante, and a few others. Its intent was to revive republican fascism inspired by the Verona Charter of 1943. Romualdi had been the highest-ranking member of the Republic of Salò to have survived the reprisals of 1945. He had served as vice secretary of the party and had been condemned to death *in absentia* but had escaped. Almirante was a journalist who had served in the Ministry of Popular Culture. Before the war, he worked for the racist newspaper editor Telesio Interlandi in the notorious journal, *La Difesa della Razza* ("Defense of the Race").

The founders of the MSI hoped to revive a movement based on the social principles framed in the Charter of Verona. This was not shared by all the early members of the MSI. The movement quickly split into right and left factions. Those on the right, like Augusto De Marsanich and Arturo Michelini, wanted a more conservative vision of neofascism that more closely resembled the regime of the *Ventennio* (1922–43) rather than that of Salò. After 1950, the party fell into the hands of the conservatives, where it subsequently enjoyed some success at the polls. The turn to democratic politics further split the movement, as some members of the MSI wanted neofascism to be a revolutionary and clandestine force rather than a parliamentary movement. In effect, neofascism in Italy needed to find an identity, and significant amounts of energy were spent on defining fascism or finding its "true soul."

In 1953, the MSI found some success in the Italian general elections, picking up more than 1.5 million votes and scoring twenty-three deputies and eight senators.

To be sure, these tallies were very distant from those of the mainstream parties, the Christian Democrats, the communists, and the socialists, but they did signify the continuing presence of those who looked back on the fascist era with some nostalgia. The MSI was also helped by the ongoing crisis over the fate of Trieste, a city which was still in limbo between Italy and Yugoslavia. The MSI, led by its youth wing, had been active in demanding that Trieste remain Italian, carrying out frequent demonstrations in the streets. After 1954, the party was led by Arturo Michelini, who moved the party further into the mainstream, advocating that the MSI "insert" itself into the party system, an approach that eventually led to schisms within the movement in 1956. In 1960, Michelini put the policy to the test when the MSI supported the Christian Democratic government led by Fernando Tambroni, a move that led to widespread street protests in the northern city of Genoa and an eventual end to the so-called Tambroni Experiment.

The MSI's shift toward the mainstream met opposition from within and without the party. Despite a law prohibiting "apologias for fascism," the party maintained much fascist baggage, keeping the one-armed salutes in their public meetings, fascist imagery in their posters, and constant tributes to Mussolini. One of the MSI's senators, Domenico Leccisi, had been the leader of the gang that had exhumed Mussolini's body from its unmarked grave in Milan, taking it to a monastery in Pavia, where it remained until it was repatriated to the Mussolini family crypt in Predappio (Luzzatto 2005). The repatriation, which happened in 1957, had the "blessing" of the Christian Democratic Party and was the result of the MSI's support in parliament. The very public ceremony of the reinterment in Predappio was noted for its fascist salutes, slogans, and songs and was given ample coverage in Italian newspapers.

The rise of the MSI in Italian politics raised some key questions and concerns. If they had now accepted democracy, did that make the movement non-fascist? Most of the MSI's support came from the south, and not the north, which had been fascism's historic base of support. The fact that most support came from the south suggested that voters were less attracted to neofascist ideology and more to protest votes against the mainstream parties. Support in the south also led to some bizarre electoral alliances at local levels; one such alliance was made with the communists in Sicily. By the late 1960s, many neofascists left the MSI to create more radical and "authentic" movements untainted by compromises with monarchists, Christian Democrats, and socialists. This splintering led to a decline in MSI support. In 1969, after the death of Michelini, who had orchestrated the party's shift to the mainstream, the party elected Giorgio Almirante as secretary. Almirante, a founder of the MSI, had also been one of its dissidents in the 1950s and had left the party briefly. His return suggested a more leftward shift in the party back to its Verona Charter days; however, Almirante proved to be more moderate. He was able to rally the party, though, especially when the MSI supported local protests in Calabria in 1970 after the national government decided to move the capital of the region. In 1972, Almirante steered the MSI to its greatest electoral success, picking up 3.2 million votes and winning 56 seats in the Chamber and 26 in the Senate. Almirante's winning formula was to broaden the appeal of the MSI by bringing back dissidents on both sides of the political spectrum, like Pino Rauti (on the left) and the Monarchist Party (on the right).

This broad coalition, which he called *Destra Nazionale*, was cemented by one overarching issue: anti-communism. It was this policy that also allowed a party like the MSI, with its clear origins in historic fascism, to function as a mainstream party in Italy, a country at the forefront of the Cold War. Italy had the largest communist party in the West and was, by the 1970s, consistently the second party in Italy behind the Christian Democrats. Bolstering the right thus became a priority especially for the Christian Democrats' most important foreign allies, the United States (and to a lesser extent the Vatican). Since the 1950s, the MSI had openly supported the so-called Atlantic Pact. Despite the anti-Americanism that characterized fascism and neofascism, the party led by Michelini and subsequently Almirante held fast to its support of NATO, which lost the party some support among its more radical members (Mammone 2015, 63). Cold War exigencies, therefore, provided a space for a neofascist to exist and grow in strength in a country that was in the frontlines of the struggle against Soviet communism. A similar, albeit less obvious, situation would exist in postwar Germany.

Since Nazi parties were effectively banned by the 1949 West German constitution, former Nazis who wished to continue carrying the flame in Germany established clandestine networks aimed at influencing mainstream politics from the shadows. Two shadow organizations made up of former Nazis emerged in West Germany and Austria in the late 1940s. They were the Brotherhood and the Spider, respectively (Breitman and Goda 2010). In both cases, the men who made up the movements hoped to latch onto right-wing nationalist parties and get involved in debates over such issues like German rearmament. The Brotherhood rejected the American alliance. Neither movement lasted long, though the Spider network did associate itself with the far-right Federation of Independents Party (VdU) that won sixteen seats in the 1949 elections.

Clandestine existence was the only realistic option for neo-Nazis and many neofascists after the war. However, shadow organizations also proved useful in the Cold War, as some of these networks would be used by secret services to fight Soviet communism. One example of this was the cooperation between the U.S. Counterintelligence Corps (CIC) and the Ukrainian Insurgent Army (UPA). The UPA included a group of Ukrainian fascists known as the Organization of Ukrainian Nationalists (OUN). Founded in 1929, the OUN carried out terrorist activities and was also involved in anti-Jewish pogroms (Breitman and Goda 2010). Making use of contacts in West German and Italian secret service organizations, Bandera's group conducted a series of anti-Soviet operations in Eastern Europe until Bandera was assassinated by a Soviet agent in Munich in 1959.

Western intelligence organizations found it useful to rely on clandestine neofascist networks because of their knowledge of communist groups and their willingness to engage in violent activities. If caught, the secret services could also claim plausible deniability (Bale 2017). In the 1950s and 1960s, with communist parties active in Western European countries like Italy, Greece, and France, Western security services created so-called "stay behind" organizations to engage in internal repression using neofascist networks (Bale 2017). These were paramilitary groups that mixed professional soldiers with young neofascist thugs. At times these groups bled into organized crime groups and involved shadowy financing. Not much is known about these networks, and their existence is often surrounded by sensationalism and exaggeration.

Neofascists were already engaged in clandestine and violent activities before their collaboration with secret service groups. A year before they founded the MSI, Pino Romualdi and Giorgio Almirante helped create the *Fasci d'Azione Rivoluzionaria* (FAR). In 1951, this group, renamed the Black Legion, carried out a series of bombings against the US Embassy in Rome and the Italian Foreign Ministry. In the 1960s, the Italian secret services, supported by the United States, formed the stay-behind Gladio Network. With the blessing of the Italian president and the chief of the armed forces, a plan was put into place in case of an uprising by the Italian left (Greene and Massignani 2004). A key figure in this network was Junio Valerio Borghese, a former commander of the *Decima Mas* anti-submarine forces in the Republic of Salò and former president of the MSI. During the war, Borghese's troops engaged in brutal anti-partisan activity, which got him put in prison briefly after the war. In the late 1950s, angered by the MSI's pro-democracy platform, Borghese left the party and formed the *Fronte Nazionale*.

In 1970, during an event which remains shrouded in mystery, Borghese nearly pulled off a coup with the help of neofascists and members of the Italian armed forces. Borghese believed Italy was on the cusp of a communist takeover, due to the unrest caused by prolonged labor union strikes and the youth riots of 1968. He was also inspired by the right-wing military coup in Greece in 1967, which enjoyed tacit approval from the US Borghese's goal was to establish a similar military *junta* in Italy that would crack down on communism and create a new constitution based on a strong president, in line with De Gaulle's reforms in France (Greene and Massignani 2004). In order to get the coup off the ground, Borghese enlisted the help of Delle Chiaie's *Avanguardia Nazionale* neofascist group, his own Fronte Nazionale (which now boasted some three thousand members), members of the armed forces, and some criminal elements from the Calabrese underworld (Cento Bull 2010). Borghese also received some support from the shadowy P2 Masonic network led by another former fascist from the Republic of Salò, Licio Gelli.

Despite his own background and the involvement of neofascists, Borghese's coup was not an attempt to reestablish a fascist state, at least not at first. The statement he prepared in case of success called for a return to order and the reinstatement of the military to a place of honor in Italian society. To be sure, these are goals fascists would have shared but this did not entail a return to the *Ventennio* or to the Italian Social Republic. Downplaying the fascist elements may have been a means of maintaining US support, however. Under the Nixon administration, money was being funneled to the MSI via the new ambassador to Rome, Graham Martin, but there was no guarantee American support would have extended to the more radical elements supporting Borghese (Greene and Massignani 2004). In the end, the coup was called off, after which Borghese left Italy to go live in exile in Spain, along with Delle Chiaie. While in Spain, Borghese mixed in with the colony of ex-Nazis surrounding Otto Skorzeny.

Terrorism and the Strategy of Tension

The Cold War provided cover for neofascism to grow, owing to the West's overarching desire to stop Soviet communism. Although they were critical of American hegemony, neofascists were able to ally themselves to the American cause, thanks to their common enemy. A more complicated dynamic came with the end of the European empires overseas and the student riots of 1968. Both events provoked ambivalent and contrasting reactions among the various neofascist groups in France and Italy. One of the outcomes of these complicated events was a further radicalization and splintering of these groups into what Roger Griffin has called "disaggregation and groupusculization" (Griffin 2022). Responding to the New Left and the radicalization of far-left groups, the new neofascist groups, led by Delle Chiaie's *Avanguardia Nazionale* and others, resorted to violent, terrorist activities.

In the fallout after the 1968 student riots, a group of Italian and French neofascists attempted to form a so-called "Black International," a development that echoed the CAUR organization in the 1930s. Inspired by the writings of the French author Maurice Bardèche, these groups moved away from fascism's traditional focus on nationalism to a Europeanist sensibility. This "Eurofascism" as it was called had the support of some of the old guard fascists like Sir Oswald Mosley and Otto Strasser, as well as younger neofascists who were less interested in the "national conservatism" promoted by groups like the MSI in Italy (Mammone 2015). Many of these groups would find an outlet in neofascism's cultural turn, which will be discussed in the next chapter. For others, it fueled a turn to violence.

In France, this violence was inspired by the events of decolonization. Like other European powers, France had lost its colonies in the 1950s and the 1960s. Unlike many others, the French put up a fight in Indochina and Algeria. Out of this struggle to keep their empire came a clandestine group of army officers called the *Organization Armée Secrète* (OAS). Founded in Spain in 1961, this group aimed at protesting President Chales De Gaulle's referendum on Algerian independence. The OAS staged a failed coup in Algeria in response to the overwhelmingly favorable support for Algerian independence demonstrated in the referendum. Consequently, the OAS resorted to terrorism both in France and in Algeria, killing and wounding thousands of people. Out of this organization came Yves Guillou, also known as Yves Guerin-Sérac, a former paratrooper who had fought in Indochina and in Algeria. While the OAS was eventually dismantled by the French government, Guerin-Sérac, a far-right sympathizer, turned to clandestine activities, supporting neocolonial movements elsewhere. In 1966, he founded a press agency called Aginter Press, purportedly designed to provide alternative journalism but really a front to train individuals in counterinsurgency methods. In this operation, Guerin-Sérac made close contacts with the Portuguese security service, the paramilitary Portuguese Legion, and the Portuguese Security Agency (PIDE) as well as the CIA (Ferraresi 1996).

Aginter Press was instrumental in creating a network of operatives in France, Portugal, Spain, and Italy, many of whom were neofascists, like Stefano Delle Chiaie, and members of the French group *Jeune Europe*. In effect, Guerin-Sérac laid the groundwork for a Fascist International, especially through *Ordre et Tradition* and its clandestine arm, the *Organization Armée contre le Communisme Internationale* (OACI). The aim of these organizations was to fight communism on a global scale, paralleling the official Cold War activities of the United States and its allies. The operatives trained by OACI would not only fight against communism but also participate in neocolonial wars like those in Angola and Mozambique. Another aim was to promote the Mediterranean authoritarian model found in Salazar's Portugal, Franco's Spain, and the Greece of the Colonels. The hope was that Italy might follow their example, which explained Delle Chiaie's support of Borghese's ill-fated coup in 1970.

It was out of this clandestine network that the so-called "strategy of tension" developed in Italy. Apart from Delle Chiaie, Aginter Press also included among its staff Pino Rauti, founder of *Ordine Nuovo*, and Guido Giannettini, once leader of the MSI's youth wing. These Italian neofascists appropriated Guerin-Sérac's program to engage in terrorist activities to spark an authoritarian reaction on the part of the Italian government. This strategy was enacted at a time when the left was making gains in Italian politics, beginning with the Christian Democrat's "opening to the left" in 1963 and culminating in the Historic Compromise between the Italian Communist Party and the DC in the mid-1970s. The key was to blame the far left for the terrorism so that public opinion would demand a crackdown on communists and socialists, thus tanking any openings to the left and hopefully ushering in a more authoritarian system. This campaign of disseminating terror (*stragismo*) began in December 1969, with the bombing of a bank in Milan's Piazza Fontana, which killed seventeen people and wounded eighty-eight (Cento Bull 2007). In subsequent years leading up to 1974, several more bombings occurred throughout Italy, killing hundreds of people and wounding many more.

The Piazza Fontana bombing was immediately blamed on left-wing anarchists. One of them, Giuseppe Pinelli, was arrested and interrogated in police headquarters before he mysteriously fell to his death out of a window. It was ruled a suicide. Ultimately, it was neofascists from Rauti's *Ordine Nuovo* (ON) who were arrested, tried, and convicted but eventually exonerated in a series of trials that lasted into the 2000s. It was not until 2017, after a series of similar convictions and acquittals, that members of the same group were imprisoned for the bombing in Brescia's Piazza della Loggia in 1974, which killed eight people (Figure 11.3). Convictions and acquittals also marked the trials of neofascists for the *Italicus* bombing of 1974. The *Italicus* was a passenger train hit by a bomb attack near Bologna killing twelve people. These series of convictions and acquittals suggested government and secret service interference and possibly even participation in the bombings, although this has never definitively been proven.

The general perception is that neofascists were involved in these bombings, including the deadliest bombing of all at the Bologna train station in August 1980, which killed over eighty people. Here, too, a series of trials and retrials took place, and two neofascists were eventually sentenced to life imprisonment. They belonged to a new group called the *Nuclei Armati Rivoluzionari* (NAR) founded in 1977 by Valerio Fioravanti. This group of avowed terrorists often worked with members of Rome's criminal organizations like

Figure 11.3 The aftermath of a terror bombing perpetrated by neofascists in Brescia in 1974. Credit: Getty Images.

the *Banda della Magliana*, which, in turn, had connections with the underworld and possibly members of the P2 Masonic organization led by Licio Gelli. In fact, Gelli and other members of this group were tried in connection with the Bologna bombing but eventually acquitted.

It is important to keep in mind that a complete picture of these events has not yet been revealed. The trials, retrials, and acquittals have made it difficult to give a clear picture of what happened during the period known as the Years of Lead in Italian history. It should also be noted that the far left was carrying out its own terrorist activities in these years through groups like the Red Brigades, who may have had a similar agenda, namely, that of short circuiting any possibility of left-wing parties working with the Chrisitan Democrats. Furthermore, bombings like that of Bologna do not easily fit into the strategy of tension (deliberate provocation of violence to force government intervention) narrative since by 1980 the so-called Historic Compromise was dead. This is further complicated by suggestions that the bombing may have involved Palestinian terrorist groups and even the Ghaddafi regime in Libya, scenarios that are unlikely, but that would need to be researched more before they are definitively disproved (Hof 2020). Moreover, the two NAR members convicted of the bombings have always maintained their innocence.

Despite the murky and yet unknown full truth of what happened in these bombings, it can be argued with some degree of assurance that neofascism was involved and that there was a strategy of some kind to destabilize Italian politics in favor of an authoritarian solution. This was admitted by the one incident that had a clear conviction due to the culprit's confession of guilt. In 1972, a local ON cell in northern Italy killed three members of the Carabinieri. It was not until 1987 that one of the ON's members, Vincenzo Vinciguerra, confessed to the killings and even gave a statement outlining his motives, aiming to "set the record straight" (Ferraresi 1996, 125). In his brief statement, Vinciguerra alluded to the "stay behind" networks like Gladio established by the Italian secret services and the CIA. He also claimed that the bombings had a direct political purpose, namely, "to arouse, by means of the most 'savage' provocations, an enraged popular reaction that would have justified repressive countermeasures" (Ferraresi 1996, 125).

Beyond the strategy of tension, the neofascist violence that afflicted Italy in the period between 1969 and 1984, when the Italian government forcibly liquidated movements like the NAR, demonstrated one of the key features of neofascism and fascism: a willingness to indulge in violence and fight extra-parliamentary battles in "low-intensity civil wars" (Cento Bull 2007). The parallels with the Italian situation after the First World War were obvious. Like the post-Great War era, neofascism in Italy worked on a clandestine and official level, as terrorist activities ran parallel to the parliamentary activities of the MSI. Although these two groups were officially distinct, with the former made up of dissidents from the MSI, there were some connections, especially after 1969, when Pino Rauti, the founder of the ON, reconciled with the MSI after Giorgio Almirante became the new party secretary. Almirante also reached out to similar groups elsewhere, acting as an unofficial advisor to Jean Marie Le Pen's *Front National* (FN) in the early 1970s, a party that enjoyed the support of former members of the OAS in France.

Conclusion

The Cold War, which came to an end in 1989–91, provided the space in which neofascist movements thrived. Not surprisingly, Italy, the birthplace of fascism, served as the main site of neofascism, due to the Cold War and the presence of a large Communist Party that nearly won Italy's first postwar general election. The convergence of these two factors made Italy fertile ground for the continuation of fascist nostalgia and the development of new fascist groups, both clandestine and official. Cold War politics also allowed former Nazis to escape justice either through the lack of priority given to denazification after 1946 or through active collaboration with Allied secret services. While most of these individuals faded into anonymity, some got involved in far-right politics in Latin America, while some others collaborated with Arab nationalist regimes in the Middle East. For the latter, it was a continuation of contacts made with Arab nationalists during the Second World War (Herf 2009).

Whatever the practical implications of these were in the grand scale of Cold War politics, the postwar world allowed fascism to continue under the guise of anti-communism. Franco's Valle de los Caídos is a monumental example of how a grandiose Catholic space expressed the idea of Spain as a bulwark against atheistic communism. The notion that it was a site of reconciliation also allowed Franco to present Spain as a friendly partner to the West without emphasizing the fascist crusade that was the Spanish Civil War. Inside the basilica, however, the fascist element can be seen both in the burial site of Primo De Rivera (since removed) and the imagery. In a similar way, the Italian MSI reinvented itself as a parliamentary force in line with Italy's pro-NATO policy, thus emphasizing its anti-communist credentials. Notably, the MSI never renounced its fascist past, nor did it ever criticize the regime of Benito Mussolini during the Cold War years. Indeed, these postwar fascists continued to harbor antidemocratic and socialist ideals that made them strange bedfellows with the capitalist and democratic West. For the moment, many of these neofascists put away their anti-Americanism to fight the more urgent war against communism (Mammone 2015, 63).

It would be a mistake to view these neofascists as merely nostalgists or as muscle in the proxy wars of the Cold War. The postwar era, with its threat of worldwide communism and impending nuclear apocalypse stoked fascism fantasy. Not all neofascist terrorism was aimed at Cold War interests, however—some of it was driven by violence for its own sake or in the interests of an "accelerationism" that would help bring about a New Order. This fantasy, like that of historic fascism, was buttressed by new ideological and cultural impulses that developed in the postwar era. These new ideas were sometimes a continuation or renewal of the old fascism, while, at other times, there was a repudiation of the Mussolinian and Hitlerian era. It is to this new constellation of ideas and impulses that we now turn.

CHAPTER 12
HOBBITS, SKINHEADS, AND GURUS: NEOFASCISM AFTER 1968

The Thin White Duke

April 1976 at Victoria Station in London. A man in an open-top Mercedes waves to a cheering crowd. A photograph shows the man standing in the vehicle and giving what appears to be a stiff-arm salute with a look of defiance on his face. He is David Bowie, a rock superstar just returning from a successful world tour. The photograph appears in several newspapers, raising serious questions about Bowie's intentions. Was he giving a Nazi salute? Or was he simply waving to his fans? Normally, celebrities who often wave at fans would have been given the benefit of the doubt, but Bowie was different. In the album that Bowie was promoting for this world tour, there were songs that suggested far-right sensibilities. The album is filled with Nietzschean references and Nazi intimations, such as the smash-hit "Golden Years" and its lyrics that refer to a golden "thousand years" (Jantine 2018).

All of this may have been a stretch had not Bowie been known for using far-right allusions in his songs. As far back as his *Hunky Dory* album (released several years previously), listeners could discern Bowie's interests in Nietzsche and even references to Nazi Germany. The song, "Quicksand," for example, is about Hitler in the bunker, dreaming about what might have been (J. Pearce 2013). The fact that Bowie had once visited the site of Hitler's bunker and was a collector of Nazi memorabilia further raised suspicions around Bowie's political views. An interview he gave with *Playboy* magazine that same year appeared to confirm these suspicions. In that notorious interview, Bowie openly showed admiration for Hitler and suggested that Great Britain could use a fascist dictatorship (Jantine 2018). A few months later, Bowie moved to West Berlin where he would record a series of critically successful albums. The first was titled *Heroes*. Bowie's flirtation with Nazism came through a persona he created called the "Thin White Duke," found on his 1976 album and in the film, *The Man Who Fell to Earth* (1974) where he played the lead character.

References to Nazism were nothing new in the world of British pop music. The Beatles were once photographed in Australia giving Nazi salutes from a hotel balcony in an ironic commentary on the oceanic crowd of fans that had appeared. Critics had often compared the impact of Beatlemania on teenage girls to the fanaticism of Nazi crowds. A notorious painting of the Rolling Stones had shown the band members in SS uniforms drinking tea while one of its members, Brian Jones, once posed in an SS uniform with his girlfriend Anita Pallenberg in a photograph that deftly mixed Nazi imagery with eroticism. The protagonist of Pink Floyd's *The Wall* is a rock and roll star who fantasizes about being a fascist dictator. In 1976, the same year that Bowie outed himself as a Nazi sympathizer, Eric Clapton gave a xenophobic rant at a concert in Birmingham, where he told his fans to vote for Enoch Powell, the Conservative MP who had given a notorious anti-immigration speech called "Rivers of Blood," calling for an end to immigration. Clapton's rant was so shocking that it inspired other pop artists to begin the Rock against Racism festivals (J. Pearce 2013).

Fascinating Fascism

The flirtation between pop culture and neo-Nazism did not go unnoticed. In 1975, Susan Sontag published her landmark essay, "Fascinating Fascism," in the *New York Review of Books*. Ostensibly a review of Leni Riefenstahl's picture book on African tribes, the essay was a meditation on why Nazi symbols had become widespread in sexual subcultures. In her far-reaching analysis, Sontag examined the fascination with all things fascist in popular culture. She noted how fascist aesthetics continued to appear in the most unlikely places. In the 1930s, Walter Benjamin had argued that fascism aestheticized politics. In the 1970s, according to Sontag, fascism had anesthetized pop culture. "Fascist art," Sontag claimed, "glorifies surrender, it exalts mindlessness, it glamorizes death" (Sontag 1980, 91). Moreover, Nazism was much sexier than the two alternatives offered by the Cold War, communism and capitalism. Nothing exemplified this more than the black SS uniform in which its "stylish" look was both "dramatic and menacing" (Sontag 1980, 99).

Sontag's article dealt with the paradox of a pop culture that celebrated permissiveness, individuality, and freedom, appropriating the symbols and style of a repressive ideology. Why did gay subcultures use the images of a movement that murdered gay men? Why did rock stars ape Nazi gestures through a style of music that the Nazis would have considered degenerate? Sontag argued that youth culture found something exotic in Nazism that was missing in communism. Horror and irrationality were fascinating, as evidenced by the popularity of horror films in the 1970s. Digging deeper, Sontag found that fascist ideals continued to have a grip on the Western imagination despite the defeat of the movement in 1945. Nazism's late Romanticism with its "ideal of life as art; the cult of beauty; the fetishism of courage; the dissolution of the alienation in ecstatic feelings of community; the repudiation of the intellect," all appealed to a "youth/rock culture" looking to transform "diverse modes of cultural dissidence" into "new forms of community" (Sontag 1980, 96).

The proliferation of Nazi symbols in pornography on the one hand and sexually transgressive acts like sadomasochism on the other hand spoke to those who found the theatrical nature of fascism appealing. Sadomasochism was performative, theatrical, and violent. Like pornography, it played on fantasy, and SS uniforms, with their transgressive look, suited a form of sexuality that went beyond biological function. According to

Sontag, Nazism transformed sexual energy into a spiritual force and the dictator into an object of erotic desire. David Bowie, with his sexually ambivalent image and his grounding in "glam rock," a genre that encouraged performers to take on personas—like the Thin White Duke—and hide behind flashy costumes and makeup, seemed to capture the Nazi aesthetic. The power the performer held over his audience only confirmed for many the easy slide into fascist aesthetics. Power, domination, and violence were the flip side of the 1960s' desire for freedom and liberation.

Rock against Communism

Sontag's essay did not deal extensively with music, but her view that fascist aesthetics could inform youth and rock culture was prescient, especially in the United Kingdom, where, in 1976–7, the punk rock phenomenon was exploding. Like the glam rock movement that preceded it, punk rock musicians were not averse to using swastikas and other Nazi symbols openly. Johnny Rotten of the Sex Pistols frequently displayed Nazi symbols on stage and made Nazi salutes. The anarchic nature of punk lent itself to Nietzschean obsessions, with images of destruction and annihilation that frequently appear in punk lyrics. The denigration of liberal and traditional institutions and the assault on bourgeois sensibilities easily played into far-right (and far-left) political ideals.

To what extent did fascist ideals penetrate pop culture? Was it merely an ironic appropriation of the Nazi aesthetic or something deeper? Sontag suggests that there was a more substantial ideological affinity, an argument that would later have its critics, but her essay became a seminal work, as it inspired the study of fascist and Nazi aesthetics as essential to, and not separate from, Nazi ideology. The continued appeal of Nazi and fascist symbols in pop subcultures was evidence that historic fascism was not simply based on terror and repression, argued Sontag—it was also based on exciting fantasies, held by many as a rejection of the primarily economic ideals of the Cold War era.

While performers like Bowie, Clapton, and the Sex Pistols flirted with fascist ideals and, in the case of Bowie, later repudiated as a drug-and drink-fueled fetish, Nazi ideals did become firmly grounded in the 1970s in the skinhead culture of Great Britain. This subculture combined with punk music found its way into the youth culture of British neofascism. In 1979, a group of skinheads attended the first Rock against Communism concert in London. Organized by Joseph (Joe) Pearce, the concert was a response to the Rock against Racism festival, which had attracted some eighty thousand attendees to hear bands like The Clash. RAC attracted significantly fewer concert goers and featured less-well-known bands like Homicide and White Boss (Shaffer 2013). By the 1980s, RAC had outgrown the small London clubs—partially due to the increasing unwillingness of club owners to host these events, which often became violent, but also due to the increasing number of attendees, many of whom came from the continent. The festivals

Fascism in Europe and Beyond

Figure 12.1 Nazi salutes for Ian Stuart and his band Skrewdriver in Stockholm, 1986. Credit: Alamy.

were held on the Suffolk estate owned by Nick Griffin, an increasingly important figure in the National Front. The festivals featured several skinhead bands, but the marquee act was always Skrewdriver, a neo-Nazi group led by the charismatic Ian Stuart Donaldson (stage name Ian Stuart) (J. Pearce 1987) (Figure 12.1).

Skrewdriver became the most famous neo-Nazi skinhead band not just in England but internationally by the late 1980s. Stuart had started the group as a Rolling Stones tribute band but by 1977 had switched to punk music. From a middle-class background near Blackpool, Stuart became the leader of the local youth chapter of the National Front, mixing political activism with his music career. A talented songwriter and musician as well as a charismatic frontman, Stuart was able to build a substantial fan base among London's skinheads. His song, "Voice of Britain," released in 1983, became an anthem at the RAC gigs, as was "Smash the IRA." As is obvious from the song titles, the emphasis was on British nationalism; however, by the late 1980s, Stuart emphasized neo-Nazi, white supremacist, and pan-European themes. He also made the switch from punk to heavy metal (J. Pearce 1987). He eventually started recording with Rock-O-Rama, a West German label that focused on White Power music before starting his own label, Blood and Honor, which also became a fanzine. Killed in a car accident in 1993, Stuart has become a cult-like figure in the neo-Nazi subculture, which has become international, thanks in part to the efforts of Stuart and his band.

The National Front's Cultural Turn

A key part of Stuart's success was the cultural turn taken by neofascist movements in the UK and elsewhere beginning in the 1970s. Founded in 1967 as a conglomeration of smaller groups, the National Front was led by A. K. Chesterton, a cousin of the more famous Gilbert Keith Chesterton, the Catholic writer. A. K. had been a member of Mosley's BUF before the war but had become disillusioned with the movement over its pro-German sympathies. A British nationalist, Chesterton founded the League of Empire Loyalists (LEL) in 1955. This was one of the groups that formed the National Front (NF) along with some neofascist groups.

The NF emerged as part of a growing xenophobic sentiment in the United Kingdom because of non-white immigration from the former British colonies. Race riots in Notting Hill in the 1950s helped stoke these xenophobic sentiments. Apart from anti-Black racism, the NF also promoted antisemitism. In the early 1970s, neo-Nazis from the British Movement (BM) started to join the NF and eventually took over its leadership. Like the Italian MSI, the NF took to electoral politics, enjoying some minor successes at a local level, thanks to a spike in membership fueled by increasing anti-immigrant sentiment in the mid-1970s. Much of the support came from disaffected Labor voters in the working-class districts of the major cities (Gable 1991). The upward momentum stopped, however, with the rise of Margaret Thatcher and the Conservatives, who coopted the NF's anti-immigration rhetoric.

After the 1979 general election, the NF went through a leadership change that witnessed the rise of members from the Young National Front (YNF). Founded in the late 1970s, the YNF was reluctantly accepted by the front's leadership, wary of the skinhead culture the YNF exalted and its involvement in football (soccer) hooliganism. Joe Pearce was one of the leaders of the YNF after having independently created a newspaper called *Bulldog*. The paper was intensely xenophobic, railing at Blacks and Jews, and drinking deeply from neofascist and neo-Nazi ideas. To this end, the paper was not much different from the official organs of the NF. Where it differed was in its focus on culture and sport to incite racial hatred (J. Pearce 2013). Next to screeds against non-English ethnic groups were found football reports, especially those concerning the two most popular teams with the most far-right skinhead fans, West Ham United and Chelsea. Significant space was devoted to culture, especially music. Pearce's interest in the punk scene led him to organize the RAC events and eventually write the official biography of Ian Stuart and Skrewdriver.

The turn to culture proved decisive in renewing the NF in the wake of the movement's electoral failures. Culture was viewed as a means of appealing to the young, a group the NF old guard regarded warily. Intergenerational tensions flared up over the hooligans and skinheads who found Pearce's commentary more in line with their own interests as opposed to the older leadership who sometimes looked nostalgically on the past and preferred classical music to punk. Recruitment of youth came at concerts and football games, which the young preferred to old-style political meetings (Shaffer 2013; J. Pearce 2013). Pearce and the YNF also looked to recruit from the state schools by launching a campaign against communist indoctrination in the classrooms. In the early 1980s, Pearce, along with other YNF alumni like Nick Griffin and Derek Holland, took over the leadership of the party and moved away from active political engagement to put an emphasis on culture. This included the RAC festivals, which reached a high point in the latter part of the decade. It also marked the NF's embrace of the International Third Position movement that will be discussed later in the chapter.

The Impact of 1968

In turning to culture over politics, the NF was following a path that had earlier been laid out by French and Italian neofascists in the wake of the 1968 student riots. For neofascists, the Cold War offered little opportunity for growth; indeed, the neofascists remained weak and impotent (Griffin 2018, 100). Modest electoral gains by the MSI in Italy and the National Democratic Party (NPD) in West Germany did not amount to much in the end. For a neofascist, the choice seemed to be (a) either play a minor role in electoral politics or (b) go subversive and work with secret services (as discussed in the previous chapter). Another option, however, was terrorism. For many young, idealist neofascists, especially those in universities, none of these seemed attractive. Moreover, student activism was confined to the left, and this was especially evident with the student uprisings in 1968 beginning in France but also spreading to West Germany and Italy, among other places.

One of the factors that drove the student protests was an ideological package provided by intellectuals of the New Left. This movement represented a rejection of the old Marxism that focused exclusively on economic and political issues. For the New Left, cultural issues mattered just as much if not more in attracting youth. New Left thinkers, inspired by members of the so-called Frankfurt School like Theodor Adorno and Herbert Marcuse, turned their attentions to subjects like music and sexuality. Others focused on supporting the anti-colonial movements that were spreading throughout the world in the 1940s and 1950s. Fashion, art, music, and philosophy rather than bread and butter labor issues now became more important, as did protesting colonial wars, like those in Algeria and Vietnam. Some on the New Left also found inspiration in Mao Zedong's Cultural Revolution in China. The universities became the focal point of this New Left activism, resulting in the student uprisings in the spring of 1968.

The events of 1968 proved divisive in the ranks of the far right in Italy. The leaders of the MSI opposed the riots and demanded a "law and order" crackdown on the students (Mammone 2015, 136). This approach was criticized by members of the MSI's university association, the *Fronte Universitario d'Azione Nazionale* (FUAN), some of whom took part in the protests. The need to bring youth into the MSI and not alienate those already in it became a key concern for Giorgio Almirante, who returned as Party Secretary in 1969. Anxious to form a new coalition of allies called the *Nuova Destra*, and eager to suppress those who looked back nostalgically on historic fascism, Almirante encouraged a more cultural emphasis within the party. This was left to youth and the *Fronte della*

Gioventù (FdG). Formed in 1971 under the leadership of Massimo Anderson and Pietro Cerullo, the FdG aimed at recruiting youth by focusing on issues that mattered to them. The aim was to train the MSI's future leaders, as the founding generation was getting older and their politics of accommodation with the liberal democratic system was not paying off, despite some success in the 1972 general election.

Rejecting parliamentary politics, many of the members of the FdG were involved in the violence and extremism of the Years of Lead in the 1970s, as several became "martyrs" in their clashes with the far left. The background for this activism was shaped by cultural, rather than political, indoctrination. The militants of the FdG were less concerned with political theory than they were with cultural and philosophical discussions. This was partly due to the influence of the followers of Rauti. Pino Rauti had rejoined the MSI after Almirante became leader, and he brought many of his disciples with him from the *Ordino Nuovo* (ON), the splinter group he had created in the 1950s (discussed at the end of the last chapter). Rauti considered himself an intellectual as well as a political activist, and under his leadership, the ON became a "study group" that spent much of its time reading and discussing the works of conservative intellectuals, such as Nietzsche, Spengler, Jünger, and others. By far the most important figure was Julius Evola, the so-called "Black Baron" of Italian neofascism.

Julius Evola

Instead of looking to political or military leaders, the neofascists fashioned their cults of personality around intellectuals like Julius Evola. Born in Rome in the 1890s, Evola was an aristocrat of Sicilian background. After having served in the Great War, he became a Dadaist painter before dropping art for philosophy in the late 1920s. Inspired by Nietzsche, Evola gravitated to the philosophy of the German conservatives like Oswald Spengler. He became a neo-pagan, denounced Judeo-Christianity, and called for the return of the Roman Empire, a call that put him in sympathy with Mussolini's fascist regime. His hostility to the Roman Catholic Church, however, ensured that he could never become a card-carrying member of the Fascist Party, and he largely remained on the margins of the regime, despite his support for fascism in general. Evola called for a pure fascism, devoid of compromise with bourgeois institutions. He wanted a "radical, more intrepid Fascism, a really absolute Fascism, made of pure force, inaccessible to compromise" (Sedgwick 2004, 101).

By the 1930s, Evola was looking beyond Europe toward the Near East. Coming under the influence of the esoteric philosopher, René Guénon, Evola began to dabble in Eastern philosophy. In 1934, he published his first major work, *Revolt Against the Modern World*, in which he argued that the Western world was in a period of decline due to the embrace of materialism. Once ruled by a race of heroes, the West was now dominated by economic values and a spirit of egalitarianism. The West, once guided by uranic (male) values, was now ruled by telluric (female) ones. The warrior hero was gone and the feminized collectivist masses now ruled (Sedgwick 2004). Evola's ideas showed a clear influence of Nietzsche and Spengler, but equally important was his dabbling in Hindu philosophy. Such influence convinced him that the West was now going through the Kali Yuga, the fourth and final cycle of Hindu eschatology. This Age of Darkness, filled with conflict, sin, and misery would one day end and the cycle would be reborn. In the meantime, Evola called for a spiritual, aristocratic elite in anticipation of the collapse of the age and rebirth of the new age. This warrior caste needed to be ready to take charge once the new cycle began and a new dawn appeared for humanity.

Evola's mixing of Eastern mysticism with Western neo-paganism came to be called Traditionalism, a combination of "rationality and myth" that would have an enormous influence on neofascism (Eatwell 1995, 254). He had little influence before the war, however. Mussolini had little time for his esotericism, and Evola thus remained an outsider, though he did collaborate with Roberto Farinacci's journal *Il Regime Fascista* for a time until he was ousted for his heterodox views. Only when it came to antisemitism did Evola enjoy a brief period in the sun. Evola was a racist, but his idea of racism was spiritual, not biological. Mussolini, eager to distinguish his antisemitic policies from Hitler's, embraced Evola's ideas for a time, though this collaboration did not last, as Evola insisted that Italian fascism was not pure enough. Although the Germans preached a biological racism, Evola began looking to the SS as an example of Traditionalism in the world of the Axis. Here too he would eventually be disappointed, but the SS and its esoteric ritualism, and especially the pan-Europeanism found in the *Waffen-SS* divisions, gave him hope that an authentic fascism could yet be found.

These hopes, however, were dashed by the victory of the Allies in 1945. Evola himself barely survived the war, as he was wounded in a Russian bombing of Vienna, where he found himself in the final months of the war. But while fascism may have been dead, the postwar period provided an opportunity for Evola's ideas to flourish. Evola's estrangement from Mussolini and Hitler's regimes meant that he was not tainted by collaboration with them in the same way as others. It also meant that his fascism was not one of compromise. He could present his view of fascism as one that had never existed in practice; he thus became a guru for those looking to resurrect the idea of a pure fascism during the Cold War. In other words, he became a source of continuity between interwar and postwar fascism—but without the baggage (Griffin 2008).

It was during the postwar period that Evola's notoriety began to increase. In the 1940s, he became a mentor to those neofascists who had split from the MSI and engaged in terrorist activities. He was tried for being an accessory to terrorism but eventually acquitted. This brought Evola's name to national attention, and the philosopher responded by becoming a recluse in his swanky apartment on the Corso Vittorio in Rome. His apartment became a site of pilgrimage for young neofascists like Pino Rauti and his ON group; here, Evola held informal seminars on his Traditionalist ideas. Only a few short steps from Vatican City, Evola taught his disciples to reject the Catholic Church and embrace neo-pagan ideas and symbols. He taught them about the cycles of history and told them they were living in a decadent society destined to collapse. They were, literally, men among the ruins, the title of a book he published in the 1950s, which called for a rejection of both dominant ideological systems in the Cold War. Both communism and capitalism were part of the decadence and decay they were living in. These were two sides of the same coin, part of the same "syphilis of the spirit" that was crippling the West and that had taken away its virility (Laqueur 1996).

Evola's most influential work for his young neofascist disciples was *Ride the Tiger: A Survival Manual for the Aristocrats of the Soul*, first published in Italian in 1961. By this point, Evola had published numerous works that ranged from Tantric Sex to the Mysteries of the Holy Grail. In *Ride the Tiger*, Evola advised his acolytes to retreat from engagement with the modern world, especially politics, and concentrate on forming themselves as a spiritual aristocracy, standing aloof from the world and its materialism. The book posed a challenge to neofascists, as it effectively meant withdrawing from political activism into a state of *apoliteia*. Neofascists should become apolitical and therefore oppose the MSI's strategy of engaging in electoral politics. Notably, the book was published a year after the failure of the Tambroni Experiment, during which the MSI briefly supported the Christian Democratic government, only for anti-fascist riots to tank the experiment in 1960. The failure of the MSI's strategy served as a lesson to neofascists hoping to work within the rules of liberal democracy. For Evola, such activity was futile since it compromised the essence of fascism, a movement that was most pure on a metaphysical and spiritual plane.

Evola's influence did not necessarily mean passivity, though. Out of his "salon" came figures like the terrorists Stefano Delle Chiaie and Pierluigi Concutelli, both of whom spouted Evolian ideas as justifications for their acts of violence (Preparata 2013). Another neofascist terrorist who counted Evola as a teacher and guide was Franco Freda, who was implicated in the Piazza Fontana bombing of 1969, an event that inaugurated the so-called Years of Lead. These men viewed violence in metaphysical terms as an act of purification. More importantly, it also contributed to accelerationism, a means of hastening the catastrophe that comes at the end of the Kali Yuga. The "strategy of tension," discussed in the previous chapter, provided such an opportunity for terrorist activity to hasten the chaos.

Evola died in 1974, but his influence has grown among the far right, not only in Italy but internationally. For the generation of 1968, Evola had the effect of turning attention away from the cut and thrust of parliamentary politics and electoral alliances, focusing instead on metapolitical and cultural issues that transcended daily politics. When Giorgio Almirante returned as leader of the MSI in 1969, he was able to convince Rauti and his followers to rejoin by promising to bring in Evolian influences to the party. Rauti's journal, *Linea*, and the satiric newspaper, *La Voce della Fogna*, founded by Marco Tarchi in the year of Evola's death, all carried the distinctive marks of Evola's ideas. But his influence has spread beyond Italy. Most of his works have been translated into several languages, and his ideas appear to have enjoyed a renaissance in the twenty-first century, despite their hermetic nature. Notably, leading figures of the alt-right in the 2010s have rediscovered Evola and have disseminated his ideas in cyberspace (Griffin 2018; Jones 2022).

Alain de Benoist and the *Nouvelle Droite*

Julius Evola's most important work predated 1968, giving young neofascists a body of literature they could fall back on. In the case of Alain de Benoist in France, 1968 proved an inspiration to shift neofascism into intellectual gear. The product was a movement called the *Nouvelle Droite* (New Right). De Benoist was born during the war and thus had no direct experience with interwar fascism. As a student he became a French nationalist and a supporter of France's efforts to keep Algeria. With the loss of Algeria and the student protests of 1968, de Benoist began to explore new ways of renewing the right in the face of the New Left's challenge among French youth. In the same month the students of the Sorbonne were rioting in the streets of Paris, he founded *Groupement de Recherche et d'Études pour la Civilisation Européen* (GRECE), a think tank designed to explore the updating of right-wing thinking. This organization soon attracted several other thinkers and spawned numerous journals aimed at presenting far-right ideals, using the same methods as the left.

De Benoist's most innovative concept was to adopt the methods advocated by Antonio Gramsci, the Italian Marxist who had died in one of Mussolini's prisons. Before his death, Gramsci had outlined his concept of hegemony in his *Prison Notebooks*. Gramsci argued that capitalism had managed to maintain a hold on culture using so-called "organic intellectuals" placed in universities and other institutions. This hold on culture had prevented the proletarian revolution from taking place. The remedy, argued Gramsci, was for left-wing intellectuals to infiltrate elite institutions and create their own hegemony as a means of laying the groundwork for the future Marxist revolution. Inspired by this notion of hegemony, de Benoist argued that this is what was needed with right-wing intellectuals in the 1960s, since the "organic intellectuals" were now from the left and increasingly in control of elite institutions. According to Benoist, "When in May 1968, the New Right emerged ... there was a Left hegemony, quite evident within university circles and, generally speaking, among intellectuals" (Mammone 2015, 159–60).

De Benoist's project was a cultural one, aimed at transforming France's intellectual culture to be receptive to thinkers who had been marginalized, largely due to their associations with fascism and Nazism. De Benoist's strategy, based on the methods of the New Left, was to achieve "cultural power" for the New Right via academic and other intellectual institutions (Mammone 2015). Channeling Evola's apolitical stance, party politics were to be avoided. Instead, the thinkers of the New Right had to find their way into schools, academic presses, and journalism through rigorous intellectual work. In the late 1970s, de Benoist and his circle would achieve a degree of mainstream success when he began publishing regular columns in *Le Figaro Magazine*, a weekly supplement to the conservative newspaper of the same name. The influence of GRECE was demonstrated by the fact that some of its exponents became part of the magazine's editorial team (Shields 2007).

De Benoist's essays became a vehicle for reintroducing forgotten conservative intellectuals like Spengler and Carl Schmitt, but he also discussed intellectual figures from the left like Gramsci, Debord, and others, preventing him from descending into a far-right silo. He also aimed at modernizing the right, opening it up to sociological and leftist ideas, such as anti-globalism (Camus 2019). Despite these "openings," de Benoist's main ideas remain firmly on the far right and have made him, alongside Evola, one of the key intellectual fathers of modern neofascism. His views were succinctly spelled out in the book *Vue de Droite*, published in 1977, and subsequently given an award by the prestigious *Académie Française* (Johnson 1991). The award, and de Benoist's subsequent work for the mainstream press, has demonstrated that his work was more accessible than Evola's. Whereas Evola lived a semi-hermit's existence in his Rome apartment, rarely making public appearances, de Benoist fit into the mold of the "public intellectual." Despite these differences of comportment and methodology—Evola showed little interest in New Left approaches—the two men share much in common, such as the turn to culture.

De Benoist's influence on neofascism has been significant and has accompanied the work of Evola, shifting neofascism's focus on culture and the intellect and away from active political engagement in the existing liberal democratic structures of Western European states. Roger Griffin has distilled de Benoist's ideas into six concise points: (1) The protection of racial and cultural diversity; (2) the recognition that Europe is made up of distinctive national cultures but can be traced back to a common Indo-European heritage; (3) this common heritage of Europe is under threat, especially from globalism; (4) the two main threats come from American capitalism and Soviet Communism; (5) the presence of immigrants is a danger to national health; and (6) European decadence can be reversed through the cultural hegemony of heroic virtues (Griffin 2008).

De Benoist's key innovation in neofascism was his argument that "ethno-pluralism" or "differentialism" was something to be protected. He argued that all cultures were unique, and all should have their own protected living space. His belief in the diversity of cultures was something he shared with the New Left, but the neofascist element came in his argument that a hierarchy of races did exist and that European culture was superior to others. In other words, all cultures were different, but they were *not* equal (Mammone 2015). Moreover, different cultures and races should not intermix and should live separately. Immigration of non-white peoples to Europe should be stopped and reversed, if possible. Like Evola, de Benoist also argued for an elitist society where superior individuals would have absolute authority. These individuals would be intellectuals who had been prepared to implement a "gnostic revolution" (Griffin 2008). De Benoist rejected the economic values that undergirded liberal democracy and called for a "new anthropology" that recognized ethnic differences as the guiding force in history, not the values associated with Christianity and Marxism with their moral and economic precepts, respectively (Johnson 1991).

De Benoist's ideas, shared by the GRECE group of intellectuals, gained increasing mainstream acceptance into the 1980s, as immigrants from former French colonies in Africa and the Middle East flooded into France. These intellectuals were also embraced by youth movements in the French and Italian far right (Schir 2022). De Benoist's Identitarian views have been especially influential in the development of neofascism in the twenty-first century, as he remains a public figure on the French Right.

Europeanism

The Evola–de Benoist influence was especially strong in one area of neofascist thinking: Europeanism. In the wake of the Axis defeat in 1945, nationalism had largely gone out of style in Europe, and one of the factors that kept neofascist movements like the MSI in Italy was a focus on Italian nationalism. In France, it was the Gaullists and the Resistance tradition that had a monopoly on patriotism, while the fascist supporters of Vichy were tagged as collaborators and traitors. Neofascism, if it was to provide an alternative to Cold War dualisms, needed another way to keep some ties with historic fascism while also providing something new—an attachment to a European identity that served as an alternative to the bipolar world of the postwar. Europeanism was neofascism's true innovation with respect to historic fascism, argues Griffin (Griffin 2008, 164). However, Europeanism also shared some continuity with the interwar years, notably with Mussolini's attempt to create an International Fascism, discussed earlier in the book. The Axis fight in the Second World War also provided an important link, especially through the myth of the *Waffen-SS*.

It was during the war years that figures like Oswald Mosley, languishing in a British prison, and Maurice Bardèche, a professor of literature and supporter of the Vichy regime, began to dream of a Eurofascism that transcended national particularities. Disappointed in his country and its alliance with the Soviet Union against Germany, Mosely stepped back into the political arena in 1948 with the creation of the Union Movement (UM), a party that advocated a United Europe. Bardèche brought a more influential movement to the development of European neofascism. A Vichy apologist and a self-proclaimed fascist, Bardèche spearheaded the formation of the *Mouvement Sociale Européene* (MSE) in 1951. Whereas Mosley appealed to economic policies, Bardèche advocated culture as the basis for a pro-European movement to counter the two competing, and alien, ideologies of the Cold War. A close friend and relative by marriage of Robert Brasillach, the writer and collaborator executed by the Resistance after the war, Bardèche looked to the arts as the best vehicle to express European identity.

Working with neofascists from Italy's MSI, as well as Mosley's UM and other far right movements, Bardèche participated in a congress held at Malmö, Sweden, in 1951. The congress produced a ten-point program on the recommendation of Per Engdahl, the head of the Swedish delegates. A poet and the leader of the New Swedish movement, Engdahl has been sanctioned for his antisemitism and was banned from Switzerland and West Germany. In his ten points, Engdahl called for the formation of a united Europe under a common market, a common currency, and a unified military. Engdahl called for equality before the law and protection of rights, such as free speech. Moreover, each country within the nation was assured of its independence. Nothing was said about racial matters.

The restrained and liberal-sounding program caused a rift in the movement, resulting in the emergence of a dissident group calling itself the New European Order (NEO) led by René Binet, a former communist who had converted to racism during the war when he joined the Charlemagne Division of the *Waffen-SS*. A collaborator of Bardèche, Binet stormed out of the Malmö Congress when it refused to recognize white supremacy as a cornerstone of a united Europe. The group's name was created in 1954 and attracted the more radical and racist neofascist personalities such as Delle Chiaie. It also provided the language that would be used by Europeanist extremists on the Right, such as Black International.

These movements in the 1950s established the foundation for neofascism's Europeanism and its ethno-cultural drive. In 1952, Bardèche founded the journal *Défense de l'Occident* (Defense of the West) along with Jean-Louis Tixier-Vignancour, a lawyer and former Vichy administrator. The journal concerned itself with pan-European neofascist movements and ideas. It also defended Vichy and promoted Holocaust denial. The journal became the most important site for those who promoted a neofascist Europe. It also advocated a modernized neofascism that was less concerned with nations and more focused on a "European community" (Mammone 2015). Not surprisingly, given Bardèche's occupation as a literary critic, the journal emphasized culture with ample space given to literary and art reviews. Excerpts from the writings of prewar French fascists like Brasillach, Drieu la Rochelle, and others were also included, thus forging a link between neofascism and the cultural production of French fascism. Writings by Evola and German fascists were also included. Emphasis on culture placed the journal in a position to benefit from the post-1968 cultural turn. Bardèche continued to edit the journal until its folding in 1982.

A central element in the work of Bardèche and the early neofascist Europeanists involved historical revisionism. Bardèche became one of Europe's first Holocaust deniers. In 1947, he stated that the gas chambers at Auschwitz were used only to disinfect clothing and that documents and photographs were all forgeries (D. E. Lipstadt, 1994). Holocaust denial was one way to present the Axis on the "good" side, defending Europe from communism and Zionism. This required a positive view of the *Waffen-SS* and the War on the Eastern Front. Rather than being a genocidal war of conquest on the part of the Nazis, the invasion of the Soviet Union was one of defense against Judeo-Bolshevism. For European neofascists, the war against the Soviet Union became Europe's "Lost Cause" myth, analogous to that of the defeat of the Confederacy in America (Smelser and Davies III 2008). The international units of the *Waffen-SS* were viewed by some as the first truly European army and was composed of volunteers coming from thirty-seven nations, comprising over three hundred thousand men (Mosse 1991). While not all these volunteers could be considered Nazis, most held in common opposition to communism and shared some form of European ideal, according to the neofascist revisionists. One of the most eloquent apologists of the *Waffen-SS* was Adriano Romualdi, a neofascist intellectual and the son of one of the MSI's founders. In the preface to a biography of Drieu la Rochelle, Romualdi paid tribute to Hitler's move to create a European army to fight against "Yankee capitalism and Asiatic Bolshevism," thanks to the "sacrifice of a few hundred thousand of international SS fighters" (Griffin 2008, 170).

Behind the revisionism, which was often presented as objective truth, lay fantasy. The Europe envisioned by the neofascists was a product of an imagined past. Evola's dream was of a pagan Europe dominated by a warrior caste. His was ideally a Roman Empire before the advent of Christianity and informed by esoteric philosophies. Evola also fantasized about the Middle Ages, seeing the Axis as a reincarnation of the Ghibelline empire and the search for the Holy Grail (Sedgwick 2004). Evolian fantasies were further developed by one of his most ardent disciples, Romualdi, who published a series of books on the Runic traditions of Europe, proposing them as a blueprint for the future. For de Benoist, Europe needed to rediscover its Indo-European roots, the same group of people the Nazis called Aryans. These fevered dreams of a future Europe based on an imagined past formed a continuity with historic fascism. It also introduced a spiritual component, especially through the works of Evola, who, despite his paganism and hatred for Christianity, was an admirer of Corneliu Codreanu's Legion of the Archangel Michael. These elements made up Traditionalism and were subsequently expressed in the International Third Position.

International Third Position

Founded in Italy by far-right terrorists, these neofascists called themselves "political soldiers" and based their activism on the writings of Evola, Bardèche, de Benoist, and other gurus who had fashioned the cultural thrust of post-1968 neofascism. Third Positionism was a Europeanist movement that included a spiritual element combined with a decentralized vision of politics and the economy. It advocated violence when necessary but also promoted religious contemplation in a rural, primitive setting. At the center stood the Political Soldier, a kind of warrior monk, steeled against the forces of modernity by living a virtuous life on the land.

Third Positionism was a development in neofascism that envisioned working with groups that were previously considered anathema. Evolians now became open to Christianity, while neo-Nazis contemplated left-wing ideas that evoked the National Bolshevism of the 1920s. Meanwhile, white supremacists and Europeanists made alliances with pro-Arabs in Libya, Iran, and Iraq and with Louis Farrakhan's Black Nationalism in the United States. One of the inspirations behind ITP was the American neo-Nazi, Francis Parker Yockey. A supporter of the European Social Movement, Yockey's book *Imperium* called for the "liberation of Europe" from the yoke of the United States and Soviet Union, returning to an "age of Authority" led by a "culture-bearing" heroic elite (Lee 2000, 94–5). To advance this cause, Yockey advocated an alliance between the far right and far left to bring down American domination—this even meant supporting anti-colonial movements in the third world (Coogan 1999).

Yockey's ideas were shared to some extent by the Belgian neofascist Jean-François Thiriart. A former member of the *Waffen-SS*, Thiriart aimed to bring together far-right and far-left activists in a campaign to undermine the American and Soviet dominance of Europe, opening the way for a white racial paradise stretching from the Atlantic to the Pacific. In pursuing a united Europe, Thiriart founded *Jeune Europe* (Young Europe), a movement that predated the post-1968 far right youth groups. His manifesto for the group called for a renewed Europe independent of the Cold War powers. In a 1960 speech, Thiriart called for a "genuine Europe ... The Europe of the beautiful conceptions, the Europe of salons, will emerge from the Europe of guns, from the Europe of will power ... The Fourth Reich will be Europe, the Reich of the people from Brest to Bucharest" (Lee 2000, 170–1).

The Europe Thiriart fantasized needed a new class of men—which he called Political Soldiers—to bring it about. Based on the vanguard idea pioneered by Lenin's Bolsheviks, these elite soldiers would fight against American imperialism, often allying with left-wing subversives and third-world revolutionaries. Thiriart gradually shed the overtly Nazi symbols of *Jeune Europe* and began advocating for anti-colonial movements in his monthly magazine, *La Nation Européenne*. Eventually Thiriart began rejecting the term neofascism altogether, but, as Martin Lee has pointed out, he could never disassociate himself entirely from the far right, no matter how far he may have shifted to the left (Lee 2000, 172).

A similar alliance between the far right and far left was advocated by the Italian neofascist terrorist, Franco Freda. A product of Rauti's ON, Freda called for a Nazi–Maoist movement that fused ideas of Mao's Cultural Revolution and Evola's philosophy. In 1969, Freda published *The Disintegration of the System*, where he called for a strategic alliance between neofascists and far-left groups against American capitalism and Soviet Communism. In the book, Freda noted that large systems were breaking down and argued that the solution was for small cells to come together and form a common anti-capitalist front to oppose the political parties and institutions of the modern state and engage in "armed spontaneity." This book became the manifesto of *Lotta di Popolo*, a Nazi–Maoist group Freda founded in 1968 (Mammone 2015). Lest anyone think that Freda was shifting to the left, he advocated the Political Soldier idea as the model for his neofascists. According to Freda, the Political Soldier was driven by "cold and lucid fanaticism ... He must neither hate nor love ... He must keep *pure*, eschewing even hatred. Enemies must be eliminated as a simple matter of hygiene" (Ferraresi 1996, 182).

Freda's sketch of the Political Soldier and his willingness to make strategic alliances with non-fascist groups in a common front against the ideological powers of the Cold War prefigured, in some ways, the formation of *Terza Posizione* (TP) in Italy. Founded in Rome in 1979, the group called for a "popular revolution" that was neither reactionary nor red but inspired by Freda's call to attack the "system," which comprised the state and its ancillaries. TP aimed to harmonize cultural initiatives with terrorism. It was structured in a manner like the Romanian Iron Guard and Codreanu's Legion, with small cells called *cuib*. Not all who joined TP engaged in violence, as most members belonged to the open structure, while a select elite formed the secret "aristocracy of the aristocracy," or future ruling elite. Meanwhile, a clandestine group engaged in acts of violence (Ferraresi 1996). Its leaders—men like Giuseppe "Peppe" Dimitri, Roberto Fiore, and Gabriele Adinolfi—had all been associates of Delle Chiaie and the NAR.

Political Soldiers

In 1980, some of these men were implicated in the Bologna Train Station bombing that killed over eighty people (mentioned in the previous chapter). To avoid prosecution, Roberto Fiore and other members of the TP fled to the United Kingdom and helped found the International Third Position with leading members of the National Front. As discussed earlier in this chapter, the NF had fallen into the hands of a younger generation of leaders who had helped engineer the NF's cultural turn in the late 1970s. These included Nick Griffin, Joe Pearce, and Derek Holland, who immediately established connections with the exiled Fiore and his group (Copsey 2008). In his memoirs, Joseph Pearce describes how the NF leaders were seduced by Fiore and his sophistication and cultured manners. "Whereas the NF's membership was becoming more proletarian," writes Pearce, "our Italian confreres were clearly better educated and more cultured" (J. Pearce 2013, 114). Fiore, recalls Pearce, could play Beethoven on the piano. He also led military exercises in Hampshire where he developed his skills in the martial arts. Furthermore, Fiore seemed to be interested in spiritual matters, telling Pearce that he was a nonbeliever but knew a great deal about Catholicism.

By the mid-1980s, Third Positionism had become the dominant ideology of the NF. This was clearly demonstrated in the manifesto of the ITP, authored by Derek Holland of the NF. Like Pearce and Griffin, Holland came up through the ranks of the YNF. In 1983, frustrated by the hesitancy of the NF's leadership to adopt revolutionary principles, Holland founded a semi-clandestine magazine called *Rising*, in which he promoted Third Position principles. In 1984, Holland pulled his ideas together and issued the Political Soldier Statement along with the Declaration of Principles.

In the statement, Holland presents the Political Soldier as a spiritual warrior, in line with the teachings of Evola—except that Holland is inspired by Traditionalist Catholicism, an ideology that rejected the reforms of the Second Vatican Council (1962–5) and aspired to Integralism. The tract is peppered with quotes from Catholic writers, such as G. K. Chesterton and Hilaire Belloc. Holland begins with the customary view of contemporary Europe: a continent in decline due to its unfettered materialism, which has upset the balance between the material and spiritual required for a healthy society. Channeling his Catholicism, Holland identifies societal estrangement from the Catholic past as the source of these ills: "When we look at the great Cathedrals," writes Holland, "that are to be found throughout Europe and built many hundreds of years ago, we are overawed by their immensity, their complexity, their beauty" (Holland 1984, 1994, 7). The death of Europe will also be the end of the White peoples, argues Holland, but the situation is not irreversible. For Holland, inspiration to reverse the decline of Europe can be found in the historical mythical models of the Spartans, the Roman centurions, and especially in the medieval Crusaders, since the knight-warriors were a pan-European force.

In an updated version of the Fascist New Man, Holland proposed that the Political Soldier will be sustained by Catholic virtues like justice, faith, humility, and compassion. "He will be stirred to action by the physical rape of our beautiful country and the destruction of our rich culture," argues Holland, and "his compassion will be such that he will cloak the weak and the needy of our nation with his towering strength. His love will be pure and refreshing, reviving and inspiring everyone and everything it touches" (Holland 1984, 1994, 11). The "enemies" of the Political Soldier are the classic ones of fascism and neofascism, namely the banks, the communists, the Freemasons, the Zionists, and the capitalists. Like a religious missionary, the Political Soldier needs to be both realist and idealist if he is to accomplish his goals.

In Part Three of his statement, Holland makes the connections between the Political Soldier and the Catholic more clearly. He begins the section with an epigraph from Thomas à Kempis' *Imitation of Christ*. In it, Holland gives some spiritual and physical advice, such as not watching television and avoiding excessive drinking. He also presents the making of a Political Soldier as akin to spiritual formation where the acolyte will stumble and fail often but must keep going and be satisfied with small accomplishments along the way. Developing virtuous habits like reading, self-improvement, and even a sense of humor is vital. The Political Soldier, claims Holland, must laugh at his trials. Learning martial arts and practical skills like other languages and driving are also crucial, especially if one is to make connections with foreign soldiers. Ultimately, the Political Soldier needs to master the three cardinal virtues of TP: patience, calmness, and self-discipline. He even provides an oath modeled on Corneliu Codreanu's Legion of the Archangel Michael's ideal of the medieval Crusaders. It ends with the exhortation: Long Live Death!

The connections between Traditionalist Catholicism and neofascism are made even more explicit in Holland's Declaration of Principles for the ITP. He lays out 10 principles that define the ITP, beginning with the Primacy of the Spirit, where he makes the following claim: "It is equally the belief of the Third Position that the splendor of Europe, viewed historically and culturally, has its roots in the doctrine and practice of the Christian faith" (Holland 1984, 1994, 19). Accompanying this point is a traditional devotional image of the Archangel Michael slaying the dragon. In the other points, Holland emphasizes the "Moral Order" and claims that only truth has rights. He sets up a series of moral absolutes where there is no gray. Here he also lays out opposition to abortion, artificial birth control, euthanasia, divorce, and homosexuality, all of which conform to Catholic teaching. In the "Ideal of Popular Rule," Holland argues for decentralized political structures that all political principles derive from God's law, which echoes Catholic social teaching and Integralism.

In other principles, Holland states his opposition to Zionism and support for the Palestinians, in a move that harmonizes with leftist positions. In "Preservation of the Environment and the Menace of Bankerdom," Holland echoes leftist ideals. Furthermore, in the last principle, National Revolution Worldwide, Holland calls for all peoples around the world to work together toward a New Social Order that resembles the leftist call for anti-colonial struggles and the liberation from Western and Soviet empires. Finally, the Third Position called for an end to the unjust concentration of wealth found in capitalism and socialism and, instead, for the building of an economy based on small, decentralized, ownership. Here, Holland is promoting the ideas of Distributism advocated by the Catholic thinkers Belloc and Chesterton, whose ideas reflected a Left Catholicism that was opposed to big business and big landowners.

Where was neofascism? Should anyone doubt Holland's commitment to the far right, the sixth principle, "Racial and Cultural Diversity," reflected the neofascist belief that the world was and should be divided by race, that it would be best if there were no multiracial societies or mixing of races. In other words, in an argument that resembled that of de Benoist and the New Right, each culture needs to be rooted in its own place. Once again, Holland attempts to impose a religious meaning on this, arguing that it is "both healthy and divinely ordained that people should have a genuine love for their own kind" and that "Racial Separatism" is the best antidote to the "abyss of multi-racism" (Holland 1984, 1994, 22). Holland leaves no doubt that, should ITP ever achieve power, the resettlement of races (forced deportations) will be undertaken to "build a more peaceful world," which means racial homogeneity.

In some ways, Holland's manifesto reflected a personal vision of ITP that may not have been shared by all neofascists, especially those uncomfortable with Catholicism. However, Holland did not state in his manifesto that the Political Soldier could also be found in the Iranian Revolutionary Guard. Holland, along with Pearce, Griffin, and Patrick Harrington in the NF, had no qualms about reaching out to pan-Arab nationalists and other rulers in the Muslim world like Muammar Gaddafi, who espoused an ideology called Third International Theory, which mixed Arab nationalism with elements of socialism and anti-imperialism. They also made contacts with Black Nationalists in the United States.

Most of the NF TP adherents supported Strasserism, a Nazi Left ideology which resembled Distributism. Strasserism was named after the Strasser brothers, Gregor and Otto. Early members of the National Socialist Party in Germany, this pair had been kicked out by Hitler when the Nazi Party's wealthy contributors began to feel threatened by their leftist ideas. The Strasserite wing of the NSDAP went underground and were able to reemerge after the war. Like Evola in Italy, they had benefited from being marginalized during the interwar years. Unlike his brother, who had been murdered during the Night of the Long Knives (first discussed in Chapter 5), Otto Strasser survived the war and went on to support a movement called the Third Front, a precursor to Third Positionism. He maintained his antisemitism but moved closer to Christianity in his later years. An opponent of parliamentary government, Strasser continued to promote the ideal society as one based on small, rural land ownership where political power was decentralized. Becoming a Strasserite was convenient for those in the NF who were not comfortable with Hitler worship but still wanted to find something positive in Nazism. Strasserism would also provide some common ground for Catholics, like Holland and Joe Pearce, who found Strasserism to be like the Catholic concept of subsidiarity (J. Pearce 2013).

In some ways, ITP represented the culmination of the cultural turn in post-1968 neofascism. By the 1980s, it had managed to bring together the cultural and philosophical ideas associated with Evola, de Benoist, and earlier far right authors like Spengler, Nietzsche, and Jünger, together with political activism, social and economic ideas, and internationalism. It was an innovative initiative but one that made connections to prewar fascism without indulging in nostalgia. It found its greatest appeal, however, in the youth. It was the YNF that made ITP the dominant ideology in the National Front. In Italy, *Terza Posizione* grew rapidly, as new cells sprouted up and down the peninsula from its home base in Rome (Ferraresi 1996). The popularity of this radical neofascist movement lay in its willingness to make contacts with non-fascist groups, including those on the far left, and to entertain ideas from a broad spectrum of thinkers. It also was not afraid to link up with pop culture movements and underground youth groups like the skinheads. It was the cultural scene that shaped post-1968 neofascism and permitted groups like the ITP to flourish.

Skinheads and Hobbits

The group that took over the NF in the 1980s was the same group that had introduced skinhead culture into the movement and organized Rock against Communism. Skinhead culture was born in England in the late 1960s in predominantly white, working-class youth in the cities (Laqueur 1996). They were gangs, in the tradition of Teds, Mods, and Rockers, other youth gangs that had sprouted up in the UK after the war. Like these other groups, the skinheads wore distinctive clothing like t-shirts, heavy jackets, and boots, their heads shaved. They did not have any specific political orientation apart from a general rejection of conventional society and its institutions. Of those who did show an interest in politics, some went to the far left and became anarchists, while others gravitated to the far right. To shock, many wore swastikas or Iron Crosses and shouted Nazi slogans (Laqueur 1996). Their days were spent hanging around in packs and causing general mayhem.

It was these groups that became devoted followers of punk music in the mid-1970s, and it was to them that the YNF appealed. They could also be found in football stadiums where they became part of the general hooliganism that marred English football in the 1970s and 1980s. Bands like Skrewdriver and concerts like RAC appealed mostly to these groups, who for a time became the foot soldiers of British neofascism. From Great Britain, skinhead culture, particularly the far-right variety, spread to other countries, notably West Germany and the United States. The appeal remained almost exclusively to white men, who could be counted on for a healthy dose of xenophobia. The skinhead bands mentioned earlier in the chapter played to a sense of white grievance and white identity, which marginalized the bands and their music from the mainstream. Despite this, or because of it, skinhead bands sprouted up in these countries, in Scandinavia and, to a lesser extent, France and Italy.

When the NF dissolved in the late 1980s, Griffin and others went on to lead the British National Party, an attempt to mainstream neofascist ideas to participate in elections. Skinhead culture was left behind as bands like Skrewdriver moved toward overt neo-Nazism. Griffin had been one of the founders of White Noise Records in 1983, and it was on his estate that the RAC festivals took place. However, by the late 1990s Griffin denounced skinhead music and declared his preference for folk music (Shaffer 2017).

Griffin's rise in the NF and that of Holland, Harrington, and others had come on the back of this skinhead presence in the movement, making it of fundamental importance in the eventual success of the BNP in elections. It was evidence that the post-1968 youth movement and cultural turn had created a thriving subculture of neofascism that allowed its proponents to later exploit opportunities in the post-Cold War era.

A similar, if seemingly more innocuous development came within Italian neofascism and the embrace of Tolkien's Hobbits. The establishment of the *Fronte della Gioventù* by the MSI in the early 1970s proved remarkably successful in recruiting youth to a party that had seemed to become a bastion of old fascists. Almirante's opening to youth and to the more radical elements around Rauti created a space for young people to explore cultural avenues within the movement that had previously been ignored. Once again, it was the left that led the way when, in 1977, a substantial group of young communists broke off from the established party and the unions to create the Movement of 1977. Influenced by developments in the UK, the Movement embraced the punk subculture.

Inspired by this, young neofascists came to identify with the same subculture, at times sharing the same interests as those on the left. For example, a study of FdG posters in the 1970s showed that they copied those of the leftist youth groups (Cheles 1991). Like the left, these neofascist youth spent more time on cultural activities, such as reading groups, theatrical performances, and especially musical concerts. Punk music and skinhead culture were not as popular, though there were some Italian examples. The more popular form of music among Italian neofascists was the singer-songwriter genre, a folksy style like the leftist protest music of the 1960s. One of the leading artists was Massimo Morsello, a member of the terrorist NAR and implicated along with Roberto Fiore in the Bologna bombing of 1980. Morsello's style echoed the left-wing music of Francesco De Gregori. His songs revolved around themes that struck a chord with young neofascists. In songs like, "*Noi non siamo uomini d'oggi,*" he laments the fact that neofascists are living in the wrong era. Another song declared democracy to be a tyranny, while another protested abortion. A notable recording was his 1981 album, *Nostri Canti Assassini*, which evoked his experiences during the Years of Lead and included tributes to fallen comrades. The album was composed and recorded in England and Germany during his fugitive years.

In 1977, Morsello was one of the headline acts at a new festival organized by Marco Tarchi in Benevento. The festival was the first *Campo Hobbit*, dedicated to J. R. R. Tolkien's *Lord of the Rings*, and another example of how neofascist youth were opening to the left through a work that had been popular with hippies of the 1960s (Mammone 2015). The embrace of Tolkien's fantasy work became a distinctive feature of neofascist youth, and the Hobbit Camps attracted large crowds. Three of them were held between 1977 and 1980, where they became generational markers for men and women who would eventually become leaders of the movement. The atmosphere was one of a pop festival mixed with summer camp. Music performances alternated with discussions on Tolkien, and the attendees slept in tents. One could be mistaken for seeing these events as innocuous if it was not for the menacing security staff wearing Celtic Cross armbands (Last 2017).

The festival was a great success. It allowed the attendees to dress up in Hobbit costumes, dance, and browse the book stalls filled with titles from the authors of the right, such as Evola, Spengler, Romualdi, and others. Set in a field near some ruins, the campers could imagine themselves in a neofascist playland. The areas of the camp were named after heroes of the Italian neofascists, such as the *Porta* Adriano Romualdi, who had died young in a car accident several years before the first camp. One of the pathways was dedicated to the French fascist Robert Brasillach. Murals of Crusader knights were painted on the walls, while banners read "Gandalf Lives!" Shockingly, at least for the old guard, there was nudity and sex. In fact, Tarchi hinted at possible orgies in his satirical magazine *La Voce della Fogna*. "What do you think about…a true, alternative, two-day musical event, with tents and sleeping bags," wrote Tarchi, "we cannot guarantee you some orgies: yet our female readers might know us in person" (Mammone 2015, 173).

This strange mix of Tolkien, sex, and neofascist Traditionalism was part of the experience that many neofascist youth craved in the 1970s. It allowed them to enjoy the same kind of communal experience that had been the exclusive preserve of the left and distinguished them from their fascist elders who were still hanging on the reins of the MSI. However, like their elders, these young people escaped into a world of political fantasy. Tolkien's world seemed fitting for those neofascists looking to escape the contemporary world and fantasize about a world shaped by racial and ethnic determinism and where good and evil were unambiguous (Last 2017). The hobbits of middle earth were good, simple people like the rural peasants who fascists and neofascists idealized. They lived in a world of moral clarity and simplicity called the Shire. The orcs, on the other hand, were an evil and brutish race, easily identifiable as monsters.

Tolkien's Catholic sensibilities and the neo-medieval setting of the stories made the stories more attractive to neofascists steeped in the mythologies purveyed by far-right philosophers. Furthermore, Tolkien's story bore some striking similarities to Richard Wagner's Ring Cycle. There too, there is a magic ring and an evil character, Alberich, who, according to some critics, was made up of antisemitic stereotypes. Like Wagner for the Nazis, Tolkien served up a fantasy world made up of heroes and villains and magic rings. Tolkien, like Wagner, knew his folklore and mythologies, and his stories appealed to those who had read Evola and his musings on the Holy Grail. Dabbling in Tolkien also connected neofascists with pop culture, one that they could share with their adversaries on the left albeit taking away some very different meanings. The antimodern and Traditionalist reading of *Lord of the Rings* was the product of Elémire Zolla, an Italian philosopher who specialized in esoteric religions and Eastern mysticism and who wrote the introduction to the first Italian translation of Tolkien's work in 1970. Whatever Tolkien's own politics were, his traditional Catholicism stood him in good stead with some neofascists, especially those who belonged to *Terza Posizione*.

Conclusion

Neofascism's cultural turn after 1968 revitalized a movement that seemed stuck in a nostalgia for historic fascism and that was having difficulty appealing to youth. By appropriating pop culture themes, the neofascists and neo-Nazis were able to mask their continued fidelity to historic, interwar fascism. When he introduced the *Nuova Destra* in 1972, the MSI leader Giorgio Almirante told his followers to put away the obvious fascist gestures and slogans and adopt a language that was more palatable to a mainstream audience (Cheles 1991). This especially applied to the recruitment of a younger generation that had not been alive during the war. Almirante was looking to create a modernized neofascism that could speak to those living in the contemporary world in a manner that would build for the future but also look back to the past for renewal. He called this "nostalgia for the future."

The cultural turn did provide innovation for neofascism by bringing in popular music, fashion, and styles that were shared by youth in the West. Ian Stuart of Skrewdriver began his musical career playing Rolling Stones cover songs. His White Power career showed experimentation and development beginning with punk rock and then shifting to heavy metal. Many of the British neofascists supported mainstream pop artists like David Bowie. Italian neofascists listened to left-wing folk singers like Francesco De Gregori. Hippies on the left shared the right's interest in Tolkien and the comic book style adopted by the FdG in its publications demonstrated strong influences from pop art. The looser sexual behavior at Campo Hobbit would not have been approved by the first generation of neofascists, but it was precisely in this that the young fascists found common cause with their opposite numbers on the New Left. Far right thinkers like Alain de Benoist had no problem adopting the methods of Gramsci and publishing left-wing thinkers in his magazines.

However, alongside these innovations and crossovers, there remained a strong link to the past, and even a renewal of original fascism. De Benoist's *Nouvelle Droite* was a throwback to the cultural focus of French fascism, especially in the tradition of Charles Maurras and the *Action Française* (Johnson 1991). French fascism had also been heavily into literature, and the young neofascists were rediscovering the work of Brasillach, Drieu La Rochelle, and Céline. Crossovers from left to right evoked the history of Jacques Doriot, not to mention the Italian anarcho-syndicalists like Mussolini and other founding members of the PNF. Interest in Roman Catholicism was also nothing new, recalling the clerical fascism in the French leagues, Tiso's regime in Slovakia, and the *Ustaša* in Croatia, not to mention Codreanu's League of the Archangel Michael, which inspired neo-pagans like Julius Evola. The rediscovery of the German Conservative intellectuals of the early twentieth century cannot be ignored, nor can the dabbling in esoteric ideas like those that circulated the beer halls in post-Great War Munich.

The post-1968 neofascists understood the deep connection between culture and politics that had informed the birth of fascism in the early twentieth century and, like those early founders, rejected liberal parliamentary traditions and materialist ideologies, like communism. In a sense, this new generation searched for an authentic and spiritual fascism, much like Evola had sought in the 1930s but did not see in the actual fascist and Nazi regimes, except partially. Like Evola after 1945, the neofascists at the end of the twentieth century were poised to take advantage of the end of the Cold War, and the return of ethno-cultural identity politics that followed the collapse of the Berlin Wall.

CHAPTER 13
FASCISM IN THE NEW MILLENNIUM

"Jews will not replace us!"

The scenes were shocking. A gray Dodge Challenger plowed into a crowd of protesters in the college town of Charlottesville, Virginia. After hitting a parked car and several people, the Challenger reversed at high speed, striking several others and leaving chaos in its wake. Bodies were left sprawling on the road and sidewalk while the significantly damaged car made its escape. One woman, thirty-two-year-old Heather Heyer, a paralegal who worked in Charlottesville, was dead, while several others were injured. Heyer had been participating in an anti-fascist demonstration, and the perpetrator was a part of the Unite the Right rally, held that day to protest the removal of a statue of Robert E. Lee from the city's Emancipation Park. James Alex Fields, Jr., a native of Ohio, was a white Nationalist who had been seen earlier that day marching with the neo-Nazi Vanguard America group.

These events of August 12, 2017, were captured by cell phone cameras and made the evening news, shocking Americans who were seeing an open display of the various neo-Nazi and neo-Confederate groups who previously had merely a virtual footprint on the internet. A *Vice* documentary was created by an embedded reporter who interviewed a leading member of Stormfront, a neo-Nazi website. The Stormfront interviewee claimed the rally was an example of the far right "slowly unveiling our power level" (Elle Reeve, dir 2017). The ostensible reason for the rally was to protest the removal of the statue, but it seems that the real motive was to take advantage of the moment and show the world the movement was on the rise. The time had come to reveal the existence of white Nationalism as a political and cultural force aimed at protecting America's heritage from those who wanted to "erase history" by removing statues. The drive to take down statues of Confederate generals was the result of the actions of a white Nationalist, Dylann Roof, who, in 2015, had murdered nine black churchgoers in Charleston, North Carolina.

Like Fields, Roof was motivated by white supremacy. He was wearing a jacket with Confederate patches, the emblems of Rhodesia, and the number 88, a reference to Adolf Hitler. He had made anti-Black statements on social media and had been radicalized online via white Nationalist websites. Significantly, he had never met another neo-Nazi in person. He was emblematic of the twenty-first century neo-Nazi, a lone wolf activist, a product of the "leaderless resistance," someone who decided to take matters into his own hands (Belew 2018, 237–8). Fields's attack was in keeping with this lone wolf tactic, which had become standard for neo-Nazis since the 1990s. It indicated the changes that characterized neo-Nazi and neofascist movements in the new millennium. The mass movements of the interwar era were now replaced by individuals committing terrorist acts as a means of accelerating the chaos that would usher in a new golden age of fascism.

The specter of fascism hung heavily over the events of Charlottesville. Aside from the ubiquitous Confederate flags were numerous neo-Nazi symbols on flags and shields. Swastikas, SS lightning bolts, and runic symbols (popular with neofascists) were on clear display, and its members wore helmets and shields (Kaplan and Lipstadt 2020). The march presented a who's who of what became known as the alt-right, a name coined by Richard Spencer, a white Nationalist and leader of the National Policy Institute. Spencer had become notorious for leading a "Hail Trump" chant at the CPAC convention in 2016. Organized by Jason Kessler, the Unite the Right rally involved various groups, ranging from neo-Confederates to members of the Ku Klux Klan, like David Duke. Also present were members of various militia groups. The most prominent of the groups, however, were neo-Nazis. They included Vanguard America, the Traditionalist Worker Party, the National Socialist Movement, and Identity Evropa (sic), among other smaller groups. Their symbols ranged from pagan runes to Crusader symbols and slogans like *Deus Vult!* ("God wills it"). The Crusader imagery was abundant. The symbols of the Knights Templar linked the Catholic Middle Ages to the post-Civil War activism of the Ku Klux Klan (Gabriele 2019).

Taking advantage of Virginia's open carry laws, these groups were armed, many of them carrying AR-15s, the weapon of choice for lone wolf, far-right terrorists. Indeed, inspired by the events of Charlottesville, the next few years would witness far-right terrorists carry out mass shootings in El Paso, Texas, Buffalo, and New York and at a synagogue in Pittsburgh. Synagogues and mosques were targeted in San Diego, Pittsburgh, and Christchurch, New Zealand. All of them came in the wake of the violence in Charlottesville, and the perpetrators had all been radicalized online by neo-Nazi ideology (Kaplan and Lipstadt 2020). They were connected by a conspiracy theory: they believed a Great Replacement was underway, a plan to replace the white race by immigrants, a plan put in place by Globalists—that is, the Jews.

The Great Replacement Theory (GRT) was one of the main themes holding these groups together—and it was on full, terrifying display the night before the rally. On the night of August 11, dozens of men carrying tiki torches dressed in polo shirts marched through the University of Virginia's campus. They were influenced by a similar event that occurred the previous May, when Richard Spencer led a similar march through Charlottesville chanting "you will not replace us," a reference to the Great Replacement Theory. In August, the marchers changed this to "Jews will not replace us," an obvious reference to their belief that GRT was a Jewish conspiracy to destroy America. The nighttime torch ceremony, the chanting, and the "uniforms" had clear echoes to the Nazi marches of the Third Reich. Antisemitism was on full display. There were other chants, like the Fourteen Words: "we must secure the existence of our people and a future for white children" (Kaplan and Lipstadt 2020). The Fourteen Words, along with GRT, are standards in the White Power movement, which was aggressively on display in Charlottesville. To further prove the point, the marchers on that Saturday surrounded the local synagogue with armed men and forced the congregants to leave by a back door, taking the Torah scrolls with them for safekeeping.

To be sure, the Unite the Right marchers met with counter-protesters, like Heather Heyer, both on Friday evening and Saturday. In the clashes, some of the alt-right protesters were hit by pepper spray. The counter-protesters often outnumbered the Unite the Righters, and the potential for escalating danger led the Governor of Virginia to declare a state of emergency. When Jason Kessler, one of the organizers, attempted to hold a press conference, he was shouted down by the counter-protesters. This was the immediate context of Fields's terroristic act on Saturday afternoon.

The events at Charlottesville demonstrated that neo-Nazism was real and existed beyond the world of the internet. It also demonstrated that opposition to white Nationalism was real and that any fantasies the alt-right might hold would be strongly countered. Despite this, the reaction from federal authorities remained ambiguous. When President Donald Trump was asked about these events, he gave an equivocal answer that suggested that the Unite the Righters might include some "fine people." Whatever Trump's own views were, his statements fit a pattern that suggested that these extreme ideas were becoming more mainstream in American life. While most Americans were shocked by what happened at Charlottesville, the rally merely made visible what had been stewing on the American right for several decades. Many of the groups at Charlottesville had been formed in the 2010s, but others existed since the 1980s and beyond. Furthermore, the symbols, chants, and the violence demonstrated in 2017 were part of an international network of extreme right movements that had been festering in Europe since the fall of the Berlin Wall. Many of these groups had connections with similar groups in Europe, giving rise to a new, virtual "anti-Black International."

Charlottesville was a revelation. It revealed not only the various groups found on the alt-right, but also their guiding ideas. The chants, the tiki torches, the shields, and the flags represented the great coming out party of the extreme right. They showed that the new fascists and the new Nazis made up an archipelago of small groups, each with their own distinctive style and symbols. No longer interested in building the mass political parties of the interwar period, neo-Nazis and neofascists were now a "disaggregation" of small cells, developed through a process of "minisculization" (Griffin 2022). Furthermore, they had no obvious leadership. Instead, the rally was led by independent organizers, all of whom lacked the charisma of a classic fascist leader. These were small groups of uncertain membership. Fields's group claimed that they did not belong to these other groups, even though he was wearing the same outfit as the other members. This is plausible, as these alt-right groups are mostly driven by online networks where individuals can "belong" to a group without knowing each other in person.

Apart from the shape of these movements, it is their ideals that hold them together and see that they are guided by certain core principles. The most prominent "myth" at Charlottesville was the GRT, a conspiratorial fantasy that integrated both white ethno-nationalist and antisemitic sentiment. This was Identitarianism on full display, one of the most prominent features of the modern far right. At the heart of this movement is the belief that liberal institutions, run by an international cabal of "globalists," are using democracy to replace white people with immigrants. This process is meant, ultimately, to destroy white identity. Other, less racially motivated groups replace white with Western identity. At Charlottesville, most groups were racially motivated.

Apart from these more obvious messages, other factors were on full display that weekend in the summer of 2017. Most of the participants at the rally were men. The car that Fields used to murder Heyer and injure other demonstrators was a symbol of hypermasculinity. The alt-right is driven by masculinist beliefs, as is made clear by many of the popular manifestos and books making the rounds of these groups, such as *Bronze Age Pervert*. The misogynist Incel movement, which preaches the superiority of men over women, favors extremist violence and promotes terroristic acts, such as the Toronto van attack in 2018 (O'Donnell and Shor 2022). The violence of Charlottesville, both actual and potential, reflected the hypermasculinity of their beliefs. This was evident in the presence of groups like the Proud Boys, a vigilante movement of which Kessler was a former member. The Proud Boys are a group that attributes the ills of the white working class to feminists and women in general, who "have defied what they [the Proud Boys] believe to be the natural order of things" (Kutner 2020).

Underlining the hypermasculinity, the appeal of violence, and the penchant for conspiracy was fantasy, easily seen in the cosplay of the marchers, many of whom were dressed as medieval Crusaders or Axis soldiers from the Second World War. If it wasn't for the deadly seriousness of the event, one could mistake this for a Halloween party. The marchers wore uniforms that established their Identitarian cause and allowed them to play out their fantasies as Crusaders defending Western civilization. A similar crew of people would show up at the "Capitol Insurrection" in 2021 (Gabriele 2021). It was an imagined attempt to unify the "groupuscules" that make up the alt-right into a cohesive and unified group. It also revolved around a fantasy to preserve the memory of the Confederacy, an appeal to the Lost Cause myth that had permeated Southern culture since Reconstruction. Like all neo-Nazi and neofascist groups, revisionist history—motivated by a fantasy of redemption, racial superiority, and ethnic purity—defined the costumes worn by the participants. The Crusades were turned into a heroic enterprise, while Robert E. Lee was held up as an ethno-nationalist icon. Permeating these myths were darker visions of a civilization that was degenerating under the influence of liberalism and controlled by a worldwide cabal of Jews, emboldened by the myth of the Holocaust. The ultimate dystopian fantasy was of a world where the white race was being attacked. Many of the groups at Charlottesville fantasized about an end-times race war and hoped to accelerate this ultimate showdown, which would determine the fate of the West. These scenarios have been played out in works of literature, as in William Pierce's *The Turner Diaries*, which provides a six-step strategy to starting a race war (Belew 2018). Also notable is the influence of James Mason's *Siege*, a compendium of essays that provides a handbook for accelerationism.

Making a show of force and giving some concrete shape to these fantasies of the alt-right was not an original idea of Kessler and company. The Unite the Right Rally was the American manifestation of neo-Nazi and neofascist rallies that had been gathering momentum in the West since the early 2000s, rallies that have picked up steam with the refugee crisis of the 2010s. Some of them, like the "Watch on the Yser," have roots that go back to the post-Great War era. The Yser Tower was built to commemorate the Flemish soldiers who had died in the First World War and was originally intended as a "peace march." After the Second World War, the Flemish had been pegged as Nazi collaborators by French-speaking Belgians, and the tower was bombed (Bekers, De Meyer and De Kooning 2021). Rebuilt in the 1960s, the tower has become a totemic site for neo-Nazis from across Europe who support the ethno-nationalist secessionist claims of the far right *Vlaams Blok* ("Flemish Bloc"). The march increasingly attracted extremist groups, and, when these marches were banned, they organized their own march beginning in 2003 (The Yser Tower: The Legacy of the First World War). The site is an attractive one for those on the far right with its two hundred and seventy-six foot cross made of concrete and brick. Here, neo-Nazi movements, with their pagan, runic symbols mingle with the strongly Catholic imagery of the site. The original tower bore the slogan of the Catholic Flemish Movement, "All for Flanders—Flanders for Christ" (Bekers, De Meyer and De Kooning 2021, 538). The current site, which includes the "Trench of Death" and memorial stones to individuals, retains a strong Catholic symbolism that can easily overlap with neo-Nazism's cult of martyrdom and redemption (Van den Dries 2014).

Similar marches have appeared in Eastern Europe since the end of the Cold War and inspired Unite the Right in Charlottesville. Since 1997, far-right nationalists in Hungary have been commemorating the Nazi resistance to Soviet encirclement in 1945. Known as the Day of Honor, it has attracted neo-Nazi and neofascist groups from around Europe. In 2022, the Hungarian government finally banned the rally, citing extremism and fears of public order (BIRN 2022). Despite this, commemorations are still held in Budapest and have led to clashes with anti-fascist demonstrators. On a much larger scale—even enjoying some government support—are the Polish Independence Day rallies, held annually on November 11 to mark the independence of Poland in 1918. In 2017, the event attracted an alarming number of far-right groups from across Europe. Some sixty-thousand demonstrators marched through the streets of Warsaw, waving flags, carrying torches, shouting anti-immigration slogans, and calling for a "Pure Poland, white Poland" (Taylor 2017). Antisemitic slogans could also be heard. The event attracted prominent far-right figures from other countries such as Tommy Robinson, leader of the English Defense League, and Roberto Fiore, of Italy's neofascist party, *Forza Nuova*. Significantly, the march seemed to draw approval from members of the Polish government, as the interior minister called the march a "beautiful sight."

These marches, which brazenly displayed far-right slogans in great numbers, were the European equivalent of Unite the Right. Like that march, it was made up of heterogeneous groups united by common cause: to demonstrate a common ethno-nationalist front against what they perceive as the threat from mass immigration and the Jewish conspiracy. As in Belgium, pagan symbols mixed in with the Catholic heritage of these countries, which reigning conservative governments played up in their nationalist platforms. Revisionist history, driven by fantasy rather than historical fact, was also on display, legitimizing the Nazi war against the Soviet Union as a "defense" of Europe from

Bolshevism. Using national holidays, like the one in Poland, also helped facilitate the increasing mainstreaming of the newly emboldened far right.

In all cases, the neo-Nazis and neofascists have exploited more mainstream issues to reveal themselves. In the United States, it was the debate over Confederate monuments, while in Hungary it was the discussion over Hungary's Cold War history. In Poland, the demonstrations took advantage of a recent visit by former American President Donald Trump, who openly supported Polish nationalist aspirations and the consolidation of power of the Law and Justice Party, a right-wing party that was attempting to rewrite the history of wartime Poland by criminalizing anyone who suggested that some Poles had collaborated with the Nazis in the Holocaust. This mainstreaming has become increasingly prevalent since the end of the Cold War in the 1990s, which reopened discussions of the past, especially the events of the Second World War, suppressed by the exigencies of the Cold War. Much of this mainstreaming took its cue from a country that seemingly did not have a fascist past: the United States.

Terror in America

Americans woke up to right-wing extremism on April 19, 1995, when a powerful bomb exploded outside a federal building in Oklahoma City, killing one hundred and sixty-eight people and injuring more than five hundred. The dead included nineteen children from a daycare center in the building. The culprit was a Gulf War veteran, Timothy McVeigh, arrested later that day after a routine traffic stop. McVeigh would later be tried, found guilty, and executed. The bombing was categorized as an act of domestic terrorism by a man who had been radicalized by the White Power movement. Although it was depicted as the act of a "lone wolf," the bombing revealed a network of far-right movements, like the Michigan Militias, to which McVeigh belonged, and the presence of a White Power willing to commit terrorist acts after years of training. One year after McVeigh's act, another individual with White Power sympathies, Eric Rudolph, set off a pipe bomb at the Atlanta Olympic Games, killing two people and injuring over a hundred others. Rudolph had expressed antisemitic and homophobic ideas and was a Holocaust denier (Belew 2018). On the run for the next five years, Rudolph would go on to bomb two abortion clinics and one gay nightclub.

These acts were the product of a period of economic recession and the return of war veterans from the Gulf War. It was also an era when the White Power movement was growing in numbers and helped by the spread of networks on the internet. Books, like Pierce's *Turner Diaries*, were finding a new audience thanks to the internet. McVeigh was a fan of the book. A copy of it was found in his car when he was arrested, and he had sold copies of the book at various gun shows (Counter Extremism Project). Pierce's novel proved influential behind revolutionary action in the 1980s led by Louis Beam, a Vietnam veteran and former member of the Ku Klux Klan. In 1983, the Aryan Nations World Congress held in Idaho declared war on the US government. In subsequent years, Beam, pioneering the use of internet networks, preached "leaderless resistance" as the

Fascism in the New Millennium

form that war would take. In effect, small, autonomous cells of radicalized individuals would take the war to the government through terrorist acts, hoping, in the process, to start a race war that would lead to the ultimate victory of the white race in America (Belew 2018).

Tactics like "leaderless resistance" had been inspired by books like *The Turner Diaries* and James Mason's *Siege*. The latter book was the product of a member of the American Nazi Party (ANP). Founded in 1959 in Virginia by George Lincoln Rockwell, the ANP openly embraced Nazism, which included uniforms and symbols (Figure 13.1). Rockwell was murdered in 1967, but his movement carried on, splintering into different groups in subsequent years. Mason belonged to one of these groups. Mason also became a devotee of the cult leader and mass murderer Charles Manson, both collaborating to form the Universal Order movement in the 1970s. Manson was a white Nationalist and neo-Nazi who had inspired his followers to commit a series of ritualistic murders in 1969. The killers made it appear as if the murders of affluent white people were committed by black rebels in the hopes of touching off a race war. Mason's collection of essays, which included pro-Manson pieces, was published in 1992, but his ideas were already well known within the White Power movement. The essays advocated terror attacks by individual cells on federal targets as a means of starting a race war and bringing about the collapse of the "system" (Counter Extremism Project). Mason's work influenced

Figure 13.1 George Lincoln Rockwell makes a speech at an American Nazi Party rally in Chicago, August 21, 1966. Credit: Alamy.

McVeigh and the Atomwaffen Division; a neo-Nazi terrorist group formed in the 2010s proclaiming "siege culture" as its main ideology.

Authors like Mason and Pierce were, in effect, the spiritual guides of the "leaderless resistance" neo-Nazi, White Power movements that spread in the United States after the 1990s. They joined already existing white supremacist movements like Aryan Nations, founded by Richard Butler in Idaho in the 1970s, and the Ku Klux Klan. By the turn of the millennium, these groups were organized and networked (thanks to the internet), and they developed international links with similar movements in Europe and elsewhere. Inspired by Mason and Pierce, they advocated direct terrorist attacks led by small cells or individuals (lone wolves) on specific targets. These were designed to stoke fear and provoke a major crisis calling for radical solutions. This strategy of accelerationism was formed amid a general apocalyptic worldview based on the belief that American society was corrupt and on the verge of collapse. Chaos thus presented an opportunity for Armageddon out of which a pure, white, ethno-state could finally be established. In the meantime, the enemies of the white race, such as blacks, Jews, and liberals, would be destroyed. This was laid out in one of Mason's essays, in which he describes a "healthy state" as one that will "expel—or kill—the Jew," since the "Jew corrupts the nation" (Counter Extremism Project n.d.).

Fascism in America

Neo-Nazi and neofascist sympathies seemed to arise out of nowhere in late-twentieth-century America, but they were nothing new. Sympathies for far-right extremism had, in fact, a long history in the United States. The debate revolves around whether fascism in America was a foreign import or whether there exists an indigenous form of fascism that can be traced back to the nineteenth century (Rosenfeld and Ward 2023). The various manifestations of the Ku Klux Klan have been seen, by some, as protofascist movements, at least in their tactics (violence directed at minorities) and ideology (white Nationalism). In the interwar period, several groups emerged in the United States that mimicked the European fascist movements. The American Civil Liberties Union has identified over one hundred such groups in the 1930s, a time when the Great Depression brought the American economic system to the verge of collapse (Gordon 2023).

One of the more notable groups was the German American Bund, made up of German expats, many of whom worked for the Ford Motor Company. The Bund was funded by the Nazi regime in Germany. Though small, this group held a notorious rally at New York's Madison Square Garden in 1939, where thousands of supporters listened to rousing speeches by the movement's leader, Fritz Kuhn. Behind Kuhn was a large image of George Washington flanked by American flags. The rally was meant to convince Americans to remain neutral in the impending war in Europe. The Washington image was there to remind Americans of his famous nonintervention speech when he left office in the 1790s. The Bund did not advocate violence, though during the rally Kuhn's bodyguards, dressed as Stormtroopers, brutally manhandled a protester who tried to climb on the stage. This was all captured on film, much of which can be seen in the documentary, *A Night at the Garden* (2017, Marshall Curry, dir.) What the footage did not capture were the more than one hundred thousand protesters outside the arena, vastly outnumbering the Bundists in attendance. Much of the Bund's activities centered on social occasions such as picnics and campouts held on land owned by the organization in New Jersey and Long Island. These events attracted as many as eighteen thousand people, many of them youth, who wore uniforms and brandished swastikas (Gordon 2023).

While the Bund was a foreign effort, the Silver Legion was a more indigenous product. Originating in the 1920s but not formally established until 1933—the year Hitler came to power in Germany—the Silver Legion was created by William Dudley Pelley, a Boston journalist and screenwriter in Hollywood who claimed to have had a religious epiphany wherein he was given a vision of Nazism's rise. Pelley's politics mixed Evangelical Christianity, occultism, and Nazism in a manner that prefigured many of the neo-Nazi movements of the postwar era. He believed in the "Aryan Christ"—that is, a Jesus who was not Jewish, an idea taken from the English writer Houston Stewart Chamberlain, who also influenced Hitler. Pelley's views were strongly antisemitic, and he came to advocate the elimination of Jewry in a genocidal vision that echoed that of the Nazis. His hatred of the Jews fit into an "eschatological" vision, which appealed to white, evangelical Christians, a demographic that made up most of the Legion's membership (Steigmann-Gall 2023). Pelley's schemes ranged from sowing conspiracy theories to planning an armed insurrection against the Roosevelt administration, planned for May 1934. He hoped to get the support of the U.S. Marines, but the insurrection never got off the ground. By then, the Silver Legion could boast some fifteen thousand members, making it the largest of the Nazi groups in America (Gordon 2023).

The mixing of religion and right-wing extremism was a salient feature of another significant far-right group of the 1930s, the Christian Front (CF). The CF was the brainchild of the Canadian-born radio priest, Fr. Charles Coughlin, who became a major celebrity in the 1930s. Coughlin used radio to regale his millions of listeners with anti-Roosevelt messages laced with virulent antisemitism. A highly charismatic figure, Coughlin used his radio addresses to fund the construction of a Catholic shrine in Michigan. The so-called Shrine of the Little Flower in Royal Oak, Michigan, was completed in 1936 at the height of the Great Depression, funded almost entirely from the proceeds of his radio show. The shrine, designed in the Art Deco style, included a massive tower with a twenty-eight-foot Crucifix at the top of its front tower, prefiguring a Catholic triumphalism that would later be seen in the Valley of the Fallen.

Inspired by Coughlin and by the Catholic crusade against the Republican government in Spain, a group of laymen in Boston and New York created the CF to combat what they saw as the communist agenda of the New Deal. The CF was motivated by the "theological anti-communism" of the Catholic Church and informed by the doctrine of the Mystical Body of Christ (Gallagher 2021). These doctrines, combined with Coughlin's antisemitism and teachings about certain social justice issues derived from Pius XI's encyclical, *Quadragesimo Anno* (1931), shaped a radical and subversive movement that planned an armed insurrection. Appealing to mostly Irish American immigrants in Boston and New York, this group stockpiled arms and plotted violence and made connections with officials in the German Consulate in Boston. In 1940, its leaders were arrested and placed on trial, officially ending the movement. Many of its adherents remained militant, however, and during the war years would conduct violent expeditions in the Jewish neighborhoods of Boston, attacking Jews. The so-called Antisemitic Crisis, which erupted in Boston in March 1943, saw members of the South Boston Citizens' Association (a front group for old CFers) unleash violence on the streets (Gallagher 2021).

The Second World War put a crimp in the pro-Nazi cause in America, but did not extinguish it. Many of its leaders, like William Dudley Pelley, were imprisoned for subversion, while others faded into the background. Far-right extremists decided to hide behind more seemingly mainstream organizations like the America First Committee (AFC). Created in 1940 at Yale University, the AFC included various groups, all with different political persuasions, coming from all walks of life. Its aim was to pressure the Roosevelt administration to not join the Second World War, a tactic that was successful until the Japanese attack on Pearl Harbor in 1941. The face of AFC was the famous aviator Charles Lindbergh, who led a series of rallies across the United States, usually with framed images of George Washington behind him. Lindbergh was a celebrity, an aviation hero who traversed the Atlantic in 1927 in a solo, non-stop flight in an airplane of his own design. It was an incredible achievement that captured the world's imagination and made him an overnight sensation. However, in the mid-1930s Lindbergh began to show signs of pro-Nazi sympathies, as did his wife, the writer Anne Morrow Lindbergh, who, in 1940, published a bestseller that laid out the case for nonintervention. In 1941, Lindbergh delivered a notorious speech in Des Moines, Iowa, suggesting that the Jews who controlled the media and Hollywood were pressuring Roosevelt to enter the war against Germany. This speech demonstrated that the AFC was more than just a policy pressure group and that it shared some ideological affinities with the far right.

The AFC was one prominent example of an attempt to create a "right wing popular front" in the 1930s, a movement that involved wealthy business lobbyists like Merwin Hunt, a Franco supporter, as well as politicians, journalists, and celebrities like Lindbergh. From the start, this movement displayed clearly anti-democratic tendencies and favored some form of authoritarian regime not unlike that of Franco's Spain (Walsh 2024). This "popular front," which brought together conservatives and extremists on the right, laid the groundwork for similar attempts to mainstream the far right in American politics during the Cold War. With anti-communism as its glue, far-right activists were able to influence public opinion and the outcomes of events, such as the Great Sedition Trial of 1944, in which thirty-three people charged with subversion were eventually let off despite strong evidence of Nazi cooperation. Elements of this group were also involved in the Nuremberg Trials and the Malmedy Trials in 1946, where seventy-three members of the *Waffen-SS* were put on trial for the execution of American prisoners of war in 1944 (Remy 2017). Unsubstantiated claims that the defendants had been tortured by Jewish-American interrogators were circulated in the press. A subcommittee of the U.S. Senate was set up in 1949 to investigate these allegations. The main figure on this committee was a Republican Senator from Wisconsin, Joseph McCarthy, who used the hearings as a launching pad for his later campaigns against communists in government. The claims were untrue, but the subcommittee hearings provided an opportunity for neo-Nazi sympathizers and admirers of the *Waffen-SS*—which were many—to publicly defend war criminals (Smelser and Davies III 2008).

One of the most notorious figures to emerge from these trials as a lobbyist for Nazi war criminals was Francis Parker Yockey, a war veteran and neo-Nazi who became a leading supporter of the European Liberation Front (ELF) and the author of its manifesto. Influenced by European neofascists like Julius Evola, Yockey's book, *Imperium*, became the bible of American neo-Nazis. Influenced by Spengler and others of the so-called German Conservative school, the book presented a spiritual-biological defense of the West that presented Jews as parasites who aimed to destroy authentic culture. The book was dedicated to Hitler, "the hero of the Second World War." The book attacked not only Jews but also Liberalism, which he claimed was "entirely negative … a disintegrating force … Liberalism is an escape from hardness into softness, from masculinity into femininity, from History to herd-grazing" (Mostrom 2020). Yockey was more than just a theorist, however—he also became a secret agent who attempted to sell atomic secrets to Arab countries and made extensive contacts with former Nazis in South America and the Middle East (Coogan 1999).

Yockey was also a Holocaust denier whose influence would be paramount among American deniers, such as Willis Carto, the last man to see Yockey alive before the latter committed suicide in a federal prison in 1960. Carto was a neo-Nazi and fervent disciple of Yockey's. In the 1950s, he spearheaded the campaign to mainstream far-right views by creating a lobbyist group called Liberty Lobby. He also established a publishing company that reissued Yockey's book as well as other Holocaust denial books and pamphlets. He also published an anti-Zionist newspaper called *Spotlight* that boasted a circulation of more than three hundred thousand by 1981. He was, according to the Anti-Defamation League, the "most important and powerful antisemite in the U.S." (D. Lipstadt 1994). In 1978, Carto was one of the founders of the Institute for Historical Research, a pseudo-scholarly organization that published a journal presenting revisionist accounts of the Second World War. Couched in scholarly euphemisms, the institute used subterfuge to organize conferences and symposiums aimed at mainstreaming Holocaust denial on an unsuspecting public.

Carto used similar tactics in politics. His Liberty Lobby was organized as an umbrella group that included various persons who wanted to push the Republican Party further to the right. Using advanced organization skills to make expansive mailing lists, Carto's group attempted to oust Dwight D. Eisenhower as presidential nominee in 1956 in favor of McCarthy. In the 1960s, Carto's group prominently supported Nixon, Barry Goldwater, and George Wallace (Walsh 2024). In 1960, Carto's newspaper claimed that the Presidential election was stolen. A one-time member of the John Birch Society, Carto appealed to conspiracy theorists on the right who claimed that the Civil Rights movement was inspired by communists. Significantly, Carto was also able to make contact with international movements, as did his mentor Yockey. For example, he helped cofound the Institute for Historical Review (IHR) with a former member of the British National Front, David McCalden. His writings and the work of the IHR proved influential in the United Kingdom, especially through the writings of the historian David Irving and the German Holocaust denier living in Canada, Ernst Zündel. Through these networks Holocaust denial, antisemitism, and ethno-nationalism would find a wide audience in the decade that followed the end of the Cold War.

Back to Origins: Germany and Italy

The 1990s saw neo-Nazi and new neofascist groups emerge in Italy and Germany, the birthplaces of historic fascism. Fascism never went away in Italy, as we have seen with the development of the present-day MSI and other far-right groups. In Germany, Nazism was banned, but this did not mean it disappeared with the end of the war. The Socialist Reich Party (SRP), founded in 1949 by an ex-Wehrmacht officer whose claim to fame had been to help stop the July 1944 plot against Hitler, could claim some fifty thousand members by the early 1950s, many of whom were former Nazis and other nostalgists. The party adhered to the pan-European project started by Rene Binet and supported by American neo-Nazis like Yockey. The party was banned in 1952 by the West German government, which invoked Article 21 of the Basic Law (the West German constitution). There is some evidence that the SRP received financial and other support from East Germany, despite its neo-Nazi leanings (Burleigh 2000, 481–2).

In the mid-1960s, just as the German Economic Miracle was slowing down, a new party created by Adolf von Thadden made its appearance. The National Democratic Party (NPD) enjoyed some success in local elections, winning seats in state elections in Bavaria, Lower Saxony, and Hesse, areas that felt the economic crunch and were receptive to the party's anti-immigrant and anti-American views. The party lay dormant in subsequent decades but revived in the 1990s, thanks to the reunification of Germany, which saw the economically backward former Eastern Germany territories absorbed into the new Germany. Unification proved traumatic for the former territories of the east. The economic success of the west did not translate and many *Ossies* ("Easterners") emigrated to the west, looking for opportunities they did not find. They were also often greeted with hostility by westerners.

Into this breach stepped the NPD, renamed *Die Heimat* (The Homeland) in 2023. Some success came in state elections, though they never achieved the heights of the 1960s. The NPD did succeed with unemployed youth and with xenophobes opposed to the presence of immigrants from the Middle East. Using the slogan, "Work, Family, Fatherland," the NPD called for a return to the borders of 1937 Germany, supported the Boycott, Divestment, Sanctions movement against Israel and called for the expulsion of all immigrants. They especially targeted asylum seekers, whom they blamed for committing crimes. Although the *Heimat* has attempted to present itself as a legitimate parliamentary party, its supporters have engaged in violence against immigrants, and some members go on "patrols" in Berlin, targeting immigrants. In 2014, the party won enough support to send one member to the European Parliament. That member, Udo Voigt, was on record making Holocaust denial claims.

The NPD was never able to mainstream fully and never achieved the parliamentary breakthrough that seemed possible during the economic uncertainties in the 1990s. Part of the problem came with divisions within the movement, as some called for more moderate stances, while others wanted to become more radical and reject liberal democracy completely. In the early 2000s, the party was largely pushed aside by other forces on the far right that were forming what has been called the "New German Right" (Ponso 2022). This New Right formed around anti-Islamic and Identitarian ideas, especially *völkisch* ideas. Mixing populist sentiment with far-right ideology, movements like *Pegida* have grown in the early 2000s.

Out of this has emerged a new political party, the Alternative for Germany (AfD). Founded in 2013 by two economists, the party was quickly taken over by far-right activists. Although it has tried to distance itself from extremists, the party has housed several neo-Nazis such as *Der Flügel* led by Björn Höcke. This more extremist wing has focused its attention on sanitizing Germany's recent history, which has involved looking for more "positive elements in the Nazi past" (Ponso 2022, 309). This has included fighting back against the so-called "Auschwitz Myth" that has left Germany with a culture of shame no other country has had to endure. Höcke's revisionism is part of a general trend in works that have tried to give a different slant on German history, even offering an apologist view of the Nazi era. This is a trend that could be traced back to the *Historikerstreit* debate in the 1980s when some West German historians attempted to "historicize" the Nazi era.

The AfD's efforts at becoming a "normal" parliamentary party has reaped some rewards. In 2017, the party won 12.6 percent of the national vote, good enough for third place behind the Christian Democrats and Democratic Socialists, Germany's two establishment parties. Although they lost some support in the 2021 elections, the AfD has remained strong in some state elections. In 2024, the AfD won 16% of the national vote in the European Parliament elections, second only to the Christian Democrats. This success in elections has made the AfD a mainstream party but it has retained some extremist language and positions. It has made frequent use of a vocabulary that traces itself back to the ideology of German Conservatism and the Nazis from the early twentieth century. Adjectives like *völkisch* are frequently invoked as well as *lügenpresse* ("the lying media"), a term used by the American white Nationalist Richard Spencer during his notorious CPAC appearance in 2016, and *abendlund* ("the West as under threat"), among others (Ponso 2022).

The electoral gains of the AfD have come after several years of extreme right violence against immigrants, guest workers, and asylum seekers. While parties like the AfD have mainstreamed, the more violent groups of skinheads have unleashed waves of violence in Germany on several occasions since Reunification. Far-right skinhead culture had grown since the 1980s, as evidenced in the success of skinhead music influenced by the

British neo-Nazi singer Ian Stuart. His Blood and Honor record label, founded in the early 1980s, helped spawn a legion of imitation bands in Germany under the Hammerskin Nation, a neo-Nazi umbrella group founded in the United States in 1988 but with several chapters in Germany. The neo-Nazi skinhead culture has grown to encompass not only music but also mixed martial arts events, like the Fight of the Nibelungs. These events are organized by former skinhead band members, like Stefan Hammer, and they are whites-only events. Designed as festivals with a distinctively Wagnerian feel, the mixed martial arts provide not only entertainment but also an arena where fighting skills are perfected. During the COVID-19 outbreak, a mixed martial arts neo-Nazi group in the state of Thuringia (an AfD bastion) attacked police in protests against pandemic restrictions (Edmondson 2023).

The skinhead movement has gone beyond just mixed martial arts and music, however. In the early 1990s, bands of these groups led violent attacks against hotels and hostels housing migrant workers and asylum seekers. Taking advantage of the high unemployment in parts of the former Eastern Germany, neo-Nazis focused their rage on immigrants, who numbered some six million, including two million Turkish guest workers (Lee 2000, 264). Between 1991 and 1993, neo-Nazis unleashed a wave of violence on immigrant communities in cities like Rostock, burning down buildings and assaulting immigrants as they tried to escape. In actions that resembled those of Nazi stormtroopers from the 1930s, violent groups of skinheads firebombed dwellings in incidents that some said resembled a civil war. In 1992, the year of the attacks in Rostock, German officials estimated that there had been at least four thousand five hundred racist attacks that left at least seventeen people dead (Lee 2000, 275). In many cases, police often stood by and intervened only when things got out of hand. Residents often stood by and watched at times even cheering the neo-Nazis on.

Against this backdrop, the German government responded by placing restrictions on immigration and even amending the German constitution, making it more difficult for refugees to seek asylum, leading one dissenting member of the ruling Christian Democratic party to proclaim that the "real cause of these crimes (the terrorist attacks) lies in the radical right's acceptance into the mainstream" (Lee 2000, 276). Despite the German government's appeasement of anti-immigrant sentiment, in a bid to sway more conservative voters, the hostility against foreigners by neo-Nazis has been absorbed into the New German Right and can be found in the party platform of the AfD, which claimed, in its 2016 manifesto, that "Islam does not belong in Germany" and demanded a ban on any public manifestation of Islam, including burqas, calls to prayers, and minarets (Bellon 2016).

Italy: Back Home

In Italy, the end of the Cold War brought substantial political upheaval. Political parties were completely redefined—and there was a revival of neofascism. Italian politics since the Second World War had been dominated, on the one hand, by the Christian

Democratic Party (DC) and, on the other, the Communist Party (PCI). The DC ran virtually every government since the Second World War. With the end of the Cold War, the DC's justification for power largely collapsed. In the early 1990s, under pressure to join the European Union (EU) (formed in 1992), a series of scandals brought the whole party system down. For decades, corruption had largely remained untouched due to the exigencies keeping the DC in power and the PCI out of power. Now, that system, called *partitocrazia* (Partyocracy), was no longer needed, and a series of judicial investigations began looking into the corruption that had propped up that system. Called Operation Clean Hands, this investigation resulted in the arrests of hundreds of politicians and the collapse of the parties.

Tangentopoli (Bribesville) opened the door to a reorientation of the political landscape, which resulted in new parties, like *Forza Italia*, led by the Milanese media magnate, Silvio Berlusconi, to emerge. In 1994, Berlusconi, a political neophyte, won the national election and, in a shocking move, invited the neofascist MSI to join his government in a coalition. For the first time since the MSI had been founded in 1946, neofascists were back in government, much to the dismay of anti-fascists, who believed that one of the foundations of the Italian Republic was the memory of the resistance against fascism. Responding to this, the MSI changed its name to the *Alleanza Nazionale* (AN) and, at the party congress in 1995, officially renounced its fascist past, declaring itself to be a "postfascist" party.

Not all agreed with this shift, and at the congress, those who wanted to retain the fascist heritage of the MSI split off from the AN. Their leader was Pino Rauti, who returned to the MSI in the late 1960s. Rauti remained beholden to the MSI's original vision and its link to the Republic of Salò (RSI). His new party, *Fiamma Tricolore*, maintained the "social" aspect of the RSI and would find most of its support in the Italian South and among the working classes (Campani 2016). The AN, on the other hand, led by Gianfranco Fini, adopted neoliberal positions that put it closer to Berlusconi's conservative *Forza Italia*.

Rauti's party appeared to be nothing more than a remnant of the past. It never achieved any significant support in Italian elections compared to the AN, which went on to be a significant party until it dissolved in the 2000s. Neofascism appeared to be a spent force, a relic of the past that was destined to disappear as the veterans of the RSI died off. Neofascism as a movement metamorphosed into two new groups by the early twenty-first century: *Forza Nuova* and *CasaPound*. These two movements are both products of Italian neofascism but are also significantly different. Together, they form the two distinct characters of contemporary neofascism in Italy—characters that resemble, in many ways, the different strands of Italian neofascism going back to the 1940s. On the one hand, there is the socially conservative *Forza Nuova*, while on the other hand, there is the socially conscious *CasaPound*. Both oppose the neoliberalism of Italian conservatism, but from different angles. Both movements pay close attention to cultural issues, largely renouncing biological racism, but one is tied to traditional Roman Catholicism, while the other looks to neo-paganism. These are the two faces of neofascism today.

Forza Nuova

The FN was born out of the ashes of the terroristic neofascist groups of the 1970s. The two men who founded the party in 1997, Roberto Fiore and Massimo Morsello, had once belonged to groups that participated in the so-called Years of Lead. Both men belonged to the *Nuclei Armati Rivoluzionari* (NAR), which had been implicated in several bombings, like the one in Bologna that killed eighty-five people in 1980. The subsequent crackdown by the Italian authorities led Fiore and Morsello to escape to the United Kingdom, where they befriended members of the British National Front (J. Pearce 2013). While in the UK, Fiore and Morsello picked up two strategies that the FN would later use; they learned to recruit from football (soccer) fans and make arm's length connections with skinhead groups (Campani 2016).

No longer under suspicion for the Bologna bombing, the two men returned to Italy in the 1990s, where they found a very different political landscape. With the MSI no longer existent, one option was to join Rauti's *Fiamma Tricolore* party—but that party had embraced too many left-wing social positions that offended Fiore's Catholic tastes. Rauti's movement also did not embrace culture war politics, preferring instead to focus on social and economic issues. Morsello was a folk singer who had performed at the Hobbit Camps in the 1970s, while Fiore was more interested in social issues, such as opposition to abortion. Morsello died in 2001, and under Fiore's leadership, the FN became closely connected to integralist Catholicism.

Fiore's charismatic leadership has not helped the FN achieve any significant electoral success, but he has made important connections with far-right groups outside of Italy, including Russia and the United States. His relationship with the Catholic Church has put him in contact with radical traditionalist groups like the Fraternity of St. Pius X (SSPX), a schismatic group opposed to the Second Vatican Council. The SSPX has long sheltered antisemites and Holocaust deniers, like Bishop Richard Williamson. A former member of the SSPX, Fr. Giulio Tam, has been close to the FN and often gives blessings at their rallies. The FN has also forged a close alliance with the pro-life lobby group, *Pro Vita*.

A look at FN's 8-Point Manifesto clearly reflects the party's attachment to traditionalist and integralist Catholicism. It calls for pronatalist policies, the abolition of abortion, the banning of Freemasonry and usury, a renewal of the 1929 Lateran Accords, and the formation of corporations based on Mussolini's corporatist system. In effect, the FN wishes to return the Catholic Church to a place of power in the nation's political system. In doing so, it reflects some of the ideals of the Tradition, Family, Property (TFP) sect that has increasingly gained influence in Catholic circles in Europe. Founded in Brazil by Plinio Corrêa de Oliveira, a wealthy landowner, Catholic integralist, and supporter of Brazil's authoritarian regimes in the 1960s, the TFP advocates a counterrevolution against the liberal heritage of the Enlightenment and the French Revolution. It calls for a Catholic integralist state that restores a medieval vision of society based on hierarchy. Like its founder, the TFP groups are willing to work with dictators and neofascists in a new version of clerical fascism (Pollard 2007).

The party also maintains some of its more radical, far-right positions inherited from Fiore's history in *Terza Posizione*. The FN is an ethno-nationalist party, and its pronatalist positions are driven by a fear that ethnic Italians will one day be replaced by immigrants. As a result, the FN opposes immigration and calls for mass deportations. It also does not oppose violence. The party's cultivation of the violent *ultras* among Rome's two football (soccer) teams, Lazio and Roma, has been largely successful, as has its connections to skinhead groups, especially in the north. Although this seems to contradict the party's cultivation of Catholic morality, Fiore has been able to keep a balance within the party. During COVID lockdowns, Fiore mobilized some of these forces in an attack on the headquarters of one of Italy's leading labor unions after it tried to enforce masking and social distancing regulations (Della Porta and Lavizzari 2022). Although the FN has made efforts to distance itself from historic fascism, many of its posters (a specialty of the movement) hark back to Nazi and Italian Fascist imagery. In 2019, the FN produced a poster with an image of Mussolini and a quotation from Tolkien. Other posters have used images that resembled the superman statues of Arno Breker, the Nazi sculptor. Yet another poster, aimed at stopping immigration, showed an image of a barbed wire fence, evoking memories of the concentration camps.

Although it has stood for parliamentary elections, the FN is profoundly opposed to liberal democracy. Like the neo-Nazi groups in Germany, the FN has been at the forefront of organizing vigilante groups in so-called "security walks" aimed at protecting Italians from criminal activity, stemming from immigrants. This is designed not only to intimidate immigrants, but also sends a clear message that the liberal state is not doing enough to protect Italians (Castelli Gattinara 2019). The resemblance to Mussolini's *squadrismo* is not accidental. By exposing the supposed weaknesses of the liberal state, the FN is creating a scenario that could justify, one day, overthrowing that state. In this, the FN has an ally in integralist Catholicism's rejection of liberalism and its embracing of post-liberal views, especially in the United States, where so-called post-liberals like Steve Bannon and others have made connections in Italy and elsewhere in Europe. Indeed, Fiore's alliance of Catholic integralists and neofascists has been instructive for a new crop of post-liberal intellectuals in the United States (Patterson 2020).

CasaPound

For those neofascists who are not attracted to the radical traditional Catholicism of the FN, there is an alternative—*CasaPound*. Founded in 2003 by a rock singer, Gianluca Iannone, frontman for the band *Zetazeroalfa*, the "House of Pound" is a squatter's community based in an unoccupied state building in the *Esquilino* district of Rome. In contrast to the FN, *CasaPound* looks to the pagan heritage of fascism, from the traditionalism of Julius Evola to the poetry of the American poet Ezra Pound, who supported Mussolini during the Second World War (Mammone 2015). Taking a page from de Benoist's New Right playbook, Iannone imitated the left-wing *centri sociali* (social centers) movement in Italy, sites of left-wing dissent that appealed to young people. *CasaPound* also focuses on young people and on helping Italians who are struggling socially, attempting to implement social benefits for working mothers and others who are being neglected by the state (Mammone 2015).

Like the FN, however, *CasaPound* focuses on culture and society, and less on getting involved in parliamentary politics. The house is a place of socializing and entertainment, and Iannone's band often heads the bill. Appealing to the young crowds that frequent the house, Iannone has come up with dances like the *Cinghiamattanza*, a wild number to which men dance while whipping each other with their belts.[1] The dance denotes the violence of the *CasaPound* movement. The target of *CasaPound* violence typically focuses on journalists and left-wing activists. The violence is usually carried out by squads reminiscent of the early *squadrismo* of Italian Fascism (Campani 2016). Various other CPs have opened throughout Italy since the early 2000s, with the emphasis on occupying urban space and fostering a political community, rather than getting involved with existing political institutions. Indeed, the aim of the CP, like the *Forza Nuova*, is to overthrow the liberal democratic state and institute an authoritarian "ethical" state like that proposed by Giovanni Gentile in the Manifesto of the Fascist Party in 1932 (Campani 2016).

While the CP focuses more on social issues than the FN, the former shares that movement's ethno-nationalism, and both subscribe to the Great Replacement Theory, blaming global elites (i.e., the Jews) for conspiring to replace ethnic Italians with immigrants. Borrowing from Evola, the CP advocates a "spiritual racism" and supports the "differentialism" preached by de Benoist and the New French Right. Unlike Fiore's party, the CP does not have a strong Islamophobic stance and has established ties with Muslim political movements, like the Hezbollah and the Palestinian cause (Albanese 2022). Like the FN, the CP is anti-globalist and shares a link to the Third Position movement from the 1970s and 1980s. Despite their anti-liberal and antidemocratic stance, the CP has participated in elections but without success. While it garnered several hundred thousand votes in the 2018 national elections, it only boasts around five- to six thousand members scattered throughout the peninsula. It has managed to garner a great deal of attention, however, through its concerts, squats, and "showpiece" protest events (Castelli Gattinari and Froio 2014).

Although the *CasaPound* has distanced itself from Mussolini's fascism, like the FN, there are important links to Italian fascism. The symbolism, imagery, and references to the regime's Labor Charter of 1927 and the social charter of the Republic of Salò all indicate this (Castelli Gattinari and Froio 2014). Moreover, there is a heavy reliance on rituals reminiscent of Italian fascism. It is mostly *CasaPound* militants who make up the annual pilgrimage to *Acca Larentia* in Rome. This was the site of the old *Fronte della Gioventù* headquarters of the MSI, where, in 1978, three militants of the section were murdered by left-wing opponents. In a massive show of force, hundreds of CP members meet at the site on the anniversary and give resounding salutes of "*Presente!*" at the reading of the

---

[1] A video of the dance and the accompanying song can be seen here: https://www.youtube.com/watch?v=drsUhWuyA9I.

names of the "martyred" neofascists. Calls to shut down these demonstrations, as well as the *CasaPound* squats, have largely been ignored by the Italian authorities, especially when right-wing governments have been in power. Through actions such as these, along with the periodic violence against the left and all other opponents, the CP has become the most visible manifestation of "millennial" neofascism in Italy.

Fascism in the New Millennium

The revival of fascism in the twenty-first century, apart from demonstrating the persistence of an idea, is also a reflection of how fascism requires exceptional circumstances to flourish. With the end of the Cold War and the formation of the European Union, many hoped the past would have been firmly left behind. Instead, the challenges of the new millennium have seemed to "reawaken the beast." In Europe, the refugee crisis that reached a critical point in 2015 has stoked anti-immigration campaigns, which has led to the rise of neofascist and neo-Nazi groups, including the Golden Dawn in Greece and the Jobbik in Hungary. Moreover, the failures of the European Union to deal effectively with this crisis, along with the EU's struggle to govern democratically, have favored the rise of a far-right populism, which has slipped into neofascism (Traverso 2019). In the United States, the aftereffects of the 9/11 attacks and the economic downturn of 2008—along with the unprecedented election of an African American as president that same year—has fed/fueled far-right extremism. All this has led to increased American involvement in foreign wars and contributed to the rise of the alt-right and the events at Charlottesville.

In 2012, the neo-Nazi Golden Dawn party (GD) become the third largest party in Greece following national elections. The movement was founded in the 1980s by Nikolaos Michaloliakos, a violent individual who admired the parafascist Metaxas regime in the 1930s and called for a rebirth of Hellenic civilization based on Aryan racial superiority (Griffin 2018). A Holocaust denier, Michaloliakos invested his movement with neo-Nazi rituals and symbols, including torch-lit parades. The Golden Dawn aimed at attracting youth through martial arts and athletic clubs and focused its resentment on immigrants and homosexuals. Until its electoral breakthrough, the GD had been a small group, notable only for its acts of violence and its celebration of Nazism. Some of its members had fought for the Bosnian Serbs and participated in the ethnic cleansing of Bosnian Muslims in Srebrenica in 1995.

Its breakthrough came in 2009, thanks to the Greek Debt Crisis. Owing to the economic downturn that hit the West in 2008, Greece's economic fragility, and its excessive spending, the EU hit the Greek government with austerity measures. This caused a backlash, which resulted in the GD's electoral breakthrough in 2012. The GD's anti-EU and anti-German views found great appeal among Greeks who resented the EU's measures. This, combined with an influx of Syrian refugees fleeing the Arab Spring in the Middle East, shifted Greek politics sharply to the right, placing the previously obscure GD in a position to exploit the crisis. Further success came in the EU elections of 2014, where the GD, previously unrepresented in Brussels, gained nearly nine percent of the vote and won three seats in the European Parliament. The party appealed not only to working-class males, like most other far-right parties, but also middle-class professionals, university professors, lawyers, surgeons, businesspeople, and even a former NATO commander (Counter Extremism Project).

Despite this turn to respectability through elections, the GD remained a violent, criminal organization. In September 2013, a member of the GD murdered a popular rapper named Pavlos Fyssas. Known for his left-wing sympathies, Fyssas was attacked by a mob outside a café in Athens, allegedly after a dispute over football. The murder came during a period of heightened crisis in the Greek capital, as protesters were assembling to contest the EU's decision to cut thousands of public sector jobs as part of its austerity measures. Known by his stage name, Killah P, Fyssas used his music and celebrity to promote anti-fascist views, making him a target for the GD. Although the GD had committed numerous murders in the past, mostly of immigrants, the assassination of Fyssas forced the Greek authorities to act by arresting one of the GD's members, Giorgos Roupakias. The incident led to a backlash against the GD and forced the Greek government to crack down on the party. In 2020, thirteen of its leaders were found guilty of leading a criminal organization, while over fifty others, including eighteen former members of parliament, were convicted of participating in criminal activity. In the meantime, the party's support had declined in the EU elections of 2019 and in the Greek legislative elections of the same year when it lost all its MPs. Before its fall, the GD had fostered international connections with other far-right movements in Europe, like the *Forza Nuova* and the British National Party. It had also forged links with Greek diaspora groups and police forces in Greece.

Both the sudden rise and precipitous fall of the GD shocked Europe and beyond. It served to demonstrate how sharp crises can reignite far-right sympathies in Europe. The crises of the 2000s hit all European countries to a greater or lesser extent, with the border regions and the Mediterranean countries bearing the brunt of the refugee crisis in the 2010s. This inflamed anti-immigrant sentiment and stoked the rise of new far-right groups. Among these was the Jobbik Party in Hungary. In the same EU elections that introduced Europe to the Golden Dawn, the Jobbik scored nearly fifteen percent of the vote in Hungary. In the national elections of the same year, the party garnered one million votes, making it the third largest party in a country already dominated by the right-wing Fidesz Party of Viktor Orbán, whose own anti-EU and anti-immigration measures should have lessened the space for extremist, right-wing parties like the Jobbik (Griffin 2018, 107). Founded in 2003, the Jobbik emphasized antisemitic and anti-Roma sentiment while at the same calling for a revision of the Treaty of Trianon (1920). Irredentism and racism aside, the Jobbik also commemorates the Arrow Cross, Hungary's fascist movement, which in the 1940s collaborated with the Nazis, deporting hundreds of thousands of Jews to Auschwitz (discussed in Chapter 9). In 2011, the Jobbik's website also celebrated the memory of Miklos Horthy, who is credited for raising the pride of Hungarians after the Treaty of Trianon. "Under Horthy," the website claimed, "Hungary had a strong and impressive elite, which pursued the goal of the appeal of the unfair Trianon peace diktat" (Counter Extremism

Project). The Jobbik also created its own paramilitary arm, the Hungarian Guard, which the Hungarian government banned in 2009, declaring it a hate group.

The Jobbik has been successful in Hungarian elections, gaining forty-seven seats and becoming the official opposition in 2010. Since then, leadership problems and divisions led to a decline, not to mention Orbán's appropriation of many of the Jobbik policies. In 2024, the Jobbik failed to win any seats in the European elections, while in 2022, its representation in the Hungarian parliament was whittled down to just ten seats. In the case of the Jobbik, attempts to mainstream the party and deradicalize its message since 2016 under the leadership of Gábor Vona has led to the party's electoral deterioration. It seems moderating the party's image has left it bereft of the rich symbolism and ritualism of the radical right, thus leading to a loss of appeal (Hyttinen 2022).

The pressure to address immigration since 2010 has also allowed far-right forces to emerge in Scandinavia. Founded in Sweden in 1997 by former members of the white Aryan Resistance movement, the Nordic Resistance Movement (NRM) grew by a third in 2015, largely due to its anti-immigrant stance. Since then, the movement has spread to other Scandinavian countries and has made important allies with other neo-Nazi and neofascist groups in Europe and the United States. The NRM revels in esoteric ideas associated with Norse mythology. It also celebrates the memory of Adolf Hitler. In its manifesto, titled "Our Path," the NRM praised Hitler as the only leader to have fought Zionism (Counter Extremism Project). Hoping to unite the Scandinavian countries in a common cause against Zionism and immigration, members of the NRM have committed terrorist acts, such as bombings and homicides.

Neo-Nazi and neofascist groups have proliferated in Eastern Europe and Russia since the millennium, some of them tied to organized crime groups that grew unchecked during the prolonged economic crisis of the post-Cold War era. In the chaos and confusion of the early 1990s in Russia, when the Soviet empire was collapsing and fledgling attempts to establish a liberal democracy were failing, neo-Nazi groups like the Russian National Unity Party (RNU) emerged. Led by Alexander Barkashov, a Slavophile and Hitler admirer, groups like the RNU and the Russian National Assembly (RNA) began a campaign to reunite the over twenty-five million Russians who found themselves in the newly independent republics that remained of the old Soviet empire. The rise of the far right in Russia was rapid and quickly divided into two camps: Slavophiles and Westerners (Lee 2000, 308). Another group that emerged in Russia was the National Bolsheviks, founded by the Soviet dissident, Eduard Limonov, who hoped to revive the so-called "red-brown" alliance forged by Lenin in the 1920s. The key intellectual figure behind this was the Eurasianist philosopher Aleksandr Dugin. Inspired by de Benoist's New Right in France and by the German Conservative Revolution of the 1920s, Dugin introduced Russians to the work of Julius Evola and other far-right, esoteric figures. He was also a leading conspiracy theorist (Lee 2000). Dugin preached a palingenetic that called for Russia to lead a geopolitical revolution in order to get out of its current decadent state (Shekhovtsov 2008).

In 1993, the different far-right groups were able to put aside their differences momentarily to attempt an insurrection against the Boris Yeltsin government. The insurrection occurred because Yeltsin refused to work with Russian nationalist groups in parliament. The protesters included Barkashov's gang as well as Liminov's NSF group. Also involved were members of the French European Liberation Front (EFL), the group founded by Jean Thiriart. The insurrection failed and was followed by a crackdown on the far right, involving tanks and arrests. Hundreds were killed and the leaders jailed (Lee 2000).

The failure of the insurrection and the subsequent crackdown opened the door for a new charismatic neofascist leader named Vladimir Zhirinovsky. He was the leader of the Liberal Democratic Party, a name that concealed its neofascist ideology. Zhirinovsky was a white supremacist who appealed to the *völkisch* traditions of Russian culture. He quickly became known not only for his charismatic appeal, but also for his eccentric behavior. Behind these lay irredentist aspirations and genocidal attitudes toward the non-Russian subjects of the old Russian Empire. In December 1993, Zhirinovsky's party scored a quarter of the national vote.

In the late 1990s, Russia turned sharply to the right, thanks in part to the success of the Liberal Democrats. The coming to power of Vladimir Putin in 1999 further consolidated this shift, along with an increasingly authoritarian form of rule that appropriated many of the ideas of the far right. However, the neo-Nazi character of some of these groups, like that of Barkashov, were eventually suppressed, since the celebration of Hitler and the Nazis did not fit in with Putin's Russian nationalism, a major part of which involved a celebration of the resistance against Germany in the Second World War. Zhirinovsky died in 2022, but his party continues, loyally supporting the Kremlin. Zhirinovsky was honored on several occasions by Putin. Meanwhile, his Jewish background made him immune to charges of being a neo-Nazi, but he and his party were neofascists whose ideas have largely been mainstreamed by the Putin regime.

Traces of neo-Nazism have remained, however, and some have reemerged since the Russia–Ukraine War. Since the outbreak of the war against Chechnya in 1994, Russia has been in an almost constant state of war—against Chechnya first, then Ukraine— which began with the seizure of Crimea in 2014. In 2022, Russia invaded Ukraine to take control of Eastern Ukraine, which hosts a sizable pro-Russian population. Putin's regime has often relied on mercenaries, like those in the Wagner Group, founded in 2014 by a neo-Nazi named Dmitry Utkin, a veteran of the Chechen Wars. The group got its name from Utkin's call sign "Wagner," inspired by Hitler's favorite composer. Neo-Nazism has not been the exclusive preserve of the Russians, however. The Ukrainian Azov Battalion is also known to harbor far-right activists. Founded in 2014 as a volunteer paramilitary group, Azov was the product of far-right, neo-Nazi racists. It was later integrated into the Ukrainian National Guard (Umland 2019). The Azov Battalion has played a prominent role in the fight against the Russian invasion of Ukraine in 2022. It has also provided fodder for Putin's claims that Ukraine is a neo-Nazi state.

The alternating fortunes of far-right movements in Eastern Europe and Russia demonstrate that the post-Cold War era opened a space for neofascist and neo-Nazi groups to emerge in those challenging times of transition. These successes have risen from sharp moments of crisis, especially economic struggles and mass migration. Many believed these crises threatened the ethno-nationalist foundations of their respective groups, foundations which had, for decades, been suppressed by the Soviet Union. They have also been able to forge transnational links with other neo-Nazi groups in Europe and elsewhere. The Golden Dawn was particularly successful in this endeavor (Tipaldou 2015). Their failures, however, demonstrate the difficulties these parties have when it comes to building mass followings, especially when they attempt to moderate their beliefs, at least outwardly. The mainstreaming of many of their platforms by conservative, right-wing governments have clipped their sails somewhat.

Conclusion

The future of neofascist and neo-Nazi movements in the twenty-first century seemed to lie in another direction: in the creation of groupuscules, movements forged mainly online through "leaderless resistance" and the promotion of "lone wolf" actions. In this way, the secrecy and the purity of the movement's cause can be maintained. Should the authorities crack down, these movements could easily metamorphose into other groups with different names. The advantage of this groupuscule existence is that it allows militants to infiltrate more mainstream parties and groups while still allowing these militants to promote extremism and engage in violent activities. The United States in the 2010s proved fertile ground for these movements in the run up to Charlottesville, where the new face of neofascism made itself known.

Neo-Nazi and white supremacist groups increased significantly in 2010, a development predicted by the US Department of Homeland Security. In 2009, DHS released a report warning of the imminence of right-wing extremism, due to the "economic and political climate" present at the time (US Department of Homeland Security 2009). The report noted the economic crisis of 2008 and the election of Barack Obama, America's first African American President, as the main drivers of this resurgence. These fears were exacerbated by the limitations the federal government placed on firearms. The report proved prescient, as the subsequent decade did see a backlash resulting in the emergence of new far-right organizations.

Prominent groups include the Atomwaffen Division, formed in 2015. Based on "leaderless resistance" cells, this group idolizes Hitler and preaches accelerationism. It also aims to recruit US military personnel (Ware 2019). One of its cofounders served in the Florida National Guard while another, Vasillios Pistolis, was an active marine when he participated in the Charlottesville riot. AD is a terrorist organization that has promoted many forms of violence, such as murder, arson, and bombings. It has also advocated attacks on the US power grid as a means of accelerating the collapse of the American "system." In 2023, two of its members were charged with plotting an attack on Maryland's power grid. As of 2018, the group had some eighty members and about twenty cells, but its membership continued to grow after the Unite the Right Rally (Counter Extremism Project). AD aims for an Aryan utopia to replace the decadent, collapsing American system. Its followers are inspired by the likes of James Mason and

William Pierce and by "lone wolf" mass murders, like those committed by Dylann Roof. AD dissolved in July 2020, but some of its members created new groups called the National Socialist Order and the National Socialist Resistance Front. AD has had foreign imitators like the Sonnenkrieg Division in Canada and the Feuerkrieg Division in Europe. The names, not accidentally, echo those of *Waffen-SS* divisions in the Second World War.

A similar movement called The Base was founded in 2018 led by Rinaldo Nazzaro who, using an autonomous cell organization, fostered a series of transnational networks of similar neo-Nazi groups. Like AD, The Base is accelerationist and calls for a race war to bring down the United States and establish an Aryan paradise. It too attempts to recruit former military personnel. Nazzaro claims to have served in the military, though he later denied it. In 2018, he moved to St. Petersburg, Russia, with his Russian-born wife leading to suspicions that he is a Russian agent.

Other groups like the National Socialist Movement (NSM) and the National Socialist Club (NSC-131) are openly neo-Nazi. The former traces its origins to the 1970s and according to the Southern Poverty Law Center (SPCL) is currently the largest neo-Nazi group in the United States. Its manifesto calls for an end to immigration and advances economic platforms reminiscent of early Nazism, such as the breakup of some large corporations and nationalization of others. It also calls for universal healthcare. All of this is designed to protect and foster the white race, expressed in its use of the 14 Words: "Secure the existence of our people and a future for white children" (Counter Extremism Project, 76). The latter is of more recent vintage. It was founded in 2015 in Massachusetts by Chris Hood, a former member of other far-right groups. Like The Base, the group's logo bears an obvious resemblance to that of the SS, with an "s" stylized like a lightning bolt. Hood's group was able to recruit support in 2020 during the COVID-19 lockdowns and the George Floyd protests.

Finally, another group that attracted increased attention in the late 2010s was the Patriot Front (PF). Founded by Thomas Rousseau in Texas in 2017, this group links American national identity with pan-Europeanism. It opposes a multicultural America and runs a vigorous and copious propaganda campaign, accounting for some eighty percent of all white supremacist propaganda in the United States (Counter Extremism Project, 105). Rousseau had been part of the Vanguard America organization that had been present at Charlottesville. (James Alex Fields, Jr., the man who drove his car into the counter-protesters, also belonged to this organization.) However, after a feud with VA's leader, Rousseau started PF (Southern Poverty Law Center). In 2022, the PF made headlines when Rousseau and his group were arrested in Idaho for planning to disrupt a Gay Pride event.

These groups are small, with most of their activity based online. Their memberships overlap, and they are often riddled with internal feuds—par for the course in fascist politics—but also with feuds against other extremist groups on the right and the left. None of these are close to developing a mass following, but they have been influential in promoting violence, often of the "lone wolf" variety. In many cases, these have been deliberate. While Unite the Right and other rallies and demonstrations have shown that these groups can organize collective events, they have mostly been successful in inspiring isolated acts of violence. For example, there have been numerous attacks on power grids in the United States. In 2023, the year that the two Atomwaffen members were arrested for plotting an attack, there were one hundred and eighty-five instances of attacks, surpassing the one hundred one in 2022 and the ninety-seven in 2021 (Morehouse 2024).

The most significant and deadliest of these lone wolf attacks have been mass shootings. Online radicalization and relatively easy access to assault weapons in the United States have contributed to this trend of domestic terrorism. Significant, too, has been the example of Timothy McVeigh in 1995, whose bombing in Oklahoma introduced Americans to this form of right-wing extremist terrorism. But these events have not been restricted to the US Right-wing extremist terrorism has been a transnational phenomenon, as many individuals are inspired by other shooters in different countries. In 2011, the Norwegian neo-Nazi Anders Behring Breivik murdered seventy-seven people in Oslo by a combination of mass shooting and a truck bomb. Breivik used his trial to platform his racist and Islamophobic views, claiming Europe was being transformed into "Eurabia" and that terror was the only way to stop it. He gave Nazi salutes in court. His 1500-page manifesto, titled "2083—A European Declaration of Independence," was published online, and in it, he gave a detailed description of his ideology, including his influences, which included American websites like *Jihad Watch* (Kundnani 2012).

Mass shootings by lone wolf extremists increased significantly in the 2010s. A report by the Anti-Defamation League (ADL) in 2022 noted twenty-six mass shootings by right-wing extremists between 2010 and 2022, accounting for over three hundred and thirty deaths (ADL 2023). The most notorious shootings included Brenton Tarrant's mass shooting of two mosques in Christchurch, New Zealand, in 2019. Tarrant killed fifty-one people and live streamed the massacre as it happened. His manifesto was inspired by the Great Replacement Theory. That same year in El Paso, Texas, Patrick Crusius, who had railed online against Hispanics, killed twenty-three people at a Walmart. Jews and synagogues have also been targeted. In Pittsburgh, Pennsylvania, in 2018, an antisemite named Robert Gregory Bowers murdered eleven congregants at the Tree of Life Synagogue. He was heard saying, "all Jews must die" when he entered the building. Although he was unaffiliated with any group, his online activity demonstrated a belief in right-wing conspiracy theories. He also had an account with *Gab*, an online social network that is popular with antisemites and alt-right figures (Counter Extremism Project). In 2022, African Americans were targeted by Payton Gendron, who traveled to a grocery store in Buffalo, New York, and killed ten people. His manifesto, which he published on Google Docs, described his opposition to mass immigration and his radicalization on neo-Nazi websites like *Daily Stormer*. He also blamed Jews for planning the elimination of the white race, encouraging black crime, and promoting transgenderism (Stanley 2022).

The turn to lone wolfism among extremist right-wing shooters is not accidental and has been promoted by neo-Nazi groups for some time. The clearest statement for this can be found in the manifesto of the British neo-Nazi group, Combat 18 (C18). This movement, founded in London in 1992, prefigured many of the tactics practiced by neo-Nazis in the 2010s, with its leaderless resistance and action by its autonomous cells. In the National Socialist Political Soldiers' Handbook, C18 promotes a Code of Honor based on the SS. It encourages members to live healthy and active lives, recommending boxing as the best form of training. Using at times a lighthearted approach, it exhorts its members to "get yourself in shape, Whiteman: it doesn't take much" (C18). The manifesto went on to explain the different kinds of actions a member of C18 could consider, with covert action as the best form, since it does not attract the attention of authorities. The ideal type of covert action, according to the manifesto, is the lone wolf tactic, since such a strategy involves a single agent who does not share his plans with anyone. This type of action was the most effective in achieving the goal: the complete collapse of the "system."

The form taken by extremist right-wing movements in the 2010s has favored covert actions and lone wolfism, as seen by the terrorist attacks in Europe, the United States, and New Zealand. Although the individual movements have insignificant numbers, the devastation they have caused has been significant. While they do not resemble or hope to achieve the mass movements of the 1930s, contemporary fascism can still impact political and cultural developments through mainstreaming and pushing conventional parties to the far right. They can also impact regular parliamentary practice. In the aftermath of the 2020 presidential election, several members of these groups showed up to the Stop the Steal rally in Washington, DC and participated in the storming of the Capitol Building on January 6, 2021. This pro-Trump rally attempted to influence the certification of the election by a show of force. It ultimately failed, but one person was shot dead, several others died in the next few weeks, scores were injured, and there was significant damage to property. In an editorial for *Newsweek*, the distinguished historian of fascism, Robert Paxton, observed that the January 6 riot resembled that of February 6, 1934, when various far-right groups in Paris attempted to overthrow the French government (R. Paxton 2021).

Paxton's assessment demonstrates a growing consensus: while fascism has changed in form, it has also maintained much of its substance, whether in ideology or in practice. Rather than viewing the alt-right or the European New Right as something entirely new and disconnected from its interwar manifestations, the events of the 2010s and 2020s have suggested that neofascism and neo-Nazism are revisions, not innovations (Copsey 2013). Indeed, like their ancestors, these movements remain revolutionary, looking to overthrow liberal democracies and creating ethno-nationalist states while maintaining a transnational network. While these movements are not dangerous in and of themselves, apart from the damage they cause through terrorism, the danger comes in what Roger Griffin calls the "illiberal democracies" that increasingly adopt alt-right language as their own (Griffin 2022).

CONCLUSION
ONE HUNDRED YEARS ON

An Exhibition for Tolkien

In November 2023, an exhibition opened in Rome's National Gallery. The exhibition marked the fiftieth anniversary of the death of J. R. R. Tolkien, the English writer famous for his *Lord of the Rings* Trilogy. The opening attracted a great deal of attention, as it was inaugurated by Italy's Prime Minister, Giorgia Meloni, who was just over a year into her mandate. The previous year, she had made history by becoming Italy's first female leader. She also happened to have once been a neofascist, and her party, the Brothers of Italy, traced its lineage back to the old MSI. On this occasion, Meloni was indulging in one of her passions, the work of Tolkien and his Hobbits. Not only did she inaugurate the exhibition, but it was sponsored by her Ministry of Culture to the tune of two hundred and fifty thousand euros. The exhibition took pride of place in Italy's most important gallery of modern and contemporary art and was slated to tour the country in 2024.

At the opening, the diminutive Meloni posed next to a life-size statue of Gandalf the Wizard, reminding those who read her memoir, *I am Giorgia*, of her lifelong devotion to fantasy literature. It seemed a harmless way to soften her otherwise strong image as prime minister, a means of reaching out to a generation of Italians who grew up on similar literature and movies from the 1970s onward. The exhibition included scenes from the Peter Jackson films playing on a loop, as well as other cinematic depictions of the *Rings* stories. It was nostalgia highlighted by a pinball machine and comic book illustrations. The exhibit itself was not particularly impressive, as some observers felt it was hastily put together (Phipps 2024). The quality of the exhibition did not live up to the impressive financial backing it received from official sources, which only served to raise more questions about its purpose. Why should the work of a foreign writer receive such attention from the Italian government, and why should a work of fantasy be celebrated in the hallowed rooms of the National Gallery?

The answers to these questions were to be found in Meloni's political background. As a teenager, growing up in a working-class district of Rome, she had joined the *Fronte della Gioventù* (FdG), MSI's youth wing. In her memoir, published not long before the 2022 election, she waxed nostalgic about the atmosphere of this club, noting how they would engage in impassioned debates on every issue under the sun. The FdG was a meeting place for young people to discuss politics, world affairs, and culture. Meloni's cagey approach said little or nothing about the FdG's political orientation, neofascism. Instead, this was a site where young people could meet and discuss the future of Italy, the world, and their generation. Her love for Tolkien's work, which she describes as a "sacred text," was not just a personal interest, but one shared by her FdG community, going

Figure C.1 The opening of the Tolkien exhibition sponsored by Giorgia Meloni's government. Rome, November 2023. Credit: Alamy.

back to the Hobbit Camps of the 1970s. Not long after the MSI became the post-fascist *Alleanza Nazionale* in 1995, the youth wing began organizing a yearly conference called *Atreju*, named after the main character in the book *The Neverending Story*, who spends his time fighting against "nothingness." Meloni was one of the leading organizers of the event, which continues to this day under the auspices of the Brothers of Italy.

Fantasy pervades the Italian far right and has done so since the 1970s. Far from being a fun distraction from the daily business of politics, events like *Atreju* and the Tolkien Exhibition are steeped in the politics of Italian neofascism. In fact, critics have noticed how exhibitions like this fit into one of Meloni's key policy initiatives, including the takeover of Italy's culture industry (Mackay 2023). Romeo Castellucci, a well-known theater director, claimed that Meloni, through her Culture Minister, Gennaro Sangiuliano, has made culture a "battlefield" (Pecqueur 2024). Italian governments have always had the right to make political appointments in cultural ministries, but in the past, many of these have often been given to coalition partners and even political opponents. With Meloni, the appointment of culture czars has been particularly aggressive, with far-right figures taking over events like the Venice Biennale, the MAXXI contemporary art gallery, and the national broadcaster, *Radiotelevisione Italiana* (RAI).

The world of neofascist fantasy has its fingerprints on Meloni's cultural politics. On the Tolkien Exhibition's website, a list of consultants is given (Galleria Nazionale 2023). One of them, Gianfranco De Turris, is the President of the Julius Evola Foundation. A devotee of Evola, De Turris has written numerous elegies to the neofascist traditionalist

Evola, who contributed more than others in shaping postwar Italian and international neofascism. De Turris's writings have often appeared in right-wing newspapers and periodicals, such as *Il Secolo d'Italia*, the former MSI newspaper that is currently run by the Brothers of Italy. Notoriously, De Turris also wrote prefaces for some works by another Evolian fantasist, Gianluca Casseri, who, in December 2011, shot and killed two Senegalese market stall owners in Florence in a deliberate hate crime. Casseri, apart from his traditionalist works, was also known to frequent Florence's chapter of *CasaPound*.

One Hundred Years

The election victory of Meloni's party in 2022 was expected but still came as a shock. For the first time since the establishment of the Italian Republic after the Second World War, a party with a fascist lineage was once again in power. For decades, this had been unthinkable. When the ruling Christian Democrats attempted to bring the MSI into its coalition in 1960, mass protests resulted—the DC, then, shifted its electoral strategy, opening to the left instead. In 2022, there were no such protests. In effect, the groundwork for this had been laid in the 1990s, when the media and sport tycoon Silvio Berlusconi brought neofascists into his government. There were few protests then as well, largely due to the political earthquake that had rocked the Italian party establishment in the wake of the end of the Cold War, not to mention corruption scandals, which allowed new parties like Berlusconi's *Forza Italia* to rise to power.

A significant corollary to this political shake-up was a new wave of historical revisionism, led by intellectuals such as Renzo De Felice, whose multivolume biography of Benito Mussolini claimed that the dictator enjoyed a great degree of consensus in the 1930s (Bosworth 1998). De Felice's controversial views were accompanied by a series of documentaries and other works that attempted to "historicize" the Fascist era in a manner that echoed similar debates in West Germany in the 1980s during the so-called *Historikerstreit*. The upshot of these debates is that they led to a reevaluation of Italian history that diminished the role and importance of anti-fascism as the primary force shaping the Italian Republic. This reevaluation, in turn, opened the door to the legitimization of the MSI. In 1993, the party's leader, Gianfranco Fini, very nearly won the mayoral election of Rome. Two years later, Fini led the rebranding of the MSI into the *Alleanza Nazionale* (AN), declaring that Mussolini was now a part of history and the AN was now a normal, conservative, democratic party. Hardliners, like Pino Rauti, refused to accept this new line, but most party members went along with it, since the prize was a role in the Berlusconi government.

Giorgia Meloni was one of the many who followed Fini. In 2008, she became the youngest person in the history of the Italian Republic to be appointed to the cabinet when she became the Minister of Youth in Berlusconi's fourth government. That year, she took part in a commemorative ceremony at the former FdG headquarters on Via Acca Larenzia in Rome, where, in 1978, three members of the MSI youth organization were killed in a shooting during the Years of Lead. It is at that ceremony where neofascists gather annually and give the fascist salute, "*Presente!*" Four years later, Meloni, along with other former members of the AN, created a new party, the Brothers of Italy.

Meloni's rise to prominence has been nothing short of meteoric. The same goes for her party. Rising from the ashes of the AN, which dissolved into Berlusconi's party after 2008 in the wake of schisms, the Brothers of Italy (FdI—*Fratelli d'Italia*) picked up less than 2 percent of the national vote in 2013. In 2018, Meloni's party was part of a center-right coalition with Berlusconi's *Forza Italia* and Matteo Salvini's *Lega Nord*, a regionalist, anti-European party that traded in xenophobic attacks on migrants. Meloni's party was the junior partner in the coalition, picking up only 4.35 percent of the vote. However, in the years between 2018 and 2022, when the next election was held, Meloni's pragmatic and canny political instincts came to the fore, as her party refused to support the three separate governments that ruled Italy in that time. Her coalition partners did support those governments, all of which were unpopular, thus gaining the FdI significant support in 2022, when her party took 26 percent of the vote, far ahead of her coalition partners, who lost such significant support.

Meloni's success in 2022 thus had a great deal to do with the protests against the parties that had governed previously and less to do with ideological conviction. Knowing this, Meloni's leadership has been known for its pragmatism and, on the surface, some degree of moderation. She has supported Italy's position in the NATO and supported Ukraine against Russia, despite the pro-Putin sympathies among some of her supporters—and among her coalition partners, like Salvini. Her diminutive stature and folksy appreciation for pop culture have rendered her harmless for some, despite her youthful enthusiasm for Mussolini, as demonstrated in a French television interview done in the 1990s. Supporters have also pointed out how she has consistently consigned Mussolini to history and repeatedly disavowed any nostalgia for the *Ventennio* in her memoir. However, shadows persist.

When the FdI was created in 2012, its logo restored the flame of the old MSI party. During the election campaign of 2022, Liliana Segre, Senator for Life and Holocaust survivor, asked that Meloni remove the flame and disavow any links with the MSI, a party that was founded by devoted followers of Mussolini in 1946. Meloni refused. Since coming to power, Meloni has had to deal with several controversies. These often include party members who are seen giving fascist salutes or expressing open admiration for Mussolini (Bubola 2024). Additionally, one of her main lieutenants, Ignazio La Russa, was elected President of the Senate. La Russa had a long history in the MSI's youth wing, and his father had been an important fascist official in Sicily and an MSI parliamentarian. La Russa was also known to have an impressive collection of fascist memorabilia, which he once showed off to a camera crew.

Significantly, despite Meloni's pragmatic and seemingly moderate positions since taking office in October 2022—one hundred almost to the day of Mussolini's March on Rome—are her cultural agenda, already discussed, and her plans for significant constitutional reforms. Here too, there were some disconcerting historical echoes. Prominent on the agenda of the FdI is a desire to reform the electoral system. Arguing that Italian governance has been too unstable since the postwar era—as evidenced by the over sixty governments that have ruled the republic—Meloni has proposed a first-past-the-post system, whereby the party that gains the most votes nationally will be awarded 55 percent of the seats in parliament, thus commanding a majority and guaranteeing that a government can serve a full term without relying on unstable and fragile coalitions. While Meloni has stressed the pragmatic nature of this reform, critics have noticed an eerie similarity to the Acerbo Law, Mussolini's electoral reform from exactly one hundred years previously, that called for a similar system. In that case, Mussolini's PNF was able to carry the 1924 elections and set up the scenario whereby the fascist dictatorship began its ascent (Meyer-Resende and Tsereteli 2023). Futhermore, the winning party's leader would automatically become prime minister, giving that person and their party enormous power.

Meloni's policies toward Europe also suggest an agenda. While the FdI has its share of critics of the EU, Meloni has been able to establish a working relationship with Brussels on several issues, including a deal regarding the migrant crisis that began in the mid-2010s and that has greatly impacted Italian shores. However, she has also cultivated a close bond with Hungary's Viktor Orbán and with Spain's far-right *Vox* Party; both are critical of the European Union and trade in significant xenophobia. Meloni's views on Europe, revealed in her memoir, and in her party's Trieste Theses, issued in 2017, demonstrates a Europeanism shrouded in mysticism and that celebrates the ethnic identities of individual nations. Hers is an identitarian view of Europe that has been a consistent thread in neofascism. She celebrates the Europe of Christianity with its gothic cathedrals and points out heroic moments associated with European and Christian resistance to Islam. This Europe is, according to Meloni, under siege by immigrants. Notably, the Trieste Theses references Jean Raspail's *The Camp of the Saints* (1973), a dystopian novel that deeply influenced the Great Replacement Theory that is so prominent among neofascists and neo-Nazis (Broder 2023, 22–3).

Fantasy, Culture, Politics

Meloni's *Lord of the Rings* exhibit was not just a fun face for pragmatic politics, but a set of codes. It is the face of fascism in the country that gave the movement birth one hundred years previously. While Meloni's Brothers of Italy is not the same as Mussolini's Blackshirts, there are threads that link them through a shared genealogy. Fascism lies at the heart of the modern experience. It is a product of the massive changes that took place in the West in the nineteenth century and took shape in the shocks of the twentieth century. It has persisted, albeit in different forms, into the twenty-first century. It remains strangely elusive, but its presence is felt strongly, even long after its defeat in Germany and Italy in the 1940s. Its shadow remains and inspires new disciples in Europe and America. A major part of its continued appeal lies in the way it brings together fantasy, culture, and politics into a unique synergy that liberal democratic politics have struggled with. It continues to elicit fascination despite—and even because of—its dismal record and its cultivation of violence. It has produced leaders who repel and attract at the same time. It entertains contradictions that defy reason and common sense. It produces monsters, as in Goya's *Saturn Devouring His Son*. It is rooted in fantasy.

Fascism cannot be understood outside of its historical context, as Paxton argues. It was a movement produced by the massive trauma of the First World War, but its origins lie in the epochal transformations of the nineteenth century. The sense of uprootedness and disequilibrium caused by the Industrial Revolution and the legacy of the French Revolution led some to search for a "golden age" they could return to, a time when a seemingly homogeneous and stable society shaped peoples' lives. The dramatic upheavals of that century in Europe and beyond produced proto-fascist episodes, such as the Boulanger and Dreyfus Affairs in France and the rise of Nativism in the United States. Antisemitism, a perennial feature of the West going back to the ancient world, was rekindled, as the Jews were blamed for the ills of modernity. Meanwhile, new ideologies, like nationalism, preached the virtues of an ethnic community unblemished by foreigners and Jews. Moreover, violence, thanks to the legacy of the revolutions and the rise of anarcho-syndicalism, was now viewed as a positive myth to be used to return society and culture back to premodern values. Not for the first time, techniques associated with the left were appropriated by the right.

The trauma of the First World War gave birth to fascism. In 1914–18, Europeans were introduced *en masse* to industrialized warfare, while the state demonstrated its ability to mobilize an entire nation and its resources to war. The upheavals caused by the war—most of all the Bolshevik Revolution in Russia, the sweeping away of the empires in Central Europe, and the emergence of liberal democracies in their wake—produced the context that gave shape to fascism. Many angry war veterans flocked to extremist politics. Some were driven by fantasies of revenge on civilians who the veterans felt had betrayed them, whether it was the German Jews of the "stab in the back legend," the *imboscati* in Italy, or the "Judeo-Bolshevik cabal" that gave birth to the Russian Revolution. Dark and violent fantasies unleashed from the trenches were converted into political energies that "brutalized politics" in the postwar era (Mosse 1990). What was perhaps latent in 1914 became real after 1918.

Fascism's "golden age" came in the interwar era, when Mussolini and Hitler ruled over their countries and millions wore either the black or brown shirts. Fascist-like movements proliferated throughout Europe and the Americas, as they seemed to provide an optimistic counterpoint to the struggling liberal democracies amid the Great Depression. Despite their differences, Italian Fascism and German Nazism held more in common than it might seem. Both were cult-like movements with a charismatic leader at the helm. Both produced heavily ritualized politics aimed at reassuring those traumatized by the violent eruptions of the previous decades. Both promised redemption for victimized nations. Both promised a future of power and peace based on fantasies of the past.

The Second World War and the Holocaust were the fruits of interwar fascism. The dream for homogeneous and pure nations could only lead to genocide and mass deportations. The Holocaust, driven by "redemptive antisemitism," was the natural product of Nazi fantasies (Friedländer 2007). The Axis alliance was the fascist attempt

Conclusion

to construct reality according to its own vision or worldview (*Weltanschauung*). The Second World War should be understood as the moment that Nazi and Fascist dreams attempted to remake the world in its own image, revealing a pathology that can only result in wreaking havoc on the real world (Prince 2023). The concentration camps allowed fascism and Nazism to manifest their Darwinian fantasies of survival of the master race. Holocaust survivor Primo Levi famously argued that Auschwitz was in essence a biological experiment aimed at dehumanizing inmates (Levi 1996). Nazi fantasies about colonizing Europe drove Hitler's armies along with the elimination of the Jewish people (Mazower 2009).

Fascist fantasy survived the Second World War even if the Axis regimes did not. One of its legacies was to prepare the ground for the two ideologies that contended with each other for world dominance during the Cold War. Neofascists and neo-Nazis remained largely underground, while many were rehabilitated to fight the cause against communism or against Israel. In these survivors, a new generation of far-right activists was born in the decades following the war. Nostalgia for the old regimes mixed in with fantasies of a new world shaped by Evolian Traditionalism. Esoteric and Eastern mysticism mixed with Roman Catholic Traditionalism and neo-paganism to forge movements throughout the Western world. Once the war against communism ended in 1989, new wars beckoned against the perceived decadence of the Western world. In the feverish minds of neofascists, Jews are responsible for flooding the West with immigrants in a plot to replace the White race.

Like the historic fascist movements of the interwar era, the current crop of neofascists and neo-Nazis are varied in what they emphasize and how they organize. However, clear genealogical threads can be made to the original movements. These can only be teased out through a narrative history of fascism beginning in the nineteenth century. Fascism is a historical phenomenon specific to the West and to Europe in particular. It's an expression of a perceived decline and degeneration in Western values and a desire to smash what is left to give birth to a new, palingenetic culture and community. It is a dystopian view of culture that foresees catastrophic collapse and works to accelerate that collapse. It comes from a position of perceived victimhood, but one where the victims still maintain a place of privilege and power. It is willing to make use of both left and right techniques and policies, but it rests exclusively on the far right of the political spectrum.

Ultimately, fascism is a fantasy that dreams of fighting ultimate, epic battles, whether through a clash of armies or through culture and politics. Culture wars have always been the preferred domestic battlefields of fascists. Rooted in the romantic nationalism of the nineteenth century, fascists define ethnic and national identity in cultural terms. Culture wars permit no compromise, unlike the liberal democracies they detest. These culture wars must be viewed in political terms (Traverso 2019). Fantasy itself is political. While all political ideologies deal in some way with fantasy, fascism has been the ideology most deeply invested in fantasy. All fascists and neofascists fantasize about some ideal past they wish to resurrect in the present. The Slovenian philosopher, Slavoj Žižek, has argued that the fantasies that motivate the far right are full of origin stories, shared memory traces, and a sense that something essential was once lost, stolen by some outsider or Other (Sharpe and Turner 2019). In this case, the theft involved some part of a nation's "way of life." Fascists have always fantasized about the retrieval of this lost object while, in the process, punishing those who stole it. This sense of loss—as a deliberate theft—has shaped the fascist mind since the origins of the movement. Violent fantasies of retribution—of taking something back from those who stole it—are central to all fascists, neofascists, and neo-Nazis, and they continue to flourish in the twenty-first century.

Does Fascism Have a Future?

As a movement, fascism remains elusive since it shares many of its basic elements with other political movements. It has taken on various forms. Meanwhile, the word has become a kind of floating signifier, used in various ways to denigrate one's political opponents. Yet, its presence is clear and can be seen in a variety of symbols, gestures, rituals, attitudes, and behaviors. Due to the crises of the West since the end of the Cold War—terrorism, economic uncertainties, pandemics, and the fragility of liberal democratic institutions—"fasc-ish" attitudes and ideas continue to circulate and have made their way into mainstream politics (Linker 2022). Amid this revival of fascist thinking is the legacy of historical fascism. The relics of the Nazi and Fascist regimes can still be seen in Europe. Mussolini's architecture is not only still there but it is being repurposed for contemporary use (Ben-Ghiat 2017). Meanwhile, Nazi artifacts continue to fetch high prices in memorabilia showcases around the world. Sellers claim that these items are valued based on their historical significance and have no ideological function, even as they ignore the atrocities committed by the Nazi regime and the crimes still committed, to this day, in its name. The reality of the Holocaust remains entirely unacknowledged in the buying and selling of these items (Kaiser 2023).

Fascism has a past and a present, but what is its future? This will depend on how successfully fascist ideas and attitudes have been and are mainstreamed. Since the 2000s, fascist mindsets have crept into not only mainstream politics, but also into intellectual discourses, social media, and virtual communities. The far reach of the internet has created cults of personality around neofascist and neo-Nazi figures, not to mention gaming cultures where Nazi armies once again invade European countries in virtual fantasies (Smelser and Davies III 2008). Think tanks and internet intellectuals have incorporated fascist influences for audiences who might be unaware of the origins of their views (Mishra 2018; Linker 2023; Szalai 2024).

The key to fascism's future, and the survival of liberal democracy in the West, requires an awareness of what fascism is and how it shows itself, either directly or indirectly. Resisting fascism is vital, and this requires that citizens do not participate in its growth. Historical fascism's success in the interwar era depended not only on repression and fear, but also on consent, sometimes given in advance (Snyder 2017; Stanley 2018; Ben-Ghiat 2020). One of the factors that has allowed a party like the Brothers of Italy to succeed in Italy has been the marginalizing of the anti-fascist principles that underpinned the

Italian Republic. Similar acts of historical and political revisionism have occurred in Germany and other European nations. The success of the National Rally party in France, formerly the National Front, has been prepared by a reevaluation of Vichy France in the Second World War. Historical ignorance of the Holocaust has allowed denialism to infect a new generation of people because of the reach of the internet (D. E. Lipstadt 2019). Historical awareness and defense of liberal democratic values are the only things that can guarantee that fascism will not have another one hundred years (Figure C.1).

WORKS CITED

Abel, Theodore. 1996. *Why Hitler Came into Power*. Cambridge, MA: Harvard University Press.
Ackerman, James S. 1990. *The Villa: Form and Ideology of the Country House*. London: Thames & Hudson.
Adamson, Walter L. 1993. *Avant-Garde Florence: From Modernism to Fascism*. Cambridge, MA: Harvard University Press.
ADL. 2023. *Murder and Extremism in the United States in 2022*. Anti-Defamation League. Accessed August 8, 2024. https://www.adl.org/resources/report/murder-and-extremism-united-states-2022.
Albanese, Matteo. 2022. "CasaPound and Forza Nuova: Back to the Future." In *Rethinking Fascism: The Italian and German Dictatorships*, edited by Andrea Di Michele and Filippo Focardi, 317–33. Berlin: Walter de Gruyter GmbH.
Albright, Madeleine. 2018. *Fascism: A Warning*. New York: Harper.
Antola Swan, Alessandra. 2020. *Photographing Mussolini: The Making of a Political Icon*. London: Palgrave Macmillan.
Arendt, Hannah. 1968. *The Origins of Totalitarianism*. San Diego: Harcourt.
Aufderheide, Patricia. 2007. *Documentary Film: A Very Short Introduction*. Oxford: Oxford University Press.
Bach, Steven. 2007. *Leni: The Life and Work of Leni Riefenstahl*. New York: Alfred A. Knopf.
Bale, Jeffrey. 2017. *The Darkest Side of Politics: Postwar Fascism, Covert Operations, and Terrorism*. Vol. I. London: Routledge.
Barron, Stephanie. 1991. *"Degenerate Art": The Fate of the Avant-Garde in Nazi Germany*. Los Angeles: Harry N. Abrams.
Bartov, Omer. 1992. *Hitler's Army: Soldiers, Nazis, and War in the Third Reich*. Oxford: Oxford University Press.
Bartov, Omer. 1996. *Murder in Our Midst: The Holocaust, Industrial Killing, and Representation*. Oxford: Oxford University Press.
Baxa, Paul. 2010. *Roads and Ruins: The Symbolic Landscape of Fascist Rome*. Toronto: University of Toronto Press.
Baxa, Paul. 2013. "'Il nostro Duce': Mussolini's Visit to Trieste in 1938 and the Workings of the Cult of the Duce." *Modern Italy* 18 (2): 117–28.
Baxa, Paul. 2022. *Motorsport and Fascism: Living Dangerously*. London: Palgrave Macmillan.
Bekers, Willem, Ronald De Meyer, and Emiel De Kooning. 2021. "Bricks of Wrath: (Re)building the IJzertoren Memorial (1925–1930 and 1952–1965). Vol. 2." In *History of Construction Cultures*, edited by João Mascarenhas-Mateus and Ana Paula Pires, 537–44. London: Taylor & Francis. Accessed August 5, 2024. https://www.taylorfrancis.com/chapters/oa-edit/10.1201/9781003173434-182/bricks-wrath-re-building-ijzertoren-memorial-1925%E2%80%931930-1952%E2%80%931965-bekers-de-meyer-de-kooning.
Belew, Kathleen. 2018. *Bring the War Home: The White Power Movement and Paramilitary America*. Cambridge, MA: Harvard University Press.
Bellon, Tina. 2016. "Far-Right AfD Says Islam Not Welcome in Germany." *Reuters*, May 1. Accessed August 6, 2024. https://www.aljazeera.com/news/2016/5/1/far-right-afd-says-islam-not-welcome-in-germany#:~:text=The%20chapter%20of%20the%20AfD,by%20some%20conservative%20Muslim%20women.

Works Cited

Ben-Ghiat, Ruth. 2001. *Fascist Modernities: Italy, 1922–1945*. Berkeley: University of California Press.

Ben-Ghiat, Ruth. 2015. *Italian Fascism's Empire Cinema*. Bloomington: Indiana University Press.

Ben-Ghiat, Ruth. 2017. "Why Are So Many Fascist Monuments Still Standing in Italy?" *New Yorker*, October 5. Accessed August 20, 2024. https://www.newyorker.com/culture/culture-desk/why-are-so-many-fascist-monuments-still-standing-in-italy.

Ben-Ghiat, Ruth. 2020. *Strongmen: Mussolini to the Present*. New York: W.W. Norton.

Benjamin, Walter. 1968. "The Work of Art in the Age of Mechanical Reproduction." In *Illuminations*, edited by Hannah Arendt, translated by Harry Zohn, 217–52. London: Fontana.

Berezin, Mabel. 1997. *Making the Fascist Self: The Political Culture of Interwar Italy*. Ithaca, NY: Cornell University Press.

Bergen, Doris. 2016. *War & Genocide: A Concise History of the Holocaust*. Third Edition. London: Rowman & Littlefield.

Biondich, Mark. 2005. "Religion and Nation in Wartime Croatia: Reflections on the Ustaše Policy of Forced Religious Conversions, 1941–1942." *The Slavonic and East European Review* 83 (1): 71–116.

BIRN. 2022. "Hungary Bans Annual Neo-Nazi Gathering in Budapest." *Balkaninsight.com*. February 2. Accessed August 5, 2024. https://balkaninsight.com/2022/02/02/hungary-bans-annual-neo-nazi-gathering-in-budapest/.

Bloch, Marc. 1949. *Strange Defeat: A Statement of Evidence Written in 1940*. Oxford: Oxford University Press.

Bosworth, R. J. B. 1998. *The Italian Dictatorship: Problems and Perspectives in the Interpretation of Mussolini and Fascism*. London: Arnold.

Bosworth, R. J. B. 2004. *Mussolini's Italy: Life under the Fascist Dictatorship, 1915–1945*. New York: The Penguin Press.

Bosworth, R. J. B. 2009. "Introduction." In *The Oxford Handbook of Fascism*, edited by R. J. B. Bosworth, 2–7. Oxford: Oxford University Press.

Botz, Gerhard. 2014. "The Coming of the Dollfuss-Schuschnigg Regime and the Stages of its Development." In *Rethinking Fascism and Dictatorship in Europe*, edited by Antonio Costa Pinto and Aristotle Kallis, 121–53. London: Palgrave Macmillan.

Boyne, Walter J. 1994. *Clash of Wings: Air Power in World War II*. New York: Simon & Schuster.

Bracher, Karl Dietrich. 1970. *The German Dictatorship: The Origins, Structure, and Effects of National Socialism*. Translated by Jean Steinberg. New York: Praeger.

Breitman, Richard, and Norman J. W. Goda. 2010. *Hitler's Shadow*. Washington, DC: National Archives and Records Administration.

Broder, David. 2023. *Mussolini's Grandchildren: Fascism in Contemporary Italy*. London: Pluto Press.

Broszat, Martin. 1981. *The Hitler State: The Foundation and Development of the Internal Structure of the Third Reich*. Translated by John W. Hiden. London: Longman.

Browning, Christopher, and Jürgen Matthäus. 2004. *The Origins of the Final Solution: The Evolution of Nazi Jewish Policy, September 1939-March 1942*. Lincoln, NE: University of Nebraska Press.

Bubola, Emma. 2024. "Meloni Condemns Fascist Nostalgia Amid Scandal in Her Party's Youth Wing." *New York Times*, July 2. Accessed August 19, 2024. https://www.nytimes.com/2024/07/02/world/europe/meloni-political-party-youth-wing-facism.html.

Bueno, Alex. 2014. "Valle de los Caídos: A Monument to Defy Time and Oblivion." In *Memory and Cultural History of the Spanish Civil War: Realms of Oblivion*, edited by Aurora Morcillo, 51–109. Leiden: Brill.

Burleigh, Michael. 2007. *Sacred Causes: The Clash of Religion and Politics, from the Great War to the War on Terror*. New York: HarperCollins.

Burleigh, Michael. 2000. *The Third Reich: A New History*. New York: Hill and Wang.

Calvino, Italo. 2003. *Hermit in Paris: Autobiographical Writings*. Translated by Martin McLaughlin. New York: Pantheon Books.

Campani, Giovanna. 2016. "Neo-fascism from the Twentieth Century to the Third Millennium: The Case of Italy." In *The Rise of the Far Right in Europe*, edited by Gabriella Lazaridis, Giovanna Campani, and Annie Benveniste, 25–64. London: Palgrave Macmillan.

Camus, Jean-Yves. 2019. "Alain de Benoist and the New Right." In *Key Thinkers of the Radical Right: Behind the New Threat to Liberal Democracy*, edited by Mark Sedgwick, 73–90. Oxford: Oxford University Press.

Cannistraro, Philip V. 1982. *Historical Dictionary of Fascist Italy*. Westport, CT: Greenwood Press.

Caprotti, Federico. 2007. *Mussolini's Cities: Internal Colonialism in Italy, 1930–1939*. Youngstown: Cambria Press.

Carsten, F. L. 1967. *The Rise of Fascism*. Berkeley: University of California Press.

Carter, Nick. 2010. *Modern Italy in Historical Perspective*. London: Bloomsbury Academic.

Castelli Gattinara, Pietro. 2019. "Forza Nuova and the Security Walks: Squadrismo and Extreme-Right Vigilantism in Italy." In *Vigilantism Against Migrants and Minorities*, edited by Tore Bjørgo and Miroslav Mares, 213–27. London: Routledge.

Castelli Gattinara, Pietro, and Caterina Froio. 2014. "Discourse and Practice of Violence in the Italian Extreme Right: Frames, Symbols, and Identity-Building in CasaPound Italia." *International Journal of Conflict and Violence* 8 (1): 154–70.

Cento Bull, Anna. 2007. *Italian Neofascism: The Strategy of Tension and the Politics of Neoreconciliation*. New York: Berghahn Books.

Cento Bull, Anna. 2010. "Neo-Fascism." In *The Oxford Book of Fascism*, edited by R. J. B. Bosworth, 586–605. Oxford: Oxford University Press.

Cheles, Luciano. 1991. "'Nostalgia dell'Avvenire': The New Propaganda of the MSI between Tradition and Innovation." In *Neo-Fascism in Europe*, edited by Luciano Cheles, Ronnie Ferguson, and Michalina Vaughan, 43–65. Harlow, Essex: Longman Group UK Limited.

Ciano, Galeazzo. 1947. *Ciano's Diary 1939–1943*. Translated by Malcolm Muggeridge. London: William Heinemann.

Combat 18. n.d. "National Socialist Political Soldier's Handbook." *Archive.org*. Accessed August 8, 2024. https://archive.org/details/combat-18-ns-political-soldiers-handbook_202311.

Confino, Alon. 2014. *A World Without Jews*. New Haven, CT: Yale University Press.

Coogan, Kevin. 1999. *Dreamer of the Day: Francis Parker Yockey and the Postwar Fascist International*. New York: Autonomedia.

Copsey, Nigel. 2013. "'Fascism…but with an Open Mind.' Reflections on the Contemporary Far Right in (Western) Europe." *Fascism: Journal of Comparative Fascist Studies* 2 (1): 1–17. Accessed August 8, 2024. https://brill.com/view/journals/fasc/2/1/article-p1_1.xml?language=en&ebody=pdf-117260.

Copsey, Nigel. 2008. *Contemporary British Fascism: The British National Party and the Quest for Legitimacy*. Second Edition. Basingstoke: Palgrave Macmillan.

Cosgrove, Denis. 1993. *The Palladian Landscape: Geographical Change and Its Representations in Sixteenth-Century Italy*. University Park, PA: Pennsylvania State Press.

Costa Pinto, António. 2020. "Brazil in the Era of Fascism: The 'New State' of Getulio Vargas." In *Beyond the Fascist Century: Essays in Honour of Roger Griffin*, edited by Constantin Iordachi and Aristotle Kallis, 235–56. London: Palgrave Macmillan.

Works Cited

Costa Pinto, António, and Aristotle Kallis. 2014. "Introduction." In *Rethinking Fascism and Dictatorship in Europe*, edited by Antonio Costa Pinto and Aristotle Kallis. New York: Palgrave Macmillan.

Counter Extremism Project. n.d. "Golden Dawn." *Counter Extremism Project*. Accessed August 8, 2024. https://www.counterextremism.com/threat/golden-dawn/report.

Counter Extremism Project. n.d. "James Mason's Siege Ties to Extremists." *Counter Extremism Project*. Accessed August 6, 2024. https://www.counterextremism.com/james-masons-siege-ties-to-extremists.

Counter Extremism Project. n.d. "Jobbik." *Counter Extremism Project*. Accessed August 8, 2024. https://www.counterextremism.com/threat/jobbik/report.

Counter Extremism Project. n.d. "Nordic Resistance Movement." *Counter Extremism Project*. Accessed August 8, 2024. https://www.counterextremism.com/threat/nordic-resistance-movement-nrm/report.

Counter Extremism Project. n.d. "Robert Bowers." *Counter Extremism Project*. Accessed August 8, 2024. https://www.counterextremism.com/extremists/robert-bowers.

Counter Extremism Project. n.d. "The Turner Diaries' Ties to Extremists." *Counter Extremism Project*. Accessed August 6, 2024. https://www.counterextremism.com/the-turner-diaries-ties-to-extremists.

Counter Extremism Project. n.d. "White Supremacy Groups in the United States." *Counter Extremism Project*. Accessed August 8, 2024. https://www.counterextremism.com/sites/default/files/supremacy_landing_files/U.S.%20White%20Supremacy%20Groups_072624.pdf.

Dafinger, Johannes, and Dieter Pohl. 2019. "Introduction." In *A New Nationalist Europe Under Hitler: Concepts of Europe and Transnational Networks in the National Socialist Sphere of Influence, 1933–1945*, edited by Johannes Dafinger and Dieter Pohl, 1–24. London: Routledge.

De Felice, Renzo. 1976. *Fascism: An Informal Introduction to Its Theory and Practice*. Translated by Michael Ledeen. New Brunswick, NJ: Transaction Books.

De Felice, Renzo. 1976. *Fascism: An Informal Introduction to Its Theory and Practice*. Translated by Michael Ledeen. New Brunswick, NJ: Transaction Books.

De Grand, Alexander. 1991. "Cracks in the Facade: The Failure of Fascist Totalitarianism in Italy, 1935–9." *European History Quarterly* 21: 515–35.

De Grand, Alexander. 1989. *Italian Fascism: Its Origins and Development*. Second Edition. Lincoln: University of Nebraska Press.

De Grazia, Victoria. 1992. *How Fascism Ruled Women: Italy, 1922–1945*. Berkeley: University of California Press.

De Grazia, Victoria. 1981. *The Culture of Consent: Mass Organization of Leisure in Fascist Italy*. London: Cambridge University Press.

Deakin, F. W. 1962. *The Brutal Friendship: Mussolini, Hitler and the Fall of Italian Fascism*. New York: Harper & Row.

Della Porta, Donatella, and Anna Lavizzari. 2022. "Waves in Cycle: The Protests Against Anti-Contagion Measures and Vaccination in Covid-19 Times in Italy." *PACO* 15 (3): 720–40.

Dickie, John. 2005. *Cosa Nostra: A History of the Sicilian Mafia*. London: St. Martin's Griffin.

Duggan, Christopher. 2013. *Fascist Voices: An Intimate History of Mussolini's Italy*. Oxford: Oxford University Press.

Duggan, Christopher. 2013. "The Propagation of the Cult of the Duce, 1925–26." In *The Cult of the Duce: Mussolini and the Italians*, edited by Stephen Gundle, Christopher Duggan, and Giuliana Pieri, 27–40. Manchester: Manchester University Press.

Earle, Ben. 2004. "The Avant-Garde Artist as Superman: Aesthetics and Politics in Dellapiccola's Volo di Notte." In *Italian Music during the Fascist Period*, edited by Roberto Illiano, 659–716. Turnhout: Brepols.

Works Cited

Eatwell, Roger. 1995. *Fascism: A History*. New York: Penguin.
Eco, Umberto. 2001. *Five Moral Pieces*. Translated by Alastair McEwen. San Diego: Harcourt Books.
Edmondson, Catie. 2023. "How Germany's Extreme Right Seized on the Martial Arts Scene." *New York Times*, September 17. Accessed August 6, 2024. https://www.nytimes.com/2023/09/17/world/europe/germany-far-right-mma.html.
Eksteins, Modris. 1989. *Rites of Spring: The Great War and the Birth of the Modern Age*. New York: Mariner Books.
Eksteins, Modris. 1999. *Walking since Daybreak: A Story of Eastern Europe, World War II, and the Heart of Our Century*. Boston, MA: Houghton Mifflin.
Esposito, Fernando. 2015. *Fascism, Aviation and Mythical Modernity*. Translated by Patrick Camiller. London: Palgrave Macmillan.
Etlin, R. A. 1991. *Modernism in Italian Architecture*. Cambridge: MIT Press.
Evans, Richard J. 2007. "Coercion and Consent in Nazi Germany." *Proceedings of the British Academy* 151: 53–81.
Evans, Richard J. 2004. *The Coming of the Third Reich*. New York: The Penguin Press.
Evans, Richard J. 2015. *The Third Reich in History and Memory*. London: Abacus.
Evans, Richard J. 2005. *The Third Reich in Power, 1933–1939*. New York: The Penguin Press.
Feiber, Albert A., and Thomas Schlemmer. 2022. "Obersalzberg and the Axis: State Visits between Idyll, Diplomacy, and Atrocity." In *Rethinking Fascism: The Italian and German Dictatorships*, edited by Andrea Di Michele and Filippo Focard, 185–224. Berlin: Walter De Gruyter GmbH.
Ferraresi, Franco. 1996. *Threats to Democracy: The Radical Right in Italy after the War*. Princeton, NJ: Princeton University Press.
Ferrari, Chiara. 2013. *The Rhetoric of Violence and Sacrifice in Fascist Italy: Mussolini, Gadda, Vittorini*. Toronto: University of Toronto Press.
Fest, Joachim C. 1974. *Hitler*. Translated by Richard Winston and Clara Winston. New York: Harcourt.
Fischer, Fritz. 1968. *Germany's Aims in the First World War*. New York: W.W. Norton.
Fogu, Claudio. 1997. "Il Duce taumaturgo: Modernist Rhetorics in Fascist Representations of History." *Representations* 57 (Winter): 24–51.
Fogu, Claudio. 2003. *The Historic Imaginary: Politics of History in Fascist Italy*. Toronto: University of Toronto Press.
Förster, Jürgen. 1986. "The German Army and the Ideological War against the Soviet Union." In *The Policies of Genocide: Jews and Soviet Prisoners of War in Nazi Germany*, edited by Gerhard Hirschfeld, 15–29. London: Allen & Unwin.
Friedländer, Saul. 2007. *The Years of Extermination: Nazi Germany and the Jews, 1939–1945*. New York: HarperCollins.
Fritzsche, Peter. 1999. *Germans into Nazis*. Cambridge, MA: Harvard University Press.
Fritzsche, Peter. 2020. *Hitler's First Hundred Days: When Germans Embraced the Third Reich*. New York: Basic Books.
Gable, Gerry. 1991. "The Far Right in Contemporary Britain." In *Neo-Fascism in Europe*, edited by Luciano Cheles, Ronnie Ferguson, and Michalina Vaughan, 245–63. Harlow, Essex: Longman Group UK Limited.
Gabriele, Matthew. 2019. "After Charlottesville." *Historians*, January 2. Accessed August 2, 2024. https://www.historians.org/perspectives-article/after-charlottesville-historians-tackle-white-supremacist-nostalgia-for-an-imagined-past-january-2019/.
Gabriele, Matthew. 2021. "Vikings, Crusaders, Confederates: Misunderstood Historical Imagery at the January 6 Capitol Insurrection." *Historians*, January 12. Accessed August 5, 2024.

Works Cited

https://www.historians.org/perspectives-article/vikings-crusaders-confederates-misunderstood-historical-imagery-at-the-january-6-capitol-insurrection-january-2021/.

Gallagher, Charles A. 2021. *Nazis of Copley Square: The Forgotten History of the Christian Front*. Cambridge, MA: Harvard University Press.

Galleria Nazionale. 2023. *Tolkien: Uomo, Professore, Autore*. Accessed August 19, 2024. https://lagallerianazionale.com/mostra/tolkien-uomo-professore-autore.

Gay, Peter. 2001. *Weimar Culture: The Outsider as Insider*. New York: W.W. Norton.

Geiss, Josef. 1980. *Obersalzberg: The History of a Mountain from Judith Platter till Hitler*. Fifteenth Edition. Berchtesgaden, Germany: Verlag Josef Geiss.

Gellately, Robert. 2001. *Backing Hitler: Consent and Coercion in Nazi Germany*. Oxford: Oxford University Press.

Gentile, Emilio. 1996. *The Sacralization of Politics in Fascist Italy*. Cambridge, MA: Harvard University Press.

Gerassi, John. 1963. *The Great Fear in Latin America*. Revised Edition. New York: Collier-Macmillan.

Gerwarth, Robert. 2008. "The Central European Counter-Revolution: Paramilitary Violence in Germany, Austria and Hungary after the Great War." *Past & Present* 200: 175–209.

Goeschel, Christian. 2018. *Mussolini and Hitler: The Forging of the Fascist Alliance*. New Haven, CT: Yale University Press.

Goodrick-Clarke, Nicholas, and Rohan D'Olier Butler. 1992. *The Occult Roots of Nazism: Secret Aryan Cults and Their Influence on Nazi Ideology*. New York: New York University Press.

Gordon, Linda. 2023. "American Fascists." In *Fascism in America: Past and Present*, edited by Gavriel D. Rosenfeld and Janet Ward, 141–69. Cambridge: Cambridge University Press.

Greene, Jack, and Alessandro Massignani. 2004. *The Black Prince and the Sea Devils: The Story of Valerio Borghese and the Elite Units of the Decima MAS*. Cambridge: Da Capo Press.

Gregor, A. James. 1979. *Italian Fascism and Developmental Dictatorship*. Princeton, NJ: Princeton University Press.

Gregor, A. James. 2005. *Mussolini's Intellectuals: Fascist Social and Political Thought*. Princeton, NJ: Princeton University Press.

Griffin, Roger. 2008. "Europe for the Europeans: Fascist Myths of the European New Order 1922–1992." In *A Fascist Century: Essays by Roger Griffin*, edited by Matthew Feldman, 132–80. Basingstoke: Palgrave Macmillan.

Griffin, Roger. 2018. *Fascism: An Introduction to Comparative Fascist Studies*. Cambridge: Polity.

Griffin, Roger. 2007. *Modernism and Fascism: The Sense of a Beginning under Mussolini and Hitler*. Basingstoke: Palgrave Macmillan.

Griffin, Roger. 2022. "Sempre Presente?" In *Rethinking Fascism*, edited by Andrea Di Michele and Filippo Focardi, 277–96. Berlin: De Gruyter Oldenbourg.

Griffin, Roger. 1991. *The Nature of Fascism*. London: Routledge.

Griffin, Roger. 2002. "The Primacy of Culture: The Current Growth (or Manufacture) of Consensus within Fascist Studies." *Journal of Contemporary Culture* 37 (1): 21–43.

Grosshans, Henry. 1983. *Hitler and the Artists*. New York: Holmes & Meier.

Gumbrecht, Hans Ulrich. 1996. "I redentori della vittoria: On Fiume's Place in the Genealogy of Fascism." *Journal of Contemporary History* 31 (2): 253–72.

Gundle, Stephen. 2013. "Mussolini's Appearances in the Regions." In *The Cult of the Duce: Mussolini and the Italians*, edited by Stephen Gundle, Christopher, Pieri Duggan and Giuliana, 110–28. Manchester: Manchester University Press.

Gundle, Stephen. 2013. *Mussolini's Dream Factory: Film Stardom in Fascist Italy*. New York: Berghahn.

Gutmann, Martin. 2013. "Debunking the Myth of the Volunteers: Transnational Volunteering in the Nazi Waffen-SS Officer Corps during the Second World War." *Contemporary European History* 22 (4): 585–607.

Hagen, Joshua. 2008. "Parades, Public Space, and Propaganda: The Nazi Culture Parades in Munich." *Geografiska Annaler. Series B, Human Geography* 90 (4): 349–67.

Hamilton, Richard F. 1982. *Who Voted for Hitler?* Princeton, NJ: Princeton University Press.

Hanebrink, Paul. 2018. *A Specter Haunting Europe: The Myth of Judeo-Bolshevism*. Cambridge, MA: Harvard University Press.

Hay, James. 1987. *Popular Film Culture in Fascist Italy: The Passing of the Rex*. Bloomington: Indiana University Press.

Herf, Jeffrey. 2009. *Nazi Propaganda and the Arab World*. New Haven, CT: Yale University Press.

Herf, Jeffrey. 1986. *Reactionary Modernism: Technology, Culture, and Politics in Weimar and the Third Reich*. Cambridge: Cambridge University Press.

Herf, Jeffrey. 1986. *Reactionary Modernism: Technology, Culture, and Politics in Weimar and the Third Reich*. Cambridge: Cambridge University Press.

Herf, Jeffrey. 2006. *The Jewish Enemy: Nazi Propaganda during World War II and the Holocaust*. Cambridge, MA: Harvard University Press.

Hitler, Adolf. 1992. "Speech Inaugurating the Great Exhibition of German Art, 1937." In *Art in Theory, 1900–1990: An Anthology of Changing Ideas*, edited by Charles Harrison and Paul Wood, 423–6. Oxford: Blackwell.

Hitler, Adolf, and Ralph Manheim. 1971. *Mein Kampf*. Boston, MA: Houghton Mifflin Company.

Hoare, Marko Attila. 2009. "Yugoslavia and its Successor States." In *The Oxford Handbook of Fascism*, edited by R. J. B. Bosworth, 414–33. Oxford: Oxford University Press.

Hof, Tobias. 2020. "The Bologna Attack of 1980: Italy's Unhealed Wound." *Fair Observer*, August 10. Accessed January 4, 2024. https://www.fairobserver.com/region/europe/tobias-hof-bolo gna-terror-attack-1980-right-wing-terrorism-news-16411/.

Hoffmann, Stanley ed. 1972. *The Sorrow and the Pity: A Film by Marcel Ophuls*. New York: Outerbridge & Lazard.

Holland, Derek. 1984, 1994. "Political Soldier." *Archive.org*. Accessed June 12, 2024. https://arch ive.org/details/political-soldier-a-4/mode/2up?view=theater.

Hughes-Hallett, Lucy. 2013. *Gabriele D'Annunzio: Poet, Seducer, and Preacher of War*. New York: Alfred A. Knopf.

Hynes, Samuel. 1990. *A War Imagined: The First World War and English Culture*. London: Pimlico.

Hyttinen, Anniina. 2022. "Deradicalisation of Jobbik and its Consequences—A Visual Ethnographic Analysis of the Symbolic and Ritual Change of a Hungarian Radical Right Party." *European Journal of Cultural and Political Sociology* 9 (4): 423–50.

Ihrig, Stefan. 2016. *Justifying Genocide: Germany and the Armenians from Bismarck to Hitler*. Cambridge, MA: Harvard University Press.

Ioanid, Radu. 2009. "Romania." In *Oxford Handbook of Fascism*, edited by R. J. B. Bosworth, 398–413. Oxford: Oxford University Press.

Iordachi, Constantin. 2014. "A Continuum of Dictatorships: Hybrid Totalitarian Experiments in Romania, 1937–44." In *Rethinking Fascism and Dictatorship in Europe*, edited by Antonio Costa Pinto and Aristotle Kallis, 233–71. London: Palgrave Macmillan.

Irvine, William D. 1991. "Fascism in France and the Strange Case of the Croix de Feu." *Journal of Modern History* 63 (2): 271–95.

Irvine, William D. 1989. *The Boulanger Affair Reconsidered: Royalism, Boulangism, and the Origins of the Radical Right in France*. New York: Oxford University Press.

Jackson, Julian. 2001. *France: The Dark Years, 1940–1944*. Oxford: Oxford University Press.

Works Cited

Jantine. 2018. "Golden Years: David Bowie and the Third Reich." *Medium*, April 14. Accessed June 10, 2024. https://medium.com/@fabulatext/golden-years-david-bowie-and-the-third-reich-50ec736193c2.

Jarausch, Konrad H. 2015. *Out of Ashes: A New History of Europe in the Twentieth Century*. Princeton, NJ: Princeton University Press.

Johnson, Douglas. 1991. "The New Right in France." In *Neo-Fascism in Europe*, edited by Luciano Cheles, Ronnie Ferguson, and Michalina Vaughan, 234–44. Harlow: Longman Group UK Limited.

Jones, Morgan. 2022. "How Julius Evola Became the Internet's Favorite Fascist." *Jacobin*, December 7. Accessed June 11, 2024. https://jacobin.com/2022/12/fascism-far-right-evola-bannon-bronze-age-pervert.

Kaiser, Menachem. 2023. "What Kind of a Person Has a Closet Full of Nazi Memorabilia?" *New York Times*, September 29. Accessed August 20, 2024. https://www.nytimes.com/2023/09/29/opinion/nazi-memorabilia-market-liveauctioneers.html?searchResultPosition=1.

Kallis, Aristotle. 2016. "From CAUR to EUR: Italian Fascism, the 'Myth of Rome' and the Pursuit of International Primacy." *Patterns of Prejudice* 50 (4–5): 359–77.

Kallis, Aristotle. 2014. "The 'Fascist Effect': On the Dynamics of Political Hybridization in Inter-War Europe." In *Rethinking Fascism and Dictatorship in Europe*, edited by Antonio Costa Pinto and Aristotle Kallis, 13–41. London: Palgrave Macmillan.

Kallis, Aristotle. 2014. *The Third Rome, 1922–1943: The Making of the Fascist Capital*. London: Palgrave Macmillan.

Kaplan, Roberta, and Deborah Lipstadt. 2020. *Three Years Later, Charlottesville's Legacy on neo-Nazi Hate Still Festers*. August 12. Accessed August 2, 2024. https://www.cnn.com/2020/08/11/opinions/charlottesville-three-years-later-hate-festers-lipstadt-kaplan/index.html.

Kater, Michael H. 1997. *The Twisted Muse: Musicians and their Music in the Third Reich*. New York: Oxford University Press.

Kershaw, Ian. 1998. *Hitler: 1889–1936: Hubris*. London: Penguin.

Kershaw, Ian. 1989. *The "Hitler Myth": Image and Reality in the Third Reich*. New York: Oxford University Press.

Kershaw, Ian. 2000. *The Nazi Dictatorship: Problems & Perspectives of Interpretation*. Fourth Edition. London: Arnold.

Kertzer, David. 2014. *The Pope and Mussolini: The Secret History of Pius XI and the Rise of Fascism in Europe*. New York: Random House.

Kitchen, Martin. 2006. *Europe between the Wars*. Second Edition. Toronto: Pearson Longman.

Klemperer, Victor. 1999. *I Will Bear Witness: A Diary of the Nazi Years, 1933–1941*. Translated by Martin Chalmers. New York: Modern Library.

Klemperer, Victor. 2006. *The Language of the Third Reich: LTI—Lingua Tertii Imperii. A Philologist's Notebook*. Translated by Martin Brady. London: Continuum International Publishing Group.

Koehl, Robert. 2003. "Nazi State and Neo-Feudalism." In *The Fascism Reader*, edited by Aristotle Kallis, 271–7. London: Routledge.

Kolb, Eberhard. 1988. *The Weimar Republic*. Translated by P. S. Falla. London: Unwin Hyman.

Koon, Tracy H. 1985. *Believe, Obey, Fight: Political Socialization of Youth in Fascist Italy, 1922–1943*. Chapel Hill: University of North Carolina Press.

Koonz, Claudia. 1987. *Mothers in the Fatherland: Women, the Family, and Nazi Politics*. New York: St. Martin's Press.

Kracauer, Siegfried. 2004. *From Caligari to Hiter: A Psychological History of German Film*. Princeton, NJ: Princeton University Press.

Works Cited

Kramer, Alan. 2007. *Dynamic of Destruction: Culture and Mass Killing in the First World War.* Oxford: Oxford University Press.

Kramer, Alan. 2006. "The First Wave of International War Crimes Trials: Istanbul and Leipzig." *European Review* 14 (4): 441–55.

Kramer, Alan. 2009. "The First World War as Cultural Trauma." In *The Oxford Handbook of Fascism*, edited by R. J. B. Bosworth, 32–51. Oxford: Oxford University Press.

Krausnick, Helmut, and Martin Broszat. 1970. *Anatomy of the SS State.* Translated by Dorothy Long and Martin Jackson. London: Granada Publishing Limited.

Kuna, Franz. 1991. "Vienna and Prague 1890–1928." In *Modernism, 1890–1930*, edited by Malcolm Bradbury and James McFarlane, 120–33. London: Penguin Books.

Kundnani, Arun. 2012. "The Anti-Islamist: Anders Behring Breivik's Manifesto." *The International Center for Counter-Terrorism*. April 23. Accessed August 8, 2024. https://www.icct.nl/publication/anti-islamist-anders-behring-breiviks-manifesto.

Kutner, Samantha. 2020. *Swiping Right: The Allure of Hyper Masculinity and Cryptofascism for Men Who Join the Proud Boys.* Research Paper, The Hague: International Centre for Counter-Terrorism. Accessed August 5, 2024. https://www.icct.nl/sites/default/files/2022-12/Swiping-Right-The-Allure-of-Hyper-Masculinity-and-Cryptofascism-for-Men-Who-Join-the-Proud-Boys.pdf.

Landy, Marcia. 1986. *Fascism in Film: The Italian Commercial Cinema, 1931–1943.* Princeton, NJ: Princeton University Press.

Laqueur, Walter. 1996. *Fascism: Past, Present and Future.* New York: Oxford University Press.

Laqueur, Walter. 1974. *Weimar: A Cultural History, 1918–1933.* New York: Putnam's Sons.

Large, David Clay. 1997. *Where Ghosts Walked: Munich's Road to the Third Reich.* New York: W.W. Norton.

Large, David Clay. 2000. *Berlin.* New York: Basic Books.

Lasansky, D. Medina. 2004. *The Renaissance Perfected: Architecture, Spectacle & Tourism in Fascist Italy.* University Park, PA: The Pennsylvania State University Press.

Last, John. 2017. "How 'Hobbit Camps' Rebirthed Italian Fascism." *Atlas Obscura.* October 3. Accessed June 12, 2024. https://www.atlasobscura.com/articles/hobbit-camps-fascism-italy?curator=MediaREDEF.

Ledeen, Michael. 2002. *D'Annunzio: The First Duce.* London: Transaction Publishers.

Ledeen, Michael. 1972. *Universal Fascism: The Theory and Practice of the Fascist International, 1928–1936.* New York: Howard Fertig.

Lee, Martin A. 2000. *The Beast Reawakens: Fascism's Resurgence from Hitler's Spymasters to Today's Neo-Nazi Groups and Right-Wing Extremists.* New York: Routledge.

Leiser, Erwin. 1974. *Nazi Cinema.* Translated by Gertrude Mander and David Wilson. New York: Collier Books.

Levi, Primo. 1996. *Survival in Auschwitz.* New York: Touchstone.

Levi, Primo. 1995. *Survival in Auschwitz.* New York: Simon & Schuster.

Linker, Damon. 2023. "Get to Know the Influential Conservative Intellectuals Who Help Explain G.O.P. Extremism." *New York Times*, November 4. Accessed August 20, 2024. https://www.nytimes.com/2023/11/04/opinion/sunday/conservative-intellectuals-republicans.html.

Linker, Damon. 2022. "Thinking About Fascism-Part 2." *Notes from the Middleground.* July 27. Accessed August 20, 2024. https://damonlinker.substack.com/p/thinking-about-fascismpart-2.

Lipstadt, Deborah. 1994. *Denying the Holocaust: The Growing Assault on Truth and Memory.* New York: Plume.

Lipstadt, Deborah E. 2019. *Antisemitism: Here and Now.* New York: Schocken Books.

Longerich, Peter. 2019. *Hitler: A Biography.* Oxford: Oxford University Press.

Works Cited

Love, Gary. 2007. "'What's the Big Idea?': Oswald Mosley, the British Union of Fascists and Generic Fascism." *Journal of Contemporary History* 42 (3): 447–68.

Ludwig, Emil. 1933. *Talks with Mussolini*. Translated by Eden Paul and Cedar Paul. Boston: Little, Brown.

Luzzatto, Sergio. 1998. *The Body of Il Duce: Mussolini's Corpse and the Fortunes of Italy*. New York: Henry Holt.

Luzzatto, Sergio. 2005. *The Body of Il Duce: Mussolini's Corpse and the Fortunes of Italy*. Translated by Frederika Randall. New York: Metropolitan Books.

Lyttelton, Adrian. 2004. *The Seizure of Power: Fascism in Italy*. Third Edition. London: Routledge.

Lyttelton, Adrian. 2004. *The Seizure of Power: Fascism in Italy 1919–1929*. Third Edition. London: Routledge.

Mackay, Jamie. 2023. "How did the Lord of the Rings become a Secret Weapon in Italy's Culture Wars?" *The Guardian*, November 3. Accessed August 19, 2024. https://www.theguardian.com/commentisfree/2023/nov/03/the-lord-of-the-rings-italy-giorgia-meloni-tolkien.

Malaparte, Curzio. 2005. *Kaputt*. Translated by Cesare Foligno. New York: The New York Review of Books.

Mammone, Andrea. 2015. *Transnational Neofascism in France and Italy*. Cambridge: Cambridge University Press.

Mandell, Richard D. 1971. *The Nazi Olympics*. New York: Ballantine Books.

Mann, Michael. 2004. *Fascists*. Cambridge: Cambridge University Press.

Marrus, Michael, and Robert O. Paxton. 2019. *Vichy France and the Jews*. Second Edition. Stanford, CA: Stanford University Press.

Martin, Simon. 2004. *Football and Fascism: The National Game under Mussolini*. Oxford: Berg.

Martin, Simon. 2011. *Sport Italia: The Italian Love Affair with Sport*. London: I.B. Tauris.

Matteotti, Giacomo. 1969. *The Fascisti Exposed: A Year of Fascist Domination*. Translated by E. W. Dickes. New York: Howard Fertig.

Mazower, Mark. 2009. *Hitler's Empire: How the Nazis Ruled Europe*. New York: Penguin Books.

Meyer-Resende, Michael, and Nino Tsereteli. 2023. "Meloni's Dangerous Constitutional Change in Italy." *Politico*, December 21, 2023. Accessed August 19, 2024. https://www.politico.eu/article/melonis-dangerous-constitutional-change-in-italy/.

Mishra, Pankaj. 2018. "Jordan Peterson & Fascist Mysticism." *The New York Review of Books*, May 25. Accessed August 20, 2024. https://www.nybooks.com/online/2018/03/19/jordan-peterson-and-fascist-mysticism/.

Morehouse, Catherine. 2024. "Tensions at Home and Abroad Pose Growing Threat to US Grid." *E&E News by Politico*. April 8. Accessed August 8, 2024. https://www.eenews.net/articles/tensions-at-home-and-abroad-pose-growing-threat-to-us-grid/#:~:text=of%20DOE%20data.-,The%20nation's%20power%20providers%20reported%20185%20instances%20of%20mostly%20physical,number%20of%20incidents%20in%202021.

Morena, Antonio. 2015. *Mussolini's Decennale: Aura and Mythmaking in Fascist Italy*. Toronto: University of Toronto Press.

Morgan, Philip. 2009. "Corporatism and the Economic Order." In *The Oxford Handbook of Fascism*, edited by R. J. B. Bosworth, 150–65. Oxford: Oxford University Press.

Morgan, Philip. 2007. *The Fall of Mussolini*. Oxford: Oxford University Press.

Mosse, George. 1990. *Fallen Soldiers: Reshaping the Memory of the World Wars*. Oxford: Oxford University Press.

Mosse, George. 1999. "Nazi Aesthetics: Beauty without Sensuality." In *The Fascist Revolution: Toward a General Theory of Fascism*, by George Mosse, 183–98. New York: Howard Fertig.

Mosse, George. 1999. *The Crisis of German Ideology: Intellectual Origins of the Third Reich*. New York: Howard Fertig.

Mostrom, Anthony. 2020. "America's 'Mein Kampf': Francis Parker Yockey and 'Imperium.'" *Los Angeles Review of Books*, August 8. https://lareviewofbooks.org/article/americas-mein-kampf-francis-parker-yockey-imperium/.

Mussolini, Benito, and Giovanni Gentile. 2000. "Foundations and Doctrine of Fascism (1932)." In *A Primer of Italian Fascism*, edited by Jeffrey Schnapp, translated by Jeffrey Schnapp, 47–71. Lincoln: University of Nebraska Press.

N.A. n.d. *Direct Democracy*. Accessed May 20, 2022. https://www-sudd-ch.translate.goog/event.php?lang=de&id=it011929&_x_tr_sl=auto&_x_tr_tl=en&_x_tr_hl=en.

Nolte, Ernst. 1966. *Three Faces of Fascism: Action Française, Italian Fascism, National Socialism*. London: Henry Holt.

Núñez Seixas, Xosé M. 2022. *The Spanish Blue Division on the Eastern Front, 1941–1945: War, Occupation, Memory*. Toronto: University of Toronto Press.

O'Brien, Mary-Elizabeth. 2004. *Nazi Cinema as Enchantment: The Politics of Entertainment in the Third Reich*. Rochester, NY: Camden House.

O'Donnell, Catharina, and Eran Shor. 2022. "'This Is a Political Movement, Friend': Why 'Incels' Support Violence." *British Journal of Sociology* 73 (2): 336–51.

Painter Jr., Borden W. 2005. *Mussolini's Rome: Rebuilding the Eternal City*. New York: Palgrave Macmillan.

Passmore, Kevin. 2014. *Fascism: A Very Short Introduction*. Second Edition. Oxford: Oxford University Press.

Patterson, James A. 2020. "After Republican Virtue." *Law & Liberty*, April 22. Accessed August 7, 2024. https://lawliberty.org/after-republican-virtue/.

Paxton, Robert. 2021. "I've Hesitated to Call Donald Trump a Fascist. Until Now." *Newsweek*, January 11. Accessed August 8, 2024. https://www.newsweek.com/robert-paxton-trump-fascist-1560652.

Paxton, Robert O. 2005. *The Anatomy of Fascism*. New York: Vintage Books.

Paxton, Robert O. 1972. *Vichy France: Old Guard and New Order*. New York: Columbia University Press.

Paxton, Robert. 2004. *The Anatomy of Fascism*. New York: Vintage Books.

Payne, Stanley G. 1995. *A History of Fascism, 1914–1945*. Madison: University of Wisconsin Press.

Pearce, Joe. 1987. *Skrewdriver-The First Ten Years 1977–87*. Accessed June 10, 2024. https://www.bloodandhonourworldwide.co.uk/bhww/ian-stuart-donaldson-skrewdriver/ian-stuart-donaldson-skrewdriver-biographies/skrewdriver-the-first-ten-years-1977-87-joe-pearce/.

Pearce, Joseph. 2013. *Race with the Devil: My Journey from Racial Hatred to Rational Love*. Charlotte, NC: Saint Benedict Press.

Pecqueur, Antoine. 2024. "Italy: Giorgia Meloni's Cultural Takeover." *Le Monde Diplomatique*, July, English ed. Accessed August 19, 2024. https://mondediplo.com/2024/07/14italy.

Peniston-Bird, Corinna. 2009. "Austria." In *The Oxford Handbook of Fascism*, edited by R.J.B. Bosworth, 434–52. Oxford: Oxford University Press.

Pergher, Roberta. 2022. "Italian Fascism in Transnational Historiography." In *Rethinking Fascism: The Italian and German Dictatorships*, edited by Andrea Di Michele and Filippo Focardi, 33–58. Oldenbourg: De Gruyter.

Pergher, Roberta. 2017. *Mussolini's Nation-Empire: Sovereignty and Settlement in Italy's Borderlands, 1922–1943*. Cambridge: Cambridge University Press.

Peukert, Detlev. 1987. *Inside Nazi Germany: Conformity, Opposition, and Racism in Everyday Life*. Translated by Richard Deveson. New Haven, CT: Yale University Press.

Phipps, John. 2024. "How Italy's Post-Fascists Fell in Love with J.R.R. Tolkien." *Jacobin*, February 25. Accessed August 19, 2024. https://jacobin.com/2024/02/giorgia-meloni-tolkien-fascism-fantasy.

Works Cited

Pick, Daniel. 1993. *Faces of Degeneration: A European Disorder, c. 1848–1918*. Cambridge: Cambridge University Press.

Pollard, John. 2007. ""Clerical Fascism": Context, Overview and Conclusion." *Totalitarian Movements and Political Religions* 8 (2): 433–46.

Pollard, John. 2008. *Catholicism in Modern Italy: Religion, Society, and Politics since 1861*. London: Routledge.

Ponso, Marzia. 2022. "Old Ideologies and New Strategies: German Right-Wing Populism." In *Rethinking Fascism: The Italian and German Dictatorships*, edited by Andrea Di Michele and Filippo Focardi, 297–316. Berlin: Walter de Gruyter GmbH.

Poole, W. Scott. 2018. *Wasteland: The Great War and the Origins of Modern Horror*. Berkeley, CA: Counterpoint.

Preparata, Guido Giacomo. 2013. "'The Bogeyman': The Story of a Political Soldier and Elements for the Sociology of Terrorism." *Journal for the Study of Radicalism* 7 (1): 109–27.

Prince, Robert M. 2023. "Locating the Fascist Mind." *Psychoanalytic Inquiry* 43 (2): 70–83.

Pugliese, Stanislao G. 1997. "Death in Exile: The Assassination of Carlo Rosselli." *Journal of Contemporary History* 32 (3): 305–19.

Quiggins Tiller, Ann. 1965. "The Igniting Spark-Brazil, 1930." *Hispanic American Historical Review* 45 (3): 384–92.

Ravitch, Norman. 1990. *The Catholic Church and the French Nation 1589–1989*. New York: Routledge.

Rees, Philip. 1990. *Biographical Dictionary of the Extreme Right Since 1890*. New York: Simon & Schuster.

Rees, Philip. 2017. *Charlottesville: Race and Terror*. Directed by Elle Reeve. Accessed August 2, 2024. https://www.youtube.com/watch?v=P54sP0Nlngg&rco=1.

Remy, Steven P. 2017. *The Malmedy Massacre: The War Crimes Trial Controversy*. Cambridge, MA: Harvard University Press.

Rentschler, Eric. 1996. *The Ministry of Illusion: Nazi Cinema and Its Afterlife*. Cambridge, MA: Harvard University Press.

Reuters. 2022. "Key Moments from Italian PM Meloni's Maiden Speech." *Reuters*, October 25. Accessed August 27, 2024. https://www.reuters.com/world/europe/key-moments-italian-pm-melonis-maiden-speech-2022-10-25/.

Roberts, David D., Alexander De Grand, Mark Antliff, and Thomas Linehan. 2002. "Comments on Roger Griffin, 'The Primacy of Culture: The Current Growth (or Manufacture) of Consensus within Fascist Studies.'" *Journal of Contemporary History* 37 (2): 259–74.

Roberts, David. 2016. *Fascist Interactions: Proposals for a New Approach to Fascism and its Era, 1919–1945*. New York: Berghahn.

Rosenbaum, Ron. 1998. *Explaining Hitler*. New York: Random House.

Rosenfeld, Gavriel D., and Janet Ward. 2023. "Introduction." In *Fascism in America: Past and Present*, edited by Gavriel D. Rosenfeld and Janet Ward, 1–44. Cambridge: Cambridge University Press.

Ross, Alex. 2022. *Wagnerism: Art and Politics in the Shadow of Music*. New York: Farrar, Straus, and Giroux.

Sabatino, Michelangelo. 2010. *Pride in Modesty: Modernist Architecture and the Vernacular Tradition in Italy*. Toronto: University of Toronto Press.

Sachs, Harvey. 1987. *Music in Fascist Italy*. London: Weidenfeld and Nicolson.

Sanfilippo, Matteo. 2003. *Ratlines and Unholy Trinities*. Accessed December 23, 2023. https://dspace.unitus.it/bitstream/2067/24/1/sanfilippo_ratlines.htm.

Schieder, Wolfgang. 2022. "Adolf Hitler and Benito Mussolini: The Staging of a Political Friendship." In *Rethinking Fascism: The Italian and German Dictatorships*, edited by Andrea Di Michele and Filippo Focardi, 87–105. Berlin: Walter de Gruyter GmbH.

Schir, Perine. 2022. "The French Connections to the Far Right, from the MSI to Fratelli d'Italia." *IERES Occasional Papers* 22: 1–13. Accessed June 11, 2024. https://www.academia.edu/99508481/The_French_Connections_of_the_Italian_Far_Right_from_the_MSI_to_Fratelli_dItalia.

Schnapp, Jeffrey. 1992. "Fascism's Museum in Motion." *Journal of Architectural Education* 45 (2): 87–97.

Schnapp, Jeffrey. 1996. *Staging Fascism: 18 BL and the Theater of Masses for Masses*. Stanford, CA: Stanford University Press.

Schnapp, Jeffrey T. 1998. "Fascism after Fascism." In *Fascism's Return: Scandal, Revision, and Ideology since 1980*, edited by Richard J. Golsan, 63–85. Lincoln: University of Nebraska Press.

Schorske, Carl E. 1981. *Fin-de-Siecle Vienna: Politics and Culture*. New York: Vintage Books.

Sedgwick, Mark. 2004. *Against the Modern World: Traditionalism and the Secret History of the Twentieth Century*. Oxford: Oxford University Press.

Segrè, Claudio. 1987. *Italo Balbo: A Fascist Life*. Berkeley: University of California Press.

Shaffer, Ryan. 2017. *Music, Youth, and International Links in Post-War British Fascism: The Transformation of Extremism*. Cham: Palgrave Macmillan.

Shaffer, Ryan. 2013. "The Soundtrack of Neo-Fascism: Youth and Music in the National Front." *Patterns of Prejudice* 47 (4–5): 458–82.

Sharpe, Matthew, and Kirk Turner. 2019. "Fantasy." In *Routledge Handbook of Psychoanalytic Political Theory*, edited by Yannis Stavrakakis, 187–98. New York: Routledge.

Shekhovtsov, Anton. 2008. "The Palingenetic Thrust of Russian Neo-Eurasianism: Ideas of Rebirth in Aleksandr Dugin's Worldview." *Totalitarian Movements and Political Religions* 9 (4): 491–506.

Sheridan Allen, William. 1984. *The Nazi Seizure of Power, 1922–1945*. New York: Franklin Watts.

Shields, James. 2007. *The Extreme Right in France: From Petain to Le Pen*. London: Routledge.

Skidelsky, R. 1968. "Great Britain." In *European Fascism*, edited by S. J. Woolf, 231–61. New York: Random House.

Skidmore, Thomas E., and Peter H. Smith. 2005. *Modern Latin America*. Sixth Edition. Oxford: Oxford University Press.

Smelser, Ronald, and Edward J. Davies II. 2008. *The Myth of the Eastern Front: The Nazi-Soviet War in American Popular Culture*. New York: Cambridge University Press.

Snyder, Timothy. 2010. *Bloodlands: Europe Between Hitler and Stalin*. New York: Basic Books.

Snyder, Timothy. 2017. *On Tyranny: Twenty Lessons from the Twentieth Century*. New York: Tim Duggan Books.

Sontag, Susan. 1980. "Fascinating Fascism." In *Under the Sign of Saturn*, by Susan Sontag, 73–105. New York: Farrar, Straus & Giroux.

Soucy, Robert. 1986. *French Fascism: The First Wave, 1924–1933*. New Haven, CT: Yale University Press.

Soucy, Robert. 1995. *French Fascism: The Second Wave, 1933–1939*. New Haven, CT: Yale University Press.

Southern Poverty Law Center. n.d. "Patriot Front." *Southern Poverty Law Center*. Accessed August 8, 2024. https://www.splcenter.org/fighting-hate/extremist-files/group/patriot-front.

Speer, Albert. 1970. *Inside the Third Reich: Memoirs by Albert Speer*. Translated by Richard Winston and Clara Winston. New York: The Macmillan.

Spotts, Frederic. 2003. *Hitler and the Power of Aesthetics*. Woodstock: The Overlook Press.

Stadler, K.R. 1968. "Austria." In *European Fascism*, by S. J. Woolf, 88–110. New York: Random House.

Stanley, Jason. 2018. *How Fascism Works: The Politics of Us and Them*. New York: Random House.

Stanley, Jason. 2022. "Buffalo Shooting: How White Replacement Theory Keeps Inspiring Mass Murder." *The Guardian*, May 15. Accessed August 8, 2024. https://www.theguardian.com/commentisfree/2022/may/15/buffalo-shooting-white-replacement-theory-inspires-mass.

Works Cited

Steigmann-Gall, Richard. 2023. "Fascism and Antisemitism in 1930s America: The Genocidal Vision of the Silver Shirts." In *Fascism in America: Past and Present*, edited by Gavriel D. Rosenfeld and Janet Ward, 198–220. Cambridge: Cambridge University Press.

Stein, George H. 1966. *The Waffen-SS: Hitler's Elite Guard at War, 1939–1945*. Ithaca, NY: Cornell University Press.

Steinacher, Gerald. 2011. *Nazis on the Run*. Oxford: Oxford University Press.

Stern, Randolph. 1989. "Seeing Culture in a Room for a Renaissance Prince." In *The New Cultural History*, edited by Lynn Hunt, 205–32. Berkeley: University of California Press.

Sternhell, Zeev. 1994. *The Birth of Fascist Ideology*. Princeton, NJ: Princeton University Press.

Stone, Marla. 1993. "Staging Fascism: The Exhibition of the Fascist Revolution." *Journal of Contemporary History* 28 (2): 215–43.

Stone, Marla. 2013. *The Fascist Revolution in Italy: A Brief History with Documents*. Boston, MA: Bedford/St. Martin's.

Stone, Marla. 1998. *The Patron State: Culture & Politics in Fascist Italy*. Princeton, NJ: Princeton University Press.

Storchi, Simona. 2013. "Margherita Sarfatti and the Invention of the Duce." In *The Cult of the Duce: Mussolini and the Italians*, edited by Stephen Gundle, Christopher Duggan and Giuliana Pieri, 41–56. Manchester: Manchester University Press.

Storchi, Simona. 2019. "The ex-Casa del Fascio in Predappio and the question of the 'difficult heritage' of Fascism in contemporary Italy." *Modern Italy* 24 (2): 139–57.

Szalai, Jennifer. 2024. "The Nazi Jurist Who Haunts Our Broken Politics." *New York Times*, July 13. Accessed August 20, 2024. https://www.nytimes.com/2024/07/13/books/review/carl-schmitt-jd-vance.html?searchResultPosition=1.

Sznajder, Mario. 2002. "Nietzsche, Mussolini, and Italian Fascism." In *Nietzsche, Godfather of Fascism? On the Uses and Abuses of a Philosophy*, edited by Jacob Golomb and Robert S. Wistrich, 235–62. Princeton, NJ: Princeton University Press.

Taylor, Matthew. 2017. "'White Europe': 60,000 Nationalists March on Poland's Independence Day." *The Guardian*. November 12. Accessed August 5, 2024. https://www.theguardian.com/world/2017/nov/12/white-europe-60000-nationalists-march-on-polands-independence-day.

Taylor, Matthew. n.d. "The Yser Tower: The Legacy of the First World War." *Canon van Vlaanderen*. Accessed August 5, 2024. https://www.canonvanvlaanderen.be/en/events/the-yser-tower/.

Theweleit, Klaus. 1987. *Male Fantasies*. 2 vols. Minneapolis: University of Minnesota Press.

Tipaldou, Sofia. 2015. "The Dawning of Europe and Eurasia? The Golden Dawn and its Transnational Links." In *Eurasianism and the European Far Right*, edited by Marlene Laruelle, 193–219. Lanham, MD: Lexington Books.

Traverso, Enzo. 2019. *The New Faces of Fascism: Populism and the Far Right*. Translated by David Broder. London: Verso.

Trythall, J. W. D. 1970. *El Caudillo: A Political Biography of Franco*. New York: McGraw-Hill Book Company.

Tumblety, Joan. 2009. "France." In *The Oxford Handbook of Fascism*, edited by R. B. J. Bosworth, 507–25. Oxford: Oxford University Press.

Umland, Andreas. 2019. "Irregular Militias and Radical Nationalism in Post-Euromaidan Ukraine: The Prehistory and Emergence of the 'Azov' Battalion in 2014." *Terrorism and Political Violence* 31 (1): 105–31.

US Department of Homeland Security. 2009. *Rightwing Extremism: Current Economic and Political Climate Fueling Resurgence in Radicalization and Recruitment*. Washington, DC: Department of Homeland Security.

US Federal Bureau of Investigation. 1945–7. *FBI Records: The Vault*. Accessed December 28, 2023. https://vault.fbi.gov/adolf-hitler.
Van den Dries, Luk. 2014. "The Pilgrimages of the Yser (1948–1970)." *Researchgate.net*. Accessed August 5, 2024. https://www.researchgate.net/profile/Luk-Van-Den-Dries/publication/309321373_The_pilgrimages_of_the_Yser/links/5809e6b108ae49c6a892f986/The-pilgrimages-of-the-Yser.pdf.
Vincent, Mary. 2009. "Spain." In *The Oxford Handbook of Fascism*, edited by R. J. B. Bosworth, 362–79. Oxford: Oxford University Press.
Wachsmann, Nikolaus. 2015. *KL: A History of the Nazi Concentration Camps*. New York: Farrar, Straus and Giroux.
Walsh, David Austin. 2024. *Taking America Back: The Conservative Movement and the Far Right*. New Haven, CT: Yale University Press.
Walters, E. Garrison. 1988. *The Other Europe: Eastern Europe to 1945*. Syracuse, NY: Syracuse University Press.
Ware, Jacob. 2019. "Siege: The Atomwaffen Division and Rising Far-Right Terrorism in the United States." *International Centre for Counter-Terrorism-The Hague*. July. Accessed August 8, 2024. https://www.icct.nl/sites/default/files/import/publication/ICCT-Ware-Siege-July2019.pdf.
Weitz, Eric D. 2007. *Weimar Germany: Promises and Tragedy*. Princeton, NJ: Princeton University Press.
White, Anthony. 2020. *Italian Modern Art in the Age of Fascism*. New York: Routledge.
Willett, John. 1978. *Art and Politics in the Weimar Period: The New Sobriety, 1917–1933*. New York: Pantheon Books.
Winter, Jay. 1996. *Sites of Memory, Sites of Mourning: The Great War in European Cultural History*. Cambridge: Cambridge University Press.
Wittenberg, Jason. 2014. "External Influences on the Evolution of Hungarian Authoritarianism, 1920–1944." In *Rethinking Fascism and Dictatorship in Europe*, by Aristotle Kallis and Antonio Costa Pinto, 219–32. London: Palgrave Macmillan.
Wohl, Robert. 1979. *The Generation of 1914*. Cambridge, MA: Harvard University Press.
Wright, Gordon. 1987. *France in Modern Times*. Fourth Edition. New York: W.W. Norton.

INDEX

accelerationism 12, 176, 223, 233, 250, 252, 256, 271–2, 281
Acerbo Law 72–3, 78, 279
Agrarianism *see Bonificia Integrale*
Alleanza Nazionale (AN) 263, 273, 277–8 (*see also Movimento Sociale Italiano*)
anti-immigrationism 4, 25, 226, 235, 250–3, 260–2, 265, 267–9, 272–3 (*see also* xenophobia)
antisemitism 12, 20–2, 24–7, 55–8, 65, 85–6, 90, 95, 115, 127–9, 135–6, 144, 159–66, 168, 170, 172, 177–8, 189, 193–5, 200, 211, 229, 232, 236, 242, 245, 250–1, 253–4, 257–60, 264, 268, 273, 280
architecture
 as fascist 5, 49, 71, 151–4, 204, 282, 115–17, 126–8
 modernist 25, 88, 146, 147, 150–4
 (neo)baroque 5, 158, 181, 184–5, 207
 (neo)classical 47, 49, 146–7, 151–4, 181, 184–5, 203, 205
 (neo)gothic 49, 203–4, 279
 Renaissance 49, 114–15, 184–6
Arditi 31, 37, 58, 60 (*see also* Blackshirts)
Arrow Cross *see* (neo)fascism in Hungary
art
 as aesthetic-political tool 36–8, 47, 65, 86, 114, 141–7, 154–5, 226
 avant garde 39–40, 65, 84, 143, 150
 -deco 149, 257
 Degenerate Art Exhibition and Great Exhibition of German Art 141–7, 203
 difference between Nazi Germany and fascist Italy 132, 146
 Expressionism 42, 78, 81, 87–8, 141–4
 Futurism 32, 35–42, 58, 131, 145, 212
 modernism 35, 39–42, 71, 87, 122, 128, 141–5, 151–4, 175, 275–6
 (neo)classical 5, 22, 122, 144, 151
 pop- 225–7, 245–6, 278
 Romanticism 144, 150, 226

Bardèche, Maurice 219, 236–8
Beer Hall Putsch 47–9, 53–5, 61–4, 83, 85, 166
Berghof 114, 116–17, 182–4
Blackshirts 23, 36–7, 58–61, 67–73, 77, 101, 104, 133, 150, 155, 201, 279 (*see also Arditi*)

"Blood and Soil" ideology 127–8, 135 (*see also völkisch*)
Bolshevism/Bolsheviks 12, 45, 48–55, 59, 62, 65, 69, 75, 86–7, 92, 158, 160, 164, 170, 174, 181, 185–6, 188, 190, 198–9, 237–9, 254, 269, 280 (*see also* Marxism)
Bonifica Integrale 54, 108, 125
 agrarianism/ruralization 13, 124–8, 174, 184, 199, 245
 public works projects 26, 78, 108–11, 126–8, 134, 151, 213
Boulanger, Georges 12, 15–29, 84
 affair 15, 18–22, 27, 29, 280
Boulangism 15–16, 18–22, 24, 27
Bowie, David 225, 227, 246
British Union of Fascists (BUF) *see* (neo)fascism in Britain
Brothers of Italy (FDI—*Fratelli d'Italia*) 1–2, 275–9, 279, 282
Brownshirts 23, 59, 62–3, 81–5, 88, 92, 95–7, 155

capitalism 8, 12, 21, 36, 55, 76, 111, 177, 198, 223, 226, 233
 fascist opposition to 86, 234–5, 237, 239, 241
CasaPound 263, 265–6
Catholic Church/Catholicism
 anti- 18, 28, 134, 231–2
 complicity in/support of fascism 21, 69, 91, 96, 105, 124, 161, 170, 186, 193, 210–11, 223, 257–8
 fascist appeals to 9, 22–3, 25, 35, 39, 96, 193, 200, 207–10, 223, 240–2, 245–6, 250, 253, 264–5, 279
 integralists 240–1, 264
 Lateran Accords 80, 113, 133, 264
 oppression under fascist states 73, 91–3, 107, 133, 181, 200
 Quadragesimo Anno 171, 257
 social teaching 199–200, 241–2
 (ultra)conservative/traditionalist 21–2, 40, 124, 136, 160, 198, 212, 241, 245, 257, 263–5, 281
Ciano, Galeazzo 148, 157, 181–2, 184, 199, 201
classicism, fascist appropriation of 22, 47–8, 119, 121–2, 144, 146, 149, 152, 184–5, 205
Codreanu, Corneliu *see* (neo)fascism in Romania

Index

Cold War 9, 205, 258
  anti- 230, 238–9, 241
  (neo)fascism during the 6, 13, 103, 190, 205, 207–23, 227, 230, 232–3, 236, 248, 260, 281
  post- 13, 103, 222–3, 226, 238–9, 244, 247, 253–4, 262–3, 267, 269–70, 277, 282
colonialist policy 12, 15, 18, 136, 167, 188–9, 200, 219–20
Comitati d'Azione per l'Universalità di Roma (CAUR) 157–9, 178, 191, 219
condottieri 70, 184
corporatism 77, 108–9, 166–7, 171, 176, 198–9
cult of
  beauty 121, 131, 141, 155, 205, 226
  the *Duce* 3, 77–80, 107, 113
  leader/personality 19, 23, 27, 32–3, 53, 83, 90–1, 99, 104, 106, 112–14, 117–18, 138, 160–3, 168, 174, 178, 193, 197, 213, 280
  technology 45, 141
  youth 125, 133, 229
culture (*see also* art)
  kultur 18, 43
  -wars 47–8, 65, 87–8, 141–55

D'Annunzio, Gabriele 22, 31–41, 44–5, 49, 131, 158, 202–5
  influence on Mussolini 32, 35–7, 71, 76, 80, 150, 203
de Benoist, Alain 234–8, 242, 246, 265–6, 269
distributism 241–2
Dreyfus, Alfred
  affair 12, 20–2, 24, 27, 43, 166, 280
  anti- 20–2

Emmanuel II, King Victor 67, 70, 80, 101, 115
Emmanuel III, King Victor 91, 106–7, 199
Enabling Act 96–8, 110
Europeanism 191, 210, 219, 232, 236–8, 272, 279
Evola, Julius 136, 231–8, 240, 242, 245–7, 259, 265–6, 269, 276–7

fantasy
  and fascism 5, 7, 11, 49, 54, 65, 95, 124–8, 157–9, 164, 166, 169–72, 174–9, 181–6, 189, 193–4, 198, 200, 202, 204–9, 214, 223, 226–7, 236–9, 244, 251–3, 275–82
  in Tolkien 245, 274–6
fascism *see* (neo)fascism
Fields, James Alex, Jr. 249–51, 272
film 20, 42, 59, 81–4, 99, 121, 136, 144, 148–9, 202, 225–6, 275
  as propaganda 81, 101, 121, 127, 136, 149, 182
Fiume 31–8, 44–5, 60, 71, 76, 80, 150, 158, 202–3, 205
Forza Nuova (FN) 4, 243, 263–6, 268
Freikorps 48, 50, 52–4, 59, 62, 201

Fronte della Gioventù (FdG) 230–1, 244, 246, 266, 275, 277

Gentile, Emilio 6–10, 39–40, 103–6, 134, 148, 266
Goebbels, Joseph 81, 86–8, 93, 98–9, 111–12, 116, 137, 143, 145, 148–9, 205
Gömbös, Gyula *see* (neo)fascism in Hungary
Great Replacement Theory (GRT) 250–1, 266, 273, 279, 281
Griffin, Nick 228, 230, 240–2

Himmler, Heinrich 47, 97, 111–12, 127, 136, 189
Hindenburg, Paul von 84–5, 88, 90–8, 109–10
Hitler, Adolf 3, 5–8, 23–6, 47–9, 55, 81–99, 103–4, 107, 109–19, 121–2, 128–30, 132–8, 141–55, 168, 175–6, 178, 181–200, 203–5, 214, 225, 242, 269–71, 280
  art 122, 141–9, 155, 159
  Mein Kampf 8, 26, 47, 55, 86–7
  Mussolini, relationship with 61, 99, 103–4, 135–6, 153–5, 181–5, 204
  origins 23–6
  rhetoric of 8, 25, 55, 61–2, 83, 86, 94, 99, 142
  rise of 55, 61–4, 91–7, 136
Holocaust 45, 132–3, 135, 210, 254, 261, 278, 280–2
  denial of 237, 252, 254, 259–61, 264, 267, 283
Holland, Derek 230, 240–4
Horthy, Miklós 56–7, 175–8, 185, 192, 268 (*see also* (neo)fascism in Hungary)

idealism *see* (neo)idealism
industrialists/industrialization 7, 18, 28, 39, 40, 43–4, 51, 57, 65, 76, 108, 112
  fascist opposition to/suspicion of 40, 57–9, 61, 124, 133, 170, 176
  -military complex 42–4, 51, 112, 280
integralism *see* Catholic Church/Catholicism
interwar period 6–7, 118, 159–63, 169, 178, 191–2, 198, 201, 205, 213–14, 232, 234, 236, 242, 246, 249–51, 256, 274, 280–2
Iron Guard *see* fascism in Romania
irredentism 31, 50, 57, 268, 270
Italian Social Republic (RSI) 194, 199–203, 215, 218, 263

Lebensraum ("living space") 87, 128, 185–8
Legion of the Archangel Michael *see* (neo)fascism in Romania
liberalism *see* (neo)liberalism
Ludendorff, Erich von 62–3, 85
Lueger, Karl 24–7, 61

March on Rome 2–4, 63, 67–71, 77, 101, 153, 203, 278

Index

martyrdom 9, 35
  as fascist political sacralization 31, 59, 64, 71, 88, 96, 105, 131, 174, 201, 231, 253, 267
Marxism 8, 23, 28, 38, 55, 234
  fascist opposition to 85, 89, 92, 95, 98, 105, 109, 177, 230
  opposition to fascism 8, 11, 111
masculinity, fascist 1, 54, 78, 109–10, 132, 153, 160–1, 252, 259
Matteotti, Giacomo 73–5, 92, 98
Maurras, Charles 20, 22–6, 40, 164, 166, 197–8, 246
Meloni, Giorgia 1–2, 275–80
  and neofascism 275–6, 278–9
  and Tolkien 275–6, 279–80
Mosley, Oswald *see* (neo)fascism in Britain
Movimento Sociale Italiano (MSI) 215–19, 222–3, 229–33, 236, 244–6, 260, 263–4, 266, 275–8
motorsport 128–31, 213
music 18, 38, 230
  anti-fascist 268
  (neo)fascist use of 38, 93, 148–51, 205, 225–30, 243–6, 261–2
Mussolini, Benito 2–7, 9, 12–13, 19, 32–5, 37–40, 57–8, 60, 63–83, 90–2, 97, 101–38, 144–55, 157–61, 165–8, 170–6, 181–2, 184–6, 188–92, 194, 199–205, 209–16, 223, 232, 265–6, 277–82
  rise 37, 57, 60–1, 67–75 (*see also* March on Rome)
  downfall 199–200, 203–5
mythology 29, 38–9, 54, 116, 199, 232, 240, 261, 269, 280
  as fascist tool 11, 23, 29, 70–1, 77, 90, 95–6, 131, 205, 236, 245, 251–2
  "lost cause" 190, 237, 252

National Democratic Party (NPD) 230, 260–1
Nazism/Nazi Party 2, 5–6, 12–13, 21, 23, 27, 36, 40–4, 47–9, 53–7, 61–4, 81–104, 109–13, 116–22, 127–138, 141–6, 148–50, 151–2, 155, 158–64, 168–72, 176–178, 181–2, 185–205, 209–19, 222, 225–30, 234, 237–9, 242–7, 250–1, 253–62, 265, 267–8, 272, 280–2
  and the fascist dream 54, 128, 158, 181–2, 185–6, 197–8, 202–5, 225, 236–8, 280–1
  neo-nazism 249–57, 259–60, 262–7, 269–74, 279, 281–2
(neo)fascism
  aestheticism 8, 36, 81, 88, 108, 121–2, 141–9, 151, 155, 159
    militaristic 37, 42, 64, 146
    political 33, 114, 155, 226
  in Austria 9, 161, 170–1, 178, 212
  in Britain 160, 166–8, 225, 227–9, 243–4, 246
  brutality *see* violence
  clandestine networks 165, 209, 213–15, 217–22, 239–40
  "cocktail" 7, 11–13, 19, 27, 61, 65
  continued appeal of 279–80
  in Croatia 192–4, 211, 246
  definition of 6–9, 36, 61, 103, 105, 158–9, 162, 200, 212, 215
  in France 19–23, 27–8, 161–5, 174, 192, 194–9, 219–20, 230, 237, 246, 280
  future of 5, 11, 13, 271–4, 282–3
  genealogy of 1, 279, 281
  in Hungary 175–8, 192, 268
  in Latin America and South America 211–15
  mainstreaming of 10, 98, 142, 144, 215–17, 234–5, 243, 246, 251, 254, 258–63, 269–71, 274, 282
  New Man of 10–12, 15, 32, 35–6, 41, 121, 130, 141, 143, 145, 152, 155, 174–5, 185, 240–1
  nostalgia 4, 23–4, 27, 93–4, 170, 213, 216, 222–3, 229–30, 243, 246–7, 246–7, 260, 275, 278, 281
  in Romania 9, 55–6, 157–8, 172–5, 177, 190, 192–3, 198, 239
  in Spain 13, 29, 157, 160, 165, 169, 175, 190, 207–210, 218–20, 223, 257–8, 279
  as spiritual 86, 94, 103, 105–6, 135–6, 161–3, 166–7, 173–4, 226, 232–3, 238, 240–1, 248
  symbols 11, 13, 52–3, 57–9, 119, 171, 181, 253, 269
    appropriation of 226–7, 250–1, 255, 266–7, 282
(neo)idealism 6, 39, 104–5
(neo)liberalism 7–8, 12, 21, 24–6, 33, 38–9, 43, 71–2, 101, 103–8, 109, 112, 115, 117, 158, 174, 212, 233, 259, 263, 265, 270, 279–80, 283
  anti- 25, 35, 39, 51, 58–9, 70, 72, 75–6, 98, 123, 125, 134, 137, 145, 160, 162, 169, 171–2, 187, 195, 227, 235, 246, 251, 261, 264–6, 274, 281
  failures of 12, 26, 57–9, 64, 69, 72, 75, 89, 104, 108, 170–1, 178, 236, 265, 269, 281–2
  residue in (neo)fascism 104, 106–8, 111–12, 115, 117, 125, 155, 175, 231, 235
(neo)paganism, fascist appropriation of 13, 23, 35, 40, 54, 231–2, 237–8, 246, 250, 253, 263, 265, 281
New Left 219, 230, 234–5, 246
New Right (*Nouvelle Droite*) 24, 234, 242, 261, 265, 269, 274 (*see also* radical right)
Nietzsche, Friedrich, influence on fascism 12, 35–6, 41, 44, 77, 122, 164, 204, 225, 227, 231–2, 242

Olympics *see* sport
Orbán, Viktor 268–9, 279

parafascism 160, 171, 197, 212–13, 267
Pearce, Joseph 227, 229–30, 240–2

Index

peasantry *see völkisch*
positivism 23, 105, 134
pragmatism 25–6, 51, 61, 63, 67, 107, 118, 166, 186–8, 278–9
Predappio, Italy 2–6, 216
propaganda
  as art 86
  definition of 43
  fascist 6, 21, 54–5, 62, 65, 73, 86–8, 90, 93, 95, 98, 108, 110, 113, 120, 127, 131, 136, 151, 182, 197–8, 211
Protestantism 22, 91, 93
Putin, Vladimir 270, 278

race and racism
  art 141–3
  Aryan ideal 21, 42, 54, 85, 121, 127–8, 131–2, 136, 141–2, 164, 174, 185, 189, 238, 254, 256–7, 267, 269, 271–2, 281
  difference between Nazi Germany and Fascist Italy 112–13, 135–7, 142, 160
  racist policies in fascist regimes 12–13, 25, 119, 127–8, 137, 158–9, 185, 235–7, 242, 270, 273
  separatism 235, 242
  as spiritual 127, 135, 142, 232, 266
  white supremacy 229, 249–56, 262, 272–3, 281
radical right 18, 20, 22, 56, 159–60, 175–6, 192–3, 262, 269
  rise 29, 50, 53, 57, 62, 192, 194, 262
Ratlines 209–11
Rauti, Pino 217, 220, 222, 231–3, 239, 244, 263–4, 277
Riefenstahl, Leni 137–8, 149, 226
  Olympia (1938) 121, 138
  Triumph of the Will (1935) 81–3, 99, 101, 121
ritual
  and liturgy 9, 33
  (neo)fascist 11, 33, 36, 81, 83, 88, 103, 107, 113, 133, 160–1, 171, 178, 232, 255, 266–7, 269, 280, 282
Romanità 70–1, 104, 108, 152
Roof, Dylann 249, 272
ruralization *see Bonifica Integrale*

Schloss Klessheim 181–5
skinheads 225–47, 262, 264–5
social engineering
  Aryanism *see* race and racism, Aryan ideal
  euthanasia 133, 136, 241
  Final Solution 181, 185–6, 189, 192, 197
  T-4 program 136, 189
socialism
  as economic party and philosophy 12–18, 21–2, 28, 33, 37–8, 51, 55, 58–9, 65, 75, 170, 213, 241

Hitler's 8–9, 25–6, 49, 55, 85–6, 92–3, 97
National Socialism 8–9, 25, 49, 55, 85–6, 134, 205, 242, 250, 260, 272
opposition by fascists 38, 55, 58–61, 65, 70, 105, 127, 129, 198
Soviet Union 40, 48, 51, 84, 191, 211, 236–9, 253, 269, 271
  fascist fear of 51–6, 181, 186, 188, 190, 198, 217, 219
  opposition to fascism 56, 189, 192
sport 88, 107, 121, 130–1, 229, 267
  Berlin Summer Games 119–21
squadrismo/squadristi 23, 36–7, 58–61, 67–73, 75, 147–8, 265–6
Strassers 85–6, 97, 111, 127
  Gregor 82, 97, 242
  Otto 219, 242
Strasserism 242
Stuart, Ian 228–9, 246, 262

Third Positionism 230, 238–43, 245, 265–6
"Third Way," 12, 76, 108–9
Thiriart, Jean-François 238–9, 270
Tolkien, J. R. R.
  Campo Hobbit 244, 246
  exhibition of 275–7
  (neo)fascist appropriation of 244–6, 265, 275–7
totalitarianism 8–9, 36, 103–5, 109, 112, 117, 123, 129
Treaty of Trianon 56, 175, 268
"trenchocracy," 37–44, 57, 161
Trump, Donald 250–1, 254, 274

United States
  (neo)fascism in 4, 18, 29, 43, 58, 210–13, 238, 242–3, 254–8, 262, 265, 269, 271–4, 280
  opposition to fascism
    after the Second World War 211–12, 217–18, 220, 254–8, 262
    during the Second World War 119, 121, 210
Ustaše see (neo)fascism in Croatia
utopia, fascist dreams of 11, 42, 45, 109, 121–30, 141–2, 144, 155, 189, 271

Vichy *see* fascism in France
violence
  and beauty 37, 141, 205, 226
  as crusade 174, 190–1, 198–9, 223, 238, 240–1, 245, 250–2, 257
  eroticized 225–7
  lone wolf terrorism 249–50, 254, 271–4
  (neo)fascist tool/strategy 7, 11–13, 23, 29, 36, 39, 48, 51, 55–6, 59–61, 65, 69–70, 72–8, 93, 96–9, 118, 121, 133, 137–9, 141, 150, 158, 160–8, 174, 177–8, 186–7, 193, 197, 201–3, 212,

Index

217–19, 221–3, 231, 233, 238–9, 252, 256, 258, 260–2, 265–8, 271–3, 279–82
  racially motivated 23, 44, 137, 168, 177, 193, 251, 262
  thuggery 92, 202, 218
völkisch 40–4, 48–9, 53–5, 61, 63, 86, 119–21, 127–8, 135, 175–6, 198–9, 261, 270 (*see also* "Blood and Soil"; *Bonifica Integrale*)

Wagner, Richard 40, 149–50, 185–6, 204, 245, 262, 270
Weimar Republic 62–3, 81–99, 110–12, 119, 138, 142, 144, 199
"White Terror," 47 49–57
women, in fascism/fascist states 132–3, 136, 141
  labor 42, 122, 132
  as mothers 122, 124
  rights 12, 36, 135

xenophobia 18, 27, 29, 161–2, 170–2, 226, 229, 243, 245, 250, 260–1, 267, 278–9 (*see also* anti-immigrationism)

youth
  cult of *see* cult of youth
  and culture 40, 171, 226–30, 234, 244–6, 257, 260, 267, 275–6
  (neo)fascist education of 5, 80, 95, 107, 133–5, 216, 229, 234, 235, 238